CULTURAL RESISTANCE

Samir Khalaf

CULTURAL
RESISTANCE

Global and Local Encounters in the Middle East

Saqi Books

British Library Cataloguing-in-Publication Data
A catalogue record for this book is available from the
British Library

ISBN 0 86356 814 9 (hb)

Saqi Books
26 Westbourne Grove
London W2 5RH
www.saqibooks.com

To

EDWARD SAID

Friend, colleague and mentor

Contents

Preface and Acknowledgements

A collection of one's essays could well carry a tinge of complacency, if not intellectual narcissism. I hope I have resisted the temptation to indulge in either. Since my return to Lebanon after about a decade, I am often asked by colleagues what I was up to during that happy interlude which released me from the terrors and distractions of civil strife. The decision to collect the essays in a single volume is, in part, a response to such queries. Some of the papers were published in rather obscure, often inaccessible, professional journals; others were part of conference proceedings placed on newly established Internet websites; a few are extracted from work in progress.

This venture has a wider justification than simply validating one's creative output or rendering it more accessible to potential readers. Despite the rather long time span separating the papers and the range of problems they explore, the essays are still held together by some pivotal concerns; central among them is the overriding issue of identity and the intransigent character of primordial loyalties. The polemics over the nature and prospects of postmodernity have reawakened the debate about the inveterate issues of the interplay between broad structural changes and the adaptive strategies of threatened local groups and communities. Postmodernity and globalism are, after all, associated with a growing consciousness of an emerging and fluid world in the throes of ambiguous and unsettling transformations.

My subjects – the dialectics of tradition and modernity, the impact of New England Puritanism as a cultural transplant, the radicalization of communal loyalties, the consequences of protracted and displaced hostility or prospects for the restoration of civility in a fragmented political culture – all deal with problems of forging pliable, porous and hybrid cultural bonds and identities.

Contemporary theorists, particularly those who harbour some reservations about postmodern perspectives, are inclined to argue that the older struggles of democracy and capitalism are overtaken today by a new conflict between the forces of rationality and the neo-communitarian politics of identity. Hence, one of the most urgent tasks facing plural and divided societies is to deal judicially with the conflicts of cultural identity.

In countries like Lebanon, such problems are more acute and pronounced precisely because the traditional sources of conflict are being exacerbated by a set of unforeseen and unfamiliar problems. In addition to the residues of an ugly and unfinished war, the taxing imperatives of post-war reconstruction and the multitude of unresolved regional conflicts, Lebanon is made more vulnerable today by the distant but more impervious forces of globalism: the intensification of consumerism, the demise of political participation, the fears of erasure by the intangible forces of virtual corporate structures and the scintillating technologies of digital and electronic communications. More poignant, perhaps, are the new discourses over issues of civil society, political marginalization, national sovereignty, autonomy, ecology and the politics of nature.

Since the bulk of the papers are revisions of texts or material already published or presented in conferences or workshops, I wish here to acknowledge the sources. Chapter 1 was first published in George Sabagh, ed., *The Modern Economic and Social History of the Middle East* (Cambridge: Cambridge University Press, 1989). Chapter 2 first appeared in *Diogenes*, 54 (1966). Chapter 3 was published in Ann Elizabeth Mayer, ed., *Law, Property and Social Structure in the Near and Middle East* (State University of New York Press, 1985). Chapter 5 is a revised version of an article that appeared in the *Journal of Mediterranean Studies: History, Culture and Society in the Mediterranean World*, vol. 7, No. 2 (1998). Chapter 6 was first published in *Islam and Christian-Muslim Relations*, vol. 8 (Spring 1997). Chapter 7 is a paper presented at a conference on *Altruism and Imperialism* held at the Bellagio Study and Conference Center, Bellagio, Italy (28 August–1 September 2000). Chapter 8 is a condensed version of a chapter extracted from a forthcoming book of mine, *Civil and Uncivil Violence* (New York: Columbia University Press, 2001). Chapter 9 is due to appear in Thomas Scheffler, ed., *Religion Between Violence and Reconciliation* (The German Orient Institute, 2001). Chapter 10 was first published in Paul Salem, ed., *Conflict Resolution in The Arab World* (Washington, The Brookings Institution, 1997). Chapter 11 is a revised version of a paper published in P. Rowe and H. Sarkis, eds, *Projecting Beirut* (Munich: Prestel Verlag, 1998). Chapter 12 is extracted from *Beirut Reclaimed* (Dar An-Nahar Press, 1993). Both Chapters 13 and 14 were first published as special editorials in *The Christian Science Monitor* on, respectively, 22 September 1987 and 8 August 1991. Finally, Chapter 15 is adapted from my forthcoming book, *Civil and Uncivil Violence* (see above).

Except for the reflexive essays, nearly all the papers are extracted from broader studies and, in some instances, works in progress, funded research and collaborative projects. Hence, the debts I accumulated in the process are boundless. For example, my interest in civil unrest dates back to the early 1980s. A Ford Foundation grant allowed me, along with Salim Nasr, Samir Nassif and a team of graduate students and research assistants at the American University of Beirut (AUB), to conduct an empirical survey in very trying times. The tenacity and courage displayed by our spirited research assistants (Rima Qulaylat, Françoise Ghoraiyeb, Ousama Tawil, Karma Barrage) in carrying on the work in such an extreme setting must be gratefully acknowledged. While on leave in Princeton I was a recipient of a MacArthur Research and Writing Award (1989), which gave me the opportunity to do extensive reading and research on comparable and not-so-comparable instances of collective violence and communal strife. Graduate seminars that I offered during the early 1990s at Princeton, NYU and jointly with Philip Khoury, MIT, allowed me to test some of the hunches and perspectives I was developing for the analysis of the Lebanese case.

The four chapters on New England Puritanism and its evangelical imagination as a cultural transplant are all by-products of a Lilly Endowment research fellowship that I enjoyed for three years (1990–94) while at Princeton. I owe special thanks to Sister Jeanne Knoerly for overseeing the project. She was disarmingly accommodating in allowing me temporarily to suspend my work on Protestant missionaries to pursue other more compelling commitments. I shall soon return to the task of completing this long-pending work.

Harriet Zukerman, Vice President of the Andrew Mellon Foundation, has been equally appreciative of the needs of scholars for stretches of uninterrupted research and writing. Because of the Foundation's generous grant to the Center for Behavioral Research, I was able, soon after my return to AUB in 1995, to break away from my strenuous teaching and administrative duties. During the past five summers I have been able to resume work on political violence and post-war reconstruction and rehabilitation. A forthcoming book on *Civil and Uncivil Violence*, soon to be published by Columbia University Press, is largely an outcome of this privilege.

In *Hugging the Shore*, John Updike – who should know, given his relentless and stunning output – advances the notion that 'solitude and small quarters are great inciters of literacy'. Over the years, both at Princeton and in Lebanon, I have been fortunate to enjoy such propitious settings. At Princeton, Henry Beinen, Serane Boocock, Marvin Bressler, Carl Brown, Michael Centano, David and the late Doris Dodge, the late Charles Issawi, Peter Johnson, Suzanne Keller, Woody and Elizabeth Littlefield, Jane De Long, Joseph O'Neil, Fadlou and Alison Shehadi, Walter Wallace, John Waterbury and Charles Westoff, have all been immensely gracious and helpful in a multitude of ways. Many of them, being the good colleagues that they are, reviewed drafts of my essays and unfailingly returned the comments that I solicited from them. Naturally, they are all absolved of any error in fact or judgement.

My re-entry into post-war Lebanon, a country beleaguered by lethargy, indifference and creeping mediocrity, both within and outside the University, has been disconcerting, even painfully so. Often I have had to forfeit my right to speak out, lest I offend the frayed sensibilities and paranoia of some who stayed behind. Here again, a handful of caring and equally indignant friends and colleagues have been a beneficent source of shelter and inspiration.

In various ways, not all academic, they have eased my homecoming and induced in me a modicum of hope in an otherwise discreditable and demeaning political culture. Some have stubbornly resisted the erosion of standards and the vulgarization of aesthetic sensibilities. Others decry the rampant and guilt-free corruption, the tampering with intellectual freedom and with the country's sovereignty and autonomy and the pervasive mood of servility and indifference. Altogether they act as the disinherited stalwarts of a decaying order. Safeguarding the restorative role of free and uncensored intellectual companionship serves as their last act of faith.

Within AUB, a new core of administrative and intellectual leadership has already taken measures to restore the depleted ethics of research, academic accountability and comradeship. Detached peer review is displacing clientelism. A surge of new recruits is adding a much-needed infusion of faculty resources. Outside academe, recalcitrant voices have been raised. One is heartened by them. In ways I cannot fully enumerate, the following have offered intellectual companionship and other genial, often gracious, venues for self-renewal: Touma and Layla Arida, George and Alexandra Asseily, Khalil Bitar, Myrna Boustani, Nasser Chamaa, Carol Hakim, Maher Jarrar, Asaad Khairallah, Mohamad Ali Khalidi, Munir Khani, Farid Khazin, Elias Khoury, Chibli Mallat, Riad Tabbarah, Fawaz Traboulsi, Fadi Tuéni and John Waterbury.

I wish to single out two remarkable friends who stand out in this regard: Michel El-Khoury and Ghassan Tuéni. They are not often mentioned in tandem and indeed often seem to be the antithesis of the other. To me, though, they have much in common and have been immense sources of encouragement and inspiration. As a young student I held both in awe from a distance. Tuéni's sharp, often spiked editorials and audacious tirades against an aberrant establishment roused and informed my public consciousness. Khoury's conduct in public office (both held successive portfolios in a score of cabinets) was always statesmanlike and dignified.

Circumstances have brought us into a closer and more fulfilling relationship. Both are disarmingly gracious, engaging and generous friends. While Tuéni is flamboyant, gregarious, outgoing, often headlong and impetuous, Khoury is more reserved and measured. Both are Francophone in their cultural leanings but feel equally at home in Anglo-Saxon and Arab settings. They are fluent in three languages, are avid and discriminate readers and follow world affairs with keen and professional interest. In these and much more they are leaps beyond their cohorts in public office. Dismayed by the substance and tone of political discourse, both have turned inwards to cultivate more private edifying pastimes in support of advocacy groups and civic-minded voluntary associations. Both epitomize some of the redeeming virtues of Lebanon's sadly bygone golden age or of a future that this now faltering state is unlikely to attain.

I seize the occasion to express my gratitude to Mai Ghoussoub, André Gaspard and Sarah Al-Hamad of Saqi Books, for their extraordinary efficiency in steering the book into publication. An otherwise tedious process was rendered more agreeable.

I also wish to thank Mrs Leila Jbara, my administrative assistant, for being so dutiful and meticulous in typing various versions of the draft and in preparing the final manuscript for publication.

At the risk of sounding too much of a doting father, I have been blessed by two gifted and vibrant sons: George on the tennis court and Ramzi, seven years his junior, on stage. Both are precocious and focused in honing their natural talents. It has been a delight to watch them grow into the accomplished and endearing young men they now are. America is wondrous in this regard. It exudes resplendent yet competitive opportunities for the young, particularly those longing to realize and enrich their potential.

Coming to terms with success and failure in such a universalistic and achievement-oriented culture is a humbling and sobering experience. Both boys are more mature and self-confident as a result. I was fortunate to be around to participate in their ventures at close range. In fact, drafts of these and other works were done 'on the road', as it were. When I followed them to tennis and country clubs or to theatres I took my notes and writing pad along and found working spaces in lounging rooms and back-stage studios. Fits of writing were thus sandwiched between exciting tennis tournaments and enthralling stage performances. The tedium of writing thus became more of a self-indulgent exhilarating tonic. To this day I have fond memories of places like Tanglewood, The Globe in San Diego, The Curran Theatre in San Francisco, Goodspeed and the Eugene O'Neill Theatre in Connecticut among others. The extracurricular escapades of George and Ramzi were not their only sources of stimulation. Lately they are beginning to evince a discriminating and not-so-partial concern in their father's career. I benefited from their critical and insightful reading of the first chapter of this book.

Over the years Edward Said has repeatedly goaded me to write in essay form and thus refrain from, if not temper, the arcane and stale prose of scholarly and professional articles. Clearly, very few of us ordinary scholars can match his erudition and his consummate gifts in this regard. I genuinely doubt whether the collection in this volume comes close to what he has in mind. It is, nonetheless, dedicated to him for being such a magnificent model and for setting such soaring standards for the rest of us to match. His peerless legacy is all the more formidable since it was often delivered under trying personal circumstances.

Finally, I am at a loss to express my gratitude to my wife Roseanne, who, to my delight, is now emerging as a writer and scholar in her own right. Over the years and despite the exacting demands on her already over-taxed resources – as 'stage mother', teacher, writer, colleague and homemaker – she never ceased to encourage and inspire. She also refused to surrender to shortcuts. All this was done with a refreshing measure of style and quiet elegance. She has always been a generous and unsparing listener, a probing and critical reader with an intuitive eye for crisp, lean and edifying prose. More, she was a source of uplift and cheer when I was downcast and despondent. She now knows more than she perhaps ever wanted to know about New England Puritans, collective violence, post-war reconstruction and the restoration of civility. This, like earlier works, would not have found its way into print without her selfless and boundless devotion and love.

On Constructing an Intellectual Craft

> Scholarship is a choice of how to live as well as a choice of career; whether he knows it or not, the intellectual workman forms his own self as he works toward the perfection of his craft; to realize his own potentialities, and any opportunities that come his way, he constructs a character which has as its core the qualities of the good workman.
>
> C. W. Mills, *The Sociological Imagination (1959)*

> . . . all good things – trout as well as eternal salvation – come by grace and grace comes by art and art does not come easy.
>
> Norman Maclean, *A River Runs Through it (1989)*

> Societies, like lives, contain their own interpretations. One has to learn how to gain access to them.
>
> Clifford Geertz, *The Interpretation of Culture (1973)*

During the past two decades or so my research and writing converged on four seemingly unrelated areas. I say seemingly because readers may be puzzled by the disparate drift of my intellectual concerns, but I can assure them that the topics explored are not unrelated. Some, like my continuing interest in the dialectics of tradition and modernity and the reassertion of communal loyalties, reflect pending and unresolved conceptual and theoretical issues. Others are by-products of unforeseen but compelling socio-political transformations that impinge on one's view of a fragmented society, particularly one that has been gripped by protracted social unrest and displacement and collective violence. Equally vital and pressing are considerations of viable options and strategies for post-war rehabilitation and reconstruction.

Even the essays on American Protestantism as a cultural transplant are not remote or arcane. They deal, among other things, with the socio-cultural impacts of such foreign incursions; particularly their unintended consequences on secular change, liberal education, popular culture, relief work and social welfare. Indeed, in several obvious respects, the missionaries during the first half of the nineteenth century may well be treated as precursors to modern-day international non-governmental organizations.

Except for three essays, one (Chapter 9) drawn from a forthcoming book and the other two (Chapters 5 and 8) presented at recent conferences (Brown University and the Bellagio Study Centre, Italy), all the rest have appeared in professional journals, edited volumes and anthologies not perhaps readily accessible to the general public. Some have been updated, while the rest have undergone minor editorial revisions by way of avoiding redundancy, providing added substantiation or extracting relevant inferences.

In order not to risk leaving the papers in a state of almost random suspension, this preamble attempts to identify the context of each, situate them within an ongoing conceptual debate, pinpoint their basic premises and what they purport to challenge or accomplish and, where possible, anticipate some of the significant findings.

The essays, singularly or collectively, should spur the reader into rethinking some of the received wisdom or modes of conventional analysis. Whether I am exploring the nature and direction of change, the survival and reconfirmation of communalism; the interplay between traditional–modern, local–global elements, the unfolding character of protracted and displaced collective violence in fragmented plural social orders like Lebanon, the intention is essentially two-fold: to disclose some of the shortcomings and pitfalls of conventional paradigms and to propose alternative perspectives more appropriate for understanding the issues and problems under exploration.

The order of the essays is not incidental or fortuitous. It reflects the sequence of timing during which the studies were undertaken. In other words, it is in that order that the research was carried out. Nor is the content entirely serendipitous, a by-product of the twists and turns inherent in contingent research. Like any other intellectual or creative product, the essays and the broader undertakings from which they are drawn are the outcome of socio-historical and biographical realities often beyond my control. The role of funding agencies, the lure of exotic and distant sites where conferences and symposia are hosted, the supportive academic milieux with engaging colleagues and spirited graduate students, copious library and archival resources have all been stimulants for sustained interludes of uninterrupted research and writing.

I have been privileged to enjoy the benefits of many such opportunities. Once initiated, however, the projects assumed a life of their own and took directions often unrelated to the initial driving forces that propelled them. Clearly, being a captive of and a living witness to the cruelties of an ugly and treacherous war must have aroused my interest in exploring the forces that were tearing my society apart and generating such senseless carnage of innocent victims and reckless destruction. But it was the generous support I received from the Ford Foundation, MacArthur, Andrew Mellon and the Lilly Endowment that allowed me to extend and deepen the dimensions of my research in unanticipated but meaningful areas.

In some rudimentary respects, the shape and direction of my research and the conceptual and methodological tools that informed it epitomize in part an exercise in the sociology of knowledge or, more likely, what Lewis Coser terms the 'ecology of ideas'. In explicit terms, a person's situation, social circle(s), audience and ideological affiliations affect the content and tone of his or her writing. My own case is no exception. More fateful, doubtless, were the baffling and threatening effects of the war. Outraged and shocked by its devastating consequences, I found myself at times, and with justification, abandoning the objective and value-free strictures of my discipline. I started to write impassioned and reflective pieces about Lebanon's victimization and its unwilled and unwilling descent into a proxy killing field for other peoples' wars.

C. W. Mills's 'sociological imagination' may also be invoked here, for elucidating both the distinction between private troubles and public issues and the interplay between biography, history and society. For example, many of the cruelties of collective violence remained muted and ignored because groups could not transcend their personal and parochial loyalties to transform private and personal anguish and fear into public issues that demanded collective resolution. Hence conflict was never resolved. It continued to reproduce itself and intensify.

One's personal experience, rooted in a particular socio-historical setting, is bound to inform what, how and why one writes. At the least it is destined to shape the general drift of one's intellectual and scholarly concerns, if not the specific problems explored and preferences for certain conceptual and methodological perspectives. In this sense, the accident of my birth and my residence, for much of my childhood and adolescence, between the suburban resort town of Aley and Ras Beirut, must have been instrumental in shaping many of my interests and curiosities. Indeed, the spaces and places of Aley and Ras Beirut have framed my life in concrete and indelible ways. Except for brief regional excursions, for 23 years I was literally anchored in Lebanon. More important, even by the standards of the fairly stationary lives of my contemporaries, mine seemed more sheltered and confined. For nine months of the year we lived on Jean d'Arc Street in Ras Beirut, only a block away from the American University of Beirut, where my father worked. The three summer months were spent in the resort town of Aley, the family homestead. Incidentally, both were religiously mixed, fairly open and vibrant communities, accommodating relatively peacefully and coherently the swift and dissonant transformations that Lebanon was beginning to experience at the time.

Academically, I was also coming of age in the mid- and late 1950s, perhaps the golden/gilded age of Lebanon. The country was enjoying a rather blissful interlude of political stability and economic prosperity, especially when compared with the political havoc and tumultuous ideological rivalry of adjacent regimes. As a student, my life was largely free of anxiety. I had little or no ambivalence about my career options or about the country's political future. The education that I received, the perspectives and life philosophies that I acquired – thanks to a string of inspiring and dedicated teachers, both in high school and beyond – reinforced the optimistic and sanguine visions consistent with social order and conflict-free nature of social change that then prevailed.

Even before I left for Princeton in 1958 to pursue my graduate studies, I was already interested in the dialectical interplay between the forces of change and local/traditional modes of accommodation. My senior paper dealt with the 'ecological' transformations of Aley. My MA dissertation was an empirical exploration of labour–management relations and industrial conflict. Most of my American professors at the time were avowed positivists, disciples of George Lundberg, Paul Lazersfeld, Samuel Stauffer and other quantitative and hard-headed empiricists. In all the courses, whether we were studying deviance, stratification, urbanism, political sociology or demography, the prime emphasis was always on methodology. The edict of the classroom was that, as students of society, we can be confident only of the methodology we employ, never of our conclusions. We were also taught that only science possesses the ability to bring order to disorder without having to rely on myth or delusions. Since the biological and physical sciences had made so much headway in this regard, we had no choice, or so we were instructed at the time, but to adopt the logic and analytical tools of the advanced sciences and apply them to our social and psychological natures. Anything else would result in deception, error and confusion.

Another inviolable, almost sacrosanct edict drilled into us was the notion of value-free social science. The ideal social scientist should be detached, dispassionate and thoroughly rational and objective. One's own values and sentiments should be suspended so as not to intrude and contaminate one's quest for truth or pure facts and perceptions. Paraphrasing Lundberg, Professor Armstrong reiterated in virtually all his classes at AUB that as a scientist he could not tell us where to go, only how to get there. Armstrong was also adviser on my MA thesis, which was an empirical field survey of the impact of managerial orientation on labour disputes. I received thorough, rigorous training in the construction of indeces, scales, operational tools and sampling frames and interviewing techniques but little by way of qualitative or humanistic analysis and frames of reference. Intuitions and instinctive reflections arising from my encounters in the field were always held suspect. So were my efforts to make broader theoretical inferences.

When I arrived Princeton University I had swiftly to unlearn many of the sociological tools and paradigms I had brought with me. The excessively positivist and quantitative training I had received at AUB was diametrically opposed to the notions of social action, system theory, structural-functionalism and Parsonian abstract and general sociology current in Princeton at the time. My professors in social thought and sociological theory were Marion Levy and Wilbert Moore, students of Talcott Parsons at Harvard and distinguished scholars in their own right.

The obsession of Parsonian Functionalism with general abstract theory, particularly the need to maintain social order, was in part a reaction to the anxieties of the middle class in different parts of the world. These anxieties, as several intellectual historians have noted, were an expression of common international threats or fears: the international economic crisis capitalism was facing, the communist seizure of state power in Russia (i.e. Marxism achieving state sponsorship) and the ascent to power in Europe of fascism and socialism. In this sense, Parsons's major concern with social order was parallel to the concerns of classical sociologists grappling with the unsettling transformations of the French and Industrial Revolutions.

Thus at Princeton I had to retool myself to become adept at Parsons's 'pattern alternatives of value orientations' and 'functional prerequisites' and Robert Merton's 'manifest and latent functions', 'dysfunctional processes' and 'theories of the Middle Range'. To me the redeeming and abiding virtue of my Princeton education was the thorough and laborious immersion in the classic and humanistic tradition, particularly European sociology and philosophy. I was able to put up with Parsons's forbidding style and verbal obscurity in exchange for his analysis of the works of Weber, Durkheim, Pareto and Marshall in his *The Structure of Social Action* (1949), the classic of the day. Our professors had also the good sense to insist that we read the classical tomes themselves, rather than later editions. I recall weeks and weeks on end of solitary and close readings, not only of Marx, Weber, Durkheim, Pareto, Tönnies, Simmel, Veblen and the like, but also earlier classics of both liberal and conservative traditions: Cicero, Hegel, Montesquieu, Rousseau, De Tocqueville, Kant, Condorcet, J. S. Mill, Mosca, Burke, Le Play, Marshall and Mannheim, among others. It was at Princeton, odd as it may seem, that I was exposed to Ibn Khaldun. I first read Rosenthal's annotated three-volume translation of the *Muqaddimah* before bracing myself to read the original.

Upon my return to Lebanon in 1960 to assume my first teaching appointment at AUB, I underwent another unsettling but challenging process of unlearning or relearning my sociology. In the early 1960s my research, if not my teaching, was still within the fold of empiricism. The field surveys I conducted on prostitution, labour–management relations, managerial ideology and industrial conflict were all the outcome of studies employing direct interviews, participant observation and reliance on official statistics and reports. My early studies on urbanization – both general surveys of the Arab world and the more focused studies of particular neighbourhoods in Beirut – were even more quantitative. Conducted jointly with Per Kongstad, a Danish urban geographer, the surveys relied more heavily on exacting and laborious methodological instruments such as grid-cell analysis, mapping, indexing and land-use surveys for measuring the socio-cultural, spatial and physical transformations of urban districts like Hamra in Ras Beirut. In virtually all our studies, the overall approach was behaviourist and realist. They were mostly concerned with disclosing the predisposing factors within a logico-empiricist tradition.

By the mid- and late 1960s, however, my research and theoretical orientations started to shift perceptibly towards more humanistic, subjective and intuitionist leanings. They also became more interdisciplinary. It was here that my training in the classical tradition, both European and American, came to my rescue. Virtually all the new theoretical perspectives – conflict theory, symbolic interaction,

Goffman's dramaturgy, phenomenology, rational choice, structuralism and post-modernism – involve considerable reformulations of some components or derivatives of classical sociology. For example, while American social theorists were profoundly influenced by social reformism, empiricism and pragmatism, European social theory operated far more within the context of post-Kantian and post-Hegelian philosophy. These differences, incidentally, persisted throughout the twentieth century. As I often remind students, sociology, after all, emerged twice in history: once modelled on the natural sciences and once modelled on the humanities. The French and British tradition propagated the affinity of sociology with the natural sciences. The German and Central European tradition articulated a broader concept of science that included the study of philosophy and history.

Even more relevant to my concerns at the time, particularly in exploring the patterns and directions of societal transformations in Lebanon and the Arab world, were the prophetic and insightful visions of the founding fathers. For example, they clearly were not uncritical admirers of modernity. Indeed, in my view, Marx, Weber, Durkheim and Simmel are the intellectual giants that they are precisely because they did not subscribe to the conventional story of the modern world uncritically. They all harboured strong reservations about the alleged progressive virtues claimed by modern European culture and industry. In this respect, they understood quite well the underside of progress, the havoc and anguish visited on ordinary people by a changing world.

Because of the trans-historical and cross-cultural dispositions of the classic tradition and its contemporary derivatives, they are more adept at exploring and accounting for resistance and change in various socio-historical settings. The various essays in this volume borrow liberally from such perspectives. If, at times, I seem more at home with the German tradition, it is because German thinkers (from Kant and Hegel to Weber, Simmel, Tönnies and Habermas) insist that individuals live in a world of human ideas and institutions, informed and sustained by human motivations and values. As such, any scientific understanding of human behaviour must include the study of human subjective, value-loaded and reflexive behaviour. Objective observation and mathematical analysis, no matter how rigorous and dispassionate, are not enough. Without an understanding of the ideational context, any sociological analysis of human actions is bound to be partial, incomplete and often misleading.

Indeed, some prominent sociologists, Robert Nisbet (1977) for one, have advanced the persuasive thesis that some of the most seminal and profound concepts of the discipline, which have had a lasting effect on both the empirical and theoretical character of sociology (i.e. alienation, anomie, rationalization, mass society), have not been the outcome of the application of what is termed the scientific method. More explicitly, the basic ingredients of empiricism, such as problem-solving hunches, proceeding rigorously from question to hypothesis to verified conclusions, are not visible in the works of Weber, Durkheim, Simmel and Tocqueville among others. Rather, they are mostly the consequences of intellectual processes that are more akin to art than science. One sees in their work clear manifestations of inspiration, imagination, intuition, impressions, flashes of insight but virtually no evidence of quantitative methodology and experimentation.

Inspiring as such visions are, one cannot but temper them with a more balanced and realistic consideration of the virtues of both. Neither 'artists' nor 'scientists' have a monopoly on truth or pure perception of social reality. Both, after all, are driven by the same desire to understand, interpret and communicate their understanding to the rest of the world. This is the intellectual legacy that I have inherited from the precepts of sociology as a craft, and this is the legacy that has informed my teaching and research.

Finally, in part because of my 'puritan' upbringing, my own calling as a scholar – teacher, researcher, writer, mentor – has been suffused with a Calvinistic work ethic predicated on the view that one's redemption and self-actualization are inextricably linked with one's work and the manner by which this potential is fulfilled. Very early in my schooling I acquired the notion that one has to work hard to perfect one's craft, whatever that may be. Work, particularly if accompanied by disciplined, diligent, almost ascetic norms of conduct, becomes more than just a source of self-validation or an expression of intellectual excitement and imagination. It becomes akin to a morally dutiful fulfilment of a redeeming and enabling task. In the language of Calvinists, this is what the coveted states of bliss and grace are all about.

The compulsion to plunge oneself in dutiful work in no way has meant, at least to me, that laborious research and writing is joyless or that it is essentially pursued for extrinsic rewards, such as to secure academic promotion, to validate one's professional marketability, to impress others or as a perfunctory duty, a form of 'writing up' to be judged in utilitarian terms. Yes, perhaps in my formative years, still furtive and anxious about my scholarly skills, I might have done so in the hope of gaining the favourable reactions of editors of credible journals or the mentors who taught me. Writing became a proof that their professional investment in me had paid off or that it had the effects on readers that I desired.

One of the virtues of academic tenure is that it relieves and liberates one from such perfunctory concerns, allowing research and writing gradually to acquire the more redemptive passions and joys of unalloyed creative pursuits. A good day's writing is thereby elevated to a joyous task of self-indulgence. Days are measured by the number of pages written, the connecting sentences hatched, the satisfaction of words or paragraphs falling in place, the anxious thrills of stretching ideas, insights, queries beyond the original intention or areas of competence.

A good day of writing makes one feel alive, spirited, focused; even a bit invincible. It also braces one to cope with the disheartening but inevitable bleak prospects of 'dry runs' and 'writer's blocks'. A good day of writing, likewise, can be an enormously self-affirming experience. One becomes sensitively aware of one's inner chemistry, adept at monitoring and managing mood swings. Likewise, one begins to relish and capitalize on moments when the juices are flowing, so to speak, when one is lucid and daring. After all, one needs a positive relation with oneself to write well.

To this day I still recall the sheer physical pleasure, the excitement of hunting for books in the aesthetically pleasing setting of the Firestone Library at Princeton. You look for one source and you walk away, always, with a hefty armful of books that you have never laid eyes on before. There is something almost sensual and exultant about being in a library sustained by a tangible air of self-absorbed contemplation, suspended from other mundane cares. So much so, in fact, that in moments of despondency I would often catch myself fantasizing about being taken captive or incarcerated in a library!

Within such an exuberant and enticing milieu, the virtues of discipline and self-restraint are once again needed. By discipline I mean here self-discipline and not the imposition of an external order of conduct. Such external restraints will clearly not work if one is to remain open to change and potentiality in the self. Nietzsche comes to mind here. In his *Twilight of the Idols,* he argues that passion needs and is needed by asceticism or self-moderation. Together they are the basis of life and creativity. (Nietzsche, 1976: 486–8)

More compelling, perhaps, in a socio-cultural setting like Lebanon, work becomes an antidote to idleness and entropy, where much public discourse is characterized by lethargy and withdrawal or depletion of creative human energy. The Lebanese have also become notorious for their short attention spans. They have also long displayed an insatiable appetite for festive, light-hearted and fun-loving activity. While these might provide the needed social and psychic supports to ward off symptoms of alienation and anomie inherent in modern life, they have not been very conducive to any form of intellectual experimentation or the pursuit of creative endeavours for their own sake. Any form of sustained scholarship in this context becomes doubly exhilarating. In the words of C. W. Mills, it becomes both 'a choice of how to live as well as a choice of career . . .'. (Mills, 1972: 196) Any workman, intellectual or otherwise, constructs a notion of selfhood or identity as he strives to perfect his craft and his unrealized potentialities. In a more poetic sense, Norman Maclean must have been invoking this same existential and redemptive ethos inherent in perfecting any task, be it trout fishing or eternal salvation. This hunger to perfect a craft, he tells us, 'comes by grace and grace comes by art and art does not come easy'. (Maclean, 1989)

In hindsight, as I try to recapture the elements that sustained my own intellectual output for the better part of almost four decades, modest as it is, they have much in common with the same self-indulgent enthusiasm that allowed Maclean to find grace and redemption in fly-fishing or C. W. Mills's ethics of workmanship, which informed his 'sociological imagination'. One's very identity, selfhood and self-esteem are thereby embedded in the skills of perfecting a craft.

Below is a brief overview of the four areas that engaged my intellectual interests and allowed me to hone the conceptual and research tools of my craft as a sociologist.

On the Dialectics of Tradition and Modernity in Arab Society

The literature on comparative modernization and social change has always been beset with ambiguities and tendentious polemics. This has been most visible, perhaps, in the continuing discourse regarding the nature and direction of social change and the interplay between 'modern' and 'traditional' loyalties.

When I was a graduate student in the early 1960s the so-called 'developmental model' became my regular conceptual fodder. For a while it nurtured and validated many of my perspectives on social change. It informed my theoretical paradigms, research methodologies and strategies for development. Talcott Parsons's 'pattern variables' and all their dichotomous derivatives were, of course, rooted in the Western intellectual traditions of American and European sociology; they were clearly not as relevant or consistent with socio-cultural realities in the world. At the risk of some oversimplification, developmentalists were making three allegedly universal claims or propositions, particularly regarding the pattern and direction of social change: 1) the inevitable erosion of traditional loyalties by the irreversible forces of secularization; 2) the polarization of tradition and modernity as incompatible dichotomies, and 3) the denigration of traditions as useless or nostalgic survivals.

The developmentalist model was not, of course, uncontested. During the late 1970s and early 1980s the so-called 'dependency theory' emerged to challenge some of its basic premises. While developmentalists maintained that traditions were an impediment to change, dependency theorists turned around to assail instead the disruptive consequences of rapid and total modernization. To leading protagonists of Dependency Theory, particularly Immanuel Wallerstein and some of his associates, such as Cardoso and Faletto, Benjamin Higgins and William Murdoch, the economic, social and culture life of the 'periphery' is tied to changes in the 'centres' of the world economic system. Hence, many of the socio-economic disparities and political instability in developing countries are a product not so much of the recalcitrance of the traditional order in the face of change but of the 'brutality of change inflicted on the traditional world'. (Smith, 1985: 551)

The polemics did not remain at the conceptual or theoretical level but spilled over into policy. Policy-makers and development practitioners in Lebanon, as elsewhere in the Arab world, characteristically possess one of two overarching mindsets and predispositions. The first is an inclination to perceive indigenous and grass-roots cultural agencies as a constraint on modernization with its supportive secular and institutions and progressive lifestyles. As a relic of the past, traditional loyalties and sentiments are treated as a nuisance to be eliminated, contained or bypassed. Hence groups are prodded to disengage themselves from such local heritage if they were to enjoy the fruits of modernity.

The second group, largely as a reaction to some of the disruptive and unsettling by-products of swift societal transformations and the fears of erasure by the seductive forces of globalization, are inclined to idealize, glorify or romanticize some of the traditional agencies and cultural by-products. Hence, the historical necessity of changing them, or even of rearranging them, is ignored or overlooked. The very institutions and loyalties, in other words, that were formerly devalued have become coveted and prized entities. What this in essence means is that indigenous local traditions are either denigrated or idealized but rarely taken for what they actually are or introduced in viable ways into real situations.

Virtually all Arab regimes, regardless of their ideological leanings or development strategies, are known to oscillate, often discordantly, between the two extremes. For example, the initial enthusiasm some of them displayed for radical and total change, reinforced by the desire to efface vestiges of the old order, quite often gives way to fatuous and nostalgic idealization of the past. The resurgence of Muslim fundamentalism and other essentialist movements is, to a considerable extent, a reaction to such excessive modernization, the more so when such changes are perceived to be associated with the 'impurities' of Western incursions.

There is no room in this short introduction to reiterate all the charges levelled against both perspectives. It is sufficient to note that they are patently deficient in helping us understand the nature of the interplay between the forces of tradition and modernity or local resistance to global incursions. In fundamental ways, in fact, they mystify and distort certain distinctive socio-historical realities of Arab societies. For example, at no point in the recent history of the Arab world, even in so-called radical and revolutionary regimes, have the processes of change been so all-embracing that they swept aside all traditional relics of the past. Likewise, traditional values and institutions have not been so immobile and rigid as to serve as insurmountable obstacles to social change. Nor have local or indigenous groups and associations been so enfeebled and disempowered that they could not resist some of the seamy incursions of globalism, which threaten their identity and well-being.

We clearly need an alternative approach for a better understanding of the interplay between tradition and modernity and, possibly, globalism and localism. We need a perspective that recognizes the likelihood, in certain contexts and socio-cultural settings, of the continuing coexistence and mutual reinforcement of the traditional and the modern, the local and the global.

The recent and popular upsurge in these polemics has, once again, reawakened interest in the interplay between such polarized schemes and dichotomies. The traditional-modern typology has now been displaced by the local–global confrontation. Over forty years ago Daniel Lerner prefaced his book, *The Passing of Traditional Society* (1958), a classic of the time, with the graphic parable of 'the grocer and the chief'. The meaning and crisis of modernization in the Middle East was encapsulated in the personal lives of two diametrically opposed protagonists in the village of Balgat on the southern outskirts of Ankara. The 'chief' represented all the traditional and classic Turkish virtues of obedience, courage and loyalty, re-enacted in Atatürk's republic. The 'grocer' was a very different style of man; though born and bred in Balgat, he lived in a different world, populated more actively with imaginings and fantasies – longing for whatever was different and unfamiliar. Where the chief was contented, the grocer was restless . . . 'Whereas the masterful chief was able to incorporate change by rearranging the environment, the nervous grocer was obliged to operate through the more painful process of rearranging himself.' (Lerner, 1958: 35)

To Lerner, the anxiety-ridden grocer was emblematic of this character shift taking place in the Middle East, marking the 'passing of traditional society'. Lerner goes on to remind us that it was this same great transformation, through the centuries, that allowed modernity to supplant medieval ways of life. With hindsight we now label these struggles the age of exploration, the Renaissance, the Reformation, the Counter-Reformation and the Industrial Revolution. They were all part and parcel of secular enlightenment.

A similar process, according to Lerner, is under way in the Middle East. 'The underlying tensions,' he tells us, 'are everywhere the same: village versus town, land versus cash, illiteracy versus enlightenment, resignation versus ambition, piety versus excitement.' (Lerner, 1958: 44) Modernization everywhere poses the same basic challenge: '[t]he infusion of a rationalist and positivist spirit . . . against which Islam is absolutely defenseless'. (Lerner, 1958: 45)

Since Lerner assumes that the Western model of modernization exhibits certain elements and consequences whose relevance is global, he naively proposes that the only hopeful course for the Arab world is to recapitulate the model. What he calls the 'empathetic and mobile personality' – newly mobile persons with the inner mechanism and sensibility to operate efficiently in a changing world – is a by-product of exposure to the mass media. Linked to increasing urbanization and literacy, the media becomes the 'great multiplier', which prepares the way for and generates greater economic participation (per capita income) and greater political participation (voting).

A crude way of putting this is to say that all you need do is to supply the Arabs with easy access to the digital, electronic and other technologies of the new information highway, and they will be on the road to modernity. From here it is just a short step to the excessive importance that post-modernists and proponents of globalism assign to 'infotainments', mass consumerism and popular culture in the framing of everyday life and in redefining basic values.

Many of the recent works, particularly the celebrated bestsellers of Paul Kennedy, Frances Fukuyama, Robert Kaplan and Samuel Huntington, have remained within that tradition. They continue to perceive persisting conflict in the world as a by-product of one single catchy and overarching thought, be it 'the decline of empires', 'the triumph of liberalism', 'chaos' or 'the clash of civilizations'. Robert Barber's *Jihad vs. McWorld* (1996) is essentially within the same fold of such monolithic, deterministic, black-and-white typologies. He too posits a polarized relationship in which the two are pitted irreconcilably against each other. 'McWorld' is the universe of manufactured needs, mass 'infotainment' and mass consumption, whereas 'jihad', the Arabic word for holy war, is shorthand for the belligerent politics of religious, tribal and other forms of bigotry and exclusion. The former is incited by the cash nexus of greedy capitalists and the bland and sleazy tastes of mass consumers. The latter is driven by fierce tribal loyalties, rooted in exclusionary and parochial hatreds. Rather than thinking of a possibility of reconciliation between the two forces, Barber sees instead the homogenized global world of McWorld as rapidly eroding local cultural identities.

As we shall see, both in the first and subsequent essays, there is little of such sharp dichotomies and diametrical representation in post-war Lebanon. While many of the emergent spatial enclaves are understandably jealous of their indigenous identities, they are not averse to experiment with more global and ephemeral encounters and cultural by-products. Likewise, global expectations are being reshaped and rearranged to accommodate local needs and preferences. Local and traditional groupings are not impassive, stolid groups. Just as we spoke of 'adaptive modernization' and the dialectical interplay between tradition and modernity, one can also talk about 'glocalization', particularly in post-war Lebanon. Examples of manifestations of 'retribalization' and the reassertion of communal identities are legion. Displaced and vulnerable groups use the locality and other primordial attachments as sites and resources for social mobilization, welfare and benevolent activities. Both recent and historical evidence indicates persuasively how local groups have been able to resist, avert or rearrange the seemingly irresistible powers and allures of global agendas.

The one notable exception in this genre is Thomas Friedman's *Lexus and the Olive Tree* (2000). In his view, globalization with its own defining technologies – such as computerization, satellites, communications, digitization, fibre optics and the Internet – do not displace the power of the individual, of local supermarkets or of other traditional modes of tapping resources in society. The 'olive tree' represents the longing for anchorage, roots and identity. It refers to everything that

> roots us, anchors us, identifies us and locates us in this world – whether it be belonging to a family, a community, a tribe, a nation, a religion or, most of all, a place called home. Olive trees are what give us the warmth of family, the joy of individuality, the intimacy of personal rituals, the depth of private relationships, as well as the confidence and security to reach out and encounter others. We fight so intensely at times over our olive trees because, at their best, they provide the feelings of self-esteem and belonging that are as essential for human survival as food in the belly. Indeed, one reason that the nation-state will never disappear, even if it does weaken, is because it is the ultimate olive tree – the ultimate expression of whom we belong to – linguistically, geographically and historically. (Friedman, 2000: 31)

Yet Friedman also warns that while 'olive trees are essential to our very being, an attachment to one's olive trees, when taken to excess, can lead us into forging identities, bonds and communities based on the exclusion of others'. (Friedman, 2000: 32)

'Lexus' to Friedman also represents an equally fundamental, age-old human drive for sustenance, improvement, prosperity and modernization, particularly as it is played out in today's globalized system. It represents 'all the bourgeoning global markets, financial institutions and computer technologies with which we pursue higher living standards today'. (Friedman, 2000: 33)

While Daniel Lerner saw his 'grocer' longing but unable to break away from the imperatives of the 'chief', Friedman sees the possibility of a balance between the 'olive tree' and the 'Lexus'. In fact much of his book is a vivid documentation, from every possible corner of the globe, of instances where the 'Lexus' and the 'olive tree' have managed to forge a healthy balance, as well as where they have not. Indeed, to Friedman, the challenge of globalization is to find a viable balance between the needs for identity, community and roots and what it takes to survive within the global system. But if participation in the world of 'Lexus' comes at the expense of displacing and uprooting individuals and groups from the security and sense of well-being inherent in 'olive trees', rootless people will rebel.

Much earlier than Friedman, I was in effect making a similar plea in favour of 'adaptive modernization' and the possibility of converting tradition in the process of absorbing and sustaining some of the necessary ingredients of modernization.

This is in fact the basic thesis of 'On Loyalties and Social Change' (Chapter 1). The essay argues in favour of an adaptive and reconciliatory form of modernization, achieved by assimilating some of the rational instruments of a nation-state into the fabric of social orders that are still sustained by primordial allegiances. The former are necessary for development, the latter for social and psychic reinforcement. Both, however, are necessary for sustaining modernization. But traditional loyalties and local identities come in many guises. They also operate differently in varied socio-cultural settings. As we shall see, in some instances they act as effective leavens or mediating agencies in supporting national planning, industrial development and economic entrepreneurship. In others, they have obstructed processes of social change and delayed the growth of national consciousness and civic and secular attachments. This double supportive-subversive function is readily apparent. The paper provides empirical and historical evidence to substantiate such realities. It does so by first elaborating on the dialectical character of tradition and modernity, the local and global. Second, it tries to disclose the nature of adaptive modernization and the type of agencies most effective in bringing it about.

The tenacity of communalism, kinship and other primordial loyalties has also had an adverse effect on the role of intellectuals as vectors of socio-cultural change. Such intrinsic failure or deficiency in their role comes at a critical threshold. The region is overwhelmed by momentous economic, socio-psychological and cultural problems, which continue to exacerbate sources of uncertainty and instability and threaten regional and world peace, more so perhaps than at any other period in its turbulent political history. Even basic human problems – generated by protracted imbalances in demographic, urban, manpower and other vital resources – are today worse off than they used to be.

Yet, at the very time indigenous scholars and policy-makers are called upon to advance viable strategies to cope with the adverse consequences of these changes, they languish, instead, in ineptitude and disinterest. Indeed, the level of intellectual discourse and scholarly output in the Arab world seems today at its lowest ebb.

In the context of the basic premise I shall be expounding here, one can better understand why their standing in society continues to be precarious and tenuous. The educated elite and public intellectuals are expected to be the torch-bearers of rational, secular and critical liberal thought in a society where non-rational and traditional sentiments are still pervasive. Hence, as I shall argue in 'The Growing Pains of Arab Intellectuals' (Chapter 2), some of the problems that they face differ from those of their Western or developing-world counterparts.

For example, the predicament Arab intellectuals face today is not primarily that of alienation versus involvement or how close or distant they are from centres of powers and authority. It is a by-product of their inability to reconcile the traditional and the rational expectations in society. The former demand that they give priority to particular local and parochial considerations. The latter is more transcendent and universalist in character. In a more poignant sense, they suffer tensions of fragmentation and marginality. Among other things this means that Arab intellectuals appear today to derive greater satisfaction and security, indeed much of their identity, from their kinship and communal ties rather than from their involvement in an intellectual pursuit. At least, their association with traditional networks and cliques is still more sociologically and psychologically meaningful for them. Partly because of the survival of such elements, intellectuals in the Arab world have remained fragmented and characterless as a social group. They still lack the identity, cohesion and class-consciousness visible in other social strata. They also do not serve as spokespersons for social groups or classes in conflict, or as the articulators of their ideologies. Nor are they the pace-setters in dictating standards of taste, mobilizing dissent or lobbying for civic and welfare causes or collective protest. Nor do they constitute, like perhaps their counterparts in some of the Afro-Asian emerging countries, a new elite. Traditional politicians, clerics and heads of voluntary and communal associations continue to abrogate such roles.

Though written over three decades ago, the essay exposes many issues that are still deeply felt today: the marginalization and fragmentation of intellectuals, their amorphous identity, deficient status and security and, above all, the paucity of their intellectual freedom. In the more recent and celebrated work of Edward Said, Arab intellectuals still seem bereft of that "modern critical consciousness . . . " or "oppositional criticism" to challenge all forms of hegemony and mindless authority. At bottom, the underlying task of what he calls "oppositional knowledge" is, after all, "the predilection to challenge and change received ideas, entrenched institutions, questionable values" (Said, 1983: 247). In the absence of such a critical mass of "secular intellectuals in opposition" public intellectuals in the Arab world (which I label "intelligentsia") are still in no position to provide "alternative resources, alternative readings, alternative presentation of evidence" (Said, 1996: 78). These attenuating circumstances have not, as intellectual historians remind us, been always so. Throughout its cultural development, Arab civilization managed to create rather vibrant urban centres. In its medieval and classical periods, in particular, a variety of guilds, orders, *zawiyas*, lodges, neighbourhoods and urban quarters provided a sense of cohesion and solidarity. They served almost as 'third spaces', alternative outlets for state and bureaucratic agencies or those of the market.

Little remains visible today of those robust communal and fraternal feelings. Their decline, in more than one respect, was inevitable. Rapid urbanization, the expansion of commerce and industry, itinerant labour and massive population shifts, the advent of the mass media and, ultimately, the dislocating forces of globalism and information technologies have done much to expedite the erosion or dilution of the sense of cohesion and solidarity elicited by such primordial groupings. Oddly, little is done to resist such erasure or to consider alternative outlets for their legitimate longings for the authenticity and empowerment inherent in fraternal and communal experience.

In this manner the essay has much in common with works of Franz Fanon, Raymond Williams, C.I.R. James and, of course, Edward Said. It becomes, namely an exploration into the cultures of coexistence, to disclose the histories of local cultures or groups threatened by oblivion. One of the defining precepts we can extract from such seminal intellectual heritage is that all cultural manifestations need to be read, studied, appreciated and learned as one element of a history that exists, not just alone, but in counterpoint to all others (Bové, 2000: 1–8). Within this context the essay addresses two related aspects. It provides first a broad overview of some of the salient features of intellectual life in the Arab world. Then it attempts briefly to account for the tensions arising between intellectuals and society. Only by so doing can we begin to understand the troubled lives that they lead and the weighty pressures with which they are compelled to grapple.

Three such dilemmas are explored. Foremost, they are expected to reconcile and accommodate the compatible elements of traditional and modern culture. In more concrete terms this means, as Edward Shils (1961: 64) maintains, to express 'traditional sentiments in modern idioms, to assimilate and transform traditional attributes and to mold them into modern genres'. This is particularly tricky because those entrusted with the task of reconciling such seemingly dichotomous entities are often drawn from two disparate, often polarized, extremes: the impetuous young secularists, bent on total change; and their more reserved traditional compatriots who wish to preserve the most tested institutions and norms. The former are out of touch with traditions; the latter refuse to entertain the new.

Secondly, they are also expected to reconcile their role as detached and disinterested observers with their eagerness to partake in the social and political struggles of their society. This, too, involves some critical and difficult choices. Among other things, it demands striking a balance between their ideological, political and emancipatory commitments and the equally compelling urge to be culturally creative.

As long as the hard core of a society's intellectual elite are being consumed by national struggle, political and economic problems or, worse yet, mundane bureaucratic chores, there will always be a critical shortage of brainpower engaged in creating and carrying culture. It is in this sense that I argue, at the risk of some exaggeration, that what exists today in the Arab world may be more appropriately characterized as a politically conscious and bureaucratic intelligentsia and not a culture-conscious intellectual elite.

Finally, and more perhaps than his or her counterparts elsewhere, the Arab intellectual must also guard against the seductive appeals and vulgarity of mass culture and kitsch. Indeed, as the production and reproduction of culture are being appropriated by commercial agencies, there is justifiable fear that the society might swiftly pass from illiteracy to mass culture without that blissful interlude of slow and genuine cultivation of arts and sciences.

Symptoms of such debasement of the aesthetic standards of 'high culture' are legion. Here again the Arab intellectual is caught between his inner creative impulses and modes of self-expression and the allures of popular appeal and commercialization. By succumbing to the temptations of kitsch or low culture, he betrays his own aesthetic values. By upholding the yardstick of high culture and exclusiveness, he runs the risk of not reaching a wider audience.

In 'Social Structure and Urban Planning in Lebanon' (Chapter 3) an attempt is made to explore the impact of the social structure, particularly as it is manifested in the survival of traditional ties and loyalties, on the process of urban planning. No matter how urban planning is perceived, it always involves the injection of some measure of rationality, calculus, control, forecasting and cost-benefit analysis in the process of regulating and managing the spatial environment and urban functions. Within such a context, it is meaningful to consider – by way of shedding further light on the character of the dialectic between tradition and modernity – how a relatively 'modern' notion of land-use zoning and planning has been incorporated into a socio-cultural setting in which seemingly traditional norms and loyalties are expected to militate against it.

This is not a trifling academic or conceptual query. Much of the urban crisis beleaguering Lebanon (particularly the violation of zoning ordinances and the haphazard and unguided growth of urban areas) is largely a by-product of the failure of urban planning thus far to curb some of the abusive consequences of rampant individualism and laissez-faire or the tenacious residues of communal and traditional loyalties.

This is perhaps most visible in one of the salient and defining features of Lebanon's experience with urbanization and urban planning: the egregious dissonance between the rather orderly and edifying use of private space – as seen in the care residents display for the cleanliness of their homes, quarters and neighbourhoods – and the mindless disregard for public space. The dissonance is not difficult to account for. The typical Lebanese are so consumed, almost obsessed, with the internal security, comfort and well-being of their private domain that they exhibit little or no concern for public welfare or civic consciousness.

Thus, the main focus of the study is to substantiate how certain persisting features of the social and cultural structure shape, modify and, in some instances, distort existing laws and their applications. Accordingly, the essay explores three interrelated dimensions. First, some of the striking features of urbanization, particularly as they relate to the distinction between 'urbanization' as a physical phenomenon and 'urbanism' as a way of life are elaborated. Repeated studies have shown that the swift and extensive urbanization that Lebanon has been undergoing during the past four to five decades has not been accompanied by a comparable decline in kinship and communal loyalties. Hence, in an existential sense, while significant numbers of inhabitants are city-dwellers, their interests and pursuits continue to be sustained by rural and non-urban ties. Such 'ruralization' might cushion the uprooted urban-dweller against the unsettling forces of urban anomie and alienation and provide some of the needed psychic and social supports. They do so, however, at the risk of undermining civility and the broader loyalties of public and national consciousness.

Second, an effort is made to review the successive attempts at proposing or legislating various planning schemes, master plans and building codes and thus to account for their failure to control or tame the haphazard and unregulated growth of Beirut.

Finally, the essay identifies three defining elements of Lebanon's social structure – familism, patronage and commercialism – to highlight their implications for future urban planning and zoning.

New England Puritanism as a Cultural Transplant

The second set of essays, four of them, deal with New England Puritanism as a cultural transplant. Initially, the intention was to explore the intellectual history of the American University of Beirut (AUB) within the parameters of my own autobiographical sketch. The study evolved, however, deliberately or otherwise, into an elaborate exploration of the impact of New England evangelism on socio-cultural change in the Arab world.

In 1985 a Fulbright Fellowship allowed me, along with my wife and two young boys, to enjoy a much-needed respite form the ravages of Lebanon's protracted strife. The one-year leave at Princeton University stretched, blissfully, into a decade. In the mid 1980s Lebanon was still newsworthy. My book, *Lebanon's Predicament*, had just been published by Columbia University Press. I was also at the time perhaps one of the first Lebanese scholars who managed to release himself from Lebanon's tempestuous battleground. Hence, I found myself trapped in a relentless stream of speaking engagements. Everywhere I went – mostly university audiences and on a score of occasions as keynote speaker at conventions and annual meetings of AUB's Alumni Association or chapters – I was always asked how AUB managed to survive and what were its prospects as an American institution of higher learning in a socio-political setting no longer very receptive to some of its premises as a liberal and residential college.

AUB's growth, to a considerable extent, is partly serendipitous, the result of some unintended circumstances. But it also manifests the interplay between successive generations of New England envoys, as carriers of American Protestantism, and the milieu on to which it was grafted.

Though accentuated by the unsettling events of the war, AUB's vulnerability is clearly not of recent origin. Throughout its eventful history, however, the relationship between AUB and its milieu has always been ambivalent and guarded, reflecting thereby its vulnerability as a cultural transplant. Its local and regional constituencies have been predisposed to view the University with mixed sentiments: genuine admiration of the professional skills and liberal lifestyles they were exposed to, but also timid acceptance of, at times outright hostility to, its underlying character, basic message and the political culture it espoused or symbolized as a Protestant-American institution.

The essays focus on the formative period in its intellectual and political history, roughly during the first half of the nineteenth century. It is then that the founding fathers of the College and their evangelist precursors were grappling with the underlying objectives of their mission and the changing needs and perceptions of the host culture. The broader study from which these essays are extracted is, in a sense, a case study, if not on cultural penetration, at least on the migration of ideas and their intended and unintended consequences. (Thanks to a generous Lilly Endowment I was able to devote three years to uninterrupted research and writing. The special archives at Princeton University, Princeton's Theological Seminary and the Lamont Library at Harvard were immensely helpful in this regard.)

'Cultural penetration' is invoked here because much of the discourse on the role of missionary education, particularly in the Levant, is often carried on within this context. Some historians (e.g. Antonius, 1938; Hitti, 1957; Salibi, 1965) are inclined to credit the early missionaries with the reawakening of Arab culture and the regeneration of significant social and literary movements in the entire region. Others, (Tibawi, 1961; Khalidy and Farroukh, 1957; Zahlan, 1965) are, of course, very critical and discredit all such efforts as forms of cultural penetration and a preamble to political intervention and domination.

In some respects, the cultural and political history of Lebanon does provide evidence for the standing argument of the opponents of foreign missions, that the sequence is, 'first the missionaries; then the traders; then the gunboats'. There is plenty of evidence to support such claims. (See Neill, 1966, for an exploration of the historical connection between colonialism and Christian missions.) This is not, however, the subject of these essays, vital as it may seem. My task is considerably less ambitious. By retracing the metamorphosis of AUB from an evangelical college to a secular, liberal and international university, I can better understand the interplay between its religious and secular components, or the so-called 'Christianizing' and 'civilizing' character.

Unfortunately, the bulk of the literature on foreign missions, much like the concern with the international standing of America in the region, does not probe sufficiently into the legacy of the early pioneers. Popular perception, in part because of the direct involvement of the US in the First World War, associates American's interest in the international affairs of the Middle East with the Woodrow Wilson era. There is little awareness that envoys of a different sort had, in fact, antedated and prepared the way for such diplomatic intervention almost a century earlier. Even the published books and monographs on AUB overlook much of the earlier evidence and normally begin their chronicles and accounts with the founding of the Syrian Protestant College in 1866 or shortly before. Hence, there is little systematic documentation of the visions and intentions of their precursors, nor any analysis of the social and intellectual setting from which they were drawn.

The genesis of foreign missions is, after all, in the so-called 'Great Awakening' and spiritual revival of New England between 1791 and 1858, inspired by theologians like Jonathan Edwards and Samuel Hopkins and their devoted core of young zealots. It is there that the story of AUB and all other foreign missions began.

Who were these puritans? What happened to their puritanism as it migrated from its original milieu to other, so-called 'darker' and 'alien' regions of the Arab world? What sort of intellectual baggage did the pioneers carry with them? What sparked their enthusiasm? Why and how did they end up where they did? Why did they succeed in Lebanon when they failed elsewhere in the region? How did they redefine their original intentions to suit the needs of the changing socio-political and cultural setting in which they found themselves? What vital societal transformations, not conventionally associated with educational institutions, can be attributed to such a cultural transfer?

At the turn of the nineteenth century, a handful of New England puritans, the direct spiritual descendants of original Calvinists, alarmed by the loss of religious fervour and the burgeoning secular and liberal tendencies of the period, were instrumental in bringing about a series of revivals that revolutionized the spiritual life of New England, contributed to reforms in theological education and generated an enthusiasm for foreign missions.

Sparked by the evangelist zeal of 'disinterested benevolence' and altruism, many of the early recruits (graduates of Andover Theological Seminary and other colleges such as Amherst, Dartmouth, Yale, Princeton, Williams) became the first generation of so-called 'envoys to regions of darkness', intent on besieging and converting the heathen world. The early Presbyterian missions, particularly those to the Holy Land, eastern Mediterranean and other provinces of the Ottoman Empire, had special appeal. No other region of the world stirred the evangelical imagination as much. Yet they all failed in the intended objectives of converting Muslims, heathens and so-called 'nominal Christians'. They succeeded, however, in all other largely unintended dimensions of their activities, often beyond their avowed original intentions and hopes.

From a nation that had neither colonial establishments nor imperial ambitions, the transfer of spiritual and civil values – via education, relief, welfare and other voluntary and recreational activities – came to be accomplished, as I will argue, by a kind of 'silent penetration', which exemplified some of the American ideals of cultural expansion. Indeed, the missionary outlook was gradually emerging into a pervasive popular ethos. It inspired philanthropic investment in foreign missions and informed, among other things, much of the nation's foreign policy. Indeed, the American Board of Commissioners for Foreign Missions (ABCFM), given the scale and diversity of its overseas activities, became the precursor and prototype of a modern-day international non-governmental organization.

Of all the mission fields, stations and colleges established in the region, the Syrian Protestant College (SPC), transformed into the American University of Beirut (AUB) in 1920, has for over 130 years been providing continuous liberal and professional education to about 5,000 students annually. Located at the crossroads of three continents, it boasts a student body, faculty and staff drawn from a rich variety of national, ethnic, sectarian and socio-economic backgrounds. It was, until very recently, the most truly international university in the world. It also managed to survive as the oldest and most distinguished American academic institution in the Middle East and as a profoundly liberating cultural experiment unique, perhaps, among developing countries.

The essay entitled 'Protestant Orientalism: Evangelical Christianity and Cultural Imperialism' (Chapter 4) examines the ongoing polemics regarding the link between evangelical Christianity and cultural imperialism. To some missionary apologists, the so-called thrust for 'world conquest' and the disparaging views espoused by the pioneering generation of New England evangelists, were not regarded as a form of cultural penetration or subjugation. For example, Kenneth Latourette, a prominent church historian, advances the view that, although missionaries talked about 'world conquest', what they meant thereby was not political or cultural subjugation, still less ecclesiastical imperialism.

These and other such benign views, I argue, are a reflection of the historic hindsight and revisionism that the missionary enterprise has invited over the years. In no way do they do justice to the prevailing outlook at the time, nor the images and mindsets that the envoys carried over with them. Indeed, I argue that Protestant evangelism shares much with other modes of colonial domination. This is visible in at least four features that may be extracted from their perceptions and strategies.

First, they were infused with a haughty self-image, reinforced by feelings of self-righteousness and the transforming powers of Christianity. To them the world out there was a 'ruined wilderness', in urgent need of moral uplift. They were also imbued with an almost blind faith in the superiority of American Protestantism and the New World as a 'righteous republic'. As New Englanders, in particular, they thought of themselves as God's 'choicest grain' of the most 'privileged garden', destined to evangelize and rescue the heathen world. Secondly, and mainly through the survival of medievalist stereotypes, Islam was seen as a 'broken cistern', a 'fortress of error and sin' and Mohammad as a 'false prophet' and an 'artful impostor'. Third, although one could easily depict at the time more sympathetic views of Islam, somehow New England missionaries continued to uphold these outworn perceptions. Finally, it is these overtones of superiority and prejudice that fostered imperialist sentiments and strategies.

In 'Leavening The Levant' (Chapter 5), I begin to shift my analysis to the host regions in which attempts were made to graft New England puritanism on to a local culture that was presumed to be inferior and unreceptive. The essay argues that of all the overseas missions the that New Englanders established, those in the Levant and Eastern Mediterranean became the most far-reaching in terms of the socio-cultural transformations that they generated. The region during the first half of the nineteenth century was in perpetual unrest. They faced formidable obstacles and were compelled to devise strategies to meet ever-changing political and socio-cultural exigencies. The essay explores the visions and objectives the pioneering envoys carried with them, particularly features of the 'puritan ethics' that accounted for the distinctive role that they came to play. An attempt is also made to assess the extent to which puritanism, as a cultural transplant, was receptive to interaction with belief systems and lifestyles different from its own.

In 'Protestant Images of Islam' (Chapter 6), I explore the impact of two largely overlooked factors, which sustained and reconfirmed the disparaging images American Protestants harboured towards Islam, particularly those that prefigured and informed the perceptions which New England Missionaries carried over with them in their efforts to evangelize the Orient and the Levant. First I consider America's encounter at the turn of the nineteenth century with the Barbary states of North Africa. Second, the life and thought of Henry H. Jessup, a leading missionary in the Levant, is examined as illustrative evidence of the reports and impressions relayed back by the missionaries themselves.

Given the temper of popular misconceptions of the day, it was not unusual for emissaries of New England to evoke these views in sanctifying what they termed as their 'sacred errand' into the 'degenerate Orient'. What is surprising, however, is the survival of such distorted views and the tenacity with which they were reconfirmed over the years. Indeed, as will be demonstrated, those medievalist images somehow became sharper and more vilifying in tone and substance.

There is an irony here, in that these were times of swift and far-reaching transformations and behavioural change. Also, and perhaps more intriguing, when compared with all other pertinent groups (i.e. merchants, diplomats, travellers, military and naval personnel), missionaries appear to have sustained the most direct, intimate and extended contacts with the region.

The case of Henry Jessup, one of the most prominent and influential missionaries, stands out in this regard. Despite his 53-year presence in Syria and Lebanon (1857–1910), he refused to discard or even temper his defamatory images of the Levant or his arrogant evangelistic perspectives. Indeed, by 1906, just four years before his death, Jessup was still demonstrating the same medievalist mindset, which he had brought with him half a century earlier. Whether he was bemoaning the 'spirit of intolerance' in Islam, its 'gross immorality', the 'destruction of the family through polygamy and *concubinage*' or the 'degradation of women', it was always to vindicate his three principal claims: that Muslims are engrossed in error and sin and are bereft of any provision for human redemption; that any virtues attributable to Islam are all derivative of Christianity and Judaism; and, finally, that Muslims can be saved only through the Gospel.

In the final essay, 'On Doing Much with Little Noise' (Chapter 7), an attempt is made to substantiate one of the salient features of New England puritanism as a cultural transplant; namely its ability to redefine itself as an itinerant culture. A score of intellectual historians have advanced the notion that, despite the cold austerity of New England puritanism, it demonstrated a remarkable adaptive predisposition to appear in many forms and adjust to the exigencies of divergent and changing cultural settings.

By focusing on its initial encounters in Lebanon (1820–40), an interlude characterized by chronic political unrest and hostility towards missionary incursions, an effort is made to highlight the circumstances that prompted the early pioneers to redirect their original strategies and objectives in favour of unobtrusive and non-confrontational forms of cultural penetration. Given the intimidations and outright persecutions that the missionaries were subjected to, they felt the urgent need very early in their encounters to reconsider some of the methods that they were employing to reach their potential converts.

The missionaries were not all of the same mind in this regard. Some, particularly William Goodell and Elie Smith, realized that they must have been initially impetuous and, hence, often aggressive and confrontational in the way they were prosecuting their work. Both, accordingly, were in favour of more cautious and milder approaches that showed concern for local customs, traditions and rituals. John Praxton, on the other hand, was openly indignant about the deficiency in converts and hence proposed more aggressive and forthright approaches, particularly among so-called 'nominal Christians'. To him the missionaries were much too timid and tentative in their evangelizing. They were also placing undue emphasis on education and the press.

In the ensuing controversy, the more reconciliatory and accommodating views of Goodell and Smith prevailed. Hence, it was during this period, particularly after they returned from their two-year forced retreat in Malta (1828–30) because of the Greek invasion of Beirut, that the novice missionaries started to display considerable inventiveness in their activities and programmes. Having first established common schools and promoted female education, they quickly branched out into a variety of outreach activities, welfare and relief in dark times.

Of note are the system of 'Lancastrian' schooling (which called for qualified native teachers to be involved in the propagation of vernacular textbooks of an evangelical character), establishment of the press, the training of native preachers and the translation of the Bible. Most significant, perhaps, is the emergence of missionaries and distinguished and accomplished scholars who did some ground-breaking research and field surveys, which provided much of the scholarly foundation for subsequent nineteenth-century explorations.

The essay, in some detail, considers these and other forms of 'silent penetration', which epitomized the American ideals of cultural expansion. It must be recalled that at the time America had not as yet any imperial ambitions. Hence, the transfer of spiritual and civil values could have been achieved only through such non-aggressive and unobtrusive measures.

The Spaces of War in Lebanon

The blissful shelter that I found in archival and historical research did not, alas, last for too long. By the late 1980s and early 1990s the war in Lebanon became more partisan and internecine and thus turned bloodier and much more treacherous. Hard as I tried, I could not overlook or dismiss this – to continue to take refuge in my work seemed like a defection from a more insistent and pressing calling.

I temporary suspended my work on missionaries to begin exploring what was, doubtless, a much more compelling, timely and relevant concern; namely, the renewed and escalating cycle of hostility. More specifically, I wished to shed light on the following largely overlooked dimensions: 1) the impact of resurgent communal identities on the pattern and magnitude of violence, 2) the routinization and normalization of violence, 3) strategies of enmity, 4) sources of cultural validation and 5) options for the resolution of conflict and restoration of pluralism.

Thanks to a MacArthur Research and Writing Grant, I was able to review the extensive literature on political unrest, civil violence and insurgency in developing countries, particularly in small and fragmented political cultures like Lebanon. The exercise was instructive in at least two respects. First, I discovered how much of the conventional literature is redundant and irrelevant to the exploration that I wished to undertake. But this preliminary review also revealed a few promising perspectives drawn mostly from social psychology, psychiatry, literary criticism, moral philosophy, social history and the like, which, I came to realize, could be more profitably applied to the study I had in mind. A brief elaboration on each is in order.

Much of the conventional literature on civil unrest, despite its diversity and expansion, converges on a set of recurrent and, in some instances, self-evident themes. In fact, one can identify five general perspectives, which have gained currency during the past two decades or so, to account for the sources and patterns of political violence.

1. Some scholars focus on the fragmented character of political culture in new states in transition. The voluminous output of scholars like Huntington (1968),

Eisenstadt (1964), Pye (1966), Apter (1965), Geertz (1971), Deutsch (1964), Black (1966), Shils (1965), Lerner (1962), etc., particularly during the 1960s, consisted mostly of efforts to elucidate the dialectical relationship between fragmentation and political instability. Fragmentation is, on the whole, treated here as a by-product of both traditional divisive and segmental loyalties and the asymmetrical growth and cultural differentiation generated by processes of development and modernization. Hence, vertical and horizontal divisions, particularly in plural societies like Lebanon, are prone to pull the society apart and threaten the delicate balance of forces. In short, fragmentation generates political unrest, which, in turn, accentuates the cleavages in society.

2. There are those who, armed with dependency theory and conspiracy models, advance some version of the 'inside-outside' polemic. Internal disparities, the argument goes, prompt threatened and dispossessed groups to seek external patronage. External forces, through direct forms of foreign intervention, growing dependence on world markets or patronage of local client groups, produce pronounced shifts in the relative socio-economic and political position of the various religious communities. These dislocations almost always touch off renewed outbreaks of civil unrest and political violence.

3. Drawing upon theories of cognitive dissonance and relative deprivation – as expounded by Festinger (1957), Gurr (1980), Davies (1979), Feierabends (1966) and others – some scholars tend to focus instead on the socio-psychological strains generated by the growing gaps and disparities between aspirations and opportunities. One of the most celebrated versions of this perspective is, of course, that of relative deprivation, treated here in terms of the individual's perception of a discrepancy between what he/she believes he/she is legitimately entitled to get and his/her estimation of what he is actually able to receive under existing conditions. According to this analysis, feelings of relative deprivation will produce anger and frustration, which in turn will trigger violent action.

4. By contrast, theories of so-called 'collective action' are more inclined to argue that what matters is not so much that people have grievances and unmet needs, but rather that they possess the political resources that will enable them to translate their discontent into action. Noted examples here are Tilly, Hirschman, Moore and Eckstein, who in much of their research concentrate on the conditions conducive to the mobilization of groups and their predisposition to participate in collective action.

5. Finally, a growing number of scholars in recent years have shifted their concern to the analysis of the impact of rapid urbanization on domestic political violence. Particular emphasis here is placed on the revolutionary potential of the urban poor and 'urban marginals' and the impact of communal networks on the pattern and intensity of civil strife. Theoretical reformulations by Tilly (1978), Bienen (1984) and Wilson (1979), among others, reinforced by

empirical surveys in regions undergoing rapid urbanization, are beginning to reveal some telling but inconsistent trends. For example, while the survival of communal networks in Latin American and African cities has been generally associated with a reduction in the incidence of political violence – as cited by Cornelius (Mexico), Ross (Nairobi), Cardose (Latin America), Perlman (Rio de Janeiro), Cohen (Ivory Coast) – preliminary results from a selected number of Middle Eastern cities provide evidence to the contrary (Karpat on Turkey, Kazemi on Iran, Ibrahim on Egypt and Khalaf and Denoeux on Lebanon).

Instructive as such analyses have been, they are predominantly concerned with the inception and etiology of civil unrest. Consequently, they have had little to say about 1) why violence has been sustained, 2) the forms and intensity it has assumed, or 3) how people cope with chronic unrest and unsettled times. At least in the case of Lebanon, the exercise has become rather futile; at best, a laborious and painful elaboration of the obvious. For example, it is quite common for a pluralistic society like Lebanon to display a high propensity for violence. The lack of political integration in new states has, after all, been cited over and over again as a major cause, indeed a prerequisite for violence. One could likewise write volumes about the destabilizing impact of the presence of Syrians, Palestinians and Israelis or the unresolved regional and superpower rivalries, without adding much to what we know already.

What is, however, unusual is the *persistence, growing intensity* and *shifting targets of hostility*. By the early 1990s, in fact, the conflict had escalated even further as intercommunal rivalries degenerated into intraconfessional hostilities. The ecology of violence, reinforced by all the psychological barriers of restructured enmities, began to assume more intensive forms as street and quarter in-fighting displaced and/or compounded the earlier communal violence. Hence, the former characterizations of the initial stages of civil unrest – 'Christian versus Muslim', 'right versus left' – generally became outmoded. They clearly do not help in accounting for the upsurge in the level of hostility between Sunnis and Shi'ites, Druze and Shi'ites, Kurds and Shi'ites, Palestinians and Shi'ites, Maronites and Armenians . . . or between Maronites and Maronites. Indeed, by the early 1990s, victims and casualties of intraconfessional violence had started to outnumber those generated by intersectarian or inter-religious hostility.

Considerations of this sort, along with all the other ruinous manifestations of civil unrest, clearly suggest that violence has become counterproductive and self-defeating. Contrary to what is often suggested, it has had little to do with the rebirth or recovery of justice and virtue, which are unlikely to rescue Lebanon from its deepening crisis and transform it into a secular and more civic social order. I take my cue here from Hannah Arendt (1958), who has suggested that the practice of violence, like all action, changes the world, but the most probable change is to a more violent world.

Expressed in more explicit political terms, the resort to violence has had little effect so far on 1) redressing the gaps and imbalances in society, or 2) transforming Lebanon's communal and confessional loyalties and institutions into more civic entities typical of a nation-state.

Yet, renewed cycles of violence went on unabated. Though Lebanon is often dubbed as an instance of 'low-intensity conflict', violence began to assume all the aberrant manifestations of endemic and autistic hostility. Unlike other encounters with civil unrest, which are often swift, decisive and localized, and where a sizable part of the population could remain sheltered from its traumatizing impact, the Lebanese experience has been much more protracted and diffuse. The savagery of violence was also compounded by its randomness. In this sense, there is hardly a Lebanese today who was exempt from experience of these atrocities, either directly or vicariously. Violence and terror touched virtually everyone. It was everywhere and nowhere. It was everywhere because it could no longer be confined to one specific area or a few combatants. It was nowhere because it could not be identified or linked to one concrete cause. Recurring cycles or episodes of violence erupted, faded and resurfaced for no recognized or coherent reason.

The warring communities also locked themselves into a dependent relationship with violence and chronic conflict. Violence became both protracted and insoluble, forced into a corner from which there was no egress to creative peaceful change. Violence was also sustained by a pervasive feeling of helplessness, demoralization and obsessive dependency on external patrons and foreign brokers.

Within such a context, it became more instructive to shift the analysis from the partial and almost exclusive concern with the etiology of violence and extend it to incorporate those features that sustain and escalate its belligerency. Only by so doing can we begin to understand fully some of the socio-psychological and cultural attributes of protracted violence and, more importantly, suggest possible courses of action or strategies to constrain its aberrant consequences.

More specifically, this shift in concern from the *initiating* to the *sustaining* factors accompanying protracted conflict can help us to elucidate at least two distinctive features of civil unrest in Lebanon: 1) the tendency for both pluralism and violence to become more pathological and 2) the existence of ideologies of enmity through which warring communities reinvent strategies for mutual debasement and demonization to rationalize acts of aggression, particularly when the victims of that aggression might well be their own co-religionists or groups with whom they had coexisted previously.

When we extend our concerns to those features that sustain and escalate the intensity of hostility, then we must part company with some of the conventional perspectives and consider other sources and paradigms more appropriate for the analysis of such overlooked features of protracted conflict. Fortunately, I discovered a rather substantial volume of writing, which could be more imaginatively applied to the instances of communal conflict under study.

One of the most striking features of political violence in Lebanon is the plurality of warring factions, changing targets of hostility and the reassertion of communal and territorial identities. If adversaries in Lebanon are trapped in an escalating cycle of violence, it is pertinent to explore how threatened communities resort to violence to preserve their endangered identities. Alain Touraine's (1981) analysis of violence as a 'glue' cementing social life, the socio-psychological formulations of Brockner and Rubin (1989) on ways in which collective victims of prolonged suffering become more psychologically challenged as they become more embroiled in bitter conflict, or Smith and Berg (1987) on what they term 'preconditions for stuckness' are all of relevance here.

Many of the conclusions and inferences of social psychologists in this regard are based on contrived, controlled experiments. The Lebanese case offers vivid instances to substantiate the impact of communal networks and loyalties on the ferocity of protracted hostility. For example, while surviving communal ties may be sheltering urban marginals from the anomie of metropolitan life, they also intensify the density of communalism and collective mobilization. Such evidence should prompt one to reconsider much of the received wisdom regarding the 'harmless', 'benevolent' and 'integrative' nature of informal networks based on traditional sentiments and loyalties (see Bienen, 1984).

Another striking feature of civil violence in Lebanon (and this is obviously true of other instances of protracted hostility) is not only that it persists and grows in intensity, but also that it has become normalized and routinized. In the words of Judith Shklar (1982), it has been reduced to an 'ordinary vice', i.e. something that, although horrible, is expectable, something ordinary and otherwise well-meaning citizens could easily find themselves engaged in.

Through direct observations and data extracted from personal accounts, biographies of fighters, tracts, pamphlets of the various militia organizations, graffiti and other artistic, popular and cultural expressions of everyday life, one can easily identify the manifestations and consequences of such routinizaton. The intention here is to substantiate in vivid and concrete ways how groups engaged in such cruelties feel that they have, so to speak, received permission, some kind of cultural sanction or legitimization for their evil deeds.

Of equal importance in this regard is to document how, with the collapse of state authority and governmental agencies, the war generated and institutionalized its own roles, status groups and networks. It has, as we shall see, evolved into a system of its own, with its informal economy, extortionist and protection rackets and a burgeoning underclass of new warlords and profiteers who are, understandably, reluctant to end a situation that has become their lifeline for power and wealth.

Though this dimension of protracted civil unrest remains largely overlooked, one does encounter comparative evidence of other such instances. Natalie Davis's (1975) analysis of popular religious riots in sixteenth-century France and Bowyer-Bell's (1987) of contemporary Ireland, offer rich documentation.

The aggressive and hostile bonding in cloistered communities that the adversaries in Lebanon have evolved to survive the menacing cruelties of a Hobbesian jungle is largely sustained by ideologies of enmity. All such strategies are, in effect, modes for legitimizing violence. All the rival groups have developed elaborate, often crude and not-so-subtle strategies for mutual vilification and debasement. These range from intermittent propaganda campaigns to other modes of political resocialization and rewriting of communal or national history. Each group now depicts the 'other' as the repository of all the evil, wicked and demonic attributes.

It is instructive, within this context, to identify the manifestations and consequences of such strategies. Here as well there is a wealth of literature –

mostly from psychiatry, social psychology, literary criticism and other humanistic traditions – which could be profitably applied to add insight into the nature of adversarial relationships, sectarian stereotypes and enmity between groups. John Mack (1988), Sam Keen (1986), Ofer Zur (1987), Charles Pinderhughes (1979), Herbert Kelman (1987), to name only a few, have all advanced some insightful hints for exploring the psycho-social structure of prejudice, 'differential bonding' and the 'ideologies of enmity', which sustain the dehumanization and demonization of 'others'. Similarly, the recent resurgence of 'attribution theory' and efforts to refine and extend its paradigms and research tools to cross-cultural settings have also revealed some promising perspectives. This is particularly relevant in accounting for the salience of religious and sectarian identification and the cultural dispositions to polarize in-group/out-group relations. (See, for example, Harvey and Weary, 1985; Hewstone, 1983; Jaspars, 1983; Turner, 1987.)

Finally, closely associated with the above are some of the normative and ethical predispositions that sanction and legitimize the cruelties antagonists in Lebanon are inflicting on each other. In significant respects, the experiences of the Lebanese poignantly epitomize the three socio-cultural elements Paul Ricœur (1967) attributes to any form of human veil: 'defilement', 'sin' and 'guilt'. By defiling and dehumanizing the 'other', it is much easier to sanction his killing and, hence, create conditions for 'guilt-free massacres'. Even wanton and gratuitous violence becomes, in the words of Robin Williams (1981), 'virtuous action in the service of applauded values'. One can easily offer some vivid evidence of episodes in which aggressors are given the opportunity to legitimize and rationalize their aggression. It is an attempt, in other words, to find out how and under what circumstances violence is rendered culturally acceptable and tolerable.

The war in Lebanon has produced reams of popular and idealized writing – in the form of covenants, declarations, propaganda campaigns, obituaries, sermons, editorials by public figures and personal memoirs of fighters, etc. – which lend themselves to systematic content analysis by way of documenting Ricœur's three attributes.

Some of Foucault's (1975) work, despite its obscurity and complexity, will also be of relevance, especially in explaining how spatial arrangements and confinement in cloistered communities will affect social relations, perceptions and ideas. A host of other writing on 'degradation ceremonies', 'ritual', 'symbolic deviance', 'social boundaries', 'stigma' and 'the management of spoiled identity' by H. Garfinkel (1967), Mary Douglas (1966), P. Bourdieu (1977) and E. Goffman (1968) may also be judiciously drawn upon. Of particular relevance here is R. Stivers's work (1982) on the social construction of evil and the sacrilization of violence and Mary Douglas's insightful analysis of ways in which cultural patterns are dramatized and affirmed.

Most promising, perhaps, for my purposes, is cultural analysis along the lines advanced by Ann Swidler (1986). She treats culture not as unified systems that produce action in a consistent direction; rather, it is more like a 'tool kit' or repertoire, from which individuals select differing pieces for constructing lines of action. This is appropriate for the analysis of strategies of action in unsettled and extreme situations such as Lebanon. In other words, choices are shaped not by values but by immediate circumstances; by what people find they have become good at, or at least accustomed to. By focusing on strategies of action (or ideologies) as cultural products, one begins to understand not only the changing character of violence in Lebanon but also why certain groups and not others resort to it.

Throughout the presentation here, as elsewhere, efforts will be made to employ, where feasible, some of the rich imagery, metaphors and paradigms of literary criticism and moral philosophy. In addition to some of the early classics (e.g. Ernest Becker, Mircea Eliade, Eli Sagan, Hubert and Mauss, etc.), I have consulted a few of the more recent original and path-breaking works, which make imaginative use of literary discourse to explore the ethics of political violence. Three examples come to mind: René Girard's (1977) analysis of the sacrificial act in sacred ritual; Mary Dahl's (1987) treatment of Greek drama, Old and New Testament to identify and elucidate the violent deed and its participants; and Elaine Scarry's (1985) brilliant and compelling work on the language of pain and its political implications.

The two essays selected here will, I hope, substantiate some of the striking features associated with protracted and displaced hostility. Three such features stand out: the persistence and growing intensity of violence, the plurality and shifting targets of hostility, and, finally, the ways in which violence acquired a momentum and a life of its own often unrelated to the initial sources of conflict.

In 'The Scares and Scars of War' (Chapter 8), I try to elucidate how some of the cruelties of war were normalized and domesticated. I argue that by 'sanitizing' the ugly episodes of the war and transforming it into an ordinary routine, terrorized groups were able to survive some of its ravages. By so doing, however, they also allowed it to become protracted and diffused.

An attempt is also made to demonstrate how the war managed to rearrange the country's social geography and impose its own menacing logic on private and public space. Here again, by seeking shelter in communal solidarities, traumatized groups could find temporary release from the cruelties of war. They were, however, rendered more vulnerable to some of its long-term menacing consequences. I will highlight here both the enabling and disabling manifestations of such predispositions. Clearly, by distancing themselves from the demonized 'other', they could of course release their aggression without mercy or guilt. They do so, however, at the risk of becoming more accessible targets of directed and focused acts of hostility. More disabling, the prospects for reconciliation and peaceful coexistence become all the more remote and unlikely.

Finally, I shall also try to show how various communities displayed different adaptive strategies to cope with the adversities of protracted strife. An intriguing finding needs to be accounted for: communities that were victims of a larger magnitude of trauma were not necessarily those who also displayed greater stress. This is, not incidentally, an inconsequential feature. The resilience that certain communities revealed may give us a hint as to the persistence of violence. In other words, the more adept the Lebanese become at adjusting to and coping with the cruelties of strife, the more opportunities the war had to reproduce itself. Once again, as we shall see, the enabling and disabling features become aligned together.

In 'The Radicalization of Communal Loyalties' (Chapter 9), an attempt is made to identify and account for some of the circumstances associated with the tenacity of communalism and its various manifestations. For purposes of analysis, three different layers or magnitudes of violence are singled out. First, there is social strife, which is generally the by-product of socio-economic disparities, ideological rivalries, asymmetrical development, relative deprivation and feelings of neglect and dispossession. These are largely non-belligerent in character and assume rather tame forms of social protest and collective mobilization. Second, if the socio-economic disparities and feelings of neglect persist and the resulting hostilities are unappeased, particularly if accompanied by feelings of threatened communal or confessional identities, conflict is inclined to become more belligerent. It is here that social strife in transformed into communal violence. In the apt language of Bowyer-Bell, it is then that *civil strife* passes the point of no return into *civil war*. Finally, civil violence does not always remain 'civil'. When incited by re-awakened tribalism and unresolved regional and global rivalries, it can readily degenerate into the incivility of proxy wars and surrogate victimization.

Within such a context it becomes meaningful to consider how social strife is deflected into communal violence and ultimately descends into further incivility and barbarism. Explorations of this sort are not only of historic significance. There has been recently renewed conceptual interest in the nature, manifestations and consequences of reawakened 'tribalism' and the reassertion of local and communal identities, particularly as they relate to the forces of globalization and post-modernity. Lebanon, as we shall see, offers an instructive case study in this regard.

The Restoration of Civility in Lebanon

How is Lebanon to break out of the grooves that have entrapped its embattled communities in an escalating cycle of political violence? Is Lebanon doomed to suffer such protracted and seemingly intractable hostility? What future prospects, if any at all, can one envisage that would offer less belligerent options for coexistence between communities experiencing such deepening enmity? This, in my view, remains the country's most central and overriding problem.

This is particularly acute because what Lebanon has been experiencing over the past twenty years is not only the breakdown of a political system but also the dismemberment of a society. The most elementary social ties that normally cement a society together – ties of trust, loyalty, confidence, compassion, decency – have been, in many respects, fatally eroded. It is considerably easier, under such circumstances, to create a state than to reassemble a society. A state can be reconstituted by legislation, by fiat, by covenants and pacts – as Lebanon has done a score of times in its political history – but how is one to repair the fabrics of a fractured society?

Two sets of crucial issues need to be considered if one is to entertain such prospects: 1) the interplay between internal and external sources of instability and 2) the nature and consequences of communal identities. Both have implications for the prospects of forging a more viable form of pluralism or consociational democracy. Cumbersome and destabilizing as the 'inside-outside' dialectics has been, it is thoroughly researched. It is, however, the second issue – the resurgence of communal and confessional identities – that needs to be explored and restructured. As we shall see, massive population shifts, particularly since they have been accompanied by the reintegration of displaced groups into more homogeneous, self-contained and exclusive communities, have reinforced communal solidarity. For better or worse, communal and parochial identities are much sharper today. As a result, territorial and confessional identities, more so perhaps that at any other time in Lebanon's eventful history, are beginning to converge. The uprooted and traumatized seek and find shelter in their reawakened communal solidarities. Such realities can no longer be denied, wished away or mystified. They must be recognized for what they are: strategies for the empowerment of threatened groups and their incorporation into public life. It must also be borne in mind that the coalition of confessional and territorial entities, since it draws upon a potentially much larger base of support, could be a more effective agency for political mobilization than kinship, fealty or sectarian loyalties.

It is my assumption that such communal solidarities, furtive and pathological as they seem at the moment, need not continue to be sources of fear and hatred. If stripped of their intolerance, they could be extended and enriched to become the bases for more judicious forms of power sharing and the articulation of more civil and broader cultural identities. This is based on the premise that, just as enmity has been socially constructed and culturally validated, it can also be unlearned. Group loyalties can, after all, be restructured. Under the spur of visionary and enlightened leadership, individuals can at least be re-socialized to perceive differences as manifestations of cultural diversity and enrichment; not as dreaded symptoms of distrust, fear and exclusion.

When, where and with what does one begin the process of restoration? Given the magnitude and scale of devastation, Lebanon will most certainly require massive efforts, in virtually all dimensions of society, to spearhead its swift recovery, including sustained development. Processes of post-war reconstruction, even under normal circumstances, are usually cumbersome. In Lebanon they are bound to be more difficult still because of the distinctive attributes and conditions that set the country apart from other comparable instances of post-war reconstruction.

Incidentally, in the autumn of 1991 I felt a beginning could be made, at least academically, by exploring the role of urban design in the post-war reconstruction of Beirut. With the collaboration of Professor Philip S. Khoury of MIT, we hosted a conference, which convened over 20 participants: three generations of architects and town planners, practitioners and entrepreneurs. Topics, both conceptual and empirical, ranged from the nature of incipient territorial identities, the housing crisis and reconstituting the Lebanese economy to hopes and visions of architects and businessmen. The conference publication, *Recovering Beirut* (Brill, 1993), has become a path-breaking reference and a precursor of other such symposia and workshops. It has also inspired a succession of research prospects.

Unfortunately, much of the concern with post-war rehabilitation has been almost exclusively focused on such matters as administrative reforms, demilitarization, bilateral agreements with neighbouring states, the involvement of the UN and the international community, infrastructure and economic reconstruction. Vital as these concerns are, they must be supplemented by considering the role of the voluntary sector along with other indigenous efforts, particularly in programmes that are effective in mobilizing otherwise disengaged, isolated and indifferent groups in public ventures.

Of equal importance is the impact of urban planning and design on the restructuring of the devastated and retribalized spaces of Lebanon. As will be seen, one of the most visible consequences of the war has been the redrawing of Lebanon's social geography. Massive population shifts and dislocations have generated fundamental transformations (and deformations) in spatial configurations and restructuring of land-use patterns and the composition of urban and rural agglomerations. Mixed and heterogeneous communities have diminished. Decentralization has undermined Beirut's primacy and its dominance as a metropolitan centre. The absence of government and municipal authorities has produced havoc in zoning ordinances and threatened the country's landscape and natural resources. Deepening enmity, hostility and pervasive fear have reinforced the psychological barriers and distance between communities.

Hence, the spatial reconstruction of Lebanon will most certainly require more than the physical rehabilitation and restoration of the country's devastated infrastructure and public capital, pressing as these are. More important and challenging is a consideration of urban strategies and master plans for restructuring public utilities and daily amenities in such a way as to meet the needs for diversity and unity. It is my view that inventive urban planning and architectural and landscape design can be judiciously used in pacifying and healing the fractured social order and, thereby, restoring more than a modicum of civility.

Pervasive symptoms of retribalization that have reshaped the country's social geography pose a direct and compelling challenge to urban planners and architects. How can common and public spaces be rearranged to create conditions conducive to a peaceful and creative coexistence among groups embittered by years of unresolved hostility? More specifically, how can public utilities and daily amenities be relocated in such a way as to meet the needs for intimacy and distance?

In 'From Geography of Fear to a Culture of Tolerance' (Chapter 10), I explore three related dimensions. First, an attempt is made to identify and account for some of the distinctive features of civil strife in Lebanon. Second, two unusual by-products of protracted strife are exposed, namely symptoms of 'retribalization' and 'collective amnesia', along with consideration of ways in which they could form the bases of a political culture of tolerance. Finally, I advance a few alternative options for reinforcing Lebanon's internal immunity or reducing its vulnerability to external sources of unrest.

In 'Contested Space and the Forging of New Cultural Identities' (Chapter 11), three issues pertinent to the prospects of forging a viable political culture of civility and peaceful coexistence are explored: collective memory, contested space and efforts to coalesce new cultural identities. These are not as unequivocal or self-evident as they may seem. They all involve some critical and contested elements.

For example, to some, anonymity, collective forgetfulness and shared amnesia are dreaded conditions in all societies. Indeed, as I have been repeatedly suggesting, the success of modernity over other socio-cultural arrangements has not necessitated the disappearance or erosion of pre-modern elements. 'Adaptive modernization' and 'globalization' involve after all the reconciliation of the two. Furthermore, local and traditional features do not survive only in nostalgic and artificial forms of retreat or withdrawal. They have been creatively reconstructed and rearranged to partake in processes of development and societal transformation.

Others, particularly Benjamin Barber (1996), advance the notion that successful civic nations always entail a certain amount of what he terms 'studied historical absentmindedness'. Injuries that are too well remembered, he tells us, cannot heal. (Barber, 1996: 167) What this implies, of course, is that if the ugly memories of the war are kept alive, they are bound to awaken unappeased symptoms of fear and paranoia, as they appear to be doing lately. More ominous, this also implies that, without an opportunity to forget, there can never be a chance for genuine coexistence.

What I argue in the essay is that both these existential predispositions – the urge to distance oneself from the fearsome memories of an ugly and unfinished war and the equally compelling urge to preserve and commemorate them – are present today in Lebanon. 'Retribalization' and the consolidation of communal and confessional loyalties – so rampant in post-war Lebanon – incorporate in fact both these features. In other words, many Lebanese today are impelled by two seemingly opposed forms of self-preservation: the need to remember and the need to forget. The former is sought in efforts to relocate oneself in one's community or to rediscover and reinvent its threatened roots and heritage. The latter assumes more escapist and nostalgic manifestations.

To understand this ongoing interplay between collective memory, the hankering for roots and heritage and the reassertion of spatial identities, the essay explores three related dimensions. First, it highlights briefly a few of the most striking spatial transformations associated with the war. Second, and more substantially, it attempts to identify and explain how three communities in Beirut have experimented with different modes of accommodation to some of the global incursions threatening their local heritage. Finally, the role of urban planning and design is considered, particularly in terms of its potential in formulating schemes for reclaiming and restoring Beirut's urban legacy. This naturally raises critical questions as to who is to reclaim what and how much of the old heritage should be restored and rehabilitated.

Reflexive Essays

The final collection of essays, which I call 'reflexive', includes a set of four rather light and discursive reflections, often provoked by personal circumstances. It was a sobering experience to be a witness to all the cruelty and barbarism of relentless civil strife, especially when the terror and havoc unleashed so many base and atavistic human impulses. When virtually all of one's cherished values, both private and public, are threatened, it is difficult to maintain one's cool, let alone the dispassionateness or value-neutrality demanded by the academic strictures of one's discipline.

Initially, I recall being furtive about 'violating' such ordinances. The urge, however, to expose, debunk, often dramatize the evil became forgivable lapses when pitted against all the bestiality begotten by the war. My writing started to acquire a more redemptive, often cathartic tone. It also became more expressive and evocative. I wrote not so much to validate or discharge the scholarly obligations of my academic calling but, rather, to 'let off steam', to reclaim a threatened heritage and advance a more realistic and balanced portrait of the forces disfiguring my society.

'From Aley to Ras Beirut' (Chapter 12) is a personal account, a memoir often laced with my own encounters with the swift transformations to two places most familiar to me (a salubrious resort town and a mixed urban neighbourhood) and the ways in which they had defaced their spatial and social structures. The forces of change associated with the incursions of petro-dollars, land speculation, the inflow of itinerant resort-seekers, gaudy commercialism and other global symptoms of large-scale urbanization were irresistible. They had already despoiled much of the country's habitat before the anarchy and destruction generated by the war started to compound these devastations. They spared very little of the old edifying features, particularly those that had managed to sustain a fairly open and plural character, such as Aley and Ras Beirut.

There is more to the sketchy memoir than a flight into nostalgia or a lament on the erosion of such blissful interludes. It has a more ameliorative message. I am prodding architects, town planners and practitioners to heed the idealistic, aesthetic and revolutionary sensibilities inherent in their professions and advocate schemes that could pacify some of the forces ravaging our beleaguered habitat.

The two short pieces, originally published in the *Christian Science Monitor*, were provoked by two rather startling but instructive events that my two sons faced as 'displaced' children. Both deal with the delicate and contested issues of identity, normative conflict, resocialization, the role of family intimacy, re-entry into post-war Lebanon and the forging of new national images. Both were widely circulated at the time, reprinted in a score of periodicals and textbooks, and they generated an outpouring of lively reactions from the Arab-American community and Lebanese in the diaspora.

In 'The Americanization of George' (Chapter 13), I describe an incident when our son George, at the vulnerable age of 12, returned home one day with a terse note from the principal of his Middle School at Princeton. Being in a 'university town', the Princeton public school system is noted for its liberal and progressive leanings and receptivity to pluralistic and open cultural expectations. Yet the note George brought home that day and the 'sexual instruction' he was receiving in school and among his peers indicated some disheartening and jarring misconceptions of the role of family intimacy in the life of an impressionable adolescent. As a Lebanese, George grew up in a nurturing setting of warm, close and affectionate family networks and obligations where the outward display of emotion – touching, kissing, hugging – are spontaneously given without guilt or shame.

The note cautioned George, in no uncertain terms, to report to his school counsellor if anybody at home touched him or displayed uninvited intimate gestures towards him! Given the legitimate concerns of Americans with 'intimate violence', sexual abuse and harassment in dysfunctional and broken homes, the protective measures taken by the school are understandable. Yet at the same time they alerted George to 'pathologies' all too remote from his own concerns and cherished values. They also imparted a more baffling message, namely, that he must break away from the reassuring and supportive intimacies of his family if he was to enjoy the exuberance and freedom inherent in becoming a full-fledged American boy.

While George was being de-natured and uprooted from some of the wholesome elements of his Lebanese heritage to become an 'American boy', Ramzi, seven years his junior, was to experience another unsettling dissonance in his re-entry into post-war Lebanon. He was barely two years old when we escaped the ravages of war in Lebanon in 1984 to settle in the tranquil and bucolic setting of Princeton. Hence, unlike his older brother, he had no direct experience or vivid recollection of the horrors of civil strife. Yet, as he was coming of age in America, Lebanon was drifting deeper into those avenging cycles of reckless violence. An already biased media and misinformed public opinion needed no justification to malign Lebanon further.

In 'Madonna and Mount Sannin' (Chapter 14), I reflect upon Ramzi's rediscovery of his country's sublime heritage, particularly its natural and historical endowment, and his longing to reconnect with its disinherited past. Informed by the intuitive sensibilities of a young child, particularly his reactions to the disharmony between the country's edifying geography and its boisterous political culture, I consider how reawakened territorial attachments can serve both as antidotes to fear and bases for the articulation of new cultural identities.

In many respects, the jarring experience of coming face to face with devastations of his country's habitat epitomized the same poignant tensions confounding the rest of the society. By his own infantile but perceptive reactions, Ramzi was personifying and responding to the same nagging disjunctions between the country's natural endowments, its captivating landscape and rich history, and the squalid despoliation of its urban milieu and its even more treacherous political culture. There was a gap of nearly half a century between me and Ramzi. Yet, the same realities confronted and angered us both.

Ramzi's reactions to his country's natural and historic endowments should not be dismissed as infantile. I dwell on them because I think they reflect some of the salient premises and concerns that his society is currently facing. Just as an intuitive young boy is willing to part with the ephemeral and seductive titillations to which he has been exposed in America and embrace those of a more distant and enduring order, so too his besieged compatriots (young and old) can do likewise.

Now that many Lebanese, during the past few years, have been revisiting parts of their country inaccessible to them before, it is to be hoped that they too will begin to renounce the alien and borrowed ideologies that they had embraced to sustain their territorial confinement and their belligerency.

Throughout its chequered history, Lebanon has been bedevilled by an almost

Janus-like character. During interludes of relative stability and prosperity, its admirers described it admiringly as the 'Switzerland' or 'Paris' of the Middle East. The more chauvinist went even further to depict the country, often in highly romanticized tones, as a 'wondrous creation', a 'valiant little democracy', a 'miraculous' cultural and economic experiment sustained by enviable resilience and *unfuwan*. In the late 1960s and early 1970s, when the country started to display early symptoms of political instability, it became fashionable to depict Lebanon as a 'precarious', 'improbable', 'fragmented', 'torn' society, so divided and fractured, in fact, that it would be impossible to piece it together again.

No sooner had the fighting erupted in 1975 than it became the easy target of scorn and disparagement. The ox had fallen and was ready to be butchered. To many of Lebanon's detractors, and they came out in droves, the country was a congenitally flawed entity. Others went further to argue that a deranged oddity of this sort could never have lasted, let alone ever become a viable political entity.

In 'Lebanon as a Playground' (Chapter 15), I propose another metaphor, which, in my view, is a more inclusive and neutral analytical tool. I consider both features intrinsic to a 'playground', which account for Lebanon's 'success story', along with those that render it more vulnerable to the inside-outside contradictions. Once both the enabling and disabling features of a 'playground' are recognized, the metaphor can also serve as a curative and rehabilitative vector for the restoration of civility.

PART I

On the Dialectics of Traditon and Modernity in Arab Society

CHAPTER 1

On Loyalties and Social Change

History, to borrow Fernand Braudel's expressive metaphor, is like a river. On the surface it flows rapidly and disappears, but down below there is a deep stream that moves more slowly, does not change quickly, but is the more important because it drives the whole river. Braudel urges us to study, as he himself has admirably done, such deep currents, particularly in elucidating processes of continuity and change in the evolution of societies. (Braudel, 1979: 621)

The focus of this essay – the pattern of loyalties and their impact on social change – allows us to probe into the nature and consequences of such deep undercurrents. Loyalties, particularly as they are manifested in sentiments, allegiances and affiliations, are, after all, the basic ties that motivate, hold and cement groups together within society. Accordingly, much of what happens in society may be understood by elucidating the character of loyalties and by identifying their impact on specific instances of social change. Fundamental as this matter is, there is still considerable ambivalence and uncertainty regarding the nature and pattern of these loyalties. As a result, we often misunderstand their character and misread some of their implications. Such misreading is not as benign and innocuous as is often assumed. It should not be dismissed as the inconsequential outcome of abstract scholars weaving conceptual images and paradigms in their ivory towers. In some instances misreading has generated a large measure of distortion of socio-historical realities. It has also led to some costly misadventures in schemes for socio-economic planning and strategies for political development.

To this day, planners in the Arab world, as elsewhere in developing countries, continue to receive inconsistent advice. At times, in the name of secularization and rational planning, they are asked to erode, bypass, contain or even devalue their traditional loyalties. At other times, particularly when planners become mindful of the burgeoning tourist industry and commercial value of some of the rustic and colourful features of their folklore and popular culture, they are implored to preserve their threatened natural and cultural heritage. The very institutions and loyalties that were formerly devalued become coveted and prized attributes. Little wonder that traditional loyalties are either denigrated or idealized but rarely treated for what they actually are.

In certain instances political regimes are known to oscillate, often discordantly, between the two extremes. Their initial enthusiasm for radical and total change, reinforced by an impetuous desire to efface the old order, quite often gives way to fatuous idealization of the past. The resurgence of Muslim fundamentalism and other reformist movements is, to a large extent, a reaction to excessive modernization. Such reactive movements, from quietist mystical orders to militant organizations, become more pronounced when modernization is associated with the 'impurities' of Western incursions.

Clearly, scholars are not exempt from such charges and pitfalls. This is particularly apparent in the continuing discourse regarding the nature and direction of social change. After the initial upsurge in comparative studies of modernization, the field witnessed a decline during the mid- and late 1970s. There has been in the past few years, however, a resurgence of interest and revival of some of the earlier polemics (see for example, Lauer, 1982; Gendzier, 1985). Scholars are, once again, invoking the old issues as to whether there is any directionality in the process of modernization and to what extent it is possible to justify the idea of a singular path or end to that process.

Within the context of this chapter, the issue becomes one of ascertaining the nature of the interplay between so-called 'modern' and 'traditional' loyalties. Are these loyalties as polarized and dichotomous as often suggested? Is it necessary for Arab societies, particularly those characterized by a large measure of persistence in their traditional values and institutions, to experience an erosion in these 'survivals' before they can become receptive to societal and behavioural transformations?

The literature on comparative modernization and social change is still riddled with ambiguities and often inconsistent responses to basic questions of this sort. Except for a few noted and recent departures, the bulk of the literature, as I have suggested elsewhere, has remained essentially within the fold of the Western intellectual tradition of European and American sociology. (Khalaf, 1987) Assumptions regarding the directionality of change and the inevitable erosion of traditional loyalties by irreversible forces of secularization, the polarization of tradition and modernity as incompatible dichotomies, or the denigration of traditions as useless and nostalgic survivals are clearly not the global models they are often claimed to be. The pitfalls involved in transposing such allegedly universal models on other instances of social change are serious.

There is no need to repeat here the charges levelled against these perspectives, which were prevalent during the 1950s and 1960s. This has been convincingly and amply done by a score of other writers.[1] It is sufficient to note that they are patently

---

1. Of the many criticisms of the earlier paradigms, particularly the tradition-modernity dichotomy, the following are worth noting: David Apter, 'The Role of Traditionalism in

(continued...)

inadequate in helping us understand the nature of interplay between traditional and modern loyalties. Indeed, they actually distort certain socio-historical realities so distinctive of particular Arab societies. For at no point in the recent history of the Arab world, even in so-called revolutionary and radical regimes, have the processes of change been so total and all-embracing as to sweep aside all the vestiges of their traditional past. Nor have traditional values and institutions been so immobile and obstructive as to pose insurmountable barriers to social change or to require that these values be rendered inoperative by encapsulating or neutralizing their 'polluting' impact.

The moral to be extracted form these and other critical reassessments of the extensive literature on comparative modernization is plain and clear. We need to divest ourselves of the conceptual and ideological tyranny of these models. If we are to employ the indispensable Weberian ideal-typical contrast between 'traditional' and 'modern', then, in the words of Reinhard Bendix, we should 'deideologize' these constructs in such a way as not to impart 'a spurious, deductive simplicity to the transition from one to the other'. (Bendix, 1967)

We clearly need an alternative approach for the analysis of the interplay between tradition and modernity. For neither in their antecedents nor in their patterns and consequences do processes of change in the Arab world comply with the Western experience or with the options or courses taken by other newly developing nations. We need an approach, to repeat, that neither anticipates the ultimate purgation of traditional 'survivals' nor regards traditional loyalties as

---

(...continued)

the Political Modernization of Ghana and Uganda', in David Apter, ed., *Some Conceptual Approaches to the Study of Modernization* (Englewood Cliffs, N.J.: Prentice Hall, Inc., 1968), pp. 133–5; Reinhard Bendix, 'Tradition and Modernity Reconsidered', *Comparative Studies in Society and History,* 9 April, 1967, pp. 292–346; S. N. Eisenstadt, 'Studies of Modernization and Sociological Theory', *History and Theory*, 13, no. 3 (1974), pp. 225–52; idem, 'Reflections on a Theory of Modernization', in A. Rivkin, ed., *Nations by Design* (New York: Anchor Books, 1968), pp. 35–61; André G. Frank, *Sociology of Development and Underdevelopment of Sociology* (London: Pluto Press, 1971); B. F. Hozelitz, 'Tradition and Economic Growth', in R. Braibanti and J. Z. Spengler, eds, *Traditions, Values and Economic Development* (Durham: Duke University Press, 1961), pp. 83–113; Marion J. Levy, Jr, 'Contrasting Factors in the Modernization of China and Japan', *Economic Development and Cultural Change*, 2 (1953–4), pp. 161–97; Ali Mazrui, 'From Social Darwinism to Current Theories of Modernization', *World Politics* 21 (October 1968), pp. 68–83; Fred G. Riggs, *Administration in Developing Countries: The Theory of Prismatic society* (Boston: Houghton Mifflin, 1964); Edward Shils, 'Tradition', *Comparative Studies in Society and History*, 13 (1971), pp. 122–59; Dean C. Tipps, 'Modernization Theory and the Comparative Study of Societies: A Critical Perspective', *Comparative Studies in Society and History*, 15 (March 1973), pp. 199–226. And the following papers in A. R. Desai, ed., *Essays on Modernization of Underdevelopment Societies*, vol. 1 (Bombay: Thacker and Co. Ltd, 1971); A. R. Desai, 'Need for Revaluation of the Concept', pp. 474–548; Gail Omvedt, 'Modernization Theories: The Ideology of Empire', pp. 119–27; M. N. Srinivas, 'Modernization: A Few Queries', pp. 138–48; R. Sinai, 'Modernization and the Poverty of Social Science', pp. 53–75; W. F. Wertheim, 'The Way Towards Modernity', pp. 76–94.

incompatible with modernization. That is, we need an approach that recognizes the possibility, in certain contexts, of the continuing coexistence and mutual reinforcement of tradition and modernity, and which makes for greater opportunities for congruence and overlapping, where tradition and modernity are allowed to infiltrate and transform each other. It is in this sense that the interplay between tradition and modernity is conceived more as a dialectical than a dichotomous relationship. The purpose of this essay is to provide further theoretical and empirical evidence in favour of this dialectical approach. First, the case for the dialectical character of tradition and modernity is elaborated. Second, an attempt is made to disclose the nature of adaptive modernization and the type of agencies or institutions most effective in bringing it about.

The Case for Dialectics: Sustained Change and Social Cohesion

The case for a dialectical approach requires little in the way of theoretical justification. There is no need, in fact, for elaborate models or complex reformulations of earlier conceptual schemes. Several basic but viable analytical tools already exist, which may be appropriately employed in analysing structural and institutional changes without the moral premises and ethnocentric biases inherent in some of the conventional perspectives. Concepts such as John Lewis's distinction between 'adaptive' and 'inverse' modernization, Clifford Geertz's 'involution', Rustow and Ward's 'reinforcing dualism', S. N. Eisenstadt's 'patrimonialism' or Ernest Gellner's analysis of 'post-traditional' forms in Islam are just as few instances.

John Lewis employs notions of structural differentiation and role proliferation in his analysis of the social limits to politically induced change. His distinction between adaptive and inverse modernization is particularly relevant. Adaptive modernization comprises 'the gradual, unplanned and essentially spontaneous differentiation of roles and the gradual evolution of formal modes of organization'. (Lewis, 1969) In essence, this involves the proliferation of roles and the progressive development from simple, undifferentiated, pre-modern institutions (predominantly defined according to particularistic and local standards) to more specialized, complex and differentiated ones. Since many of the pre-modern social institutions and relationships are 'carried over' – particularly those that help shape the attitudes of individuals – social cohesion is maintained during the unsettling period of social change.

Inverse modernization, on the other hand, occurs 'where the gradual processes of change are bypassed and specialized organizational forms are directly transferred to new nations under the guidance of a revolutionary or modernizing elite'. In some respects this involves the 'inversion' of those processes of development that underlie adaptive modernization. The often impetuous revolutionary elites of new nations, according to Lewis, are not only bent on a disruptive and rapid course of modernization but have consciously repudiated the pre-modern social relationships that might help sustain minimal social cohesion. In this way, 'they exacerbate disorder and destroy potential support: they thereby sow the seeds of their own destruction. Left unchecked, these difficulties would produce extreme social upheaval and a new revolutionary situation.' (Lewis, 1969: 6)

In analysing processes of agricultural and ecological change in Indonesia, Clifford Geertz borrows the interesting concept of involution from the American anthropologist Alexander Golden-Weister, who devised it to describe

> those cultural patterns which, after having reached what would seem to be a definitive form, nonetheless fail either to stabilize or transform themselves into a new pattern but rather continue to develop by becoming internally more complicated . . . What we have here is pattern plus continued development. The pattern precludes the use of another unit or units, but it is not inimical to play within the unit or units. The inevitable result is progressive complication, a variety within uniformity, virtuosity within monotony. This is involution. A parallel instance . . . is provided by what is called ornateness in art, as in the late Gothic. The basic forms of art have reached finality, the structural features are fixed beyond variation, inventive originality is exhausted. Still development goes on. Being hemmed in on all sides by a crystallized pattern, it takes the function of elaborateness. Expansive creativeness having dried up at the source, a special kind of virtuosity takes its place . . . (Geertz, 1968: 81)

Involution in the case of Indonesia was highly functional because it enabled the society to 'evade, adjust, absorb, and adapt but not really change'. Since the particular Javanese village Geertz explored was shaped by forces over which it had little control and since it was denied the means for actively reconstructing itself, it

> clung to the husks of selected established institutions and limbered them internally in such a way as to permit greater flexibility, a freer play of social relationships within a generally stereotyped framework . . . The quality of everyday existence in a fully involuted Javanese village is comparable to that in the other formless human community, the American suburb: a richness of social surfaces and a monotonous poverty of social substance. (Geertz, 1968: 103)

Certain institutions, roles and other seemingly traditional patterns of behaviour in the Arab world can be said to be 'involuted' in a related, if not completely identical sense. In Lebanon, for example, family firms, family associations and communal and voluntary organizations have displayed considerable degrees of internal adaptability while retaining their outward fixity. (Khalaf, 1986) Similar tendencies are manifested in the persistence of patron-client networks (Gellner and Waterbury, 1977) and Sufi orders, brotherhoods, urban quarters and reformist movements (Eickelman, 1981). In most of these instances the outer form, the social surface of these organizations, has remained fundamentally the same, while their inner substance managed to undergo appreciable differentiation and development. The concept of involution is relevant and useful precisely because it recognizes the possibility of internal differentiation, variety, development and a certain measure of 'virtuosity', while cultural patterns retain their definitive and crystallized form. Outward fixity and inner dynamism, in other words, coexist and reinforce each other.

Rustow and Ward (1964: 445) identify the quality of reinforcing dualism to explain Japan's classic and perhaps most dramatic instance of the systematic and purposeful exploitation of traditional institutions for the achievement of modernizing goals. They provide ample evidence to counter the conventional thesis by showing that the role of traditional attitudes and institutions in the modernizing process has often been 'more symbiotic than antagonistic'. The most conspicuous example of this reinforcing dualism is the political role of the emperor:

> Here is an institution which is not only traditional but archaic. Yet when faced with the problem of constituting a modern nation-state in Japan, it was possible for the Meiji leadership to exhume this ancient institution, imbue it with quite a new content and much higher degree of visibility and status, and emerge with an extraordinarily effective symbol and instrument of national unity, discipline and sacrifice. (Rustow and Ward, 1964: 445)

Similar instances of reinforcing dualism are evident in the economic field. The maintenance of small, traditionally organized units of production alongside the most modern factories seems to have contributed to the rapid and effective economic development of Japan. The conclusion Rustow and Ward draw from this is clear: 'many elements of the traditional society could be converted into supports for the process of political modernization. The result was added impetus of a sort conducive to modernization.' (Rustow and Ward, 1964: 445)

Eisenstadt's concept of patrimonialism, particularly as it relates to the persistence of patron-client networks, feudal and semi-feudal survivals and other personalistic loyalties and associations, can also be judiciously applied to explore concrete instances of the reinforcing character of the interplay between traditional modern forms. (Eisenstadt, 1973) According to Eisenstadt, this perspective discloses the inadequacies of some of the basic premises of the earlier theories of modernization on at least four counts:

> First, by showing that many of these societies and states did not develop in the direction of certain modern nation-states; second, by demonstrating that these regimes did not necessarily constitute a temporary 'transitional' phase along an inevitable path to this type of modernity; third, by indicating that there was nevertheless some internal 'logic' in their development, and last by emphasizing that part, at least, of this logic or pattern could be understood from some aspects of the traditions of these societies and derived from them. (Eisenstadt, 1974: 241)

Two other relatively obscure but equally telling examples of the dialectics I have in mind may also be cited. To document the adaptation of traditional Islamic movements to modern conditions, Ernest Gellner provides an insightful analysis of two other paradoxical but successful instances of so-called post-traditional forms in Islam: the Ismailis of the Shi'a, and the Murids, a Sufi brotherhood in Senegal. (Gellner, 1973). The first group operates conceptually outside the bonds of Sunni orthodoxy, the second claims to have remained within it. Neither group, however, is particularly predisposed to the allegedly rational, universalistic and achievement-oriented ethics of the modern world. Yet both have displayed remarkable entrepreneurial and organizational skills, while sustained by mystical beliefs and primordial loyalties that are the antithesis of the Weberian model of the Protestant ethic. In each case, Gellner concludes:

> A fortunate combination of circumstances has enabled a particular set of organizational and ideological elements, inherited from a tradition in which they were but slight variants of a standard pattern, to make a marked impact in novel circumstances. Shi'ism is an unpromising candidate for the Protestant Ethic, but the followers of the Aga Khan are famed as entrepreneurs, and it seems unlikely that without their Shi'a faith, they could have been as successful as in fact they have been. Sufism does not resemble socialism and looks like most unpromising ideological equipment for the formation of agricultural kibbutzim, but in its Murid form, this is just what it has achieved . . . In either case, an explanation in terms of the faith alone and its preaching is woefully inadequate, but in either case, the faith played a crucial part. (Gellner, 1973)

Finally, several other instances of the dialectical relationship between tradition and modernity are increasingly recognized lately. At least two such expressions can be noted here. One has to do with the role of informal groups, kinship networks and other primordial ties in political development. James Bill and Carl Leiden provide persuasive evidence of the pervasiveness and profound influence these networks continue to have on political loyalties, power struggle in relaying vital political information, and in arriving at consequential political decisions. (Bill and Leiden, 1984) The other focuses on the developmental potential of indigenous and other traditional grass-roots organizations in the formation of viable cooperatives, collectives and other peasant associations concerned with various rural development projects ranging from rotating credit and savings associations to the construction, maintenance, allocation and management of water schemes and irrigation projects.

For Nash, Dandler and Hopkins, cooperatives are conceived as communities that demonstrate how people direct themselves to form, out of the old human material, new institutions to cope with their changing world. They, too, speak of the 'dialectic between structure and movement' and how 'new forms of mobilization relate to existing traditional structures'. They provide supportive evidence, from various cross-cultural settings, to demonstrate 'the effectiveness of this kind of grafting of new organizations on the traditional kinship and communal organizations'. (Nash, Dandler and Hopkins, 1976)

Likewise, Cernea, Siebel and Massin, and Colletta, among others, provide further substantive evidence along those lines. Cernea is quite explicit and maintains that policy-makers or development practitioners in this area tend to develop one of two basic sets of attitudes:

> The first consists of ignoring or underestimating the development function or potential of grass-roots, production-oriented peasant organizations. This is the well-known attitude of certain national development agencies that perceive indigenous organizations and culture as a constraint on modernization, as a remnant of old times, and a nuisance to be eliminated, in order to really 'modernize'.
>
> The second consists of idealizing the traditional organizations and culture and ignoring the historical necessity of changing them too; this is tantamount to not understanding the essence of organizational forms as a cultural adaptive mechanism to change and as a socio-cultural form for absorbing and utilizing modernized technologies. (Cernea, 1981: 130)

For Cernea, clearly, neither of these two positions can guide, either in practical or in theoretical terms, an effective development policy. Instead of regarding traditional organizations as a constraint, could they not, Cernea asks, be utilized as a resource for development?

> A sound modernization policy should make the best use of all available resources . . . when they are amenable to development activities. On the other hand, the need to strengthen, change and develop these organizations themselves should not be overlooked. (Cernea, 1981: 130)

Colletta makes a similar plea for the use of indigenous culture. He concludes his Indonesian case study by writing:

> All too often development has confronted culture as a bulwark of conservatism, infrequently looking towards its potential use for positive change. Anthropologists have been quick to document the confrontation between development and culture . . . [instead of] leading the creative discovery of how long-established cultural pathways of interaction, established roles, institutions and value incentive systems might be employed as levers for positive change. (Colletta, 1975: 62)

This charge does not apply to at least one anthropologist, Elizabeth Fernea, who, after an absence of five years, revisited the Arab world in 1984 and returned to speak of 'new voices'. In her book, an edited volume of evocative essays, stories, poems, life histories and so on, she argues that, despite the rich variety of expressions, there is a great shift in the aspirations of men and women:

> No longer is the example of the West seen as the answer to the problems of the Middle East . . . People are attempting to improve their lives through indigenous traditions and customs; through the dominant religion of the area, Islam; and through their own kinship and family patterns. They are improvising

and combining the new and the old, adapting, changing, and building, trying to create their own form of independence. (Fernea, 1985)

In the Arab world, these new voices are far from new: they have always been there. Somehow, social scientists and historians failed to identify or recognize their true nature or the role that they could play in generating and absorbing change. In fact, a generation of earlier scholars had either denigrated the presence of such traditional values and sentiments or prodded Arabs to disengage themselves from them, if they were to enjoy the fruits of modernity. (See, among others, Lerner, 1982)

Further instances of the mutual reinforcement of tradition and modernity, from both developed and developing societies, can be easily furnished.[1] The foregoing examples are, it is hoped, sufficient to establish the fact that such a dialectic is much more widespread and viable than has so far been admitted by interested observers. The oversight is understandable and may be accounted for in two ways. First, as has been suggested earlier, because of the predominance of certain Western perspectives and the emergence of radical revolutionary elites in developing countries, we have either overlooked or denigrated the modernizing potential of traditional loyalties and institutions. Simply not enough social scientists have been trained to look for, recognize and document this convergence. Second, forging a blend between seemingly discordant elements is admittedly not a simple and manageable task. These historical forces – the desire for continuity and change, for coherence and dynamism, for institutional transformation and cultural reconstruction, for 'essentialism' and 'epochalism',[2] to mention but a few of the many labels applied to this interplay – are impelled after all by different sentiments and values and often derive their support from divergent and disparate social groups.

The experience of specific countries may vary, but the tensions and the broad patterns bespeak of essentially the same process or underlying concern: how to preserve cherished values and loyalties while transforming the institutional and material basis of society. Expressed more pointedly: how is social cohesion to be maintained if change is accelerated?

Rather than looking in only one of two directions – the rooted traditions of the past or the more secular and liberal components – several countries in the Arab world have been inclined to reconcile the two. The results may often seem an incoherent and precarious mélange of disparate elements. They have, however,

---

1. For added substantiation of the notion that traditional institutions may be adaptive to modern society and politics, see Joseph Gusfield, 'Tradition and Modernity: Misplaced Polarities in the Study of Social Change', *American Journal of Sociology*, 72 (January 1967), pp. 351–62; Milton Singer, *When a Great Tradition Modernizes* (New York: Praeger Publishers, 1972); Ann Willner, 'The Undeveloped Study of Political Development', *World Politics*, 16 (April 1964), pp. 468–82; Robert N. Bellah, 'Continuity and Change in Japanese Society', in B. Barber and A. Inkeles, eds, *Stability and Change* (Boston: Little, Brown and Co., 1971), pp. 377–404.

2. For a discussion of the meaning and significance of essentialism and epochalism, see Clifford Geertz, 'After the Revolution: The Fate of Nationalism in the New States', in Barber and Inkeles, eds, *Stability and Change*, pp. 357–76.

particularly at the micro and local level, been effective in generating and sustaining change while maintaining social cohesion and some measure of cultural continuity.

Features of Adaptive Modernization

Three central features of adaptive modernization may be extracted from the discussion thus far. All three are essential for understanding and justifying the need for a dialectical perspective.

1. No matter how modernization is defined, it most certainly involves the will and capacity of a society to absorb and generate change or innovation. The capability for sustained growth, however, need not involve total and radical transformation. Nor should it necessitate incessant adoption and borrowing of new ideas and practices. Innovation can take place through the restructuring and rearrangement of existing institutions. Indeed, the distinctive feature of adaptive modernization is the capacity of existing institutions and agencies to rearrange themselves to confront new challenges and cope with continuing tensions and problems. In brief, a large measure of modernization can and does take place by mobilizing traditional networks and loyalties.

2. Another distinctive attribute of modernization stands out. Whether the process follows a gradual and spontaneous course or is a more radical and revolutionary reconstruction, whether it originates from internal indigenous forces or from external social contact, modernization always generates discontinuities, imbalances and tensions, which necessitate adjustments and continuous adaptation. No mode of social interaction is free from the occasional ramifications of internal tension. Accordingly, another feature of modernity is the capacity of a society to cope with the discontinuities and discrepancies inherent in a changing social order.[1]

3. Modernity, as Rousseau poignantly realized more than 200 years ago, despite all its potential promises, remains a disruptive social process and a bitter and agonizing personal experience. To counterbalance some of its disquieting by-products – alienation, apathy, homelessness, overurbanization, excessive materialism, pollution, senseless rebellion, pointless crime and deviance and so on – there must be more cognizance of the need for stabilizing and integrative mechanisms that can provide some measure of social support and psychic reinforcement. The will to be modern, after all, and the desire to enjoy the material benefits of modernity are not the only overpowering urges among newly developing societies. Equally compelling is the will to survive with

---

1. S. N. Eisenstadt, among others, has in several of his earlier writings emphasized the discontinuities and breakdowns inherent in the process of modernization. See his 'Breakdowns of Modernization', *Economic Development and Cultural Change*, 12 (July 1964), pp. 345–67; and his *Modernization: Protest and Change* (Englewood Cliffs, NJ: Prentice-Hall, 1966).

dignity and honour, or what Mazzini called the 'need to exist and have a name'. In fact, the concern for national consciousness, cultural identity and personal autonomy appears to be assuming more prominence than the heedless craving for unlimited growth and material progress. This has became much more poignant in the wake of some of the more intimidating incursions of globalism and post-modernity.

If we accept these fundamental components, then modernization becomes ultimately a question of identifying the appropriate agencies capable of generating change and absorbing and mediating tensions without threatening national identity. The viability and effectiveness of any agency of modernization should be assessed in terms of its propensity for providing these basic elements. In this sense, modernization, contrary to what is often assumed (Huntington, 1966: 766), requires more than the expansion of production and communications, the broadening of loyalties from family, village and community to nation, the secularization of public life, the rationalization of political authority, the promotion of functionally specific organizations and the substitution of achievement criteria for ascriptive ones. These are no doubt essential for absorbing and generating change, but over and above them the system must be capable of incorporating traditional social groupings that can act as palliatives in absorbing imbalances and in maintaining some measure of political consciousness and national identity. In concluding his lucid and exhaustive survey of the economic history of the Middle East, Charles Issawi (1982: 227) singles out this contradiction as a future source of social and political unrest in the region. Peoples of the Middle East, he maintains, much like those of the rest of the world, are seeking to achieve incompatible aims: economic growth, higher living standards, national power and equality, a greater sense of community, cultural identity and political liberty.

Modernization, then, should not be taken to mean necessarily the erosion of traditional loyalties and groupings or a process of 'disengagement from traditions' (Welch, 1967). It is doubtful whether specific countries in the Arab world, or elsewhere for that matter, could ever sustain substantial change and development if these transformations were to dislodge the rooted traditional interests and loyalties. Likewise, modernization need not involve the emergence of exclusively rational and secular agencies. Ultimately it means that all groups – traditional and rational, secular and confessional, communal and national – become increasingly group-conscious and aware of their particular interests.

The central thesis of this essay is therefore an argument in favour of an adaptive form of modernization, which tackles the basic problem of modernization in many parts of the Arab world, namely the need to reconcile development with social and psychic reinforcement.

What is being suggested here is that, insofar as modernization is a disruptive process, a modernizing agency, to be effective, must possess the capacity both to absorb and generate change and to cope with tensions and discontinuities.

This is not a trivial matter. Much of the tension Arab societies face today can be attributed to their failure to meet these criteria. The specific experience of particular societies could, in fact, be differentiated in terms of their predisposition for satisfying such demands.

The roles and institutional arrangements that the Lebanese have devised at various stages of their history, for example, kinship associations, various forms of political patronage, parochial voluntary organizations, family firms and the like, are a case in point. (Khalaf, 1987) While these mediating structures have been effective in generating change and alleviating some of the tensions and disquieting effects of modernization, they have not been successful in generating the necessary conditions that sustain civic ties and national loyalties. The very factors that account for much of the vitality, resourcefulness and integration of the Lebanese are also the factors responsible for the erosion of civic ties and national loyalties.

Expressed differently, loyalties that enable in some respects disable in other respects. This notion can be appropriately applied both to account for the failure of specific instances of socio-economic planning and development and to underscore the deeper and more encompassing predicament other countries in the Arab world are also facing. It also clarifies the inherently ambivalent character of the interplay between traditional and modern loyalties. In some instances, traditional loyalties have acted as leavens in reinforcing and supporting national planning, economic resourcefulness and industrial development. In others, they have obstructed the process of social change and retarded the growth of national or higher forms of social consciousness. This double supportive-subversive function is readily apparent; a few illustrations will suffice.

The relatively low incidence of social disorganization and deviant behaviour, particularly as reflected in rates of crime and delinquency, drug addiction, alcoholism, suicide and other symptoms of alienation and anomie, may to a large extent be attributed to the survival of primordial, kinship and communal ties in the Arab world. As repeated studies have shown, the social and psychological supports people continue to derive from such ties have insulated rapidly urbanizing districts form the temporal, segmented and impersonal types of social contacts often associated with urbanism.[1] Likewise, patron–client networks, in a variety of socio-political settings, continue to offer access to vital services, personal benefits and privileges. (Gellner and Waterbury, 1977) The same is true of the role of parochial voluntary associations, urban quarters and religious orders. But it is the survival of loyalties and mediating structures that also account for much of the deficiency in civility and in higher and more encompassing forms of national consciousness from which Arab societies continue to suffer. In short, the factors that enable at the micro and communal level disable at the macro and national level.

In virtually all parts of the Arab world the pattern and direction of social change will ultimately depend on how or when this dilemma is resolved. Indeed, in some societies, in Lebanon in particular, the country's political future has become

---

1.   See Janet Abu Lughod, 'Migrant Adjustment of City Life: The Egyptian Case', *American Journal of Sociology*, 67 (July 1961), pp. 22–32; Michael Bonine, 'Urban Studies in the Middle East', *Middle East Studies Association Bulletin*, 10 (October 1976), pp. 1–37; John Gulick, *Tripoli: A Modern Arab City* (Cambridge, MA: Harvard University Press, 1967); Samir Khalaf and Per Kongstad, *Hamra of Beirut: A Case of Rapid Urbanization* (Leiden: E. J. Brill, 1973).

inextricably linked with such a predicament. At the risk of overgeneralization, I am suggesting that socio-political systems that continue to display strong tribal, ethnic or sectarian pluralism and subnational loyalties superseding national commitments have much in common. They all need those socio-political institutions of structural arrangements that will permit the average Lebanese to preserve some of his primordial allegiances without threatening the already precarious and tenuous national sentiments and loyalties. This, among other things, will necessitate the development of new political and national leadership, one that will encourage and sanction extensive political resocialization and restructuring of certain existing values and loyalties. Without restructuring or resocialization, these political entities cannot possibly develop into a full-fledged nation-state. Compared with the purely secular or traditional institutions, the adaptive agencies I have in mind could potentially be more effective as carriers of these transformations, particularly if reinforced by resocialization.

That these adaptive agencies or mediating structures have survived for so long is one indication that they continue to answer some durable and profound needs. That some of them degenerate or cannot as effectively mobilize and integrate human and other resources at higher levels of the social order is, in many respects, inevitable and predictable, given the pluralistic and multifarious nature of group affiliations in the Arab world. Such realities, as Durkheim often reminds us, are reasons to seek the reformation of these agencies, not to declare them forever useless or to destroy them. (Durkheim, 1964: 14)

Alternative Courses of Modernization

If the postulated features of modernization are accepted as central to the understanding of the interplay between loyalties and social change, then the focus of analysis should be those mediating structures that display the highest propensity for innovation, for coping with some of the imbalances and disruptive consequences of change and finally for integrating the social order and retaining a measure of group identity and solidarity. This is emphasized because there is a tendency in the literature to overrate the innovative aspects of modernization at the expense of the integrative and tension-reducing capacity of a particular agency or system. Once again, I reiterate that, because of the persistence of certain perspectives on social change, with their emphasis on rationality, growth and development, some of the integrative and socio-cultural dimensions of modernization are often overlooked or treated only obliquely. Accordingly, the central problem of how social cohesion is to be maintained if change is accelerated continues to be generally ignored.[1]

If this is the context – that is, sustained change and social cohesion – within which modernization is to be evaluated, then one of three courses of modernization becomes possible.

---

1. A notable exception in this regard is Samuel Huntington; see his *Political Order in Changing Societies* (New Haven: Yale University Press, 1968).

1. Specific Arab countries could, as some have already done, adopt a coercive and disciplined model in line with many newly emerging nations, where the state becomes the dominant agency of political socialization and modernization. In a Marxian sense, the state will presumably liberate man from his communal and primordial ties and establish collective allegiance on the basis of the 'unmediated loyalties' and devotions of individuals.[1] All voluntary associations, special-purpose groups and social identities – traditional and rational alike – will be eroded or become virtually nonexistent. This unmediated approach to modernization (as it may be called, for lack of a better expression) has not only been badly battered by academic critics, it has been faulted by events. Suffice it to note here that, given the persistently tribal and pluralistic structure of Arab societies, let alone the resurgence of fundamentalism in its various forms, this option cannot possibly gain any widespread appeal. The totalitarian or authoritarian model is certainly effective in generating social cohesion and solidarity, but only at the expense of sealing off all avenues of individuality and self-expression. Increasing centralization and state control may produce the desired goals of political stability and uniformity, but only by insulating the individual from modern life. Among other things, citizens in such a system are incapable of imagining any other values except those defined by the state. Also, this model assumes that becoming modern is inherently revolutionary, in that it seeks to dislodge all the inherited basic institutions, a process that can be carried out only by and under the guidance of a radical elite.[2]

    Durkheim, once again, can be appropriately invoked here. 'When the state,' he warns us, 'is the only environment in which men can live communal lives, they inevitably lose contact, become detached, and thus society disintegrates. A nation can be maintained only if, between the state and the individual, there is intercalated a whole series of secondary groups near enough to the individuals to attract them strongly in their sphere of action and drag them, in this way, into the torrent of social life.' (Durkheim, 1964: 28)

    The critical question, then, is what sort of groups are more effective in dragging individuals into the 'torrent of social life'. Within this context, any authoritarian or centralized model that requires the elimination of such mediating groups is clearly the most perilous option a country can choose.

2. Countries could opt for a more liberal and secular approach where change is mediated through predominantly rational agencies of modernization, and where political allegiance and loyalty are sustained by the civic instruments of the nation-state. The majority of Western scholars, particularly in their earlier writings, were inclined to favour this approach. Daniel Lerner, Edward Shils,

---

1. For a clarification of this point see Robert A. Nisbet, *The Sociological Tradition* (New York: Basic Books, 1967), pp. 132–41. This conception comes close to the sacred collectivity model outlined in David Apter, *The Politics of Modernization* (Chicago: University of Chicago Press, 1965), pp. 31–33.

2. For an elaboration of this viewpoint see Chandler Morse, 'Becoming vs. Being Modern: An Essay on Institutional Change and Economic Development', in Morse et al., *Modernization by Design* (Ithaca, NY: Cornell University Press, 1969), pp. 238–382.

Manfred Halpern, Karl Deutsch, S. N. Eisenstadt, to mention a few, all identify the agencies of political development in terms of the instruments of the nation-state modelled after the experience of some Western countries.[1] Modern man, whether through 'empathy', 'psychic mobility' or socio-economic 'mobilization', is defined in terms of psychological attitudes that predispose him towards secular, pragmatic, instrumental and utilitarian ties and contacts. He is also a 'participant', in that he experiences modern citizenship by joining political associations or special-purpose groups. Accordingly, there is extensive consideration of the role of the mass media, the military elite, political parties, civil bureaucracy and other so-called institutional vectors of modernization (Berger, Berger and Kellner, 1973), but hardly any recognition of the role of adaptive agencies in bringing about political development or promoting cultural identity and social integration. Secular institutions are seen as liberating agencies that free or disengage man from traditional loyalties and prepare him psychologically for modernity. Neither of these notions – the one of instrumentality and utilitarianism and the other of participation in secular political groups – corresponds to the realities or characteristics of social change in most Arab societies. Even if they were to exist, the rational instruments of change are of doubtful value in coping with the imbalances and discontinuities inherent in a changing society. Neither can they be effective, as suggested earlier, as integrative mechanisms.

The early experience of some of the revolutionary and radical regimes in the Arab world is instructive in this regard. Their leaders were more than eager to adopt the purely secular course of adopting programmes and projects for restructuring the socio-economic, cultural and administrative resources in their countries. Many of these projects, intended as models and showpieces of collective will and rational planning, in fact became sources of public embarrassment and failure shortly after their implementation. The Tahrir Project, during the earlier period of the Nasser regime in Egypt, was one such dramatic and costly instance. Launched in 1954 as an experiment in desert reclamation and land reform, the Tahrir Project was intended to cast the state in the role of social engineer to create new group relations and new roles, which the rest of society could emulate (Hassanain, 1975). The architects of the project were so enthusiastic in their ambitions, so utopian in their conceptions, that they overlooked some of the most common everyday life realities and basic loyalties that have characterized the life of the Egyptian peasant for so long. In a utopian, almost 'Brave New World' fashion, peasants were made to live in rows of detached residential units on grid-net streets named after war heroes. They awoke to military music and were expected to dispense their labour collectively, with elected cooperatives to process and market their produce.

---

1. Lerner, *The Passing of Traditional Society*; Edward Shils, *Political Development in the New States* (The Hague: Mouton and Co., 1962); Manfred Halpern, *The Politics of Social Change in the Middle East and North Africa* (Princeton: Princeton University Press, 1963); Karl Deutsch, 'Social Mobilization and Political Development', *American Political Science Review*, 55 (September 1961), pp. 493–514; S. N. Eisenstadt, *Modernization: Protest and Change.*

These and other equally bizarre features prompted Nasser himself, in 1965, publicly to criticize the project as an example of confused thinking and muddled planning. (Waterbury, 1983)

Other examples of excessive rationalization and corresponding insensitivity to indigenous needs and local traditions abound. For example, misguided attempts at mobilizing and structuring the labour force and creating national unions and Pan-Arab labour federations (Belling, 1960), family planning programmes and population policy (Warwick, 1982) and social welfare agencies and benevolent associations have been frequently devastating in their impact. The most striking attempt, perhaps, is in the area of urban and town planning, where the imposition of colonial principles of spatial order and subsequent urban strategies have often led to conflicting and inconsistent planning schemes. This is particularly true in North Africa, where efforts to preserve and devalue 'native' institutions inevitably created dualistic and jarring juxtapositions of striking different urban structures.[1]

3. The third and perhaps most realistic and effective alternative is the particularistic or adaptive path to modernity. This approach does not exclude the possibility of mobilizing traditional groupings in the process of modernization. It is an adaptive course in more than one sense. First, it attempts to mediate change through agencies that are not exclusively rational or secular. Second, it strives to reconcile some of the universal and rational principles with the indigenous cultural traditions.

It is primarily for these reasons that the predisposition to justify change within traditional contexts should not be dismissed as a conservative gesture to glorify the sacred traditions of the past. Recognizing the viability of some primordial ties and loyalties should not be taken to mean that one seeks refuge in heritage and communal attachments as a means of avoiding confrontation with the challenges of the modern age. The adaptive path to modernity is not a resigned and nostalgic flight. Rather, it emanates from a given socio-historical reality, a reality that cannot be ignored or simply willed away by prophetic visions of a secular social order free of all primordial attachments. Putting new wine in old bottles, to borrow a metaphor, can be quite salutary in absorbing conflict and in facilitating the acceptance of new ideas. Furthermore, the fact that an agency is traditional in form or structure does not imply that it must espouse traditional values or that it must devote itself exclusively to passing on sacred values or preserving traditional lore and skills. Conversely, implementing seemingly modern values and practices does not automatically mean that people will undergo drastic transformations in spirit and attitude and will unhesitatingly acquire modern lifestyles.

The case for adaptive modernization can be justified on at least one additional ground. There is a tendency in the literature to exaggerate the

---

1. L. Carl Brown, ed., *From Medina to Metropolis* (Princeton: The Darwin Press, 1973); Ellen Micaud, 'Urbanization, Urbanism, and the Medina in Tunis', *International Journal of Middle East Studies*, 9 (November 1978), pp. 431–47; Eickelman, *The Middle East: An Anthropological Approach* (Englewood Cliff, NJ: Prentice Hall, 1981).

differences and discontinuities between so-called modern and traditional loyalties. For example, Karl Deutsch sees the transition from one polarity to the other as a 'process in which major clusters of old social, economic, and psychological commitments are eroded and broken and people become available for new patterns of socialization and behaviour'. (Deutsch, 1961: 464) Inkeles asserts that one of the marks of the contemporary man is that 'he will no longer live enmeshed in a network of primary kin ties [. . .] but rather will be drawn into a much more impersonal and bureaucratic milieu'. (Inkeles, 1966)

The basic argument of this essay departs from the tradition of dichotomous schemes, a tempting and powerful tradition, which still occupies a peculiar place in the folklore of Western sociological theory. Indeed, we cannot begin to understand what is involved in the processes of social change in the Arab world unless we abandon the tendency to view transformation as an inevitable, unilinear movement from one end of the scheme to the other. Despite their rich insights, all such polarized dichotomies obscure and mystify the inherently dialectical character of the relationship between traditional and rational loyalties.

To repeat, then, we cannot think of modernization in terms of a qualitative decline in traditional loyalties and the emergence of modern ones. We must consider instead that the most effective modernization depends upon whether the traditional patterns reinforce or undermine the superstructure of modernity. This is certainly a far more value-neutral approach than the ones that ipso facto declare the obstructive and unchanging character of all traditional values and institutions.

Both historical and more recent evidence appears to suggest that change mediated through exclusively traditional or exclusively rational agencies is not likely to be continuous or effective. Indeed, most such efforts have only generated inauspicious and extremist reactions: either the mindless denigration of traditional loyalties or their fatuous idealization. For Ernest Gellner, the ideological consequences of this predicament are obvious. These societies are usually torn between two trends or temptations, Westernization and populism, that is, the idealization of the local folk tradition. 'The old local "Great Tradition" is generally damned by its failure to resist the West and by its doctrinal and organizational rigidity, once a source of strength, now a great weakness.' (Gellner, 1984: xii)

Quite often, in fact, the two trends are coterminous. The excessive or premature introduction of rational or secular norms and lifestyles, Western-inspired or otherwise, begets or exacerbates revivalist and fundamentalist reactions. The chasm and tension between these two extremes have been responsible recently for some of the most disruptive and turbulent episodes in Arab history. A shortcut, in one of Charles Issawi's pungent aphorisms, is often not only the longest distance but also the most perilous route between two points. (Issawi, 1973: 8)

CHAPTER 2

The Growing Pains of Arab Intellectuals

As a social group, intellectuals everywhere are almost always gripped by certain tensions and uncertainties. Some of these tensions are inherent in the universal role of intellectuals as creators and carriers of culture; others reflect the particular socio-economic and political milieu in which they live. Although, for instance, the American intellectual has been enjoying more power and status in society,[1] he still must 'avoid the twin temptations of total withdrawal and total integration' (Coser, 1965: 10–13) As intellectuals are being increasingly absorbed into and recognized by various parts of the American 'establishment', they seem haunted by the fear of selling out or losing part of their creative and critical role in society. Conversely, total detachment or alienation may also be self-defeating. Likewise, some observers have found the English intellectual 'gentlemanly, amateurish and unrigorous, too near the upper classes and to established power to exercise real independence of mind and creativity'. (Bradbury, 1964:7–9) Equally, '[t]here is no country in the world where intellectuals have more influence, attract more attention, or enjoy more prestige than they do in France. But the relationship between French intellectuals and the society to which they belong is a paradoxical one.' (Cranston, 1965: 12–14)

The dilemmas of the contemporary Arab intellectual, as elsewhere in developing societies, are of a different nature and magnitude. To begin with, the so-called 'searching, detached, yet concerned' intellectual is still a rare individual. Intellectuals in most parts of the Arab world have not gained enough sense of identity or self-awareness as a social group to exert any appreciable influence.

---

1. Both David Riesman and Seymour Lipset support the contention that intellectuals in the US have risen in power and status. See D. Riesman, 'The Academic Career: Notes on Recruitment and Colleagueship', in *Daedalus* (Winter, 1959), pp. 152–57; S. Lipset, 'American Intellectuals: Their Politics and Status', in *Daedalus* (Summer, 1959), pp. 467–73.

Neither are they radically alienated, so that from the fringe of society they could effectively criticize or rebel against the social order. Yet, and here lies the paradox, an increasing number of technocrats and university graduates find themselves in positions of power and authority. Like the salaried middle class to which they belong, they attained power before gaining status, order and security. Therefore, they use their power not to defend their status and security but to create them. (Halpern, 1963: 52)

This is indeed a revolutionary task, and the educated elite are expected to be the torch-bearers of rationality and secularization in a society where non-rational and traditional forces are still predominant. The tensions that the Arab intellectual faces are not primarily those of alienation or involvement, or of his closeness or distance from the loci of power and authority. Rather, they emerge from his underlying task of reconciling the traditional and rational elements in society. They are the tensions of a 'marginal man', a man torn between the dictates of reason and rationality and the value patterns of his traditional culture.

This essay has two goals: in a rather interpretative manner to describe some of the salient features of intellectual life and to account for the tensions arising between intellectuals and society. Only by so doing can we assess the role of intellectuals and the nature of their dilemmas in contemporary Arab society.

Some Salient Features of Intellectual Life

What sort of people qualify for the label of intellectual in the Arab world? Since the term has come to cover a multitude of persons and activities, it is extremely difficult to arrive at a single concise definition. From non-manual workers to university graduates, experts to abstract ideologists, men of action to men of reflection, philosophers, artists and journalists to bureaucrats and technocrats, all have – at different times and places – made claims to the title. To avoid such confusion, the term will here be treated broadly to include all those who create, carry and apply culture. Thus a university graduate need not, by virtue of his higher education alone, pass for an intellectual. Only if he partakes in the process of creating, diffusing or applying culture will he become one. Conversely, a person with no formal university training may, albeit rarely, qualify.

The distinction between the creative agents as opposed to those who are more involved in disseminating or applying ideas is pertinent. Ideally, the heart of any intellectual community is composed of writers, men of letters, philosophers, scientists, scholars and artists who, in the words of Raymond Aron (1957: 206), are the people who 'live by and for the exercise of the intellect'. These, in almost any society, are the passionate and dedicated few. Most of the intellectual sector, however, is composed of scholars, writers, artists and research workers who go on producing without creating original ideas or new forms. Below them are the serious journalists, political and social commentators, along with a preponderance of the people engaged in the mass media, who serve as communicating links in disseminating ideas to others. Finally, there are the popularizers – pseudo-intellectuals with commercial interests who 'cease to interpret and begin to mislead' and vulgarize the creative standards and cultural outputs in society. I f intellectuals then are defined in an exclusive manner – i.e. people who derive pleasure and perhaps profit from creating or playing with ideas, rather than applying them – then very few indeed qualify to earn such a label in the Arab world. This is why we shall widen our scope here to include those who take part in diffusing and applying culture as well. The distinction, nonetheless, should be borne in mind. To the extent also that members of the liberal professions – physicians, lawyers, engineers and other practitioners – are more interested in practical achievements than culture in general, they may be excluded from our definition.[1]

It is not as difficult to identify some of the broad characteristics of intellectual life in the Arab world. It is apparent, upon any cursory observation, that intellectuals as a social group are fragmented and still lack the identity and class consciousness common in other social strata of society. Deficient in status and security, they also do not appear to enjoy any substantial measure of intellectual freedom.

Fragmentation

Throughout its cultural development, Arab civilization thrived best in urban and spiritual centres. As far back as the pre-Islamic 'Jahiliya', markets like *ukaz* were centres where producers and consumers of goods and cultural products met to exchange their wares and ideas. With the advent of Islam, the mosque became the centre of gravity for the spiritual, temporal and cultural forces in the community. Later, in its medieval and classical periods, all sort of guilds, lodges and neighbourhoods provided appropriate outlets for integrating the intellectual life of the community.

Although the charge that 'in the historical Islamic tradition, the intellectual has been peripheral and precarious' (Smith, 1955: 196; Halpern, 1963: 19–22) is debatable, there is no doubt that intellectual communities that centred around bazaars, mosques, guilds or neighbourhoods were not rare or precarious. They played a conspicuously important part in integrating intellectual life down to the nineteenth century. After all, mystical-ascetic orders like Sufism emerged and developed around such centres. 'The greatest achievement of Sufism,' writes Sir Hamilton Gibb, 'was that the orders succeeded, deliberately or not, in creating a religious organization parallel to, and identified with, the units of which Muslim society was composed. Each village community, each guild association in the towns, each regiment of troops, in India even each caste group, had its sufi "lodge", which linked its members together in a common religious allegiance, and gave to its religious ceremonies a fraternal and communal appeal'. (Gibb, 1962: 216) The famed accounts of Ibn Battuta, the fourteenth-century North African traveller, demonstrates the significance of these 'lodges' in providing refuge and a sense of identity and intimacy among intellectuals.

---

1. Both R. Aron and J. Schumpeter justify such exclusion unless of course such practitioners talk or write about subjects outside of their professional competence, which no doubt they do, especially lawyers. See Aron, *ibid.*, p. 207; J. A. Schumpeter, *Capitalism, Socialism and Democracy* (Harper and Brothers, 1947), pp. 145–55.

Little of this fraternal and communal feeling survives today, either in form or in spirit. The decline was really inevitable. Urbanization and expansion of commerce and industry weakened these associations and diluted the homogeneity of brotherhoods and orders. Oddly enough, the advent of mass media and swift means of transport appear to have had little effect in recreating this sense of community or in bringing Arab intellectuals closer together. Neither have Arab intellectuals sought to find substitutes (for better or worse) in outlets like Greenwich Village or Saint-Germain des Près, which serve to satisfy part of their yearning for a communal and fraternal experience. The so-called 'coffee-house' intellectual, a fashionable and symbolic figure in intellectual circles in the West, is still virtually non-existent in the Arab world.

Political fragmentation also adds to the splintering of intellectual life. Cleavages among intellectuals existed in early Islam, but they were largely intellectual in character, such as the general distinction in society between the consensus of the *ulema* (scholar-jurists) and that of the *ummah* (masses). Present-day schisms and ideological rifts are predominantly political and sectarian in nature. Nothing akin to the lively debate between the 'liberal secularists' and the 'Islamic Revivalists', which consumed the intellectual energies of social and political thinkers at the turn of the last century, can be discerned today. Neither can we boast of intellectual giants of the calibre of Muhammad 'Abduh, Rashid Rida, Lutfi al-Sayyid, Butrus al-Bustani – to mention a few – who were able to transcend the parochial problems of their day and view the national crisis in a broader and more profound perspective.

Out of such debates, intellectual traditions and schools of thought were created, and intellectuals were known by their allegiances and commitments to either of these traditions. Very few of the present generation of intellectuals sustain any such labels. The overriding political differences have factionalized their loyalties and allegiances. Except on formal and ritualistic occasions there is little effective dialogue and exchange of views and cultural products. The few symposia and conventions are rarely attended by representatives from all Arab countries. Egyptian delegates, for example, often fail to attend academic conferences sponsored in Lebanon, and except for the heated exchange of incriminatory and often vulgar vilifications through the radio and the press, there has been almost no association between Egyptian and Syrian intellectuals.

Not only regionally but also locally, Arab intellectuals are torn asunder by divided loyalties and non-intellectual allegiances. Even within a small country like Lebanon there is little association between the scholars of its four universities. Perhaps by virtue of the names they carry and the cultural interests they represent (American, French, Lebanese and Arab), there has been a minimum of rapport between colleagues affiliated with these different institutions. One frequently encounters a highly cultivated American University professor who is totally oblivious to even the names of writers in his own field in, say, the French University, and certainly has no acquaintance with the intellectual milieu that sustains them.

What accentuates this fragmentation and may in turn prevent a closer rapprochement between intellectuals is the fact, observed by Wilfred Smith, 'that today's Muslim intellectual is everywhere not merely bilingual, but linguistically bicultural'. (Smith, 1955: 201) In other words, this is not simply a matter of feeling at home in two different languages or cultures. Rather, it stems from the fact that many foreign-trained Arab intellectuals think conceptually in one language and converse and write in another. It is not too uncommon, for instance, for a young scholar in Lebanon to undertake his research and writing in English, converse with his friends in French and address his parents in Arabic. This is certainly not an unmixed blessing. In some academic disciplines, particularly the social sciences, which have not yet developed a standardized conceptual terminology in Arabic, foreign-trained scholars find some difficulty in communicating with others in their native tongue. Even if they chose to, chances are the result might not be too intelligible, except perhaps to those who make the effort of retranslating it into Western concepts. Furthermore, in the absence of respectable journals and publishing houses, many a young scholar does not even bother to write in Arabic. After all, his intellectual standing in his own community very often depends on how he is judged abroad, and foreign publications guarantee a wider and more international audience.

In brief, what this adds up to is a further widening of the gulf between intellectuals. Linguistic fragmentation, along with the political and geographical, has certainly not been conducive to the emergence of a sense of cohesion among intellectuals. Without cohesion, they cannot have a unified audience, nor can they make their presence felt in society.

Class, Status and Power
As creators and bearers of culture, it is expected that intellectuals' commitment to the world of ideas and creative thought should ultimately supersede other loyalties and attachments. This tendency, at least in the West, did progressively suppress differences of birth, status and wealth, and tended to unite intellectuals on the basis of their common training and interests. (Mannheim, 1960) This is hardly the case in the Middle East. Apart from the uncertainties and ambivalences of the Arab intellectual, loyalties are still predominantly traditional in character. He or she appears to derive greater satisfaction and security from kinship and communal ties than from participation in an intellectual career. At least, association with traditional circles is still sociologically more meaningful, and he/she remains partly if not totally attached to non-intellectual pursuits. If he/she does dabble in an intellectual activity, it is at best a pastime or a diversion; it is rarely followed with gusto and total involvement. Besides – and this admittedly is expected of developing societies – knowledge and higher education in general are largely sought as a means to an end. As long as this utilitarian bias persists, there can be little hope of cultivating an interest in knowledge or an intellectual activity as an end in itself, '[f]or everything which a man fails to pursue for its own sake,' as Schopenhauer warns us, 'is but half pursued.' (Schopenhauer, 1951: 35)

Partly because of the persistence of such tendencies, intellectuals in the Arab world have remained amorphous and characterless as a social group. They still lack the identity and class-consciousness apparent in other social strata of society. They also do not serve as champions of classes or social groups in conflict or the articulators of their ideologies. Neither do they constitute, as do perhaps their counterparts in some of the Afro-Asian emerging countries, a new aristocracy or a new elite. They are not an aristocracy, because they are not as yet equipped with symbols of status and social prestige, nor do they take the lead in setting standards of taste and patterns of social behaviour. They are not an elite, in the true sense of the word, because they do not initiate or articulate the ideals and values of their society. It is the emerging intelligentsia – the technocrats, experts, social engineers, bureaucrats, the military – rather than the intellectuals, who are by and large the pace-setters in the Arab world today.

Needless to say, the plight of intellectuals did not always exist. Not only was intellectual life in early Islam more integrated and homogeneous, but the scholar-jurists (*ulema*) also enjoyed unmatched status and prestige in society. They were the accredited guardians and interpreters of theological doctrine as well as of the *Shari'ah* – the corpus of Islamic jurisprudence. They were scholars in the broad sense of the term and not simply specialists in theology as is often assumed. They frequently lectured and wrote books on several aspects of Islamic sciences and social thought.

The fact that contemporary Arab intellectuals have not yet achieved a sense of identity and class-consciousness may be a blessing in disguise. A group whose class position is relatively fixed may be more susceptible to becoming rigid and conservative in its thinking. This likelihood does not loom on our intellectual horizon. Cultural life in the Arab world suffers more from sterility of thought and mediocrity of brainpower than from class rigidities or frustrations imposed by the social order. In fact, what is needed today is not an intellectual class, not even an intellectual elite, but the commitment and dedication of people who are the bearers of intellectual activity. No matter how dedicated, however, such people cannot act and think in a vacuum. Without some cultural traditions and institutional supports, intellectuals cannot possibly perpetuate themselves as a unified group. Neither can they preserve or add much to the cultural heritage of society.

Lacking any sense of identity or self-awareness as a social group able to exercise any real independence of mind and creativity, intellectuals are also deficient in status and prestige. Depending on the intellectual traditions and needs of particular societies, the value attached to the hierarchy of brainpower is distributed differently in every country. In Germany, for example, the laurels of prestige and status have always gone to the professor and scholar; in America to the expert; in France to the *homme de lettres* or writer; in Africa to the newly emerging political ideologist. In the Arab world, because of the pending political and economic problems, it is the bureaucratic and political intelligentsia who currently occupy the top positions of the social pyramid. 'Leadership in all areas of Middle Eastern life is increasingly being seized by a class of men inspired by non-traditional knowledge, and it is being clustered around a core of salaried civilian and military politicians, organizers, administrators, and experts.' (Halpern, 1963: 52)

Lebanon, though not in all senses, is an exception. In a service-biased economy, where the mercantile spirit still thrives and material and pecuniary values are highly coveted, it is the manipulators of men and money who seem the most privileged in society. Intellectuals – the manipulators of ideas, people who 'live by and for the exercise of the intellect' – are still relatively lower on the totem pole. That intellectuals then should harbour some hostility to businessmen is no mystery. By virtue of their functions, the two groups are impelled by entirely different motives and aspirations. What is surprising is that in Lebanon the two groups seem perfectly compatible at times. Scholars enjoy extended sojourns into the business world, and successful business firms affect scholarly interests to boost their public image in the community. The status of any group is in part a function of its size and utility. For if scarcity breeds value, then excess must depreciate it. With increasing educational opportunities, there has been an enormous expansion in the intellectual sector. In fact, there has been an excess of high-talent manpower. It is true that enterprises like public relations, market research and mass communications have recruited heavily from the pool of people with quasi-intellectual interests and training. But there are still many individuals who feel that their training and intellectual powers are in excess of opportunities or jobs available. This creates a characteristic pattern of frustration and hostility clearly evident among the young generation of foreign-trained intellectuals. Because of their precarious position, Arab intellectuals seem particularly predisposed to what Nietzsche terms *ressentiment*. Although they feel angry and hostile, they are overwhelmingly powerless to direct those feelings against their social causes. The discontent remains latent and hostility impotent. Although there is cause for rebellion, few have in fact rebelled; even fewer have become 'angry young men'. They are not uprooted and alienated in the same mould as the Russian intellectual of whom Dostoyevsky wrote. Neither do they refuse to be reconciled to native culture or to cooperate with legitimate institutions in society. Instead, they appear to have resigned themselves to an apathetic, defeatist attitude: to continue to re-experience this sense of 'impotent hostility' and thereby earn the occasional rewards of docility.

If Arab intellectuals have not acquired the status of a privileged class endowed with political influence and social prestige, it is little wonder that they have remained powerless. There is a danger, in fact, in enjoying the status and power of privileged positions before attaining enough intellectual maturity. For if they lose political power, as is likely to happen when they attain it prematurely, they will have little else to fall back on. It should also be remembered that this new breed of intellectuals – people with Western education – is of relatively recent vintage. It made its appearance in the Arab world around the beginning of the nineteenth century. The other two traditional groups of intellectuals – the scholar-jurists and the Sufi shaykhs, who for centuries competed to control the ideas of the masses – never enjoyed much political power. There have been, of course, a few exceptions. At certain times in the seventeenth century, for example, the scholar-jurists were the most important class politically in the Ottoman Empire. But then, in concentrating on political power, they lowered their intellectual standards and thereby forfeited the respect of other sections of the community. (Montgomery Watt, 1961: 248)

Thus only on rare occasions has the pen been stronger than the sword in the Arab world. The rivalry between men of letters and men of power is not like sibling rivalry. Intellectuals have not been too readily admitted into the ranks of the body politic. When they are, it is normally not on the intellectual merit, but rather through adoption or sponsorship by some traditional political figure. In a way, the feelings between the two groups are mutual. Politicians have not sought intellectual leadership, nor have intellectuals expressly craved political leadership. This need not be a cause for alarm. On the contrary, it may work to the benefit of all. Intellectuals, after all, in the words of Harold Laski, may prove to be 'invaluable servants but impossible masters'.

When intellectuals fail to maintain power or recognition by the political regime, they often seek it indirectly through their participation in any of the instruments of political change – for example, labour unions, political parties and pressure groups. But such voluntary associations are still ineffective as agencies of social and political change in the Arab world. Except for a few instances, they have failed to attract any radical cadre of intellectuals. In fact, this may account for their failure thus far. Furthermore, open opposition to the ruling group is still risky and difficult, especially in one-party states or autocratic regimes. Those who choose the hard and uncompromising way of open opposition often end up either jobless or in political exile. This, among other things, has contributed to a sizeable brain drain.

Intellectual Freedom?
What Western intellectuals lack in terms of security, status and power, they gain in freedom of inquiry and thought. Their counterpart in the Arab world appear deprived on both counts. What they lost in status (compared with the scholar-jurists of early Islam) they have not gained in freedom. They still do not enjoy any substantial measure of freedom in the social role of discoverer and disseminator of knowledge. In some parts of the Arab world, because of political and other considerations, there are restrictions on the scope and nature of free inquiry. In Lebanon, for example, a social scientist, fearful of upsetting the proverbial sectarian balance, is often inclined to ignore any consideration of the religious factor that might otherwise be significantly correlated to some other variable under study. In a preliminary meeting about a prospective book on the politics of Lebanon, to cite one instance, the editors and contributors – all young scholars in leading Lebanese universities – implicitly agreed to avoid inviting controversial figures or handling issues that may touch some delicate and sensitive aspect of the society. Similarly, little of the critical thought of native Egyptian scholars – of whom some must surely harbour a few misgivings about the present regime – has as yet found its way into print.

The historical roots of this phenomenon, which run deeper than its political and sectarian manifestations, may be inherent in the very nature of personalized and authoritarian society. One of the obvious features of such a society is the lack of freedom to express feelings or articulate thoughts. Since the Arab in general is extremely sensitive to public pressure and keen on preserving appearances, one frequently encounters a striking contrast between outer social behaviour and inner thinking and feeling. What a person says or does may often be at variance with what he or she thinks or feels. In intellectual life this discrepancy manifests itself in a lack of frankness in expressing views or in criticizing others. Dispassionate criticism of the ideas of a colleague is invariably confused with a personal affront. Rarely are people dissociated from their ideas. Consequently, an attack on their ideas is also interpreted as an act of personal vilification.

In an authoritarian society people are also afraid to defy elders or to challenge the sovereignty of sacred norms. Little of the pent-up hostility is verbalized or released. 'Resentment, dislike, even hate are masked by outward compliance . . . The mask becomes the man, the man the mask.' (Khatchadorian, 1961: 18) The net result of all this is the decay of spontaneity and individual freedom. Nothing could stifle more the creative impulse of a generation.

Tensions and Dilemmas

Deprived of the privileges of status and power normally enjoyed by a cohesive, self-conscious elite, and constrained in the ability to express themselves spontaneously and independently, the Arab intellectuals are also pinned on the horns of some dilemmas. Their growing sense of crisis, to repeat, need not be only a reflection of the socio-political milieu in which they live. It is in part inherent in the role of intellectuals as torch-bearers of knowledge and reason in society.

Rationality vs Traditionalism
The tension with which the Arab intellectual has to grapple is the discrepancy between the dictates of reason and rationality, which ideally form guidelines, and the non-rational and traditional forces rooted in the culture. This tension is particularly felt by foreign-trained intellectuals, who return home so thoroughly steeped in Western ideas and ways of life that they often remain misfits in their native land. Their dreams of national and personal advancement are so ruthlessly shattered that they are left bitter and frustrated.

This bitterness is due not only to the disparity between their youthful dreams and the woeful reality that they have to face but also to the growing realization that their knowledge and training are not being adequately used. They burn with a crushing sense of failure and defeat: failure, because they seem unable to function creatively in society, defeat, because they are often compelled to compromise and seek jobs below their intellectual level or interest. If their bitterness and hostility remain impotent, there is a danger of their becoming perennial misanthropists. A mind defeated by the strains of contemporary problems can either become increasingly alienated or seek refuge in the glories of the past or in communal attachments. None of these defence mechanisms is conducive to the creative and cultural life of society.

This is the dilemma that nags at the minds of Arab intellectuals: how to reconcile the rational premises of the present with the secure and tested traditions of the past? The dilemma is intensified because the people entrusted with the task of bringing about this fusion are often of two extremes: the ruthless young secularists, bent on change at all costs; and their traditionalist compatriots, who seek to preserve the familiar without upsetting the status quo. The former are out of touch with traditions; the latter refuse to entertain the new. The development offices in most Arab countries, as a result, abound with moribund projects and unimplemented blueprints for extravagant schemes. The defunct Liberation Project of Egypt is one such costly victim of this twin gift of audacious planning and administrative ineffectiveness. It was intended as a showcase for the virtues of collective farming and other socialist formulae, but the architects of the project had underestimated the resilience of some of the traditional patterns of behaviour. The average Egyptian *fallah*, notwithstanding the hopes of eager political ideologists, could not be transplanted overnight into an impersonal and rational world.

The failure of this and many other such projects demonstrates, among other things, the failure to bring about a compatible fusion between the traditional and rational elements. It is interesting to note in this connection that, unlike contemporary Asian intellectuals, those who are unable to reconcile their rational beliefs with the persisting traditional values have not flirted with communism as a possible substitute. As an ideology or technique of political action or economic development, communism does not seem to have been in particular favour among Arab intellectuals. It has, as elsewhere, attracted the malcontents of the depressed classes in society but relatively very few of the alienated intellectuals. This is further evidence that kinship, fealty and other traditional loyalties are still stronger than some of the secular and ideological commitments.

Naturally not all intellectuals are seeking alternative substitutes. A few may even be unconscious of the implications of such a dilemma. The majority, and here lies the paradox in our intellectual life, seem to want to have their cake and eat it too. While they commit themselves to a life dedicated to reason and rationality, they harbour very few strong antipathies to traditional authority and 'sacred' institutions in society.

Intellectuals vs Intelligentsia

In most developing societies, there has been an intimate association between higher education and government employment. The Arab world is certainly no exception. In fact, with increasing nationalization and state control, the government is increasingly becoming the major employer of all kinds and levels of university graduates. The attractions of a government job, particularly in areas where the private sector is shrinking, are self-evident. In Egypt, observes Morroe Berger, it has been an irresistible combination of need, tradition and deliberate planning that has turned the ambitions of the educated elite towards government jobs.

> The need has been apparent in the oversupply of educated youth in certain fields in an agricultural society. The tradition was created early in Egypt's modern era when secular education was established to train skilled civil servants. The deliberate planning cemented these effects by the creation of special job incentives to acquire formal education. (Berger, 1957: 70)

This tendency, irresistible or otherwise, has certainly left its mark on the broad intellectual life of society. While giving an impetus to the growth in the numbers of technocrats and bureaucrats, it has stifled the variety of intellectual development that thrives best in the independent and liberal professions.

Even where non-political and independent intellectuals continue to exist as a minority, political upheavals consume the bulk of their intellectual resources. They seem totally engrossed in the effort of accounting for political instability or in defending a particular form of government. That this is expected in a society undergoing so much political and social change is not to be denied. After all, intellectuals would be guilty of burying their heads in the sand if they were apathetic or insensitive to symptoms of political malaise within their society. But then they are also intellectually myopic if they perceive only this.

I am not for a moment decrying the political role and concern of Arab intellectuals. The nature of present-day Arab society no doubt justifies such political consciousness. But this, I maintain, is happening at the expense of broader and more creative cultural activities. That an *intelligentsia* – defined in Seton-Watson's (1964: 6–8) terms as people with 'a modern education who live for and by political and social ideas' – is vitally necessary in the Arab world today is not being disputed. This should not be confused, however, with communities of *intellectuals* who create, carry and apply culture. Furthermore, since both groups are drawn from the same supply of the educated elite, the one can exist only at the expense of the other. It is the intelligentsia, and not the intellectual elite, who are walking away with the lion's share of society's privileged and powerful positions.

This dilemma generates several tensions. To begin with, and in no way is this peculiar to the Arab world, the intellectual feels the tensions inherent in the dual nature of his role. Should he remain a 'man of reflection', a detached scholar pursuing and defending a life of reason in its purer and abstract forms; or a 'man of action', eager to participate in the social and political struggles of his society? To say that there is room for both types of men does not alleviate the tension. The Arab world today is in desperate need of enlightened action. The pressures on, and public obligations of, the educated elite to participate in reform movements and development programmes are immense. Only the insensitive few can remain oblivious to such civic callings. Even where intellectuals manage to enjoy a relative amount of detachment, they are invariably drawn into the social and political affairs of their communities when the conduct of politicians and policy-makers begins to have serious cultural implications. To remain then a disinterested observer is to invite lay and inexperienced action. On the other hand, to become increasingly absorbed into the various parts of the growing government bureaucracy may ultimately spell the progressive obsolescence of the free and unattached intellectual.

It is true that one need not be too dogmatic in asserting that public or political involvement invariably corrupts intellectuals. Yet many of the younger intellectuals are afraid, and recent historical trends justify their fear, that in becoming state employees they may cease to be truly creative and critical. If his European counterparts (particularly French and to a lesser degree British intellectuals) feel relatively free in the service of the state, it is because they enjoy comfortable and well-remunerated positions. Apart from the civil service, a large number of them have contracts with the state radio, television monopoly or some other comfortable places such as museums and other national and cultural institutions. Furthermore they have had intellectuals such as André Malraux and C. P. Snow as ministers of culture – distinguished people passionately dedicated to the task of promoting culture. Very few Arab intellectuals are employed in appropriate cultural institutions, and fewer still benefit from association with such inspiring superiors as Malraux and C. P. Snow. Imagine Taha Hussein as minister of culture; he would certainly succeed in recruiting the support and sympathy of intellectuals who might otherwise have some misgivings about rallying behind a mere politician. But then very few can or are willing to play such a dual role. Those who do are bound to lose some of the prestige that belongs to the unattached and independent intellectual.

In another respect, contemporary Arab intellectuals appear to be caught in an equally awesome impasse. They are torn between loyalties to Arab nationalism and an urge to be culturally and artistically creative. As citizens they cannot possibly avoid his involvement in the economic and political crises of the day. As intellectuals, they realize that this involvement will ultimately curtail their contributions to culture. Here lies the dilemma. Arab culture will retain its value only if the national goals and aspirations are successfully maintained; and if intellectuals wish to partake in this national process, as most of them seem bent on doing, they will have little to contribute to culture.

From whatever angle the dilemma is viewed, the cultural life of society stands to diminish. As long as a society's best minds are being consumed by either petty bureaucratic chores or political problems – no matter how vital and immediate they appear – there will always be a shortage of people capable of creating a culture. At the risk of some exaggeration, it may be said that what exists today in the Arab world is a politically conscious and bureaucratic intelligentsia, not a culture-conscious intellectual elite.

'Mass Culture' vs 'High Culture'

The invasion of the mass media has not spared the cultural life in the Arab world. More people now than ever before have access to television, radios, paperbacks and other inexpensive periodicals and magazines. With increasing exposure, Arab intellectuals are beginning to share the anxieties of their Western colleagues about the vulgarity of popular culture in a mass society. True, with strong communal and kinship ties, Arab society is certainly far from becoming a 'mass society', yet there is a danger in entrusting culture to commercial agencies. Some of the spirited young intellectuals are justifiably concerned lest their own countrymen pass swiftly from illiteracy to popular culture without an intervening period of slow and genuine cultivation of the arts and sciences.

Symptoms of this danger can already be discerned. To many university graduates, such popular periodicals as *Time*, *Life* and *Newsweek* are their prime links with the external world. They are not only an information medium, but a source of new tastes in consumption, styles of life and ideas. Furthermore, in a highly mobile society, any object charged with social meaning can readily serve as a symbol of status. Culture, or the appearance of being cultured, is increasingly becoming (at least among the more modern segments of urban Beirut) a status symbol. In the course of a mundane conversation people can casually drop names like Baudelaire, Proust and Kafka without ever having read any of them. We patronize the arts and attend musical festivals just to be seen there. We invest in encyclopedias and home libraries as mantelpiece ornaments or conversation pieces. In short, intellectual snobs feign an interest in intellectual concerns as a shortcut to status.

In much the same way, the utilitarian interest in higher education is evident not only in the predisposition for practical, empirical and technical training, but also in the way educational qualifications are coveted for the prestige they carry. In Lebanon, for example, academic titles are so passionately sought after that one cannot help but feel that it is their prestige value and not the inherent value of the education associated with the title that is the prized object. The deference with which people act towards holders of such titles and the almost flagrant exhibitionism with which they are indulgently displayed are further proof of the snob appeal of higher education. Almost everyone becomes an *ustaz* (teacher or master), and the qualification for admission to such a title is often no more than a non-manual job, with or without a college degree. Many people carry visiting cards with whatever symbols of status they can claim ostentatiously displayed. Special licence plates carry the insignia of doctors, lawyers and pharmacists; other professional groups are enviously beginning to claim similar privileges. Letterheads, even nameplates for homes and apartments similarly boast such claimed degrees and titles. Men, even scholars in academic communities where titles abound and should be taken for granted, are careful to address each other in a pompous and ceremonial fashion.

The helpless intellectual views all this with mixed feelings. They recognize the virtues of the mass media as agents of social and cultural change, yet they are also painfully aware of their corrupting influences in debasing the standards of 'high culture'. They are torn between loyalties to their own creative impulses and modes of self-expression and the temptations of popular appeal and commercial success. By yielding to the temptation of mass appeal, they betray some of their intellectual values; by maintaining the standards of quality and exclusiveness, they run the risk of not reaching a wider audience. In a society where intellectual resources are scarce, the tensions inherent in this dilemma are understandably more acute. If Arab intellectuals feel troubled, it is because they find it difficult to reconcile their inner promptings as an intellectual with civic obligations to be socially useful.

Concluding Observations

Like other societies in transition, the Arab world today is in the throes of deep and continuous change. Numerous new processes and events underlie its social structure. Some changes have happened with alarming swiftness: new forms of communication, increasing exposure to the mass media, decline in kinship and other forms of traditional authority, emergence of new social movements and power elites, emancipation of women, increasing economic and political participation have all created new problems that require comprehension and adjustment. Naturally these changing processes require new solutions and experimentation. The fact that Western societies underwent this very same change earlier does not mean that we have to adopt the same yardsticks or frames of reference and apply them indiscriminately. Selective adaptation and not wholesale application is required.

In this time of transition and uncertainty we need intellectual power and virtue more than ever before. We need the critical support and dedicated energy of people with an overriding passion for reason; people who live for and by the exercise of the intellect. After all, it was the intellectuals and the middle class from which they emerged that were responsible for most of these transformations.

Perhaps the new generation of foreign-trained and college-bred intellectuals imbued with the values of rationality and freedom can fill this gap in our cultural life. Thus far this has been more promise than achievement. As was shown, intellectuals not only lack the cohesion and self-awareness of a social group, they also enjoy relatively little status and practically no freedom to exercise any real independence of mind and creativity. They are also subject to some underlying dilemmas, which strain their role in and relationship with society.

To begin with, they are expected to fuse the compatible elements of traditional and modern culture. In concrete terms this means that they need to express 'traditional sentiments in modern idioms, to assimilate and transform traditional attitudes and to mold them into modern genres'. Second, they are expected to reconcile their role as detached scholars or disinterested observers with their eagerness to participate in the social and political struggles of their society. This is also a difficult task. Among other things, it involves striking a balance between their loyalties to Arab nationalism and the equally demanding urge to be culturally creative. Finally, they have yet to discover how to diffuse culture to the widest possible audience without debasing its aesthetic content.

All these are forbidding tasks, which tax the meagre supply of brainpower. Only by maintaining a kind of balance or reconciliation between these efforts can we ease the tensions or guarantee a more equitable distribution and fruitful utilization of intellectual resources in society. So far we are still far from realizing this goal, and it is unlikely that we can get any closer to it if we persist in our present course of channelling all the emotional and intellectual energies of younger intellectuals towards economic and political problems. When one considers the sacrifices that our developing societies undergo in producing a single intellectual, and when one considers the wastage and rapid obsolescence of brainpower, one cannot but lament such an imbalance of intellectual resources. In a sense, the decline in the cultural level of Arab civilization may in part be a reflection of the preoccupation of Arab intellectuals with the political and social struggles of their societies. Since this is an inevitable, but probably a transitional condition, little is gained by acquiring an apologetic attitude. Indulging in intellectual chauvinism, whether by idealizing the heights of our past cultural glories or debasing those of others, can be of little help either. Instead we should avoid the confusion of culture and politics altogether. A rootless class of half-educated technocrats and political intelligentsia is no substitute for an intellectual elite – the creators and carriers of culture.

Finally, in spite of the troubled life they lead and the heavy claims they are saddled with, the longings of Arab intellectuals are not too demanding or unrealistic. They are not longing for Plato's Republic, one in which philosophers would be kings and kings philosophers. Neither do they harbour visions of a Machiavellian sort of world where intellectuals consort with princes. All that they long for is some modest recognition of the values of rationality and freedom. Not only intellectual freedom from indiscreet censorship boards or tyrannical bureaucratic structures, but also some 'elbow room' to seek spontaneous outlets for self-expression and self-definition. These longings, it must be remembered, cannot be quelled by the slogans for social reform, economic prosperity and political stability.

CHAPTER 3

Social Structure and Urban Planning in Lebanon

Introduction

To anyone concerned with the interplay between urban planning and social structure, Lebanon poses a curious and instructive case study. There are several general reasons why this is so.

First, no matter how urban planning is defined, whether in its narrow physical perspective or in a broader social context, it connotes the injection of rationality into a particular area of human life. In its narrow sense planning is predominantly concerned with issues surrounding the physical form of the city, the spatial arrangement of urban functions and the control and allocation of land. In its broader sense, urban planning represents 'deliberate efforts to order the environment so as to realize certain common goals and values. As such, it is concerned not merely with the rational allocation of resources but, more importantly, with the selection of goals and values toward which these resources should be directed.' (Weaver, 1963:97)

In both definitions, however, attempts are made to control the environment, by eliminating such hazards to health and well-being as slums or traffic congestion and by adjusting future growth to a master plan. Thus zoning, along with other ordinances, traffic regulation, urban renewal and the provision of public amenities, becomes an integral part of urban master planning. They are all efforts to exert control over the distribution of land use and the allocation of other resources. (Willhelm, 1962: 2) Implicit in all this are issues such as the ideal size of cities, the optimum ratio of primary to other cities and the impact of increasing urbanization on existing social institutions and values. These and other such issues involve the introduction of a certain degree of calculus, rationality control, forecasting and cost-benefit analysis into an area previously left to private initiative or to the chance combination of other societal changes.

Within such a context it becomes meaningful to consider how a relatively modern notion of land-use planning and zoning has been introduced and incorporated into a socio-cultural milieu in which seemingly traditional values and loyalties are expected to militate against their introduction.

The second consideration is the dialectical nature of the relationship between urban planning as a rational strategy for controlling and allocating resources and some of the persisting features of pluralistic society such as Lebanon. This discloses another poignant dilemma. The very elements of the social structure that are sources of viability and solidarity – such as kinship and communal loyalties, patron–client networks and other primordial attachments – are also sources of vulnerability. While the average Lebanese continues to derive social and psychic supports and some tangible benefits from cultivating such traditional ties, it is also these ties that impede or distort urban planning and zoning. In other words, norms that enable in some respects can disable in other respects. This insight, attributed to Thorsten Veblen, John Dewey and Kenneth Burke, and more recently used judiciously by Bennett Berger, Bruno Bettelheim and William F. Whyte, can be appropriately applied in accounting for the failure of urban planning in Lebanon (see Berger, 1966; Bettelheim, 1960; and Whyte, 1943).

A third distinctive and persistent feature of Lebanese society, particularly when compared with adjacent Arab regimes, has been its laissez-faire and liberal tradition. In mobilizing and managing its human and economic resources, successive governments in Lebanon have continued to pursue policies that encourage free enterprise and private initiative in virtually all sectors of the society. Such rampant liberalism manifests itself in an excessive degree of individualism at the personal level and the near absence of government intervention at the state level. Conscious perhaps of both its own limitations and the resourcefulness and enterprise of its citizens, the government has reduced its interference to a minimum. While such a liberal tradition may have served well the interests of private enterprise and is consistent with the political realities of a pluralistic society, it is certainly not compatible with the requirements of urban planning.

One of the basic tools of urban planning is, after all, the promulgation of orderly legislation dealing with the just and equitable conveyance of property from private to public use. By its very nature, such process involves restrictions on certain freedoms. The Lebanese in general have always resisted such restrictions and have continued to perceive any plan as an unwarranted infringement on the private use of property.

Once again, it becomes pertinent within such a context to explore how such seemingly incompatible traditions – laissez-faire, freedom and nonintervention as against the growing need for planning, coordination and control – have been reconciled in Lebanon. As will be demonstrated, such a reconciliation has not yet been effectively attained. Much of the urban crisis Lebanon is facing is attributed to the failure of planning thus far to curb or restrain some of the inauspicious consequences of individualism and laissez-faire.

A fourth consideration is that, in addition to these internal factors, there are economic and political forces originating outside Lebanon that also account for the failure of urban planning. Massive internal migration generated by Israel's unremitting bombardment of southern Lebanon in 1978 and 1982, the successive migrations of Palestinian and other refugees and their convergence on already congested urban districts, the influx of Arabian capital and foreign remittances and the consequent speculation in real estate and soaring land values have all disrupted the government's ability to implement general master plans or specific zoning schemes. Any analysis of the interplay between planning and the social structure must take into account the implications of such external factors.

The fifth factor is that Lebanon's urban crisis is a reflection of yet another unresolved problem: the persisting discrepancy between urban legislation and ordinances and actual social behaviour and spatial patterns. In all human societies, even the most civic and orderly, the two rarely converge. In Lebanon, however, the gap between the two is more visible than elsewhere. As will be seen, Lebanon has never been short of master plans and blueprints. As early as 1930, long before the increasing scale and intensity of urbanization began to appear, the country experimented with several planning schemes, although none of these master plans was approved or implemented. The gap between audacious planning and executive ineffectiveness has continued to characterize all subsequent efforts at master planning and zoning. Even after town planning legislation was passed in 1968, certain provisions of the plans were regularly transgressed and violated.

Underlying this persistent discrepancy is an unresolved controversy regarding the relationship between social processes and spatial forms. The fashioning of spatial forms can influence social processes, and conversely, a particular spatial environment can reflect certain social and normative considerations. The interplay between these two forms of consciousness, the 'geographic' and the 'sociological', as they have been labelled by David Harvey (1973), continues to generate considerable controversy.

Early city planners such as Ebenezer Howard and Sir Patrick Abercrombie and more recently architects such as Lynch (1960) and Doxiadis (1968), trained in a tradition of spatial consciousness, have sought to show how the modification of spatial forms can mould the social process. Others, particularly Jacobs (1961), Webber (1963) and Gans (1970), attack this form of 'spatial environmental determinism' and support instead an alternative perspective in which a social process is viewed as possessing its own dynamic, which often – in spite of the planner – achieves its own particular spatial form.

Though in a different context, some of the earlier writings of Levi-Strauss (see, for example, 1963) reflect this same general perspective, particularly when he shows how the spatial layout of a whole village in a primitive culture may reflect the mythology of the people and their pattern of social interaction. Likewise, Lowenthal and Prince (1964) have demonstrated how each age fashions its environment to reflect existing social norms.

While one should recognize the complementary and dialectical nature of this process, it is appropriate, in the case of Lebanon, to give greater weight to exploring the impact of the social system on land-use patterns and other spatial arrangements rather than the other way around. Given the nature of urbanization, the relative recency of planning and the tenacity of certain social and normative elements, it becomes more meaningful to document how the social structure has affected planning and zoning ordinances rather than to consider the impact of such laws on the social structure. More specifically, an attempt will be made in this study to demonstrate how certain enduring features of the social and cultural structure shape, modify and even distort existing laws and their application.

It is necessary, however, first to consider some of the striking features of urbanization and the nature of urban planning and zoning in Lebanon.

The Nature of Urbanization and Urbanism in Beirut

Two general features of urbanization in Lebanon have concrete implications for the present study, namely, the relatively swift and recent character of urbanization and the persistence of traditional ties and communal attachments.

Despite its compelling site and favourable geographical location, for centuries Beirut remained a curiously small and insignificant agglomeration. As recently as the late eighteenth century its population was estimated at only 6,000 and in 1848 at not more that 15,000. After 1860 the incessant flow of rural migration began and has never ceased. The first evidence, however, of the increasing scale of urbanization – as measured by the intensity of construction activity – did not really appear in Beirut until the early 1950s. Before that time, the city maintained its horizontal and even skyline and the urban scene consisted overwhelmingly of traditional suburban villas. As in most European towns before industrialization, people in Beirut from the turn of the twentieth century until the 1940s continued to live and work within the same area of the city. Daily routines were carried out within clearly defined quarters and the neighbourhood survived as an almost self-sufficient community with which the individual identified. There was a strong sense of neighbourliness and patterns of behaviour were largely regulated through kinship and religious ties. Physical space and social space, in other words, were almost identical. Ethnic and religious affiliations created relatively homogeneous and compact neighbourhoods, *harat* or *ahya*, which until recently continued to provide security and a deep sense of community. More important, these neighbourhoods offered the urban dweller a human scale and types of social networks that he/she could comprehend and in which a uniquely individual space could be found.

With rapid urbanization (the consequence of both internal migration and natural growth rates in the population) this pattern naturally could not sustain itself. Since nearly two-thirds of the rural exodus was directed towards Beirut, the capital trebled its residential population between 1932 and 1964 and grew by nearly tenfold between 1932 and 1980. This rapid growth of Beirut was due not only to internal demographic factors but also, to a large extent, to external pressures, which generated added demand for urban space. The waves of Palestinian refugees after 1948 and the political instability in neighbouring Arab countries intensified this demand, as did the subsequent inflow of capital from the Gulf states and foreign remittances, which poured into the already lucrative real-estate and construction sectors of the economy. The building boom of the 1950s and 1960s, with its manifestations of mixed and intensive land-use patterns and vertical expansion, was largely a by-product of such forces. The resulting uncontrolled and haphazard patterns of growth were maintained during the early 1970s. Shortly before the outbreak of civil disturbances in 1975, greater Beirut was probably absorbing 75 per cent of Lebanon's urban population and close to 45 per cent of all the inhabitants of the country. In addition, its already overcrowded 101-square kilometre area had to accommodate an estimated 120,000 daily commuters from adjoining suburbs. (Ragheb, 1969: 110)

By the early 1970s Beirut's annual rate of growth was estimated at 4 per cent, which implied that the city was bound to double in less than twenty years. The magnitude of this change may be expressed in more concrete terms: if the current rates of growth are maintained, Beirut has to accommodate and provide housing, schooling, medical services, transport and other services for at least 40,000 new residents every year. Consequently, Beirut is associated with the phenomenon of primacy and overurbanization. Insofar as the degree of urbanization is much more than would be expected from the level of industrialization, Lebanon is among the few countries – along with Egypt, Greece and Korea – that may be considered overurbanized. (Sovani, 1969)

This is not the place to explore the implications of primary loyalties and overurbanization. Suffice it to note that this is one of the most critical problems Lebanon faces, a problem with serious social, psychological, economic and – as recent events amply demonstrate – political implications. Urban congestion, blight, depletion of open spaces, disparities in income distribution, rising levels of unemployment and underemployment, housing shortages, exorbitant rents, problems generated by slums and shantytowns, and, to a considerable extent, urban violence are all by-products of overurbanization. In short, the scale and scope of urbanization have outstripped the city's resources to cope effectively with continuously mounting demand for urban space and public amenities.

These problems have been compounded by another peculiar feature of Lebanese urbanization: the survival of communal and traditional loyalties. Repeated studies have shown that the swift and extensive urbanization Lebanon has been experiencing has not been associated, as is the case in most other societies, with a comparable decline in kinship and communal loyalties (see, for example, Gulick 1967; Khalaf and Kongstad 1973: Khuri 1975), nor with a proportional degree of urbanism as a way of life.

What this suggests is that a considerable proportion of the urban residents are, in an existential sense, in but not of the city. To both recent migrants and relatively more permanent urban settlers, city life is predominantly conceived as a transient encounter, to be sustained by periodic visits to rural areas or by developing rural networks within urban areas. In practice, urbanization in Lebanon has not meant the erosion of kinship ties, communal loyalties and confessional affinities and the emergence of impersonality, anonymity and transitory social relations. As in other dimensions of social life, the network of urban social relations, visiting patterns and the character of voluntary associations still sustain a large residue of traditional attachments despite increasing secularization and urbanization. In many respects Beirut – and Tripoli, Saida and other major Lebanese cities – are more 'mosaics' of distinct urban communities than 'melting pots' of amorphous urban masses.

Often neighbourhoods emerge that consist of families drawn from both the same village and the same religious group, resulting in patterns of segregation in which religious and village ties are reinforced.

Lebanon shares with other countries in the region, and possibly with other developing countries, the disjunction between overurbanization and underurbanism. These traditional survivals may determine spatial patterns such as functional neighbourhoods, homogeneous quarters and expedient pedestrian alleyways and courtyards. These in turn can serve as viable sources of communal solidarity and social and psychological reinforcement. Partly because of the bias in Western models and perspectives, there has been a tendency in the Arab world to denigrate such traditional forms and spatial arrangements as useless and nostalgic residues of the past. Extended kinship networks, family associations and parochial and communal organizations are treated with nearly the same disregard. This is a serious and costly error, one that is based on a misunderstanding of the adaptive role that traditional and smaller organizations or systems can play in alleviating some of the disquieting features of rapid urbanization.

The experience of other Arab cities with urban planning demonstrates equal shortsightedness. In the name of urban zoning and master plans, traditional neighbourhoods and residential quarters, have been wilfully by-passed, destroyed or allowed to atrophy by gradually siphoning off their functions. Belated attempts have been made to recreate artificially and by fiat what could have served as a natural and viable alternative means of coping with some of the unanticipated consequences of rapid urbanization.

Surviving traditional features have been a source of communal solidarity, providing much of the needed social and psychic supports, but they also account for much of the deficiency in civility and the erosion of public and national consciousness. More important, perhaps, they may obstruct rational urban planning and zoning.

The protracted civil crisis since 1975 has not only reinforced the communal character of neighbourhoods but also generated other problems of a far more critical magnitude. Vast areas, in addition to the central business district, have been totally or partially destroyed. Massive population shifts have generated further disparities and imbalances between the various communities and intensified religious hostilities and urban violence. The virtual collapse of state agencies and legitimate institutions has created further opportunities for the violation of zoning and construction ordinances.

In summary of the discussion thus far, it can be said that swift and extensive urbanization and the survival of many traditional norms characterize Beirut and are factors that have contributed to the haphazard and unguided growth of the city.

Historical Survey of Planning in Beirut

Proposed Plans
In the early 1930s public officials in Beirut began to display considerable concern for the physical development of the city. Lebanon, it must be recalled, was then

under the French Mandate, and all the early plans were inspired and undertaken by French experts. Successive teams of such specialists were engaged to prepare the necessary guidelines to direct the future growth of Beirut. Arrayed against the planners were local interest groups and politicians, who saw in the plans threats to their ability to use private property freely. A brief survey of the salient features of these plans is instructive, since they set the pattern for later town-planning schemes and development.

The earliest city plan for Beirut was prepared by the French consultant Danger, in 1932. This was the first attempt at comprehensive planning taking into account the geographical, geological, demographic and human features of Beirut and its adjacent communities. The plan established three main traffic arteries (Beirut–Damascus; Beirut–Tripoli; Beirut–Saida) and proposed other new roads and by-passes. More significantly, it outlined zoning coefficients and varying densities for various occupations and recommended residential developments along the lines of garden cities. Danger, half a century ago, had the foresight to treat Beirut and its suburbs as one unit. He also demonstrated a judicious concern for conserving and promoting some of the environmental and aesthetic attractions of the city. His plan proposed measures for the protection of elevated areas, the development of public parks and gardens, the building of sanitary sewers, the organization of refuse collection and slum clearance. Unfortunately, the Danger Plan was never approved and its recommendations were never implemented. (For further details, see the Executive Board of Major Projects for the City of Beirut 1968; and Salam, 1972.)

The Ecochard Plan of 1944 did not fare any better. It too was based on exhaustive studies and maintained that the planning of Beirut should extend beyond its limited administrative boundaries to encompass the coastal stretch from Bahr el-Maout in the north to Ouzai in the south. Like the Danger Plan, it outlined the major traffic arteries and the highway network and displayed the same concern for the protection of natural sites, open spaces and public gardens. It even went so far as to provide an inventory of the valuable trees that should be maintained in Beirut. It also went into great detail in proposing zoning ordinances, the location of the airport and other civic centres, industrial zones and popular housing. The city was divided into twelve zones – commercial, industrial and residential in character – with varying densities. Like its predecessor, however, this plan was never approved, although many of its recommendations were incorporated in later plans.

The Egli Report or Plan of 1950 was essentially a reappraisal of the earlier Ecochard Plan. It recommended the adoption of most of the Ecochard proposals, particularly the layout of the highway system, but reduced the number of zones from twelve to five. Again, this plan was never approved – probably because, like the others, it met resistance from local interest groups and politicians – although some of its recommendations formed the basis for further studies, which resulted in the General Master Plan of 1951–54.

The General Master Plan
This General Master Plan – the only officially approved plan and the one

responsible for the subsequent development of Beirut – was nothing but a network of roads derived essentially from the Ecochard Plan. It neither provided zoning nor did it consider any of the factors that could affect future development, such as the location of industry, airports, harbours and tourism. It also failed to make any effort to preserve the natural sites and historic monuments of the city. More important, perhaps, it failed to consider Beirut within its broader metropolitan and regional context. The results of its deficiencies became painfully obvious as Beirut's growth accelerated: commercial centres invaded residential districts; ground floors and front gardens were converted into shops and pavement cafes; offices were located in apartment buildings; streets were congested with traffic; soaring land values made it impossible to provide for green areas and open spaces; and the lack of protection for natural sites and monuments eroded the little that remained of the national and architectural heritage. Conditions in the suburbs were even worse. Since there was no plan or zoning legislation for the outskirts before 1963, no limits whatsoever were imposed on building up outlying areas. Entire suburbs mushroomed overnight and started to close in on the city. Stretches of virgin land were subjected to parcelization schemes to enhance their value for commercial speculation.

In short, at the very time that Beirut and its suburbs were experiencing their most intensive demographic pressure and urban expansion, planning schemes were either totally absent or deficient. Until the two town planning acts of 1963, the only control was the obsolete building code, but by then it was too late to curb or redirect the previous chaotic growth.

Since the building code of 1932 and the town planning laws of 1963 were the two legislative documents most responsible for planning and zoning in Lebanon, a word about each is in order.

The Building Code and Problems of Enforcement
The Lebanese Building Code, which has been subjected to four substantive amendments since its enactment in 1932 (1940, 1954, 1964, 1971), like all other official schemes in Lebanon, leaves little to be desired except its implementation. The code was inspired by the French and is very explicit in its provisions. It contains specific requirements and regulations regarding matters such as construction and occupancy permits; the overall envelope within which a building must be contained; the unobstructed visual distance between the facade of a building and the boundaries of a plot (this is usually a minimum of 4.5 metres to ensure a 'clear view', that is, to permit the opening of a window for ventilation and lighting); setbacks from both the road and neighbouring property; plot ratios specifying coefficients of surface and total exploitation; the appearance of buildings and their structural safety; parcelization or subdivision of land; parking space; and penalties for noncompliance (for further details see Abi Nader, 1972).

Most of the provisions are very stringent in their requirements and, if applied, could have safeguarded the urban environment from further abuse, or at least contained some of the ugly manifestations of the dehumanization of living space that Lebanon witnessed since the 1960s. In the absence of its application, the damage has been irreparable because to permit the misuse of a parcel of land, insignificant as it may seem initially, has irreversible consequences.

For example, the non-application of Article VII of the code should be considered. This article specifies that a newly constructed building cannot be supplied with electric power, water and telephones until the proprietor secures an occupancy permit verifying that the actual specifications of the construction are consistent with the approved original design of the building. If implemented, this regulation could impose effective controls on rampant construction violations. Municipal authorities, however, have not been able to detect, let alone contain or prevent, the ingenious strategies the Lebanese have developed to transgress this and other construction ordinances. Quite often, for example, proprietors, after securing the occupancy permit, add another floor, violate setback regulations or convert the use of floor space from residential to commercial. Most such constructions take place stealthily at night to avoid notice. Even if detected, penalties and fines are nominal and insubstantial compared with the benefits that the offenders derive from such transgressions. Often a modest bribe to a municipal clerk or inspector is sufficient to have the infraction concealed or ignored.

Article XVIII of the Building Code, which is concerned with the outside appearance and aesthetic quality of buildings, requires that proprietors periodically restore, paint and embellish the facades of their buildings. If they neglect to do so, the appropriate authorities are empowered to undertake such beautification at the owner's expense. This regulation too is never enforced, and the result is an ugly and blighted urban environment. In contrast, while the exterior and facades of buildings are neglected, the interiors are generally cared for better.

The proclivity of proprietors to ignore code requirements and the reluctance of municipal authorities to enforce them are both expressions of deficient civility and the pervasive lack of concern citizens in general display for the quality of public space.

Probably no other part of the Building Code is subject to as many violations as the provisions regulating the coefficient of exploitation of land. The code makes a distinction between zoned and unzoned areas and specifies the total and surface coefficients for each, along with the height of the building, number of floors, setbacks and so on. Because of soaring land values and the eagerness of the Lebanese to exploit every square metre of space they can lay their hands on, the extent and nature of violations of these provisions are staggering. Violations are committed by large entrepreneurs, contractors and speculators, but also by ordinary homeowners keen on maximizing their private gain. The strategies they have developed for circumventing the law are both subtle and ingenious.

For example, Article XIV of the Building Code specifies the areas normally excluded in calculating the coefficient of exploitation, such as open terraces and balconies that do not exceed 20 per cent of the surface area of the floor, basements and pillar floors, attic projections and protrusions added for decorative and other purposes. Proprietors, particularly once they have secured their occupancy permits, manage ultimately to extend their construction to exploit such areas, thus exceeding the optimal coefficient required by law. The conversion of pillar and attic space into full-fledged floors is one of the most recurrent and visible violations in suburban and rural areas where zoning regulations restrict the number of floors to three. The hilly terrain and the often steep incline of construction sites in the suburbs necessitate the use of pillars as structural supports. The law also encourages the construction of traditional red-tiled roofs by reducing municipal taxes for them. By filling in the pillar floor and by slightly rearranging the attic space under the traditional roof, an owner can convert a three-storey building into a five-storey one. Only nominal fines are imposed for these violations.

Regulations governing parking space and garages in the basements of apartment buildings are similarly circumvented. Article XII of the Building Code requires that all buildings, irrespective of their use, must provide garage space exclusively for parking. The area set aside for parking is 25 square metres per car; the law also details the amount of parking space in buildings that may be used for different purposes[1] and the circumstances in which exceptions to the normal parking space requirements will be allowed. Despite the strictures of the code, most proprietors find their way around such restrictions and end up leasing the space for commercial use. The excuses resorted to are legion and easily concocted. All that is needed is some proof that the passage leading to the basement is too steep or narrow to permit the entry of vehicles. In some instances proprietors actually contrive pillars or other structural barriers to obstruct such passages. They are then more than willing to pay the substitute fee to secure the release of the basement. In nearly all such instances, what should have been legitimate parking space for tenants is leased as warehouse space, disco clubs, bars or for other commercial uses. More than any other factor, this practice has compounded the parking problems and traffic congestion afflicting Lebanese cities.

Recent estimates reveal that there is one motor vehicle for every 4.5 persons in Lebanon. Given the small size and high density of the country, this is a notably high ratio and one that is bound to have adverse implications for the quality of urban life. As it is, public areas such as pavements, alleyways, courtyards and other pedestrian and open spaces are being mindlessly eaten up and transformed into parking lots. Since municipal authorities are normally lax in detecting and penalizing such transgressions, they have increased considerably in number, particularly since the mid-1970s.

Public parking garages are not currently a viable alternative to the problem. Only a few public parking ventures succeeded in Beirut before the civil war, and they were inadequate. Article XIX of the Building Code stipulates that the income generated by municipalities from payments made by owners of buildings when converting parking space to other uses is to go towards establishing public garages. Although some plans for such garages have been made, none has been implemented, in large measure because skyrocketing land values have made appropriation of land for garages prohibitively expensive.

---

1.   For example, residential apartments whose size does not exceed 125 square metres must provide space for one car. Parking space for larger apartments is calculated on the basis of one car for every 125 square metres of living space, with a maximum of four cars for every apartment. Parking space for offices and other commercial uses is calculated on the basis of one car for every 100 square metres of built-up area, while that for recreational centres, auditoria and hotels is one car for every 20 persons. For industrial uses and warehouses, it is one car for every 200 square metres.

The reasons for the failure to enforce the strict provisions of the Building Code are manifold, but underlying them all are the pervasive deficiencies in civic consciousness and the soaring land values that have made it impractical to expropriate private land or even to protect existing public spaces from further abuse. There are other more specific reasons for the failure to penalize code violators. The inspection system is inadequate and inspectors are subject to bribery. Where violations are detected, there is no follow-up by the municipal authorities or internal security forces, who are entitled by law to remove the offending structures.

Agencies empowered to safeguard public safety and security have been reluctant to exercise their responsibility. Municipal authorities, judges and magistrates, in the absence of institutional support, harbour legitimate fears about initiating any legal or criminal proceedings, and in any case they see such proceedings as largely futile in the present circumstances. As the level of anarchy and the erosion of state sovereignty have increased since 1975, the prospects for enforcing the code have grown even poorer.

Planning Legislation of 1963 and Problems of Implementation
The town planning legislation of 1963 stands out as an important landmark in Lebanon's chequered history in urban planning. This first serious attempt at comprehensive planning and legislation was the product of a commission appointed by the government in 1961. The commission produced the so-called Plan Directeure de Beirut et sa Banlieue,[1] which established densities for the various zones, particularly on the outskirts of Beirut; set the locations for industry and governmental centres; and protected the coast, beaches, woods and other natural sites. More important, the commission also produced the first body of planning legislation, which was to apply to the whole of Lebanon and which has been in operation since that time.

In brief, the 1963 legislation concentrated all matters related to town planning in one single authority, the Directorate General of Town Planning, attached to the Ministry of Public Works. It also established a Higher Council for Urban Planning (HCUP), a totally independent body formed of representatives of interested ministries.[2] Both the Directorate and the Council are expected to follow priorities set by the government, but they are nonetheless given the full right to decide on the areas that need planning.

On the whole, by tightening control over building permits, architectural aesthetics and land parcelization, the new legislation has so far been moderately successful in filling some of the earlier gaps inherent in the obsolete Building

1. The studies for the plan were directed by Ecochard in cooperation with a team of local professional architects. Although the plan continues to bear his name, Ecochard at the time publicly dissociated himself from the officially approved plan.

2. The composition of HCUP was modified in June 1977 to include the following: the General Director of Town Planning, one representative each from the Ministry of the Interior, the Ministry of Public Works and the Council for Reconstruction and Development, as well as the president of the Syndicate of Engineers and a university sociologist. The Council meets weekly.

Code. For example, in March 1981 HCUP submitted a draft proposal to amend articles of the Building Code that dealt with violations, rendering them more stringent. If and when the proposed amendments are approved by Parliament,[1] it will become theoretically impossible for a violator to persist in his transgression unless he is willing to pay a heavy fine. The proposed law calculates the fine at five times the cost of the required construction permits on all the built-up area on the violator's property in addition to the price of 'imaginary land' affected by the violation. To give a concrete instance, suppose a proprietor unlawfully constructs an additional floor and by so doing increases his built-up area by 500 square metres beyond the coefficient allowed by law. This area will be treated as imaginary land. In certain areas of Beirut, where the land value is as high as $3,000 per square metre, the fine might easily reach $200,000.

Theoretically, such penalties could act as effective deterrents. In practice, however, they are likely to remain futile unless supplemented by new executive powers to implement them. Given the erosion of state powers and the rampant lawlessness currently besetting Lebanon, they are unlikely to be enforced.

The effectiveness of the legislation and HCUP itself has been seriously handicapped by some other persistent shortcomings. There is, first, the ubiquitous conflict with other government agencies, which are reluctant to relinquish prerogatives they once enjoyed.[2] More grievous, perhaps, is the failure to reform the existing system of land taxation or to control land speculation. Given the usual collusion between private entrepreneurs and the political establishment, it is the substantial entrepreneurs and businessmen with political connections who are in a position to benefit from unfettered land speculation ventures. They are frequently privy to vital tips as to the areas that are about to be subjected to zoning. Exploiting their inside information, they purchase vast stretches of land in advance of their being zoned. Such speculation is highly profitable, since zoning almost always generates a sharp increase in land values.

Speculation has adverse consequences. With soaring land values it was prohibitively expensive under the Building Code of 1932 to expropriate land for any urban redevelopment on a large scale. To deal with this problem, a 1954 law (reconfirmed in 1964) provided for the establishment of mixed real-estate companies (public and private) in which the government is a 25 per cent shareholder and which can expropriate up to 25 per cent of a piece of private property without compensation to the owner if the part taken is for public use; the private segment of the company receives the remaining 75 per cent. The mixed

---

1. Because of the civil war and the involvement of Parliament in more pressing issues, the proposed amendments had not been approved as of October 1982.

2. These conflicts involve various government agencies and departments such as municipal councils, the Department of Buildings and Roads and the Ministries of Public Works and Planning. Municipal councils, which are often under the control of local interest groups, normally favour more intensive forms of exploitation of land and are therefore likely to oppose HCUP-imposed restrictions on land use. The councils tend not to implement HCUP master plans, which zone certain areas as green belts or public parks, on the grounds that they lack the funds to expropriate the necessary land. After a delay of ten years, the land originally allotted for green belts and public parks can be released for commercial use.

company undertakes the planning of an entire zone and then proceeds to sell the property, reimburse the owners and develop the site in accordance with the master plan for the zone, which must include open areas, parks, schools and other common facilities. If widely implemented, such a system would protect individual landowners from being exploited by speculators and would mean that appreciation in land values resulting from such projects would be shared by every owner in proportion to his share of land. Although the law has been in existence since 1954, mixed companies have rarely been effective because of the interference of large property owners interested in land speculation in districts where mixed companies were created. Such entrepreneurs oppose the purchase of land by mixed companies because they could limit their own free and uncontrolled speculation. Unfortunately, only three such projects, all in the suburbs of Beirut, have actually been implemented. Studies for four other areas – Tripoli, Saida, Hammanah, and Sofar (the latter two being mountain resorts) – have been completed and await approval by the authorities.

Finally, and perhaps most important, although HCUP was established as an independent and central authority to consider all matters pertaining to urban planning and zoning, it is only empowered to 'express its opinion' (Article IV of the Urban Planning Legislation) and hence can act in an advisory capacity only. Many of its decisions and deliberations are overruled or ignored by the Council of Ministers or the president of the Republic. Indeed, the president has exceptional powers at his disposal, enabling him to enact special decrees by which he can modify the zoning or land-use pattern of any area without reference to HCUP. On several occasions successive presidents are known to have made opportune use of such extraordinary prerogatives. Needless to say, a mere reclassification of a zoned area from, for instance, residential to industrial, increasing the coefficient of exploitation, is enough to generate an increase in land value. Presidents have resorted to such reclassifications to benefit cronies and relatives.

The foregoing discussion has treated some of the salient features of urbanization and the nature of urban planning and zoning in Lebanon, and an attempt has been made to show what factors impeded the government's ability to control the haphazard growth of urban areas. The successive schemes and master plans, many of them nothing more than a network of roads on paper, remained unimplemented. Even the plans that were officially adopted, the Building Code of 1932 and the Urban Planning Legislation of 1963, with their stringent provisions and restrictions, failed to impose effective controls on the abuses of the urban environment.

Another factor that must be taken into account is the small area reached by planning. Even today it is estimated that not more than 7 per cent of the total built-up area of Lebanon has been zoned or planned. In all these unplanned areas construction is not controlled and maximum exploitation is authorized. Furthermore, in sizeable portions of the planned areas, the plan simply confirms already existing trends. In other words, rather than anticipating and directing the course of future developments, planning has often meant the reinforcement of already established spatial patterns. For example, the growth of the industrial belt around the suburbs of Beirut was largely the by-product of such forces. The heavy rural–urban migration of the 1950s and 1960s and the consequent availability of a large reserve of cheap labour in the suburban zones prompted many industrialists to locate their firms and establishments in the adjoining areas. The Master Plan of 1963 simply confirmed this reality by assigning a high coefficient of exploitation to such periurban areas.

Not only have certain areas grown without a master plan, but others have developed contrary to the specifications of rigid planning schemes. Hamra, the once fashionable and cosmopolitan middle-class urban district in western Beirut, is one such dramatic instance. It grew despite the general concept in the Master Plan that urban development should be diverted along the southern axis of metropolitan Beirut. Because of the absence in Hamra of traditional patterns of landholdings that would have involved collective ownership of land by an extended family and thus impeded its division into separately owned lots, the transfer of land was rendered possible through cadastral legislation. There is evidence that parcels in the Hamra district were individualized as early as 1928, a tendency that must have encouraged land transactions and speculations in real estate as viable economic ventures (for further details, see Khalaf and Kongstad, 1973: 30). This same pattern has been repeated in a score of other districts and suburbs.

Another factor to be considered in assessing the reasons for the failure of planning in Lebanon is the existence of cultural biases and deficiencies in the plans themselves. The borrowed schemes, which, as elsewhere in the Arab world, were designed by foreign experts, were often insensitive to the particular needs and interests of local groups and communities. Had the successive master plans evinced more responsiveness to local sentiments and traditional elements of Lebanese society, they would have been more effective and avoided some of the hostility and resistance they incurred. No matter how planning is defined, it must always involve a certain degree of congruence between planner and user; when this congruence is lacking, the user will violate the plans.

An example of the way in which planning has been thwarted by indigenous cultural patterns may be seen in the failure of plans for a limited-access highway around Beirut's periphery. To the average Lebanese, who tends to be in no particular hurry to get anywhere, a road is not necessarily valued as a quick route between two points. Instead, it may be perceived as offering a chance for leisurely excursions, shopping trips and recreation. Thus the plans for the limited-access highway were set aside; shopping and recreational facilities mushroomed on its flanks, the flow of traffic was impeded and it was converted into a multi-access highway.

Familism, Patronage and Commercialism

The failure of urban planning in Lebanon is not only a product of the factors discussed in the preceding sections but also a reflection of certain persistent features of its social structure. This final section explores the impact of three features of Lebanon's social structure – familism, patronage and commercialism – on the spatial structure. The discussion will necessarily be brief. The intention is simply to highlight some of the obvious implementations of such traditional elements for urban planning and zoning.

Family Loyalty

The survival of family loyalty, with its associated norms and institutions, as repeated studies have demonstrated, continues to have a visible impact on the spatial structure and physical layout of urban areas. The family in Lebanon, despite the inevitable decline in the sense of kinship generated by increasing urbanization, mobility and secularization, continues to have a social and psychological reality that pervades virtually all aspects of society. There is hardly a dimension of people's lives that it does not touch. To a considerable extent, a person's status, occupation, political behaviour, personal values and critical periods in the lifecycle are defined by kinship affiliation. For the average Lebanese, kinship attachments are intense and encompassing.

The pervasive familism not only manifests itself in particular architectural features that survive in traditional urban quarters, such as the inward-looking house, the arched doorway, the *dar* or *harat* (clusters of houses whose inhabitants are linked through kinship) and courtyard, but also determines the location of residence, visiting and shopping patterns and much of the associational behaviour of people, even in highly mobile and modern urban districts. Patrilocal residence, extended family obligations, the desire to retain control of family homesteads and real estate and the system of inheritance, which permits the divisibility of property into a potentially infinite number of shares, determine features of the urban environment that are difficult to reconcile with modern models of urban renewal or redevelopment of traditional urban quarters. Much of the confused look, irregularity and anarchy of labyrinthine quarters and the unusual lot shapes and sizes are attributable to such kinship norms and primordial loyalties. It should be noted here that the layout of the traditional neighbourhoods is not by itself necessarily incompatible with urban planning standards. Despite their seemingly confused look, many of the older neighbourhoods would have survived as viable and colourful forms of human association had they been preserved by the new plans. Unfortunately, many of the new schemes display little sensitivity to such spatial arrangements. Hence, rather than rerouting throughways to protect some of the graceful and edifying features of such communities, the new expressways often disfigure their natural layout and destroy their communal and intimate character. It is then that the neighbourhoods and quarters begin to assume some dysfunctional features.

Patron–Client Relationships

A pluralistic society like Lebanon, marked by persistent disparities in status and opportunity and sustained by highly personalized networks of reciprocal obligations and primordial loyalties, favours the development of political patron–client relationships. To a large degree, much of the socio–political history of Lebanon may be viewed as the history of various groups and communities seeking to secure patronage: client groups needing protection, security and vital benefits, and patrons trying to extend the scope of their clientele.

Patronage appears in many guises and is certainly not unique to Lebanon. In virtually all known societies, with or without diffuse and ascriptive loyalties, individuals and groups normally seek to advance their private ends in particular ways. In Lebanon the most viable and visible form of patronage is the middleman, or *wasit*, a broker who provides greater access to opportunity and benefits for his clients in return for political support and loyalty. Patron–client ties involve the reciprocal exchange of extrinsic benefits and therefore both patron and client have a vested interest in maintaining this reciprocity. As has been demonstrated elsewhere (Khalaf, 1977), clients in Lebanon have no way of securing certain services and favoured treatment except through their allegiance to a patron, and patrons can maintain their power only by extending the size of their client support.

This pervasive feature of Lebanon's social structure affects the process of urban zoning in substantive and concrete ways. Patronage, it must be remembered, rarely appears alone. It carries with it a host of other unsavoury features: endemic corruption, bribery, graft, nepotism, executive and administrative incompetence, private interference in public decisions and exchange of quid pro quos. The prevalence of these features suggests that private and particular ends are being promoted at the expense of public concerns. Government bureaucracy is overstaffed with incompetent and inept civil servants, most of whom owe their careers to the favouritism, or *wasta*, of a political or communal leader. When they are in a position to return the favour, they do so in tangible ways.

The result is that virtually everyone within the government civil bureaucracy – from the simple municipal clerk who overlooks a minor transgression to a high government official who intervenes on behalf of either his client or patron to reroute a road network or rezone a certain area – is placed in a strategic position to affect the redistribution of rewards and benefits in society. Such manipulations are especially frequent when the case involves land or real estate, which in Lebanon provides one of the most viable sources of commercial speculation. Examples of this sort are legion.

Commercialism

Finally, in a mercantile culture like Lebanon, excessive commercialism and its concomitant bourgeois values have always been given a free hand. Commercialism has become so rooted in the ethos of the average Lebanese that he is inclined to reduce every relationship and dimension of his life to a cash nexus. Practically everything and anything is for sale in Lebanon. Every entity and human capacity is conceived as a resource for the acquisition of profit or as a commodity to be sold to the highest bidder in a competitive market. Land is certainly not spared, and such features as shorelines, green belts, public parks and private backyards, suburban villas and historic sites and monuments have all been subjected to the most intensive and profitable forms of exploitation. Indeed, the commercial traffic in land (particularly since the 1950s) has become one of the most important sources of private wealth. The attendant commercialism has brought about a ruthless plunder of Lebanon's scenic natural habitat and the dehumanization of much of its living space.

The impact of commercialism has also meant that municipal and other civic authorities are no longer able to provide the necessary funds to expropriate vital areas for public use, making it impossible to prevent some of the choicest parcels of land, often earmarked as public parks and green areas, from being converted to commercial use. Unfortunately, legislation in Lebanon permits such conversion. Urban planning regulations stipulate that after a lapse of ten years from the time a zoning plan has been proposed for a particular district, all areas designated as prospective green areas can be released and converted to private use. Indeed, this is what actually happens in most instances because of the failure to implement zoning plans within the ten-year period. Since municipal councils cannot afford to pay the exorbitant expropriation compensation, they usually welcome such conversion.

As previously noted, the expropriation law also provides that 25 per cent of a property can be expropriated without compensation if it is affected by planning, as happens when a parcel of land is intersected by a proposed road network. However, because of delays in implementation, such proposals obstruct rather than facilitate comprehensive planning. An anticipated passage of a road almost always generates a manifold increase in the value of land, and thus leads to speculation in the affected land.

The outcome of commercialism is painfully clear: by placing a cash value on every relationship, the moral and aesthetic restraints that could control the growth of cities and shape their human habitat are completely eroded and sacrificed. People have scant concern for whether cities are ugly, whether they debase their inhabitants, whether they are aesthetically, spiritually or physically tolerable, or whether they provide people with opportunities for authentic individuality, privacy and edifying human encounters. What counts is that commercial transactions occur on a scale and with an effectiveness to meet the only criteria of bourgeois survival: economic growth and the insatiable appetite for profit.

As long as such materialistic values remain dominant in Lebanese society, zoning is more likely to be a reactive rather than an independent social force for controlling urban land use. Indeed, short of a fundamental change in the basic values underlying kinship, patronage and commercialism, which could help transform Lebanon into a more civic and secular society, planning and zoning can do little to protect the urban environment from further abuse.

Conclusion

The urban growth of Beirut has been shaped more by the forces of the free market and fortuitous circumstances than by planning and zoning. Beirut's plans have failed to realize basic goals of urban planning such as comprehensive zoning, balanced population density, proper relationships of land use and landscape design. They have also failed to anticipate the consequences of the increasing scale of urbanization in terms of the Lebanese cultural ethos and traditional modes of behaviour. As noted, the increasing scale and intensity of urbanization in Lebanon – involving traditional loyalties, high population density, mobility and mixed land-use patterns – has not been accompanied by a corresponding degree of genuine urbanism as a socio-cultural and psychic phenomenon. This has meant that many non-urban ties and loyalties have survived and are reflected in certain communal forms of spatial patterns. Both in Beirut and in its suburbs, much growth has proceeded independently of any master plan.

The process of rational urban planning has also been undermined by the persistence of patron–client relationships in politics and elsewhere. These allow strategically placed individuals to control the distribution of benefits achieved through the manipulation of zoning laws and ordinances. Since good connections and political ties open many avenues for engaging in speculation connected with anticipated planning or rezoning schemes, even the ordinary citizen can secure favoured treatment or protection from the law.

What inferences can be made regarding the interplay between urban planning and social structure in Lebanon? One should not generalize from the Lebanese experience, since the nature and particular milieu within which its urban planning has occurred are in many respects unique. For example, the deep-seated weakness of state agencies and the consequent deficiency in civility and public consciousness – all of which have direct implications for urban planning – are exceptionally pronounced in Lebanon. The Lebanese state, compared with other forms of primary loyalties and communal allegiances, has always been an enfeebled and residual institution. Likewise, as a fragmented political culture, Lebanon has experienced a comparatively high incidence of repeated episodes of civil unrest and social disorder. The rampant chaos and lawlessness generated by such protracted episodes renders any effort to enforce the law vain and futile. Furthermore, when normlessness becomes so widespread, offences such as the confiscation of property and the violation of construction and zoning ordinances become legitimate and forgivable.

Examination of the Lebanese experience reveals a curious but poignant contrast: a dissonance between the rather orderly and viable regulation of private space in homes, neighbourhoods and quarters, matched by a mindless and almost total disregard for public space. In other words, the average Lebanese is so preoccupied with the internal comforts of his family and private domain that he evinces little concern for public welfare and civic developments and becomes correspondingly more inclined to violate zoning ordinances. These contrasting attitudes towards the private and public spheres are clearly symptoms and sources of the deficiency in civility pervading Lebanese society.

PART II

New England Puritanism as a Cultural Transplant

CHAPTER 4

Protestant Orientalism

Evangelical Christianity and Cultural Imperialism

> . . . A great desire in my breast to demolish this mighty empire of sin . . . Woe to me if I ever leave this sacred calling. Ever may it be the language of my heart, 'Conquest or death'.
>
> Levi Parsons, *The Dereliction and Restoration of the Jews* (1819)

> For almost a century American public opinion concerning the Near East was formed by the missionaries. If American opinion has been uninformed, misinformed and prejudiced, the missionaries are largely to blame. Interpreting history in terms of the advance of Christianity, they have given an inadequate, distorted, and occasionally a grotesque picture of Moslems and Islam. While consciously preaching good-will, they sometimes have unconsciously sowed the seeds of misunderstanding.
>
> Edward Earle, *Early American Policy Concerning Ottoman Minorities* (1927)

> Cultural aggression not only threatened the self-image of the violated nation but fed the self-righteousness of the intruders.
>
> Arthur Schlesinger Jr, *The Missionary Enterprise and Theories of Imperialism* (1974)

Pliny Fisk and Levi Parsons, as first envoys and archetypes of 'disinterested benevolence' and romantic adventure, sailed from Boston (in 1819) armed with the instructions of the American Board of Commissioners for Foreign Missions (ABCFM) and boundless faith in their divine mission for converting the world to Christianity. They were so buoyed by their zeal, so longing to go, that they didn't really care which 'heathens' were to receive the beneficent rewards of their heroic labour. These glowing endorsements of Christian benevolence, which were assuming manifestations of militancy among a growing segment of New England college students during the first half of the nineteenth century, were not uncharacteristic of the time. As vanguards and forerunners, Fisk and Parsons were doubtless a cut above the ordinary youth of the day. They shared much, nonetheless, with that devoted core of enthusiasts. The blessed Gospel, they were convinced, had commenced its 'irresistible' progress. National pride in America's spectacular growth and accomplishments as a 'righteous republic' reinforced its 'manifest destiny' to play a significant role in disseminating the Gospel throughout the world.

Since at least the beginning of the nineteenth century this evangelical zeal had acquired a global perspective embracing all mankind. Samuel Mills, who was one of the most creative spirits in the American missionary enterprise at the turn of the twentieth century, is said to have declared to one of his friends, 'though you and I are very little beings, we must not rest satisfied till we have made our influence extend to the remotest corner of this ruined world'. (Spring, 1829: 25) In his own person, incidentally, Mills did much to embody that ideal. In his brief life (like many of his pious cohorts, he died in his early thirties while on a mission to Africa), he was one of the architects of the ABCFM and served as a role model, inspiring other spirited young evangelists in the crusade of 'Christianizing the world'. Samuel Worcester, another founder of the ABCFM, speaking at the ordination service for six missionaries, exclaimed, 'my brethren, the heathen do need the Gospel. There is no other remedy for them . . . All other world religions were utterly worthless and their adherents were without hope, salvation or eternal light.' (Worcester, 1815: 8)

This drive for 'world conquest', supported by the benighted view espoused by the pioneering generation of New England evangelists, was defended and justified by some missionary apologists. Kenneth Latourette, for example, maintains that though the missionaries talked about 'world conquest' they did not mean by that 'political or even cultural subjugation, still less ecclesiastical imperialism. They sought to bring into being the world around self-governing, self-supporting, self-propagating churches which could be knit together with other churches in all lands on the basis of equality.' Latourette goes further to assert that the missionary enterprise 'has contributed a particular kind of world-mindedness. It has encouraged thousands of Americans to think of the rest of the world not as a field for political or commercial empire but as an opportunity for brotherhood.' (Latourette, 1949: 30–26)

These and other such benign views are doubtless a reflection of the revisionist and historic hindsight the enterprise has invited over the years. In no way, however, do they realistically represent the prevailing outlook at the time, nor the images and perceptions that the emissaries carried over with them. Indeed, the main thrust of this essay is to demonstrate that, despite its diverse origins and evolving forms and manifestations, one can still discern consistent and inveterate polemics that underlie New England evangelism. I believe this is particularly evident in the basic premises and perceptions that informed its missionary enterprise to the Orient and eastern Mediterranean. The missionaries' haughty self-image, contempt for the 'worthless' others and ardent belief that redemption and salvation can come only through the Gospel all bespeak of an imperialist, often arrogant and militant ethos, which far exceeded the bounds of mere cultural penetration. I shall argue here that, both in its disparaging views of the 'other' and in its intrusive strategies to undermine and deprive 'native' groups of their spiritual inheritance and cultural identity, Protestant evangelism shares much with all other modes of colonial domination. At least four striking features, extracted from the perceptions and strategies that the Protestants carried over with them, reinforce this overwhelming imperialistic thrust.

First and foremost, this was apparent in their belief in the transforming and elevating powers of Christianity. More particularly, it found expression in their abiding faith that as New England Puritans they were 'special, 'chosen' people, destined, through some divine intervention and as heirs of their own 'righteous Republic', to uplift 'perishing souls' and other species of 'wretchedness' and 'ruined' worlds.

Secondly, largely through the survival of some medievalist stereotypes, Islam was seen as a 'broken cistern' and Mohammad as an 'impostor'. Neither the false prophet nor the 'degenerate' and 'wicked' faith was, naturally, capable of uplifting itself, let alone act as uplifting agencies. Hence Muslims needed the knowledge of Christ and could be saved only through evangelical Christianity.

Thirdly, although other more charitable, or at least moderately sympathetic, views of Islam were prevalent at the time, somehow New England missionaries continued to uphold and reinforce these outworn perceptions. Some went further to assert that by pitting 'degenerate' Islam against the superior and 'righteous' forces of Christianity, the 'decrepit' needs of the former were destined to be undermined and supplanted.

Finally, such overtones of haughty superiority and prejudice fostered and legitimized imperialist sentiments and strategies, particularly those associated with forms of cultural penetration.

My intention is to elaborate on these interrelated components.

Protestant Self-Righteousness

One inescapable and general inference can be readily deduced from the massive literature dealing with Protestant perceptions of its role in uplifting the heathen and non-Christian world. All the proselytizers shared an overriding mindset: namely, that America as a 'righteous republic' was a 'peerless' country called upon through divine intervention of Providence to mobilize its 'manifest destiny' on behalf of the degenerate in regions of darkness elsewhere in the world.

Perhaps no theme has ever dominated the minds of the founding fathers and spokesmen of the New Republic to the same extent as this notion that America occupied a unique place and had a special destiny among the nations of the world. America's manifest destiny to uplift, civilize and Christianize the heathen and backward world was a curious blend of patriotism, chauvinism and spiritual beliefs. It evolved into something akin to an early and pure version of the 'white man's burden' of protecting and bestowing good upon so-called 'perishing souls'. From then on New England Puritans behaved as though they were a 'covenant people' spurred by a messianic obligation towards the rest of the world.

As early as the Puritan migration of the seventeenth century one could discern concrete manifestations of such messianic sentiments. To some it was akin to a God-given right of discovery and occupation. John Winthrop and his company launched, after all, an 'Errand into the Wilderness' to establish a 'New Canaan', where God's latter-day chosen people could worship free from danger and error. (Segal and Stineback, 1977) To other Puritan stalwarts this was seen as though God had intentionally opened the land for the Puritans so that they could subdue the wilderness, plant colonies, erect towns and establish churches. (Beaver, 1966: 25–6)

This same sense of cultural arrogance permeated much of the effusive spiritual and national consciousness underlying the belief in the New World as a 'righteous republic'. The revolutionary struggles with Great Britain during the 1770s led the early Calvinists to see the hand of God in nearly all events. One sees manifestations of such lofty sentiments as early as 1765, before the enthusiasm generated by the Second Awakening or the resurgence of national consciousness in the post-revolutionary struggles of the 1770s. John Adams, for example, was already considering the settlement of America 'with reverence and wonder, as the opening of a grand scheme and design in Providence for illumination of the ignorant and the emancipation of the slavish part of mankind all over the earth'. (Adams, 1856: vol. I, 66)

In its first Address to the Christian Public immediately after the ABCFM was organized in November 1811, this overbearing sense of self-righteousness and the accompanying urge to promulgate the Gospel among the heathen was very much in evidence. The Address asserted in resounding terms that 'no nation is more inviting in the exertion of this mission than the people of New England'.

No nation ever experienced the blessing of the Christian religion more evidently, and uniformly, than the inhabitants of New England, from its first colonization till the present time, through nearly two centuries. Of all our social and civil enjoyments, scarcely one is worthy to be mentioned, which is not derived directly, or indirectly, from this holy religion; and all the enjoyments, which concern us as immortal beings, spring directly from this source. If we were deprived of all the civilization and liberty, all the present consolations and future hopes, which we receive from the Gospel, what should we have left? Where is the Christian who would not mourn day and night, were he told, that at some future time, this favoured land should sink into the superstition, corruption, and impiety of Paganism; that the Sabbath should become extinct, our churches moulder to ruin, no voice of supplication ascend to Jehovah, no children be dedicated in baptism to the triune God, and no memorial be observed of the Redeemer's sufferings, atonement, death, and resurrection; that instead of the rational worship of Christian assemblies, future generations should behold some horrible idol receiving the adoration of deluded millions? Where is the person of common humanity, who would not lift up the voice of lamentation, at the certain prospect of such an apostasy from the truth, and such a debasing all into the cruelties and debaucheries, the sins and miseries, of heathenism? If we should feel so intensely at the prospect of these evils befalling our own country, can we avoid being touched with compassion at the sight of many populous nations, which have been subjected for ages, and are still subjected, to the power of the most degrading idolatry? Are we not called upon in a peculiar manner, to exert ourselves in dispelling this worse than Egyptian darkness? (ABCFM, 1834: 28–9)

No wonder that such lofty sentiments should inspire poetic writing, often of epic proportions. Joel Barlow, William Lynch, Ezra Stiles, Timothy Dwight, among others – all extremely popular among seminarians and college students at the time – wrote some of their most evocative prose and poetry to shore up evangelist fervour and nationalist zeal (for a sampling see Sha'ban, 1991: 16–63). Barlow, perhaps the most prolific of the group, invoked this ennobling blend of spiritual and patriotic propensities to call on all mankind to emulate the distinctive traits of the New Republic.

But now no more the patriotic mind,
To narrow views and local laws confined,
Gainst neighboring lands direct the public rage,
Plods for a clan or counsels for an age;
But soars to loftier thoughts and reaches far
Beyond the power, beyond the wish of war;
For realms and ages forms the general aim,
Makes patriot views and moral views the same
Works with enlighten'd zeal, to see combined
The strength and happiness of humankind. (Barlow, 1970: II, 348)

The naval prowess Americans displayed in their confrontations with the 'infidels' of the Barbary States (1800–15) reconfirmed such haughty sentiments. There was, clearly, more than just trade or the desire to navigate the Mediterranean that prompted the US to entertain imperialist designs towards the Orient. The Protestant-American sense of Manifest Destiny, spurred by religious fervour and patriotic zeal, also sustained this expansionist form of cultural penetration. Incidentally, this self-righteous sentiment was apparent among those who were disparaging Islam as a 'fortress of error and sin' and dismissing Mohammad as an 'impostor' as much as among those who entertained more deferential attitudes towards some of the basic tenets and founder of its faith.

Scarcely had the 13 states gained their independence than it was taken for granted that what they had achieved would be a spur and inspiration to the victims of tyranny in other countries. It must also be recalled that Calvinism was so overpowering at the time that even groups that were not affiliated or had no direct contact with Calvinist churches could not entirely escape the effects of its pervasive influence.[1]

Herman Melville, far from being an uncritical admirer of missionary ventures, was still, like many of his generation of American writers, a proponent of America's manifest destiny as a chosen or peculiar people. Americans were, in the rhetoric of the day, treated as though they were preordained to transform domains of political paganism and 'wilderness' into 'cities on the hill' and 'the Israel of our time'. In language suffused with biblical idioms he too was astonishingly explicit in heralding Americans as the 'advance guards', the pioneers sent on through the wilderness to break new paths:

> We Americans are the peculiar, chosen people – the Israel of our time; we bear the ark of the liberties of the world. Seventy years ago we escaped from thrall; and, besides our first birthright – embracing one continent of earth – God has given to us, for a future inheritance, the broad domains of the political pagans, that shall yet come and lie down under the shade of our ark, without bloody hands being lifted. God has predestinated, mankind expects, great things from our race; and great things we feel in our souls. The rest of the nations must soon be in our rear. We are the pioneers of the world; the advance guard, sent on through the wilderness of untried things to break a new path in the New World that is ours. (Quoted by Sha'ban, 1991: 142)

Islam as a 'Broken Cistern'

Another universal component in Evangelical Christianity was, obviously, its deeply entrenched antithetical attitudes towards Islam, largely a residue of the ancient hostility between them. Such antipathies were often part of the broader disdain Protestantism harboured against the 'idolatry' and 'infidelity' of all non-Christian faiths. As Albert Hourani argues, it is easy to see the historical relationship between Christianity and Islam as one sustained by intermittent hostility, suspicion and outright holy wars, i.e. of Crusades and jihad. The historical justification of such enmity is fairly easy to discern.

The first great Muslim expansion in Christian lands, Syria, Egypt, North Africa, Spain and Sicily, the first Christian reconquests, in Spain, Sicily and the Holy Land; the spread of Ottoman power in Asia Minor and the Balkans; and the spread of European power in the last two centuries: all these processes had created and served to maintain an attitude of suspicion and hostility on both sides and still

---

1. Even an 'ungodly' Puritan like Benjamin Franklin, in a letter to Thomas Paine, asked him to consider how great a portion of mankind consists of weak and ignorant men and women – who have need of religion to restrain them from vice and to support their virtue. 'If men are so wicked with religion,' he asked, 'what could they be if without it?' (Bigelow (1887), vol. IX, p. 355)

provide, if not a reason for enmity, at least a language in which it could express itself. (Hourani, 1974: 5–6)

In successive declarations of the ABCFM and justifications for convening world missionary conferences one sees much evidence of this polar differentiation between the moral and ethical features of Christianity and the 'degeneracy', 'ruin' and innate 'inadequacy' of all other non-Christian faiths. Is this not after all what epitomizes all forms of ethnocentric and racist sentiments? The self-proclaimed uniqueness or superiority of one's culture or group can be sustained, in other words, only by debasing and downgrading the other. The former cannot exist without the latter. Those who idealized Anglo-Saxon supremacy – diehards like Jessup, Lynch and Curtis, who unabashedly spoke of 'Anglo-Saxonizing' and 'Americanizing' the Orient – were naturally more prone to employ equally strong language in depicting the moral flaws and foibles of native cultures. (see Curtis, 1856; Lynch, 1853; Jessup, 1879).

The three monumental volumes of James Dennis (published between 1897 and 1906) were illustrative of such ethnocentric perspectives. Incidentally, Dennis was no ordinary or obscure scholar. He served as a lecturer on missions at Princeton University (1893–96) and a member of the Presbyterian mission in Beirut (1869–92). Nor was he a dispassionate theologian. His widely circulated volumes, written as classroom lectures, were very influential 'in vindicating the beneficent results of Christianity as a sublime force in the social regeneration and elevation of the human race'. (Dennis, 1897: ix) The incipient discipline of sociology was gaining academic credibility at the time and this was, perhaps, the first such effort to apply analytical and conceptual paradigms, crude as they may seem, to substantiate what Dennis termed 'the power of renewal and the capacity for expansion inherent in Christianity'. (Dennis, 1897: 51) He outlined the parameters of what he termed 'Christian sociology' as distinct from a purely scientific or non-biblical sociology, one that recognized the role of Christian missions as 'sociological agencies' for reforming and rescuing man from these 'great and brooding wrongs' that oppress and dominate the 'social deserts' inherent in heathen societies. For that purpose Dennis constructed an elaborate typology of 'the social evils of the non-Christian world'. These were meticulously classified under six alleged universal categories with a detailed inventory of the 'evils' inherent in each.

The Individual:	Idleness and improvidence; excessive pride and self-exaltation; the blighting effects of untruth and dishonesty; the habits of intemperance, opium smoking, and gambling; immoral vices, self-torture, and suicide.
The Family:	Polygamy, adultery, and divorce; child-marriage and widowhood; infanticide.
The Tribe:	Slavery, cannibalism, human sacrifice, cruelty in war.

The Social Group:	Ignorance, quackery, and witchcraft; neglect of the poor, insanitariness, caste.
The Commercial Group:	Lack of business confidence; commercial deceit and fraud, financial irregularities, primitive industrial appliances. (Dennis, 1897: 733–39)

Of course New England evangelists did not remain abstract and detached in disparaging the religious tenets and practices of others. Islam to them, often in very riveting language, became incarnate and embodied all the 'evils' attributed to all non-Christian faiths. As W. M. Watt, in his most recent study of the perceptions and misperceptions of Muslim-Christian encounters, reminds us, once distorted images become firmly rooted in the collective image or general outlook of a community, they are difficult to change. (Watt, 1991: 111) Hence one need not be astonished by the survival and profusion of the medievalist warped judgement of Islam and of Muhammad. All the opprobrious appellations, derogatory clichés and epithets – such as Muhammad as a 'false prophet', 'anti-Christ', and Islam as a 'wretched heresy' spread by 'fire and sword' and sustained through 'fraud and perfidy' and other forms of cruelty and injustice – became, like all hackneyed stereotypes, irrevocably embedded in the public image that was already rampant in the early nineteenth century. Others went even further to claim that, given all its inherent deficiencies, Islam was bereft of any talent for rational science and philosophy, was hostile to fine arts and that whatever spirituality it acquired was derived from other sources. Such a degenerate, fanatical and corrupt faith becomes futile and powerless as an uplifting agency. It cannot elevate its own people and can be rescued only through evangelization.

Those who continued to study Islam or condoned expeditions to facilitate access to empirical and more intimate knowledge for understanding it did so only to expose its foibles and inadequacies. For a century (from 1820 to 1920), the reports and impressions missionaries were relaying back laid the foundation for much of America's knowledge and perceptions of the eastern Mediterranean. The intention in undertaking such studies was not to produce knowledge for its own sake but to work out strategies for undermining the basic tenets and modes of life of 'perishing souls' and 'deluded people'.

Others still went further, rejecting calls for a modus vivendi with Islam on the basis of mutual concession and recognition, and maintaining that the sublime mission of all emissaries to the East was to 'supplant the dead forms and the outworn creed of Islam'.

No Christian missionary is sent to the Moslem World to establish a treaty of peace with Islam. He is sent there to carry the Gospel of salvation to the perishing Moslem. He is God's messenger to the deluded people . . . He is an ambassador of the Cross, not an apologist for the Crescent . . . The Moslem world shall be open to the gracious entrance of the Saviour and the triumphs of the Gospel. The spell of twelve centuries shall be broken. That voice from the Arabian desert shall no longer say to the church of living God – thus far and no longer. The deep and sad delusion which shadows the intellectual and spiritual life of so many millions shall be dispelled, and the blessed life-giving power of Christ's religion shall supplant the dead forms and the outworn creed of Islam. (The Missionary Review of the World, 1889: 20–1)

In successive world missionary conferences, convened to shore up enthusiasm for the evangelizing ventures of New England missionaries, such images of 'the spiritual destitution of Islam and its failure to elevate the peoples who profess it' were pronounced more forcibly. During the first conference held at Cairo in 1906, in one paper after another, all the delegates expressed similar sentiments. One declared how Muslim nations are 'without exception sunk in almost every kind of immorality . . . How Islam excites a great deal of religious fanaticism . . . and how the followers of the Prophet of the Sword, with incredible courage and bloodthirstiness, slaughter all who will not acknowledge Mohammed to be the Prophet of God.' (Tisdall, 1907: 207–8) The delegate from Saudi Arabia, Rev. S. M. Zwemer, in almost identical terms to those Dennis used to identify the typology of universal social evils, had this to say about the emergence of the Wahhabis:

Wahhabism is a strong argument that Islam, even when reformed into its original principles and practices, has no power to save people or introduce permanent progress. There is no better polemic against Islam than a presentation of the present intellectual, social, and moral condition of Arabia. Cradled at Mecca, fostered at Medina, and reformed in the Nejd, the creed of Islam has had indisputed possession of the peninsula almost since its birth. In other lands, such as Syria and Egypt, it remained in contact with a more or less corrupt form of Christianity, or, as in India and in China, in conflict with cultured paganism, and there is no doubt that in both cases there were and are mutual concessions and influences. But in its native Arabian soil the tree planted by the Prophet has grown with wild freedom and brought forth fruit after its kind. As regards morality, Arabia is on a low plane. Slavery and concubinage exist everywhere; while polygamy and divorce are fearfully common. The conscience is petrified, legality is the highest form of worship, virtue is to be like the prophet Mohammed. Intellectually there has been scant progress since the time of ignorance. . . .The Bedouins are nearly all illiterate, and, in spite of the Wahhabi revival and the attempt of Turkish officials to open schools, there is little that deserves the name of education in even the larger towns. Kufa, which was once the Oxford of Arabia, now has one day-school with twelve pupils. Fatalism, the philosophy of the masses, has paralyzed progress, and injustice is often stoically accepted. Cruelty is common, lying is a fine art, and robbery a science. Islam and the Wahhabis have made the noble, free-hearted, and hospitable Arabs hostile to Christians, and wary of all strangers. Doughty and Palgrave, who both crossed the heart of Arabia, have given it as their verdict that there is no hope for this land in Islam. It has been tried zealously for thirteen hundred years and piteously failed. (Zwemer, 1906: 109–10)

During the Lucknow conference, five years later, the epithets became more abusive and encompassing. The 'degradation', 'neglect', 'disintegration', 'stagnation' of Islam and its 'supreme need for Christ' were attributed to virtually every country touched by Islam (from Morocco to China, India, Malaysia and Africa) or those exposed to corrupt forms of Christianity:

> Morocco (one of the dark places in the world to-day) is typical of the *degradation* of Islam; Persia of its *disintegration;* Arabia of its *stagnation;* Egypt of its attempted *reformation;* China shows the *neglect* of Islam; Java, the *conversion* of Islam; India, the *opportunity* to reach Islam; Equatorial Africa, its *peril*. Each of these typical conditions is in itself an appeal. The supreme need of the Moslem world is Jesus Christ. He alone can give light to Morocco, unity to Persia, life to Arabia, rebirth to Egypt, reach the neglected in China, with Malaysia, meet the opportunity in India, and stop the aggressive peril in Africa. (Wherry, Zwemer and Mylera, 1911: 42)

As late as 1925 James Barton, the prominent Senior Foreign Secretary of the ABCFM, was still heralding the impending disintegration of Islam and calling for a more adequate substitute. Islam, he asserted, is 'inflexible, unprogressive, stationary, incapable of adapting itself to new conditions . . . It repudiates all change, all development. Whatever savours of vitality is by that alone convicted of heresy and defection.' (Barton, 1925: 3)

The Ratification of Medieval Distortions

The perception of Islam with which the missionaries set out were those of the ordinary Europeans of the time, namely one in which its medieval distortions still played a large part. Given the state of knowledge and what was available at the time, some are inclined to argue that such perceptions were legitimate. Yet there were other more charitable views of Islam. Somehow, many New England evangelists (both early and late), despite their extended contacts with Muslim communities, refused to part with or modify their initial perceptions. They clearly overlooked the more ennobling or moderate views, those of Carlyle, Gibbon and their Transcendentalist followers (and the equally popular figures of Emerson and Thoreau), subscribing instead to the benighted images tenaciously upheld by Muir, Cromer, Palgrave, Houghton and Lane-Pool among others.

While America's evangelical encounters with the so-called barbarians of the Barbary States helped to reinforce all the despicable stereotypes of Muslim and Oriental cruelty and despotism, travel literature, which was becoming more popular during the first quarter of the nineteenth century, was inclined to dwell on the exotic, mystical elements of the Orient, Levant and the Holy Land. The former, a relic of medieval Christendom, reconfirmed the urge to tame, contain or save the heathens from their own bigotry and degeneracy. The latter, part of the Enlightenment or Romantic tradition, evoked an exaggerated sense of wonder, exuberance and enchantment in the contemplation of exotic, far-away places. Both were misrepresentations of the world out there. Both continued to be invoked by Europeans and Americans in their encounters with the Orient or the tales and impressions that they relayed back.

Such mindsets, as Edward Said reminds us, are common among travel writers. 'Almost without exception these narratives, and literally hundreds like them based on the exhilaration and interest of adventure in the colonial world, far from casting doubt on the imperial undertaking, serve to confirm and celebrate its success. Explorers find what they are looking for . . .' (Said, 1993: 187)

In fact, to many of the early generations of missionaries, both these myths – the myth of the orient as a place of foreboding and degeneracy but also of wonder, healing and spiritual rebirth – fired their enthusiasm and longing to go. Diaries and memoirs of the early emissaries, fresh out of college or seminaries, exuded a curious blend of a sense of adventure but also of peril in undertaking this pilgrimage into wastelands and dark regions of the heathen world. The more challenging the prospects, the more redeeming was the venture. New England missionaries clung relentlessly to such images, reinforcing the benighted perceptions of their medieval predecessors.

The romantic image of the Orient inevitably started to languish as the economic and political penetration of the Ottoman Empire by the European great powers sustained itself with greater vehemence. Napoleon's Egyptian campaign of 1798 marked a decisive watershed in Muslim–Christian encounters in several crucial respects.

First, it generated, through scientific expeditions, consular reports, commercial treaties and direct contacts, a steady increase in 'less romance and thus more accurate' knowledge of Islam and the Orient (see Von Grunebaum, 1966: 169).

Second, it made Muslims conscious – at least at the material, technological and military level – of the unquestionable superiority of the West and ushered in epochs of Islamic reform and modernism. The two conventional Western stereotypes or attitudes towards Islam, namely, the medievalist and romantic images, were now, as J. W. Fück (1962: 304) argues, joined by a third, based on the conviction that the prevailing superiority of Europe over the Orient was 'axiomatic and absolute'. Expressed differently, this also implied that the Muslim world was no longer to be feared. Nor could Islam be a source of philosophic or scientific inspiration. It only 'provided an example and a warning of greatness fallen from high estate'. (Von Grunebaum, 1966: 169)

Finally, and perhaps most significant to New England evangelists of the period, the new century also ushered in or reawakened the perils of ascendant French and Catholic influence in the Levant. Hence, since most Protestant emissaries refused to part with their degenerate view of Islam, their pilgrimage to the Levant was now driven by a wish to rescue the Holy Land from the compounded 'evils' of both 'impostors', the pope and Muhammad. The pope was represented by the growing activity of what evangelists perceived as nominal Christians of the Eastern rites, with their corrupt church hierarchy and insolent and haughty clerics. Muhammad's evil empire, on the other hand, was manifested in the barbaric splendour, Oriental despotism and infidelity of Ottoman Turks. It is no wonder American Protestants felt providentially both destined and empowered to administer, as it were, 'the final rites to the tottering Papal and Ottoman Empires'. Such lofty sentiments were very visible in the zealotry of the young recruits for foreign missions and the 'instructions they received from their mentors on ordination and embarkation ceremonies.

The Impulse to Colonize

As a form of cultural expansion, the missionary enterprise is clearly not as benign as it seems. Initially, American Protestantism, as several observers have noted, emerged in a notion that had neither colonial nor imperial ambitions. (Phillips, 1969: 242–3; Hutchinson, 1987: 60–1) But it did not remain thus. It quickly acquired many of the premises and practices of any form of imperialistic colonialism, namely, a sense of overpowering mission and duty to spread a nation's vision of society and culture to an alien and often subjected people. A score of writers – Brookfield (1972), Davies (1973), Schlesinger (1974), Beidelman (1982), Hutchinson (1987) and, most recently, Wood (1990) – have all documented such symptoms in a variety of historical settings.

Despite their differing perspectives, they are in agreement that, as embodiments of Western good intentions in non-Western settings, all missionary endeavours exhibit 'an expansionist and proselytizing ethos' (Brookfield, 1972: 3), sustained by a sense of both 'duty and domination' and an ideology of 'paternal guardianship' (Maunier, 1949: I, 168); or they may be seen as an interaction between disproportionate social groups possessing markedly different degrees of power to dominate. (Davies, 1973) All these, according to Beidelman, involve 'an attempt to transform a subject people who are judged inferior yet capable of conversion to a higher level, albeit one judged unequal to that of their masters and teachers. While such notions are intensified in a religious mission, they appear in all such colonialistic endeavors.' (Beidelman, 1982: 4) To Hutchinson the missionary enterprise was the 'moral equivalent for imperialism', particularly among those missionaries who perceived themselves as 'chaplains and tamers of Western expansion' and professed a longing to 'displace the evil and dubious forms of expansionism . . . in favour of the fine spiritual imperialism'. (Hutchinson, 1987: 92) In short, just as Henry James sought to replace war with other avenues for loyalty, competition and animal spirits, there were among the early missionaries those who felt 'called and fitted to spiritualize a powerful force in secular development . . . and felt entirely comfortable in the role of spiritual directorship that history seemed to be thrusting upon them'. (Hutchinson, 1987: 93)

Missionary evangelism thus became the quintessential expression of 'cultural arrogance', particularly when compared with other forms of colonialist penetration. (Brown, 1944: 217) In their foreign ventures, administrators, military expeditions, planters, businessmen and, to some extent, educators generally seek limited objectives, such as law and order, cheap labour, profits, taxation or comparative advantage over other competing groups. Often these forms of cultural expansion carry with them, intentionally or otherwise, elements of psychological domination. At no point, however, do they approximate the total, radical and morally intense commitment of missionaries, who, in the words of Beidelman, 'invariably aimed at overall changes in beliefs and actions of native peoples, at colonizing of heart and mind as well as body'. Beidelman goes still further, to assert that the comparative study of overseas missions reveals that missionaries 'responded in ways which were callously ethnocentric and mindlessly romantic, at times poignantly altruistic and confusedly well-meaning'. (Beidelman, 1982: 6)

Preliminary evidence appears to indicate that the perceptions and experiences of New England missionaries in the Levant did not depart much from these prototypes. It is instructive to assess what happened to these attributes as missionaries intensified and extended their contacts with the subjects and cultures they had sworn to regenerate and redeem. Did they, in Beidelman's words, become more obdurate in their ethnocentric biases, more guileless in their romanticism and more fervent in their good intentions and Christian benevolence?

We should also consider the view of Arthur Schlesinger in his seminal analysis of the relationship of Christian evangelism to other modes of Western penetration and dominion. He too sees the missionary as 'an agent of the Western assault on non-Western societies'. In retrospect, he regards the whole Christian missionary enterprise as

> not only incredibly audacious and ambitious but also incredibly arrogant. This arrogance, however, was the simple-hearted expression of a strength of faith – a faith that galvanized the will of conquest and no doubt contributed to more secular forms of imperialism. The Faustian optimism about Western man's ability to change the world explains in part why the Christian adventures were not only intrepid but victorious. (Schlesinger, 1974: 360)

Given the overpowering combination of Protestant zealotry and national consciousness that spurred the early volunteers, the evangelical crusade had little difficulty in enlisting steadfast and aggressive men and women. The intensity of their own fidelity made them at times insensitive, if not hostile, to the psychic, cultural and spiritual needs of others. Indeed, by definition, 'missionaries were so persuaded of their possession of absolute truth that they would risk nearly anything to assure its propagation . . . They placed no limit on their own spiritual aggression, that is, their right to challenge ancient custom and authority, to denounce traditional rituals, creeds of gods, to deprive the pagans of their spiritual inheritance and identity.' (Schlesinger, 1974: 360–1)

In other words, the 'pagans' (and by evangelist standards this was taken to mean all non-Christian faiths) were not entitled to live by their own standards or to have others judge them by those standards. Early and successive generations of overseas missionaries continued to perceive the entire non-Christian world as lost in darkness. Hence all manifestations of local culture were treated with contempt; its attributes had to be crushed or supplanted if the natives were to be amenable to the virtues of Christian civilization. For example, in his efforts to establish 'praying villages', John Eliot, probably the most aggressive Puritan missionary, was not concerned simply with converting heathens to Christianity but also with bringing about a 'massive cultural change by the introduction of European social and cultural values and institutions into Indian life'. Urging the Indians to 'detach themselves from their "savage" culture, Eliot insisted that they adopt "the ways of civilizations" before being introduced to Christianity' (see Wood, 1990: 33).

Ironically, it was the missionaries who, in order to preserve the heathen from the anguish of eternal damnation, were most prepared to destroy a person's cultural identity. Herman Melville, eager as he always was to rescue hopeless natives in the South Seas and elsewhere in quaint, isolated preserves, liked to hit out at the holy excesses and prudery of the missionaries. He was particularly outraged by the arrogance they displayed in their dogged resolve to impose New England's Blue Laws on the seemingly lackadaisical and free-spirited natives. 'These gentry are undefatigable,' he howled

> at the dead of the night prowling round the houses, and in the daytime hunting amorous couples in the groves. Dancing, kite flying, flute playing, and the singing of traditional ballads fell under the missionary ban. (Anderson, 1966: 253–6)

Melville expressed his concern about the 'denationalizing' of the natives, an astonishing coinage that subsequently became current in appraising the overall strategy and tactics of overseas missions.

Even when missionaries, at least the more moderate and progressive among them, became apprehensive about the cognitive dissonance they were generating in native cultures and cautioned against such intrusive strategies, most of the transformations they brought about were unintended and unanticipated consequences of their missionary activity and could not have been contained once unleashed. This is, in fact, the basic premise of this essay. New England evangelists were there to proselytize, to preach the Gospel and to open souls to the grace of God. They did very little of that. Yet they ended up, often through unforeseen and serendipitous circumstances beyond their control, inaugurating liberal and secular transformations of great magnitude. Some of these liberal by-products are explored in Chapter 7.

In assessing the missionary experience in Turkey, A. C. Coolidge observes: 'Even if they refrain from teaching disloyalty, the whole spirit of their instruction . . . the mere presence of these protected strangers, the representatives of a higher and freer civilization, must stimulate aspirations which the Turks regard with aversion.' (Coolidge, 1908: 227)

Such realities have prompted Schlesinger, among others, to question the adequacy of conventional classical theories of economic and political imperialism. Instead he calls upon those colleagues seeking to explain the impact of Christian evangelism to move on to the ideas of 'cultural imperialism'. Cultural imperialism to Schlesinger means 'purposeful aggression by one culture against the ideas and values of another. The mere communication of ideas and values across national borders is not in itself imperialistic. Such communication becomes aggression only when accompanied by political, economic or military pressures.' (Schlesinger, 1974: 363–4) Much like Beidelman, Brown, Hutchinson and Wood, Schlesinger also maintains that such forms of cultural penetration reach deeper into the 'soul of native societies' than the essentially 'utilitarian' economic and political forms of imperialism. The latter, in Schlesinger's view, assumes little more than that one state or economy is stronger than another. Cultural imperialism, on the other hand, maintained that one set of values was better than another, and this was far more demoralizing. In other words, traders wanted only to make money or politicians to make treaties, whereas missionaries wanted to change souls and societies. (Schlesinger, 1974: 365–73)

As a form of cultural aggression, therefore, missionary incursions not only threaten the self-image of the violated native groups but also reinforce and sustain the arrogance and self-righteousness of the intruders. By the same token, evangelism, as a form of silent penetration or cultural transfer, is not as benign as it may seem. When energized by the lofty sentiments of manifest destiny, spiritual supremacy and millennial urgency, it is often infused with all the impulses and rhetoric of a crusade. As we have seen, many of the Founding Fathers and early stalwarts of New England evangelism did not shy away from such grand visions.

In the late eighteenth century, the erstwhile thirteen colonies were far from the centre of world affairs. Their knowledge of the globe and their interests outside of their own bounds were painfully narrow. These limits, however, were short-lived. Early in the life of the new republic, the impulse to colonize, sparked by the desire to expand and the zeal for discovery, took on and became almost a national obsession. This impulse, or genius, for colonizing and expansion became, of course, more ascendant during the 1880s, particularly in association with the ideas of the 'social Gospel' as propagated by evangelists like Josiah Strong. Strong, it must be recalled, believed that the characteristics of his privileged compatriots (energy, resourcefulness, inventiveness, perseverance and all the other enabling traits of 'Yankee' ingenuity) were the inherited traits of the 'Anglo-Saxon' race (for further details, see Hopkins, 1940: 40).

It was then that missionaries, to use Roy Nichols's expression, became the 'advance agents' of America's destiny to play the role of judge, jury and executioner for a sinful world (Nichols, 1956). It was also then that America's penchant for interfering in the affairs of other people became embedded in its self-image and national ethos. The degenerate 'other' had to be reinvented to sustain the self-righteousness of New England evangelists. 'From the muscular Christianity of the last generation to the imperial Christianity of the present day,' wrote J. A. Hobson, 'is but a single step.' (Hobson, 1965: 216)

Another ironical feature in this evangelistic thrust to colonize asserts itself. The so-called sacred errand, inspired and sustained by a sense of Christian benevolence, philanthropy, tenderness and human compassion for perishing souls was, paradoxically enough, not free from the militant and martial rhetoric and idioms found in more belligerent crusades. As manifestations of the 'culture of arrogance', with its overtones of racist superiority and prejudice, the impulse to 'Anglo-Saxonize' and 'Americanize' the 'other' often adopted the ruthless language of 'penetrating', 'besieging', 'subduing' and 'demolishing' all traces of native cultures. 'Regions of darkness' became 'wildernesses' sanctioned to be possessed. The more sinful the 'empires of sin' to be besieged, the more militant the call to 'invade and appropriate'.

The seminal work of Edward Said, first in *Orientalism* (1978) and more recently in *Culture and Imperialism* (1993), elucidates how this imperialistic structure of attitude and reference, whether in fiction, geography or art, acquires a continuous presence through 'actual expansion, administration, investment and commitment'. (Said, 1993: xxiii) The impulse of New England missionaries to 'evangelize' or 'Americanize' the other (particularly in overseas territories) becomes another, perhaps more unadulterated and more militant, version of the same experience. They are there to 'jostle, displace, or incorporate the other'. (Said, 1993:xv)

The day Levi Parsons disembarked at Smyrna, in February 1820, he bemoaned all those 'souls that are shut out from light and blessings of the Gospel and then went on to disclose' a great desire in my breast to demolish this mighty empire of sin . . . Woe is me if I ever leave this sacred calling; if I do not consecrate every faculty to my high profession. Ever may it be the language of my heart, '*conquest or death*'. (Parsons, 1819: 175)

In one sermon after another, especially during ordination or embarkation ceremonies, this notion of the great commission as a 'continued conquest' launched by Christian envoys as 'soldiers of the Cross', was propounded almost ad nauseam. Outright conquest became the sine qua non in the prosecution of overseas missions. Envoys were cautioned not to lose their aggression, otherwise they would cease to be true missionaries. In the ordination of the Webbs as ABCFM missionaries to India in 1845, the reverend officiating at the ceremony emphasized the same theme:

> His embassy is to the rebellious, to beseech them, in Christ's stead, to be reconciled to God. His vocation, as a soldier of the Cross, is to make conquests, and to go on, in the name of his divine Master, 'conquering and to conquer'; committing the security and permanency of his conquests to another class of men created expressly for the purpose. The idea of *continued conquest* is fundamental in missions to the heathen, and is vital to their spiritual life and efficiency. It will doubtless be found on inquiry, that missions among the heathen have always ceased to be healthful and efficient, have ceased to evince the true missionary spirit in its strength, whenever they have ceased to be actively aggressive upon the kingdom of darkness. (Beaver, 1967: 76)

Even Eli Smith, often singled out for his balanced and conciliatory views, fell prey to this contemptuous language. 'The missionary goes to raise the standard of revolt, to change, to undermine . . . to besiege the citadels of the beast and false prophet, and whose conquest is to complete the triumph of the Lamb'. In a sermon on 'the missionary character' delivered before the Society of Inquiry, Smith implored his colleagues to

> Look upon the world, and see the dark clouds of ignorance and sin that rest upon almost every land. Go forth and penetrate the gloom. Sit down in their hovels, the abodes of every species of wretchedness, physical and moral. Walk through their temples polluted with lust and blood. And let the conviction fasten

upon you, with a power not be shaken off, and a weight scarcely to be borne, that they are lost, lost forever, unless rescued by missionary effort. (Smith, 1840: 25–6)

In an earlier sermon Smith had even asserted that the task of the missionary should not stop short of 'subjecting the whole world to his will'. (Smith, 1832: 15) By the time James Munroe was calling for the 'invasion' of every corner of the world and 'appropriating all that can make us happier', this imperialist thrust clearly exceeded the bounds of cultural penetration.

Within the past fifty years we have broken through the imaginary hedge which shut us out from so much of the brightness and freedom of existence. Within the next twenty-five years we shall have become the most cosmopolitan country in the world. Adaptable, vigorous, acute, we have made that difficult first trespass upon the territory of civilizations older, richer, in many ways better than ours, and it will require but another generation for us to invade every corner of them appropriating all that can make us happier and that can add to our wealth in those things of life which endure. (Munroe, 1915: 12)

About the same time, James Barton, as Foreign Secretary of the ABCFM, was recommending a complete survey of the Muslim world to underscore its complete failure as an agency of spiritual uplift. Such a survey, he argued, 'could be of no permanent value unless it led to a mobilization of those forces for the speedy and adequate occupation of the strategic centers of Islam'. (Barton, 1918: 310)

It must be borne in mind that even when the missionaries were wary about the 'denationalizing' impact of their intervention, they were not entirely innocent of the charges that the cultural penetration they were professing amounted to colonialism. Indeed, some were quite circumspect and cautioned their colleagues against making such massive intrusions into native cultures. By their sheer presence in the region, however, at a time of intense diplomatic rivalry and political upheaval, they were invariably drawn (deliberately or otherwise) into the mired local and regional conflicts. More perhaps than other 'Orientalists', they were in a position to assist colonialist and imperialist powers to legitimize their hegemony over indigenous groups.

Missionaries developed expedient symbiotic relationships with various branches of the US government, which were mutually beneficial. Missionary literature (field reports, correspondence, results of surveys, expeditions) furnished much-needed logistical data and firsthand knowledge. For over a century, information relayed back from the missionary outfields strewn throughout the Orient and eastern Mediterranean provided the foundation for much of America's understanding of the region. Indeed, the parameters of its foreign policy and outlines for defining its spheres of influence in the region were all largely a by-product of such knowledge.

Missionaries also served as hosts to a growing stream of Western travellers and visitors at a time when public accommodation and tourist facilities were still extremely scarce and insecure. In return, missionaries expected and, often, directly sought the assistance of the US government in a turbulent political milieu. The appearance of naval warships at Ottoman ports in the Mediterranean was always a welcome sight to the missionaries, particularly when they were still persecuted or treated with suspicion by Ottoman officials and their surrogate potentates in Syria and Mount Lebanon.

During the decade of Egyptian occupation of Mount Lebanon (1831–41), missionaries were subjected to more intense repressions and were particularly delighted when American warships came to their rescue. Even a normally mild and amiable creature like Eli Smith, not known for his hawkish sentiments, went out of his way in 1835 vigorously to denounce any infringements on their rights to operate freely. He requested strong and severe measures. 'They ought to know,' he boasted, 'that we are a powerful nation. And there is no other way to teach them but to make them *feel* it.' (Quoted by Field, 1969: 210)

During successive episodes of protracted strife, when lives of missionary families were endangered, American warships often assisted in evacuating the beleaguered emissaries. In 1845, the resumption of bloody hostilities between Maronites and Druzes produced new calls for help. Ironically, the missionaries were requesting support for Maronite Christians despite the bitter anti-Catholic enmity they harboured against them. A letter of thanks, signed by ten members of the Syrian mission, stated that 'the presence of one of our noble ships of war has always had a happy influence, both upon the Turkish authorities, and upon the people generally', and earnestly solicited the repetition of such displays of naval prowess in the future (see Fields, 1969: 210–11).

The fact that the US heeded calls of intervention on behalf of missionaries in the Levant is particularly interesting in view of the prevailing overall non-interventionist policy the US had pursued in its diplomatic relations with the Ottomans. Indeed, American official policy towards nationalist minorities of the Ottoman Empire reveals no significant departures from the precepts set out by John Quincy Adams early in the nineteenth century. Even at times when America's commercial, diplomatic, naval and missionary interests in the Mediterranean were directly threatened, particularly during the Greek war of Independence (1821–29), the Cretan insurrection of 1866, the Graeco-Turkish War of 1897, Armenia's struggle for national sovereignty (all of which incidentally were confrontations between Christian minorities seeking emancipation from Muslim rule and which at the time inspired considerable popular support among American citizens), the US government did not veer away from its official non-interventionist stance. Throughout the nineteenth century and the first quarter of the twentieth, the government occasionally welcomed American popular enthusiasm in support of repressed minorities. It encouraged discreet efforts on their behalf. Writing in 1927, Edward Earle asserted that 'not once has the government of this republic signed a treaty guaranteeing the rights of minorities in Turkish dominions; not once has taken an active part, diplomatic or military, in the emancipation of Christian peoples of the Near East from Moslem rule.' (Earle, 1927: 367)

Missionaries in the field at the time welcomed and lobbied for direct Western intervention on behalf of endangered Christian minorities. Since US involvement was not forthcoming, some diehards like H. H. Jessup became enthusiastic instead about the prospects of Great Britain's intervention. This was, in fact, what had transpired during the 1860 civil strife in Mount Lebanon, the Bulgarian War of 1877 and the Arab Revolt of 1882 in Egypt. Jessup credits such interposition for checking the 'wild spirit of Mohammedan bigotry' and 'Moslem frenzy'. Like other stalwarts of Protestant evangelism, he also saw, in those cataclysmic episodes, the workings of the Providential Plan towards the Kingdom of God.

> . . . The wild spirit of Mohammedan bigotry broke out once more, and the streets of Alexandria ran with Christian blood . . . The interposition of England, the defeat of Arabi, the check upon rising Moslem frenzy, and the shattering of the Pan Islamic league which had become a menace to progress and civilization in the East, all revealed again the working of that hand which makes no mistakes, and that wise and glorious Providence of God, which overrules all things for his own glory. (Jessup, 1884: 25)

Ironically, social upheavals, wars and epidemics quickened the scriptural prophecies regarding the advent of the Second Kingdom. Missionaries, as will be seen in Chapter 7, became quite adept at exploiting such misfortunes, even the anguish of personal grief, bereavement and other private afflictions, to heighten the psychological receptivity of native groups to their spiritual messages. It was also then that the spiritual metaphor of the 'city on a hill' gained more credence in the so-called 'Land of Promise' when it was transferred to a geographical location for fulfilment in the 'Promised Land'.

In 1906, just a few years before the beginning of the Woodrow Wilson era that consolidated America's neutrality in the region, Mercure Conway (an eminent critic known for his constructive objections to the missionary establishment) drew the following portrait of the often arrogant and divisive strategies to which the missionaries resorted in deploying their messages. Incidentally, Wilson at the time was considering dividing the Ottoman Empire into autonomous regions along ethnic lines (see Garbill, 1971: 93).

> It is no joke when the youngest of nations, whose constitution ignores religion, strains itself morally with precisely that criminal complexion which was once attributed to Mohammedanism. Fifty years ago Protestant preachers were never weary of accusing Mohammed of propagating his religion by the sword; but in the opening twentieth century, our government sends warships to the chief Moslem nation and says in effect, 'Pay for the American missionary property damaged by a mob or we will murder your people and burn your capital'. And I heard a missionary, lecturing in our Century Club, New York, boast that by this menace the American mission was the only one that got its money! (Conway, 1906: 138–9)

Finally, and more unsettling, were the adverse consequences such a policy had, of generating greater tension between and among the various religious communities. With all their pious prattle about love, harmony and tolerance, New England evangelists carried with them their indiscriminate and inveterate enmity towards non-Christian faiths and more bitter and inflexible anti-Catholic sentiments. They also resorted to some of the common but pernicious ploys of playing one community against another. In doing so, they contributed, wilfully or otherwise, to sectarian discord.

Incidentally, in his book *The Arabists*, Robert Kaplan (1993) explores the changing perspective and status of representatives of this inbred and closely-knit group and the impact they have had in shaping America's perceptions and policies in the region. Based on a selection of third-generation scions of New England missionaries to the Levant (particularly those turned diplomats and State Department specialists), Kaplan attributes many of the foibles of US foreign policy in the region to the 'political naïveté', 'elitism', 'romantic adventure' and 'deferential sentiments' such misty-eyed idealists harboured towards the Arabs. He conjures up a composite profile (extracted from the diplomatic careers of such people as Philip and William Stoltzfus, Talcott Seelye, Ray Close, Herman Elits, Joseph Sisco, Alfred Atherton, Roy Henderson, Richard Parker, April Glaspie and descendants of the Blisses and Dodges among others) to account for the hegemony that such driven and self-righteous WASPs – with little other than their anti-Zionism and nostalgia for the charmed life and romance of Arab culture – came to enjoy in shaping American perceptions and policies in the region.

Kaplan is candid enough to preface his book with the caveat that it is 'neither pure history nor pure journalism'. This, however, should not absolve him from the historical distortions and journalistic mystifications that underlie much of his polemical, often shoddy treatment. Because of his obsession with showing how this 'subculture' of State Department Arabists remained inherently opposed to the State of Israel, he paints an unseemly portrait of a monolithic group driven more by their disenchantment with the spiritless and drab life of middle-class American suburbia or the pasha-like privileges that they enjoyed on their stints abroad than by the rigours of dispassionate diplomacy. Indeed, he alleges that Arabists are known for fudging political reports and reinforcing the arcane and conventional wisdom of their superiors rather than risking the consequences of speaking out in informed dissent. (Kaplan, 1993: 311)

He goes further to attribute many of the costly blunders of US foreign policy in the Middle East to the 'delusions' of Arabists; delusions born, he claims, of their naïve and effete longings to sustain their self-righteous elitism and deferential attitudes towards the Arabs. Only a new breed of non-Arabists, free of such romanticized visions, Kaplan argues, could salvage US foreign policy and steer it in more imaginative and even-handed directions.

Kaplan is, of course, correct in tracing, as many others have done, the genesis and inspiration of Arabists back to the evangelistic ethos engendered by the Great Awakenings, the Haystack episode and other religious revivals sweeping New England seminaries and colleges at the time. But the early descendants of Hopkins and Edwards were anything but deferential towards the 'natives' they had vowed to besiege and conquer. One has only to skim through the writings of Jessup, Post and others to realize how inflexible and prejudiced they were. They were also deliberately very selective in bestowing their charitable views and beneficent dispensations. They naturally targeted religious sects and communities more amenable to their message or more receptive to conversion (e.g. Greek Orthodox, Armenians). If not treated deferentially, such groups, however, were not denigrated. Others, particularly those associated with Protestants with an inbred antipathy towards Catholics and Muslims, were indiscriminately and persistently vilified. Their attitudes towards other Ottoman subjects often oscillated with the shifting tide of political and ideological transformations and superpower rivalries.

CHAPTER 5

Leavening the Levant[1]

New England Puritanism as a Cultural Transplant

> Let the Gospel Prevail among them, [Mahommedans],
> and some of the strongest fortresses of error and sin
> will be taken.
>
> *Memoir* of the Rev. Pliny Fisk (1828)

Popular perception, in part because of the direct involvement of the US in the First World War, associates America's interest in the international affairs of the Middle East with the Woodrow Wilson era. There is little awareness that envoys of a different sort had, in fact, antedated and prepared the way for such diplomatic interventions and cultural incursions.

Protestants had first made their appearance in the Near East as early as the sixteenth century. Anglicans, Calvinists and Lutherans had initiated contacts, largely as attempts to establish and invigorate their relations with the Easter (Greek) Orthodox Church. These and other such efforts continued intermittently throughout the next two centuries. They were, however, predominantly Europeans and did not have an explicitly evangelizing character. Nor did their influence amount to much.

Interestingly, it was not the missionaries but American traders and ship captains who first established contacts with the Levant. Early in the 1780s American agents had commenced trading at Smyrna (Izmir). Judging by the evidence, initial

---

1. The title of this paper is borrowed from J. K. Greene (1916), subsequently adopted by James A. Field (1991) as a title of one of his chapters on the missionary establishment in the Levant, 1835–62. The notion of the Gospel as a 'leaven', a favourite missionary parable (Mathew 13:33, Galatians 5:9), evolved as a leitmotif for self-governing and self-propagating mission. In other words, as benevolent emissaries of that 'heavenly treasure', missionaries were simply to instil the pure Gospel as 'leaven' and go home.

contacts were at first few and far between. It was not until 1800 that the first American vessel reached Constantinople. Even by then very few American merchants had established permanent headquarters in Turkey or other ports of call in the eastern Mediterranean. Most Yankee ship captains sold their cargoes through English trading houses. (Daniel, 1964: 73)

This historical variance in the cultural penetration in the Near East, patchy as it was, is often identified by historians as an attribute of the American Protestant missionary movement in the region. While it is difficult to overlook the colonizing impulse the movement came to adopt, it did not (at least initially) manifest any imperial or colonial ambitions. According to A. L. Tibawi, this distinguishes the pioneers of American missionaries from other comparable groups. 'Unlike missionaries from Imperial nations such as Spain and England, American Missionaries followed in the paths of American commercial traffic, not in the wake of conquering armies.' (Tibawi, 1963: 139)

The spiritual, evangelistic and largely non-imperialistic character was also apparent, at least initially, among the young zealots, graduates of Andover and other New England seminaries and colleges, who had inspired much of this thrust for overseas missions. Clearly, they displayed a love for their New England home and often spoke about it in their published letters and memoirs in highly evocative and romanticized tones. Yet it was not until the mid-nineteenth century, as we have seen, that notions of 'manifest destiny' and the moral and cultural superiority of American Protestantism became embedded in the colonial ethos of Christian 'spiritual imperialism', which evangelicals felt called upon to spread across the globe.

Another anomaly that highlights a feature of New England Puritanism as a cultural transplant also deserves validation. In their thrust for world evangelism, New Englanders evinced an understandable preference for the Holy Land. This fascination with the birthplace of Christ, because of its infinite spiritual associations as both a blessed and a defiled place, had inspired the young seminarians at Andover and the general public in New England colonies. Indeed, there is evidence to indicate that the American Board of Commissioners for Foreign Missions (ABCFM) may have hastened its plans for a mission to Palestine largely to take advantage of such popular enthusiasm for mobilizing interest and soliciting financial support for their missionary endeavours. (Lindsay, 1965: 67) Yet in a short while this enthusiasm for the Holy Land was abandoned. The early envoys were compelled to shift their interest to other more receptive and accessible fields in the Levant.

Here again the often grandiose schemes for evangelizing the Muslims, Jews and Oriental churches in the eastern Mediterranean ended up by being exclusively confined to 'nominal Christians'. Perhaps this is also why the Syrian Mission came to occupy a special place in the aspirations of New England missionaries.

Of all these American missionary efforts, it was their inroads into 'Syria', intentional or otherwise, that proved to be the most far-reaching in terms of the socio-cultural transformations they generated in the lives of the people they touched. Indeed, largely because of the formidable obstacles and the promise of opportunities, the mission to Syria came to acquire a mystique of its own. No wonder that 'Syria' was termed in the annals of world evangelism as the 'romance land of missions'. (Bartlett, 1872: 99) It was also there that the ABCFM was compelled to redefine its objectives and experiment with various 'instrumentalities' to meet the ever-changing political and socio-cultural exigencies they faced in the Levant.

Within this context the chapter explores four related dimensions:

1. How and why did the Mission to Palestine and the broader interest in the Levant and eastern Mediterranean get redirected to Syria? How did the glowing sentiments for global Christian benevolence take root there? What accounts for the ardent enthusiasm it inspired and the distinctive role it came to play in the region?

2. What were the original intentions of the Palestine Mission, particularly those articulated in the 'instructions' Pliny Fisk and Levi Parsons, the first envoys to the Levant, received from the Prudential Committee of the ABCFM? What mandate, visions, objectives and 'instrumentalities' did the pioneering envoys carry over with them?

3. Fisk and Parsons, when they embarked on their first mission to the Levant in 1820, epitomized many of the attributes of evangelism as a sacred errand. This is quite visible both in their private lives and in their embodiment of the stern imperatives of piety, duty and unhesitating acceptance of all the hazards and privations attendant on their mission. Accordingly, it is appropriate to focus on a few critical episodes in their lives, as prototypes of Christian 'disinterested benevolence', to find out which particular features of the Puritan ethic they carried over with them. How did they justify their burning zeal for conversions in that part of the world? How did they articulate such expectations?

4. Finally, at a more abstract and conceptual level, I consider a few salient features of Puritanism, which disclose critical issues in its role as a cultural transplant, particularly as an embodiment of Western good intentions in a non-Western setting. How disinterested were the missionaries in their benevolence? Were they receptive and open to interaction with systems of beliefs and ways of life different from theirs? These and related views can tell us much about their construction of otherness.

'Syria' as the Romance Land of Missions

In missionary parlance the 'Levant' was broadly defined to include the eastern shores of the Mediterranean, Asia Minor, Syria, Palestine and Egypt. The usage was often stretched further to encompass Greece, the Balkan peninsula, Mesopotamia and, more rarely, Persia and Arabia. (Bliss,1897: 127) However, because of its association with the Holy Land, it has always evoked, even to those who never made the journey, poignant myths and sentiments and became coveted as a favoured setting for missionary posts and stations. To many of the pioneering generations of New England emissaries, fresh from colleges and seminaries and driven by longing for personal redemption and zeal to rescue the heathen world, such places were particularly appealing. This evangelistic imagination was sustained by two overpowering impulses or images current at the time when these young zealots were embarking on their exploratory missions to so-called regions of darkness.

First, the Levant, as the domain of 'Muslim degradation and Ottoman cruelty', reconfirmed this urge to save the heathen from his own bigotry. Second, because of surviving relics of the Enlightenment and Romanticism, the Levant also evoked a sense of wonder, excitement and exoticism. This Janus-like image was reinforced by a growing body of travel literature that popularized such enticing perceptions. It was the curious blend of enchantment and foreboding, combined with the sense of stepping into a perilous wasteland, that continued to inspire successive generations of New England puritans.

The Holy Land was, after all, their primordial home; a divine place imbued with all the sacred connotations of spiritual rebirth and healing. It is not surprising that this longing to reconnect assumed the redemptive imagery of a pious exertion, a pilgrimage. One was 'returning' to one's spiritual home and promised land to reclaim it from the 'empires of sin' and 'pagan darkness'. The pious young recruits felt that they were taking the Gospel back to the land whence it came. In the Levant these forces of infidelity were, in the eyes of New England Protestants, incarnate not only in the two greatest Antichrist evils (i.e. Mohammedanism and the papacy) but also in what Pliny Fisk termed 'Turkish avarice and despotism, Jewish unbelief and hardness of heart, and the superstitions and idolatry of nominal Christians'.

The fascination with the Holy Land was deeply embedded in the popular folklore, idioms, biblical parables and motifs of early New England colonists long before the eastern Mediterranean became accessible to travellers. It did not, however, assume explicit expression until the ABCFM undertook its first mission to India in 1811. Indeed, it was problems in India that first encouraged the ABCFM to consider more viable and hospitable alternatives. Samuel Newell, a prominent member of the India Mission and an Andover graduate, first suggested a mission to Basra and other great emporia of Western Asia. Newell urged the translation of the Bible into Arabic and Persian, whose speakers he held to 'rank as high on the scale of intellect as any people in the world'. He also anticipated the success of such evangelism because Islam is no more than 'a heretical form of Christianity'. Curiously, he thought that the Wahhabi movement was friendlier to Christians than Muslims and that it was rapidly causing the downfall of Muslim power. Like many others after him, he also noted the presence of 'nominal Christians' who needed to be brought back into the fold of genuine Christianity. All these, however, seemed subsidiary to, or offshoots of, the all-consuming desire to reclaim Jerusalem as the scene of the first missionary endeavours.

We should be in the neighbourhood of Mesopotamia, Syria, Palestine, and Egypt, those interesting theatres, on which the most wonderful and important events, recorded in sacred history, took place . . . When I think of these things, I long to be on my way towards Jerusalem. (ABCFM, 1817: 112)

In addition to the encouragement of missionaries in India, the early volumes of the *Missionary Herald* were replete with appeals from travellers and merchants returning from exploratory visits to the region. British missionaries had preceded their American counterparts in establishing direct communication with virtually all parts of the Levant. Chaplains in Bengal and Malta, as early as 1811, were sending reports about the favourable opportunities for direct missionary work in the region. (Bliss, 1897: 127–28)

By 1817, and perhaps for the first time, the Prudential Committee acknowledged the recommendations of the missionaries in India, particularly the information they relayed regarding the importance and practicality of such missions. (ABCFM, 1817: 147) Hardly a year later, in the autumn of 1818, the Prudential Committee established the Palestine Mission, designating Fisk and Parsons as its first two envoys. They were commissioned by the Board, for almost a year before their departure, to tour the southern part of the country for the twofold objective of soliciting donations and interesting the public in the purposes of overseas missions. Judging by Fisk's accounts, their arduous labour was in vain and often downright embarrassing. Though he spoke of the 'formidable prejudices against northern agents', he nonetheless noted that their travels 'awakened curious inquiry and enlisted feelings in missionary objects'. (Bond, 1828: 88) He seemed more hopeful in his farewell sermon.

And, if we judge of future patronage by what has been already experienced, we may hope to see, before even a few years shall elapse, many Bibles distributed, many schools established and many missionaries employed, in this interesting field, by means of American effort and American charity. (Fisk, 1819: 37)

Lebanon in particular, was recognized as a field deeply interesting and suggestive in its historical associations. 'Every step we take in this richly historic region,' declared Rev. James Dennis, 'brings us into contact with the relics of the long past . . . Our Lord himself once trod the mission soil of Syria, when He visited the coasts of Tyre and Sidon . . . .. The heights of Hermon probably witnessed His Transfiguration. Paul touched at the Syrian seaports on his missionary journeys. This, then, is sacredly historic soil, and a tenderer interest lingers here than could be given by human history alone.' (Dennis, 1872: 4–5)

In addition to the enduring religious and historical associations the Levant and the Holy Land inspired, there was something about its strategic location and the mixed character of its population (particularly in what was termed Syria at the time) that provided perhaps the greatest inducements to establish missionary stations there. The Mediterranean Sea was not only the cross-roads of trade and culture, it also offered vital access to much of the unevangelized world of Asia and Africa. At the time Syria was infinitesimally small with barely a million inhabitants. It was, however, correctly seen as the key to the entire Arabic-speaking population.

The Arabic Bible can utter its messages to at least a hundred and twenty millions of people, spread through Barbary, Nubia, Arabia, Persia, India, Tartary, to the Philippine Islands on the north-east, and to Central Africa on the south-west. The Scriptures from the Syrian press have been sold on the borders of Liberia, and to the Mohammedans in Bombay. (Bartlett, 1872: 99)

If successful, Bartlett goes on to assert, the Syrian mission would place itself in contact with one-tenth of the human family. (Bartlett, 1872: 99)

Soon the longing to envelop the whole region, largely because of obstacles they encountered elsewhere, came to be focused on the Syrian mission. To emissaries of the ABCFM, the Syria Mission extended from below Tripoli in the north and from the shore of the Mediterranean to Mount Lebanon and the Beqà. Geographically, this is what constitutes political Lebanon today.[1] Formerly, it embraced the whole of Palestine and northern Syria, as far as Aleppo, together with the island of Cyprus. Palestine was given up in 1843 to other missionary societies. Northern Syria was transferred, in 1855, to the missions in Turkey. Cyprus, made first a separate mission in 1839, was joined to the Turkish mission in 1840 and finally abandoned in 1842 (see Laurie, 1866: 3).

The ABCFM was fully aware of the strategic importance of the region in providing access to millions of unevangelized just as Fisk and Parsons were being dispatched to Palestine (*Missionary Herald*, June 1819: 271). Of equal importance was the fact that the Near East was neither part of the British Empire nor under its sphere of influence. Considerations of possible competition with other missionary groups played a vital role in the ultimate decision of the ABCFM to locate fields of operation abroad.

For example, there is evidence of cooperation in apportioning fields and regions between the various missionary groups: New England Puritans in Syria, United Presbyterians in Egypt and Northern Presbyterians working among the Nestorians in Persia or the Armenians in Turkey. It was, however, the intense competition and bitter rivalry between American Protestants and French Jesuits and papal Catholics that was instrumental in determining not only the location of their fields of operation but also the scope, objective and direction of much of the endeavour of New England Protestants. Yes, the Mission to Palestine had been intended, as Parsons indicated in his farewell sermon, to 'rescue and restore the Jews from their dereliction', but no sooner had they arrived there than their focus was intently shifted towards the Oriental churches. Indeed, not only the dereliction of the Jews but the degeneration of Muslims, Druze, Nestorians, Assyrians and Armenians, among other potential targets, was attributed to the 'corrupt mass of nominal Christians'. The latter had to be saved and restored first before others could be reached.

1. According to Turkish official maps, the province of Syria extends from the Taurus Mountains in the north to the river Arish on the borders of Egypt, and from the Mediterranean to the Euphrates. But the territory occupied by the American Mission in Syria extends from Mount Carmel and Acre on the south to the island of Arwad in the north, and from the sea to the Jordan Valley, Mount Hermon, Baalbek and Hama in the east. The area of official Syria is about 155,400 square kilometres. (Spears, 1901: 183)

There was more to Syria, as the 'romance land of missions', than its strategic location and the mystique of numbers of potential converts. The mixed and unusual character of its population seemed singularly appealing to many of the pioneers before they even made contacts with native groups. To Bartlett, for example, the Arabs of Syria are

> a very noble race. We are not to think of them only in the guise of the shrivelled and fiery Bedouin who howls around the traveller for a bakhshish, or hovers about his pathway with matchlock and spear . . . The Arab of Syria, however illiterate and ignorant, carries with him a native dignity of address and deportment unsurpassed by the highest culture of civilized land. (Bartlett, 1872: 109–10)

Bartlett went on to highlight the distinctive promises and the powerful obstacles (both the 'darkness' and the 'light') underlying all the outward diversities and inner complexities that characterize its social fabric.

> The eye of the traveler is caught by a variety of costumes, from that of the city gentleman, with his flowing robes, yellow slippers, red overshoes, and faultless white turban, down to that of the Bedouin of the desert, with his simple calico shirt, and *kufiyeh* bound about his head by a strand of camel's hair. Beneath all outward diversities lies a still more complicated division of religious sects, offering, separately and untidily, powerful obstacles to the spread of the Gospel. Here Mohammedans, some eight hundred and fifty thousand, the mass of the people, including the Sunnites, or Traditionists, and the Shiites, or followers of Ali, together with the Ansairiyeh and the Metawileh. Here are Kurds, Yezidees, and Gypsies. Only about fifteen thousand Jews are found in all Syria, including Palestine, of whom four fifths, chiefly foreigners, reside at Safet, Hebron, Tiberias, and Jerusalem. Here are the Druzes, powerful body, with a creed long undiscoverable. And there are many sects nominally Christian, the Greek church, the most influential body, having two patriarchs and a hundred and fifty thousand members; the Maronites, the most numerous sect, comprising two hundred thousand persons; Jacobites, Armenians, Greek Catholics, and Syrian Catholics. The Moslems were found corrupt in their principles and morals as they were fierce in their religion, and when the missionaries arrived, were sustained by the death-penalty for a change of faith. The nominal Christians of association sects, equally low in morality, and formalists in religion, were despised by the Mohammedans for their picture-worship and Mariolatry, while not behind in the disposition, and formerly in the power, to persecute. The Druzes, ferocious in war, though hospitable in peace, are bound together by secret obligations so strong and so unscrupulous, that, unless quite recently, not more than three or four are known to have been effectually reached by the Gospel. And the Jews, in addition to their proverbial bigotry, are dependent on foreign Israelites for support, and are thus by their daily bread pledged to resist the truth. But in the midst of this thick-ribbed ice the fire was hopefully kindled,

and in spite of every species of extinguisher has been made to burn. (Bartlett, 1872: 100–02)

The Rev. Thomas Laurie, another noted student of early missions, credits Providence for inspiring the pioneers of the mission to locate their fields at the most opportune corner of the world. He, too, extols the virtues of the Arabic-speaking portion for their

> highest degree of development, where the body has drunk in vigour from the cool springs and bracing air of goodly Lebanon, and the mind has learned manliness under the inspiration of the freedom long maintained in those mountain fastnesses. Here, too, in this home of energetic and thinking men, is the commercial centre of Syria, offering every facility for the diffusion of the truth; while constant communication with Europe rouses inquiring minds to search into the causes of the prosperity of nations so much more favoured than themselves, and the healthy atmosphere of Lebanon offers itself to sustain the vigour of missionaries sent there from a northern clime. (Laurie, 1866: 3–4)

In his farewell sermon (31 October 1819) before his departure from Boston to the Palestine mission, Pliny Fisk was also cognizant of the privileged standing of the natives. He, too, invoked the metaphor of darkness and light to underscore their 'intellect and enterprise' when compared to the 'stupidity and ignorance of the Hindo and Hottentots'. (Fisk, 1819: 29)

Objectives, Instructions and Instrumentalities

Although much of the original impetus for world evangelism was first triggered by the enthusiasm of that devoted core of Andover seminarians, it was the ABCFM that provided much of the organizational and instrumental supports necessary to launch and sustain its activities during its formative and eventful first decades. The Board was composed largely of Congregational churches of New England, but also included a number of other Reformed groups on the Eastern seaboard. It was the first American organization to be concerned with missionaries abroad. In its first fifty years, it established eight missions to Palestine, Syria, Greece, Armenians (Turkey-Armenia), Nestorians, Assyrians (eastern Turkey-Iraq), Jews and Muslims. By 1860 it had already ordained 114 missionaries and dispatched a total of 142 (including physicians and female assistants) to the Levant alone. This is considerably more than the total of all other missionary groups in the Levant. It was also larger than other ABCFM field stations elsewhere in the world, such as India, China, Japan, Latin America and Africa. (For further details, see Field, 1974: 30–38.)

So complex and substantive were the managerial problems of recruiting, staffing and financing overseas missions that James Field appropriately labels the ABCFM the first prototype of an American multinational corporation. (Field, 1974:

39) In its heyday, the 1840s, the Board was dealing with problems previously undertaken only by the government.

> Of all American institutions, only the State Department during Jefferson's tenure as secretary and the navy during his presidency had grappled with the difficulties of creating, staffing, and supervising a transoceanic structure. In other respects, too, the situations were similar. Like the State and Navy Departments, the Board found itself obliged to issue periodic reports for the edification of its constituency. Like the government, it had to set up a tax system, reaching out in its own case through Sunday school and church collections to the creation of a network of regional agents. (Field, 1974: 39)

To add to the difficulty, the ABCFM was not only managing a novel transnational enterprise but it was also doing so in times of ambivalence and uncertainty. The countries in which it operated were largely unknown. In formulating its overall objectives, procedural instructions, their targets and the type of activities they ought to pursue, the Board was understandably vague and general. It left much to Providence. This taxed the sensibilities of their pioneering emissaries.

As I shall show, much of what they did, indeed the very location of field stations and specific outcomes of their labours was largely unintended, by-products of both their good intentions and their considerable ignorance of the areas they were seeking to evangelize. Unsurprisingly, much of what they accomplished diverged substantially from their original intentions.

The Board was unequivocal in stating its objective. The second article of its constitution declared that its object is 'to devise, adopt, and prosecute ways and means for propagating the Gospel among those who are destitute of the knowledge of Christianity. (Anderson, 1872: viii) The Board acted on the belief that its labours should not be restricted to so-called 'pagan' or 'heathen' nations. The Board's ultimate and broad objective in the Near East, as elsewhere, was nothing short of the winning of all peoples to the kingdom of God.

The scope and direction of their labour in the Near East, because of the presence of Oriental churches and what they termed 'nominal Christians', were perceived as different even before they embarked on their first mission there. At the outset the Board had also realized that its task would be difficult and that the only hope for reaching Muslims and Jews was to reclaim the 'derelict and degenerate Eastern Christian'. Thus, despite the professed aim of the Palestine Mission, its initial intent, i.e. to encourage reform within the Orthodox churches, became its immediate and ultimate goal (see Vander Werff, 1977: 102–03).

Though New England missionaries had no direct contact with the region, they were not venturing there with good intentions only. They had well-formed opinions, prefigured stereotypes and knowledge filtered through European merchants, travellers and chaplains who had predated them in the region. For example, Henry Lindsay, Chaplain to the British embassy in Constantinople, after a visit to the seven churches in Asia Minor in 1816, talked about the eagerness with which the priests there received the Bible. He implored the Board to send more books. In describing the state of Christianity he wrote that the 'extravagant tales of miracles, and fabulous accounts of angels, saints, and relics had so usurped the place of the Scripture, as to render it very difficult to separate in their minds, divine truth from human invention'. (*Missionary Herald*, June 1816: 284)

Gordon Hall, around the same time, also deplored how 'destitute' the churches were of 'spiritual life and light'.

> Scattered over these regions are not less than a million of Armenian, Syrian, and Greek Christians, in general destitute of the Bible, destitute of spiritual light and life, and on the whole but little better in any respect than their Mohammedan masters. What a field for the benevolent exertions of enlightened Christians! How much good might be effected by endeavouring to revive pure religion and Christian Knowledge in these eastern churches, venerable for their antiquity, their situation, and their origin. (Hall, 1818: 34)

As was his custom, Hall invoked divine intervention for the fortuitous location of native Christians in that favoured corner of the world. Rather than Palestine or Syria, however, he singled out Cairo and Alexandria as opportune outposts for such effort. (1818: 48–49)

The annual report of 1819 of the Prudential Committee also focused on the special role of native Christians, despite its critical view overall of the Eastern churches.

> In Palestine, Syria, the Provinces of Asia Minor, Armenia, Georgia, and Persia, though Mohammedan countries, there are many thousands of Jews, and many thousands of Christians, at least in name. But the whole mingled population is in a state of deplorable ignorance and degradation – destitute of the means of divine knowledge, and bewildered with vain imaginations and strong delusions. It is to be hoped, however, that among the Christians there, of various denominations, some might be found, who are alive in Christ Jesus; and who, were proper means employed for their excitement, improvement, and help, might be roused from their slumbers, become active in doing good, and shine as lights in those darkened regions. It is indeed to be hoped, that no small part of those, who bear the Christian name, would willingly and gladly receive the Bible into their houses, and do something towards imparting the heavenly treasure, as opportunities should be afforded, to the Jews, Mohammedans, and Pagans; and, dispersed as they are, among the different nations, they might do much, at least might afford many and important facilities and advantages for carrying into the effect the expanding desires of benevolence. (ABCFM, 1819: 230)

By focusing on nominal Christians, the Board hoped to have two results: reforming and revitalizing the Eastern churches, and in the process transforming them into agents for diffusing 'pure' Christianity. This two-pronged objective was predicated on the premise that, not until native Christians could pose as pious and illustrious examples of the evangelistic ethos of New England Calvinism, would surrounding Muslims and Jews embrace Christianity without resistance. Much of the Board's initial effort in the region was devoted to searching for, enticing, training or ordaining 'native helpers' who could become more expeditious carriers of their message to their deluded compatriots.

Of all native communities, Armenians were regarded as singularly qualified to be the recipients of divine grace and, hence, act as devoted and enterprising prosecutors of Protestant emissaries. They were perceived as a 'noble race', the 'Anglo-Saxons of the East', shrewd, industrious and persevering. (Bartlett, 1972: 2–3) Their enterprising character, wide dispersion, preservation of the sentiment of national solidarity and acquaintance with the languages of the lands of their residence all rendered them particularly privileged to receive and propagate the message of pure Christianity.

Even before New England missionaries came in direct contact with Armenians, they had been perceived as people of great promise in the evangelization of Western Asia. Shortly before the departure of Fisk and Parsons, Gordon Hall was already predicting that from Armenia the Gospel would naturally advance into Persia, Mesopotamia, Syria, Palestine and Asia Minor. Given the improbability of converting Muslims directly, Armenians could well become their surrogate targets. 'Without a Crusade,' Hall declared, 'the church of Christ might recover those long-lost regions.' Hall went further to spell out the specific activities – schools, Bible societies, printing, seminaries, etc. – through which converted Armenians could assist in 'rekindling the flame of religion and restore the light of truth.' (Hall, 1818: 38)

The unique endowments of Armenians were compatible, or so they seemed at the time to New England Puritans, with their general philosophy of using indigenous groups as instruments of their own enlightenment and self-propagation. If and when evangelized, the Armenians were seen as a most fitting 'leaven' through which other non-Christian groups may be enlightened. The industrious Armenians were particularly felicitous as a leaven because they displayed the Puritan ethos of integrity and self-reliance.

Interestingly, there was no mention in the early volumes of the *Missionary Herald* of direct conversion as a basic objective. Instead, the pioneers of New England Calvinism were seeking to foster an attitude, a vitality and a zealousness for Christianity. It was their hope, of course, a reflection of their enduring faith in New England as God's 'choicest grain' and 'righteous republic' that once the mustard seeds of such a 'privileged garden' were planted elsewhere they were destined to beget other 'cities on the hill'. Protestantism, in other words, especially in its true form, was believed to be contagious. The missionary was no more than a benevolent messenger who planted the seeds and moved on.

The experience of missionaries in India, Ceylon and Africa persuaded the Board to make better and fuller use of natives in their efforts to create self-directing and eventually self-supporting institutions. Assessing the prospects for establishing a Theological Seminary for Africans, the Board was unequivocal in its support of such indigenous efforts.

If Africa is to stand forth in its glory of Christianity and civilization, her own sons, and not the sons of strangers, must be the instructors of her youth, and her ministers of religion. No nation will ever advance far in any improvement but by the instrumentality of her own children. Strangers may make a beginning, but strangers cannot continue to support her schools and her churches. To sustain such a weight at arm's length, would exhaust both patience and power . . . Apostles and missionaries may pass over a country, but native teachers must finish the work. So it was in primitive times. So it was in every country of Europe, when it received the Christian faith. (*Missionary Herald*, January 1817: 29)

Likewise, the Board was convinced, largely because of its experience in India and Africa, of the need to preach and teach in the vernacular. Common schools were to be a chief instrument of native helpers. There was no expectation, however, that such education was going to change the social order or class structure. In other words, while it might be beneficial to society in general, education was not necessarily seen as a means for social mobility. Individuals were to be trained to better perform their roles within the confines of their inherited 'station'. On the whole, care was generally taken not to offend local customs and cultural rituals, bizarre as they may have seemed to ethnocentric missionaries (for further elaboration, see Lindsay, 1965: 59–60). For example, New England evangelists in Ceylon promised parents of the boarding students that they would not require boys to eat anything that contravened the laws of their castes. They even went so far as to assert that it was their 'duty to yield so far to the prejudices of this people as is necessary in order to make known to them, in the most favourable circumstances, of the Gospel of Christ'. (*Missionary Herald*, June 1820: 279)

Altogether the expectations and objectives of the Board may be aptly summed up in the activities and 'instrumentalities' they had hoped that their first emissaries to the Levant would undertake. At the risk of oversimplification, they were to learn languages, gather information and circulate the Bible and tracts. They were cautioned to instruct in private or as unobtrusively as possible, without offending laws and customs. Finally, as benevolent messengers of that 'heavenly treasure', they were simply to instil the pure Gospel as a leaven and leave.

These broad objectives were embodied in the often-quoted 'instructions' given to Fisk and Parsons on the eve of their departure:

The two Grand Inquiries ever present to your minds will be—What good can be done? And, by what means? What can be done for the Jews? What for the Pagans? What for the Mohammedans? What for the Christians? What for the people in Palestine? What for those in Egypt–in Syria–in Persia–in Armenia–in other countries to which your inquiries may be extended? (ABCFM, 1819: 7)

Though the 'instructions' they received from the Board were general, their mandate, however, was immense. They were to perceive their mission as nothing short of 'an extended and continually extending system of benevolent action for the recovery of the world to God, to virtue and to happiness'. The august instructions went on to remind the ardent emissaries of the formidable task ahead. 'Yours is a field of no ordinary description. It comprises, either within itself or by intimate association, all that is most affecting to Christian feeling, or most interesting to Christian hope.'

For the effective prosecution of their work, knowledge of several languages, particularly Hebrew, ancient and modern Greek, ancient and modern Arabic, Turkish, French and Italian, was deemed of vital importance. They were encouraged to give 'diligent attention to Arabic'. More important, they were also expected by 'attentive observation and diligent inquiries, to become thoroughly acquainted . . . in regard to their general state, their religious opinions and rites, their moral and civil habits and manners, their means of improvement; in a word the circumstances favourable and unfavourable to the propagation of the Gospel . . .' (ABCFM, 1819: 6)

The Board was also understandably keen on gaining first-hand information before launching any major programmes. This task, however, vital as it was, was only a means for a nobler and much more venerable calling: 'You will go to that Land – still of Promise – as Christian missionaries and as Ministers of Christ commissioned to testify the Gospel to Jews and Gentiles, to people of every nation, name and condition . . .' (ABCFM, 1819: 10) Finally, the instructions cautioned the zealous emissaries not to be impatient under embarrassments and restraints: 'You must not despise the day of small things . . . From small beginnings He can advance your work in its several parts, to extensive operations and bright results.' (ABCFM, 1819: 10)

The instructions were not only broad, but much was also left to 'Providence'. The design was that they should go first to Smyrna and reside there for a 'longer or shorter time, as circumstances shall render advisable, for the purpose of acquiring more perfectly the requisite languages, and obtaining such information, of various kinds, as will be important in their subsequent course'. Since the mission was intended for Palestine, they were to proceed to the Holy Land and establish their station at Jerusalem. Aware, perhaps, of all the uncertainties, here again the Board was judiciously flexible. 'If found practicable and eligible' they could stay there; otherwise they could consider any other place, 'within or without the limits of Judea, as Providence shall indicate'. (ABCFM, 1819: 231)

The choice of Smyrna, however, was not incidental. By the early 1820s it was already a bustling entrepot, perhaps the largest commercial emporium in western Asia. Much of the thriving American commerce with the Levant and beyond was being routed through it. As a principal port of shipment of Turkish opium, it acted as an expedient conduit for the rapidly growing American commerce with China and the Orient. (Earle, 1927: 340–41) The volume of trade, with the United States initially, was barely visible. It was not until 1800 that the first American vessel reached Constantinople. Even Smyrna, the principal port at the time, received not more than a dozen ships a year on average before 1820 (see Daniel, 1964: 72–75 for further details). American ship captains had to discharge their cargo through English trading houses.

By the turn of the nineteenth century, the Ottoman government was embarking on modernization, most notably by undertaking massive programmes of economic and infrastructural development, which relied heavily on foreign expertise. The bulk of such technical know-how was supplied by English and French entrepreneurs reinforced by their home governments, which, it seems, had regarded such ventures as an adjunct of their foreign policy. American capitalists and technicians played little or no part in such schemes.

It was New England missionaries, more particularly Andover graduates, who must be credited for at least initiating the early cultural penetrations that were to prefigure most of the subsequent American incursions into the Near East. Initially, the intention was to proselytize by converting Jews and Muslims of the Holy Land. For a variety of adverse, often unanticipated circumstances they laboured in vain. Jews remained inaccessible and indifferent and the Muslims were militantly hostile to Christianity. If measured by the number of converts, their mission was a dismal failure.

To the Levant: The Departure of Pliny Fisk and Levi Parsons

One cannot but be impressed, when reviewing the backgrounds of the first generation of missionaries, by the common and discernible set of circumstances that imbued them with the desire to dispense Christian benevolence in the 'heathen' world. The young recruits were far from ordinary. As zealous, almost fanatic missionaries, they were doubtless by-products of the rigidity and parochialism of the times.

The beginning of the nineteenth century in America, in New England in particular, was a time of religious reawakening. A pervasive mood of religiosity, marked by the primacy of the Bible and sectarian controversy, was sweeping the country. It was a time of camp meetings, conversions, revivals and belief in the millennium. As New England Congregationalists – the direct spiritual descendants of the original Puritans – the early recruits displayed an even larger capacity for religious uplift and adherence to stringent moral edicts. Faith in what God had done through Christ, as divinely recorded in Scripture, was to them the only source of redemption. Conversely, eternal damnation in hell was the punishment for a lack of faith.

New England society was still in the grip of what were termed at the time 'Consistent Calvinists'. This was apparent in the education system and normative standards of conduct. Until 1827, for example, the clergy in Massachusetts were charged by law to inspect and license schools and teachers. Many of the teachers were clergymen. Virtually all college presidents were ministers, as were most of the faculty heads (see Finnie, 1967: 112–13).

As 'nurseries of piety' some of the most prominent colleges continued to draw a disproportionate number of their students for the ministry. Up to 1860, for example, one out of every 17 students of Princeton's Seminary went into overseas missions. (Anderson, 1869: 261)

Religion, manners and everyday conduct were so intimately aligned that it was extremely difficult to distinguish the boundaries between them. Although subscribing to the Gospel was the only true means of salvation, rigid arbiters of conduct and public behaviour were often transferred into articles of faith. Hence, observance of the Sabbath, abstinence, teetotalism, thrift, asceticism, as well as other ritualistic manifestations of piety and purity peculiar to Calvinism, were strictly adhered to. They also became the standards by which all others were judged.

One should not be misled, however, by the biblical education and rather rigid theological precepts of the missionaries. Although they were largely drawn from the smaller towns and farms of New England, led narrow, parochial lives and were imbued with the spirit of Puritan saintliness and patriotism, they were, nonetheless, well educated by standards of the day. At a time when only about two per cent of Americans would have gone to college, most of the missionaries – particularly those linked to the ABCFM – would have spent four years at college (typically Yale, Princeton, Amherst, Dartmouth, Williams, Middlebury, etc.), followed by two or three years at a seminary (Andover). (See Finnie, 1967; Phillips, 1969; Lindsay, 1965.)

Like other pioneering endeavours, foreign missions attracted their fair share of mavericks, eccentrics and some extremely gifted, versatile and precocious young recruits. They all 'saw the light' rather early in life. Jonas King, for example, read the Bible at four and then once yearly to the age of sixteen. He learnt English grammar while hoeing corn, read the 12 books of Virgil's *Aeneid* in 58 days and the New Testament in Greek in six weeks. Much like the other so-called 'Seven Pioneers' (Fisk, Parsons, Bird, Goodell, Smith, Thomson), King had first gone to Williams (1816) and then to Andover (1819). The precocious farm boy from Hawley, Massachusetts, with a fierce longing for an overseas mission in the Levant, went to Paris to study with DeSacy, the prominent French Arabist. It was there that he received an urgent appeal from Fisk to replace the deceased Parsons.

They had to become proficient in foreign languages at formidable speed. Goodell mastered all the Turkish and Armenian dialects and single-handedly completed a revision and translation of the Bible into Armeno-Turkish. Pliny Fisk, like many of his colleagues, could preach in Arabic, Turkish, Armenian, Italian, Greek and French. (Jessup, 1910: 38)

Despite their humble origins, they felt they were part of a privileged, passionate core of dedicated idealists. They were also, it seems, perceived as such by their communities. Indeed, some emerged into folk heroes of a sort. In the pioneer era of American missions it was perhaps natural to glorify, almost apotheosize, the life of the foreign evangelist as the ideal life of piety; for it was he who seemed to carry out most completely the theological commitments of New England Calvinism.[1]

It was no accident that Andover graduates should spearhead the call for such a sacred errand. It was at Andover that the young seminarians were first exposed to the Hopkinsian doctrine of altruistic 'disinterested benevolence'. Though conceived in provincial New England, Samuel Hopkins's elaboration of Edwardian Calvinism imbued this first generation of evangelists with a compassionate view of a world of unsaved millions far removed in space yet potentially within American evangelical sympathies. By the beginning of the century, the secret missionary fraternity founded at Andover had managed to recruit 250 of their own

1. For biographical sketches of successive generations of missionaries, see Goodell, 1961; Jessup, 1910; Finnie, 1967; Field, 1969; Shaw, 1937.

graduates as missionaries for the ABCFM (see Goodell, 1861: 60–61).

This compassionate world view and ardent longing to spread the Gospel did not come easy. It was not arrived at in a fit of impulse or frenzy. Reading the diaries and memoirs of the pioneers, one becomes aware of considerable anguish, pain and uncertainty accompanying the burning religious zeal and fierce commitment. The greater the task and the hardships, the more arduous the labour and self-denial, the closer they were to winning God's favour. Pliny Fisk, two years before embarking on his first mission, wrote how 'the great want of men among the heathen, weighs heavily on my mind . . . Happiness to spend and be spent for the heathen . . .' and that 'the mission to that country is not for the faint-hearted, the irresolute; for him who shrinks from the shock of arms, and the fierce and long contested battle . . . (Bond, 1828: 80–81) Later in his diary he was more explicit in evoking this connection between the willingness to be damned and redemption. 'I had determined to go among the heathen in view of the risk of life . . . I would cheerfully meet all the difficulties, and bear all the pains thou shall appoint, if they may but lead me to more wisdom and humility and prepare me to do more good.' (Bond, 1928: 84)

Perhaps it was because they were armed with this Faustian sense of optimism and the mystery of venturing into unknown and unexplored regions, combined with their self-righteousness and legendary drive and commitment, that they were able at times to accomplish remarkable feats against immense odds. Missionary accounts – both their own memoirs or sympathetic biographical sketches – are naturally inclined to exaggerate their travails. Yet these missionaries did endure an immense toll of vicissitudes as well as the inconveniences and perils of a peripatetic life. Their lives were often cut short. During the first 40 years, over a quarter of the 134 Andover seminarians in overseas missions failed to return home. They died before completing their eleventh year of duty. Since virtually all the early recruits were fresh out of college, they must have been in their early thirties. (ABCFM, 1861: 274–75)

The lives, memoirs and reflections of Fisk and Parsons reflect many of these concerns. They were also, amazingly, almost identical. Both were products of austere biblical upbringing reinforced by the Puritanism of righteous parents. Parsons's father was a minister. Fisk recalls how deep were the impressions left on his mind by 'the Christian example and counsel of pious parents, favourable to the susceptibility of the stronger convictions or religious truth . . .' (Bond, 1823: 14) Both went to Middlebury College, Vermont, graduated the same year (1814) and resumed theological training at Andover a year later. Both were converted and publicly professed their 'attachment to the redeemer' at the early age of 16. Their memoirs and correspondence are infused with self-examination, often sinking into morbid self-introspection. In both style and content their writing is anything but casual or prosaic. Even their ordinary correspondence with their family is delivered in eloquent but ponderous prose. While it is well known that Puritans did not promote the pursuit of certain intellectual and artistic activities (particularly drama, religious music, erotic poetry and other aspects of Renaissance humanism), they did express considerable interest in the classics, belles-lettres and scientific research.

Fisk and Parsons, like other young seminarians, were exemplary by-products of this tradition. The written word became almost sacred to them and was elevated into an accomplished and edifying art. They took special pride in refining their prose. If, occasionally, I seem overindulgent quoting from their works, it is a tribute to their alluring style.

Of the two, Parsons seemed more preoccupied with foreboding premonitions and was plagued by longer and more intense lapses of 'darkness', 'distress' and 'anxiety' about his own piety. While still a freshman in college he was already confessing to his 'vileness' and 'spiritual blindness' and longed to

Behold a few rays of Christ's glory shining in his saints, how glorious, how unspeakably blessed will be the paradise of God! This Saviour whom my soul loveth and melteth at the sound of his voice, will be seen in all the majesty of God. O my Saviour, how have I grieved thee! But on thy kind arms fall, and rest on thy bosom. I hope to be kept by thy love, and at last see thee face to face. O blessed morning! O my Saviour, come quickly! (Morton, 1832: 21)

The journal of his four years at Middlebury often refers to such relentless anguish. In his frequent letters to every member of his family, he bemoaned how his 'heart is awfully corrupt, a sink of iniquity . . .'. He decried the 'criminality' of his life, his despondency and feelings of inadequacy and guilt. 'My mind,' he wrote, 'has been barren and frozen with stupidity.' Yet he often would admit that when these 'afflictions are sanctified, they are the richest blessings . . . they are designed to quicken the Christian in spiritual work.' (Morton, 1832: 22) During his sophomore year in college, he was already reporting that the thought of becoming a missionary 'fires me with uncommon zeal'. In a letter to his parents (May 2, 1814) he writes:

From that blessed moment, when as I trust I experienced the smiles of heaven, the deplorable condition of the heathen has sensibly affected my mind. I have desired, and sometimes resolved, by the leave of Providence, to proclaim in their ears a crucified Saviour. This spring, the subject has appeared more solemn than ever; and often I am in the centre of Asia, listening to the groans of the eastern world, which are wafted to heaven for deliverance. Indeed I converse more with the heathen, than with my own classmates. (Andover Theological Seminary, 1833: 98)

By his senior year he was still apprehensive that even his sustained studies were a distraction.

I have now commenced my last year in college. It is my desire to spend it for God, to be diligent in business, yet fervent in spirit, serving the Lord. Intense study will check the progress of piety, and lead the soul away from prayer, unless there be constant watchfulness and faithfulness. Let me not forget that the glory of God is to be the ruling motive of my conduct; that no study, however interesting or enchanting, is of any consequence any farther that that it can be made to subserve the interests of the church. (Morton, 1832: 25)

Evincing the same sense of 'deep contrition and self-abhorrence', Fisk also, in astonishingly similar terms, mourns his levity and stupidity and longs to be delivered from sin.

I will throw myself on divine mercy, and hope and wait for the consolations of religion. A ray of light enters my benighted soul. Though heavy laden with guilt, Jesus appears mighty to save. My soul again leaps for joy to see my Redeemer. O my Saviour, do I not love thee, and long to be conformed to thy image? Do I not sincerely mourn my levity, my stupidity, and my unfaithfulness? Lord, thou knowest my heart, – is not sin the burden, and holiness the delight of my soul? Let me see thy glory, and my own vileness, – be delivered from the power of sin, and assimilated to thee . . . (Bond, 1828: 27)

Gripped by such mood swings, both Parsons and Fisk entertained, at a fairly early age, the 'sweet' prospects of deliverance from despondency through the 'glorious' sacrifice of missionary labour. Once again, Parsons evoked this with impassioned prose.

I have not those qualifications, those mental endowments, which are indispensable to a missionary. I am wanting in ardent piety, Christian zeal, and almost every thing beside. When sinking into despondency, and despairing of relief, the sweet promises of Christ to his weak, yet faithful followers, give me substantial consolation. Taking all these things in consideration, what must I do? Must I no longer indulge the thought of becoming a missionary, or a minister? Then death (I speak with awe) would appear more desirable than life. Become a missionary O blessed thought! May I indulge it! Labour, toil, suffer and die for souls – O honour is too great! Its an angel's trust, – here I pause and wonder . . . Should infinite mercy grant me a crown of glory how pleasing the consideration to have it sparkle with heathen souls. Nay, father, how pleasing to labour, to toil and suffer for him, who, through infinite condescension and boundless grace, endured the pains of Calvary! (Morton, 1832: 28–29)

By the time they moved to Andover, such sentiments began to find more tangible expression. Both spoke favourably of the spiritually refreshing atmosphere at Andover. They attributed this to a score of 'revivals' sweeping the Seminary at the time to resist the rapid decline in religious piety.

Both were inspired by the lectures and sermons of Drs Woods and Worcester, read and re-read the same books and biographies (Jonathan Edwards, Henry Martyn, William Crey and David Brainerd) and avoided and berated the works of secularists and 'infidels', particularly Paine, Hume and the French philosophers.

Their autobiographical accounts, reflecting the asceticism and self-denial of their austere Puritanism, lack any signs of spontaneous play, fun, humour or vivacity, except of course for the profound joy with which they felt blessed when touched by God's grace. Journal entries were replete with recurrent bouts of religious meditation, self-examination, devotional exercises, fasting, prayers and renewed resolutions.

Even their 'vacations' were devoted to spiritual labours and duties. Of course, any manifestation of idleness or 'levity in manner, looks and words' were signs of 'vileness', 'stupidity' and 'unprofitable' life. Returning from his spring vacation in 1816, Parsons reported that he had made 127 religious family visits in Vermont, attended 30 religious meetings in five towns and that on Sabbaths he had aided the devotions of destitute churches by explaining the Scriptures. (Morton, 1832: 68)

The dispensation of such favours and duties was clearly not enough to quench their 'thirsting after holiness' and their consideration for 'souls perishing in ignorance and sin'. They were, in their own words, longing 'to go'. When they were officially informed by the Prudential Committee of ABCFM (September 24, 1818) that they had been selected as its first evangelists to the Holy Land, Fisk and Parsons received the request with their characteristic 'rejoicing and trembling'. The object of the missions, as stipulated by the Board in a meeting held at Andover, was threefold:

1. To acquire information respecting the state of religion, by correspondence or otherwise, in Asiatic Turkey.

2. To ascertain the most promising place for the establishment of Christian missions, and the best means of conducting them.

3. To inquire by what means the Scriptures and religious tracts may be most advantageously circulated. (Morton, 1832: 112–13)

The religious public responded eagerly to the prospect of establishing a permanent station in the 'vineyard of Christ'. The departure by Fisk and Parsons was delayed a year so that they could take full advantage of such enthusiasm. They travelled around the country soliciting funds and support. A score of 'Palestine societies' was established for the purpose.

What is striking in the annual reports of the ABCFM is the almost total absence of an overall strategy or programme or a preference for any particular area. Fisk and Parsons were instructed that they should not just confine their efforts to any single region and that 'if unsuccessful in one place . . . they can turn to another . . . and seize upon any promising opportunity to do good to any portion of the world'. (*Panoplist*, XV 1819: 92) Fisk and Parsons displayed this same ambivalence and did not seem to prefer one area over another.

Another irony in this whole episode, as I have pointed out earlier (Chapter 4), was that the sacred errand was infused with a rather belligerent strain, expressed in militant or even martial rhetoric.

Though their destination was Palestine, the pioneering generation of evangelists had envisioned a much greater geographic scope for their mission. In his departing sermon, Pliny Fisk was quite explicit. 'It is destined,' he stated, 'to Judea, having at the same time particular reference to Asia Minor on the northwest . . . and

Armenia on the North.' (Fisk, 1819: 24) Palestine was, in their eyes, the most sacred and favoured of all places.

> This was the spot selected from all the surface of the earth by the Creator, to be the residence of that people whom he loved above all other people. Here the Lord their God gave them a good land of brooks of water, of fountains and depths that spring out of valleys and hills; a land of wheat and barley and vines and fig trees and pomegranates; a land of oil olive and honey; a land, wherein they might eat bread without scarceness and not lack anything; a land, in which they might build goodly houses and dwell therein, and in which their herds and flocks and gold and silver might be multiplied, that they might bless the Lord God for the good land which he had given them. It would seem, that the country was originally a favoured portion of the earth; or else that a peculiar blessing was granted, that it might be a suitable dwelling for the people of God. (Fisk, 1819: 24)

Fisk goes on justify why that spot was, because of its infinite religious associations, an originally favoured portion of the world. He also asserts what was to become the familiar refrain of successive generations of early envoys to the Levant, 'the Cross as the wonder of the universe and the only hope of a ruined world'. Palestine had special appeal not only because it was the birthplace of Islam, Judaism and Christianity but also because it was inhabited by diverse religious sects and groups who violated the piety and articles of faith inherent in their religious heritage.

Fisk expressed the view, shared by his mentors and peers, that Islam or 'Mohammedans', were 'The followers of that artful impostor . . ., a fortress of error and sin propagated by the sword and the persecution of infidels and heretics. (Fisk, 1819: 26–27)

Jews did not fare any better. Notwithstanding all that they had suffered, by way of persecution and dispersion, they continued, Fisk tells us, to betray their religion 'as it was exhibited in the piety of David, Daniel and Nehemiah only to retain the unbelief and self-righteousness of those Jews who rejected and crucified the Lord Jesus'. (Fisk, 1819: 27)

Roman Catholics, Syrian Christians, Greeks, Armenians and other 'nominal Christians' were equally retrograde. 'Though they call themselves Christians, [they] are still destitute almost entirely of the Scriptures, and deplorably ignorant of real Christianity.' (Fisk, 1819: 28) Their destitution and ignorance were not, however, irredeemable. At least when compared with the more deplorable conditions that subjects in Africa, India and other parts of Asia were suffering at the time, the people of Palestine and the eastern Mediterranean seemed much more amenable to redemption.

Such themes – of degeneracy versus redemption, despair versus hope, gloom versus optimism, darkness versus light, etc – run through many of the sermons, journals and justifications of the early and subsequent generations of missionaries. Often the depravity and destitution were exaggerated. This clearly imbued their mission with sacrificial glory. But, faint as it was, there was always a glimmer of hope. In his farewell sermon, preached in Park Street Church in Boston (31 October 1819), Parsons was concerned about the extent of Jewish sustained suffering.

> After their hands were imbued in the blood of the Son of God, the Judgements of heaven were not long suspended. In less than forty years, Jerusalem was given up to be plundered; the city was demolished, and a ploughshare drawn over it as a sign of perpetual desolation . . . Their lands in Judea were sold. They were reduced to abject slavery; exposed, in vast multitudes, to public sale; subjected to most rigorous corporeal punishment; and, at last, they were not permitted to tread upon that spot where Jerusalem stood; nor to shed their tears upon that ground, where they crucified the Lord of glory.
>
> From that period, the condition of the Jews in Judea has been miserable beyond description. They have waited for the Messiah, but waited in vain. They have attempted to re-establish the religion of their Fathers, but every attempt has been marked with sword, bloodshed, and death. To this day they remain the objects of universal abhorrence, and contempt. Thus the blood of Jesus has been upon them, and upon their children; thus for ages they have been suffering the vengeance of an incensed Judge . . . (Parsons, 1819: 5–7)

The Children of Israel did not suffer only in Palestine. Their condition in the West, in the eyes of the missionaries, was no less miserable. Indeed, they used this awareness and the Jews' longing to return to Israel, as part of their justification for undertaking their mission to Palestine. Parsons, much more than Fisk, was very explicit on this. Characteristically, he invoked the savage cruelties of the Crusades, hopes of the millennium, the demise of the Ottoman Empire and the social degeneracy of Islam.

Parsons, in his impassioned farewell sermon, had much to say on each of the four themes. The Crusades invited, perhaps, his greatest scorn. They were seen as the commencement

> of a long series of inhuman and savage cruelties; the history of which is but a detail of persecutions, proscriptions, banishments, and massacres . . . Parents were torn from their children, and families; their houses were consumed; their synagogues laid in ruins. Some fled to the caves and holes of the earth; others surrendered, and were immediately murdered by a furious populace; some escaped the sword by a pretended conversion to the Christian religion; others despairing of redress came to the horrid resolution of destroying themselves. (Parsons, 1819: 8)

Like many of his peers, who were equally buoyed by the imminent millennium, revival preaching and the bestowal of human grace through conversion, Parsons cherished the hope that the 'outcasts of Israel will yet be gathered to their own land', and with it, the yet brighter prospect that they would embrace Christianity. Indeed, he provided evidence of 'increasing solicitude among the Jews with regard to the Christian's Messiah'. In Poland, Russia, Venice, Bohemia and parts of the

Mediterranean he claimed there were 'hundreds of Rabbis showing greater interest in Christ's message and his impending return . . .' and that the Jews 'are not as obdurate as they once were, and when converted prove the most active members of the Church of Christ'. (Parsons, 1819: 14–15)

Encouraged by these events, Parsons entreats the Christian to awake from his 'long and criminal slumber' to discharge benevolent duties and obligations.

> With these facts before us, we cannot for a moment hesitate. Surely the day so long desired by the people of God is beginning to dawn! The darkness and gloom of this long and dismal night are retiring before the light of truth. The blessed Gospel has commenced its gradual, yet irresistible progress. The Holy Spirit is carrying on among them a work of grace. The sacred Scriptures are circulated, and received, with the most animating prospect for success. Jewish children are receiving a Christian education; and are thus secured from the most bitter prejudices against the name of Jesus . . . We do not expect the conversion of the Jews by a miracle. The means which God hath appointed must be employed. The millions of Jews must be furnished with the word of God, and with instruction of Missionaries. But this cannot be done without charity; without the liberal, and persevering efforts of the Christian world. Say then, brethren, shall we bear a part in this work of benevolence, or must it be accomplished without us. (Parsons, 1819: 17–19)

Puritanism as a Cultural Transfer: Premises and Issues

We now need to identify and possibly extract a few broader inferences underlying the character of New England Puritanism as a cultural transfer. Puritanism thrived best as an itinerant culture. It had an adaptive quality, which predisposed it to the needs of groups in diverse cultural settings.

To understand the troubled life of any transplant, one most investigate the view that missionaries (in this case New England evangelists) held of the 'other', and how predisposed they were to recognize, if not assimilate, the distinctive attributes of foreign cultures. On the whole, while successive generations of missionaries were charitable in their compassions, they were not too charitable in their views and images. The 'heathen' was seen as lacking human dignity and moral worth.

The disparaging images that American Protestants harboured towards Islam are, to a large extent, understandable, given the temper and popular misconceptions of the day. By the turn of the nineteenth century the reading public in America was being exposed to a steady flow of knowledge about Islam, its tenets and the life and personality of the Prophet Muhammad. The bulk of this literature, be it biographies of the Prophet, translations of the Qur'an or the general Christian polemics with Islam, continued to reflect some of the medieval distortions.

'Disinterested benevolence' accounted for much of missionary zeal and was indeed the bedrock of evangelism. But how 'disinterested' were the missionaries in their benevolence? Was their glowing sentiment dispensed unconditionally to all so-called 'perishing souls'? Who were its beneficiaries? Were some recipients more privileged than others and on what grounds? The evidence here once again suggests that the missionaries were selective and partial in dispensing their favours. They did their good works only within the narrow confines of Protestant consciousness. Hence, those sects and groups that were perceived as accessible or more amenable to receiving their message were treated more favourably. The 'heathen', in other words, forfeited his privilege of being the beneficiary of any Protestant benevolence (i.e. divine grace, redemption and ultimately education, welfare, relief and other 'good works') unless he demonstrated enough 'piety' or willingness to be converted.

Such selective benevolence was very much in evidence in the new settlements before the American Civil War. Religious benevolent societies and voluntary agencies flourished at the time. Most of these agencies, however, ranging from Bible, tract and temperance societies to those concerned with the reclamation of fallen women, did their good works only within a Christian context. Presbyterian missionaries praised Indians 'only in so far as they could emulate white Christians'. (Wood, 1990: 29) Much like the legions of homeless and hungry derelicts who must sit through a sermon to receive their coveted soup bowl at a skid row mission, the heathens were the beneficiaries of tokens of Christian benevolence only if they were perceived as potential recruits.

The attitudes of New England Puritans towards other religious sects in the Levant were largely an expression of how close they were to being converted to Protestantism. Clearly, their partiality towards Greek Orthodox, Armenians, Chaldeans, Assyrians, Nestorians and other 'marginal' sects within Islam (such as Druze, Yazeedees and Allawites) was a reflection of such favourable perceptions. Conversely, the antipathies they harboured towards Maronites, Jesuits, Catholics, Syrian Jacobites, Papal Syrians as so-called 'nominal Christians' were also understandable.

Such selective benevolence invites concern about the degree to which New England evangelists were willing to recognize and interact dispassionately with spiritual beliefs and practices that were at variance with theirs. Some religions have been more indulgent of disagreement and divergence than others. Buddhists, Baha'is, Unitarians – to single out three rather obvious instances (see Wood, 1990: 6) – display comparatively greater latitude in challenging the canons and dogmas of their faith without suffering the reproving charges of heresy. The kind of evangelism New England missionaries were exporting was not hospitable to any forms of salvation other than their own – through Jesus Christ and His word as expressed in the Gospel.

Missionaries in the Levant were more open and experimental in the means they employed, but they were inflexible, indeed, often doggedly intractable in their devotion to their sacred errand. More disheartening was their obfuscating ethnocentrism, which encouraged them to patronize the other. Yet it is not too difficult to understand how New England Puritans, facing the Orient at that time, suffused with millennial sentiments and the startling accomplishments of the New World as a 'righteous paradise', could harbour such disdainful images of alien cultures. Indeed, they could not at the time have possibly imagined the existence of native societies, so distinct from their own, without also regarding them as morally inferior.

If we wish to understand evangelism as a cultural transplant, it is of profound importance to consider how they should have nurtured 'heathens', especially those perceived as 'corrupt', 'degenerate', 'barbaric', etc . Given their contemptuous regard for the 'other', the encounters between them were not intended to be an open give and take. Nor could the resultant synthesis be a congenial reconciliation between the congruent elements of two cultures. It is pertinent to invoke here the question Forrest Wood (1990: 9) advanced in this regard: 'How can one,' he asked, 'enjoy the best of two worlds if one world perceives the other's best as its worst?'

Such ethnocentrism was bound to have a lasting impact on the interplay between transplanted Protestantism and its new setting. Although missionaries gladly accepted their long exile from home, and indeed many rejoiced in this form of banishment and self-denial, they almost always considered themselves as aliens and strangers wherever they went. Evangelists resisted any temptation to get closer to the native culture or even to acquire its superficial or outward signs or practices. They were there, after all, 'to besiege a great empire of sin . . .' not to resurrect or reform it. They were there to touch but not be touched by the native culture. Hence, the burden of adjustment and adaptation almost always fell on the 'natives'.

A few of the pioneering generation of missionaries were romantically infatuated with some of the picturesque elements of the culture, such as garb, mannerisms and eccentric rituals. Such affinities, however, rarely went beyond these outward gestures. Their response to the indigenous culture, particularly to those large segments deemed beyond their reach, remained indifferent and hostile.

Such views became sharper with time. If the Calvinist image of the sinful condition of natural man reinforced the evangelists' belief in the moral degradation of the heathen, then missionary enthusiasm had to be shored up by the constant evocation of such images. Even in the light of contrary evidence, successive generations of New England missionaries throughout their extended contacts with 'native' groups rarely disarmed themselves of some of their deep-seated mindsets and stereotypes. They did not question the belief that theirs was a superior religion and that they were the beneficiaries of a higher civilization.

Issues of winning over potential converts, the means of so doing (i.e. preaching, conversion, gathering into churches, as opposed to mobilization through education, the press, welfare) and evidence of their piety consequently became matters of controversy among the missionaries. Some insisted that their responsibility did not extend beyond the winning of individual converts to the cause of Christ. Others advanced a wider perspective, which sought the restructuring of the social system of which the converts formed a part (see Hudson, 1961: 102–04).

The continuing polemics over Christ versus culture entailed other controversies. Were the 'natives', for example, to be 'civilized' first before being Christianized, or was Christian piety and grace enough to generate cultural uplift? If they were to be civilized first, how were they to ward off the unsettling consequences of 'denationalization'? Which of the accessories and appendages of Western culture should they take with them? This, too, had critical implications for cultural transfer, particularly one that involved contact between two such markedly different cultural entities.

This issue hinged not only on whether non-Western ideas values and patterns of behaviour could be assimilated intact into Western culture or whether they must be modified and eventually undermined and destroyed. It also raised other predicaments. Successive generations of pioneering missionaries, as is evident from the 'instructions' they received and their own predispositions, were cognizant of the hazards of 'denationalization'. Indeed, they spoke about it in these same explicit terms. After barely a decade in the field, they were already volunteering their own hints and 'cautionary' advice to their colleagues contemplating a career in the Mediterranean.

Such advice was not always heeded. Many of the successive generations of missionaries were not as enlightened as the pioneers. They persisted in depicting all other 'heathen' cultures as savage, barbaric and degenerate and called for their destruction. There is a contradiction here. The 'natives' were told that they must break away from their 'vile' and 'degenerate' culture if they were to enjoy the fruits of salvation. Yet they were also told that they must guard against identification with alien cultures, if they were to preserve their cultural heritage and collective identity.

One must be cautious not to infer too many progressive, well-meaning intentions from such pious assertions. Underlying this seeming concern for cultural sensitivity and the indigenization of cultural change lurk other intentions. Hence, such matters as preaching in the vernacular, language instruction, the type and level of education, the education of women, indigenous leadership, self-government, church organization, etc., were all debated and considered in the context of expediting the propagation of the Gospel. The concern, then, was not how to shelter the 'natives' from the alienating impact of Western culture, but how to render them more accessible and pliable to Protestantism. Throughout the years this professed role, i.e. missionaries as evangelists for Christ and saviours of the world, did not, in fact, undergo much change.

CHAPTER 6

Protestant Images of Islam

Disparaging Stereotypes Reconfirmed

> . . .The whole mingled population is in a state of
> deplorable ignorance and degradation – destitute of the
> means of divine knowledge, and bewildered with vain
> imaginations and strong delusions.
>
> American Board of Commissions
> for Foreign Missions (1819)

> The good works of Islam are of the lips, the hand and
> the outward bodily act, having no connection with
> holiness of life, honesty, veracity and integrity.
>
> Henry Jessup, *The Mohammedan*
> *Missionary Problem* (1879)

By the turn of the nineteenth century the reading public in America was being
exposed to a steady flow of knowledge about Islam, its tenets and the life and
personality of the Prophet Muhammad. The bulk of this literature – whether
biographies of the Prophet, translations of the Qur'an or the general Christian
polemics with Islam – continued, at least initially, to reflect some of the medieval
distortions.

Given the overall deficient state of knowledge and relative inaccessibility of
Islam and the Orient to empirical and dispassionate study or observation, it is
understandable that New England emissaries, particularly the pioneering
generations, should uphold these views and invoke them so ardently in sanctifying
their 'sacred errand'. What is remarkable, however, is the survival of such distorted
images and the tenacity with which they were sustained over the years. This is
rather ironic, since of all the groups (i.e. merchants, diplomats, travellers, military

and naval personnel), missionaries appear to have had the most continuous and direct relationships with and probably the most intimate knowledge of Islam and its way of life. Yet such close and extended contacts did not lead to any noticeable change in their perceptions. Indeed, many of the medievalist distortions they initially carried over with them somehow managed to become sharper and more defamatory in tone and content. Products of apprehension and fear, these old pejorative caricatures were being supplanted or supplemented, as several social historians have pointed out, by a new set of stereotypes, reflecting a blend of patronizing disdain and romanticization of the Orient and the Levant. Some of the older forbidding images were slowly being transformed into images of intrigue and curiosity. (Oxtaby, 1980)

It is pertinent to explore the circumstances that reinforced such warped stereotypes. This chapter briefly considers the impact of two hitherto overlooked factors that sustained and reconfirmed these images: America's encounters with the Barbary states of North Africa at the turn of the nineteenth century and the reports and impressions relayed back by the missionaries themselves, of which the life and thoughts of Henry Jessup (1832–1910) stand out as a paramount example.

Medievalist Distortions

Like much of the writing on Islam rooted in the medieval Christian tradition, the underlying purpose of such polemical literature was not to inform or understand, but to expose the blemishes and failures of Muhammad's message and to protect Christians from Muslim blandishments. At best Islam was misinterpreted as a sort of minor or lesser image of Christendom. Most of the Christian scholars responsible for this body of literature were, it must be recalled, priests or monks who were avowedly polemical in intent. Indeed, they were 'often scurrilous in tone, designed to protect and discourage rather than to inform'. (Lewis, 1993: 85–86)

Two quite typical examples suffice. In accounting for the wide appeal of Islam and the swiftness of its expansion, Hannah Adams (1817) reiterates some of the deeply rooted prejudices and misconceptions current at the time, namely, the treacherous powers of the sword and the perfidy and bestial nature of human instincts.

> This rapid and extensive spread of the Moslem faith has not only been urged as an argument in its favour, but been brought into competition with the propagation of Christianity. Two circumstances however must be brought into consideration. Mohammed contrived by the permission of polygamy and concubinage to make his creed palatable to the most depraved of mankind; and at the same time, allowing its propagation by the sword, to excite the martial spirit of unprincipled adventurers. (Adam, 1817: 157)

John Hayward (1843), some 25 years later, wrote in similar terms.

> The terror of Mahomet's arms, and the repeated victories which were gained by

him and his successors, were, no doubt, the irresistible arguments that persuaded such multitudes to embrace his religion, and submit to his dominion. Besides, his law was artfully and marvellously adapted to the corrupt nature of man, and in a most particular manner, to the manners and opinions of the Eastern nations, and the vices to which they were naturally addicted. (Hayward, 1843: 229)

In the United States it was not until the mid-nineteenth century that some of the deep-seated misconceptions of Islam and the Prophet started to be dispelled or questioned. At least one may discern a generation of writers who were not as rancorous, those who shied away from the unrestrained vitriolic attacks commonly lavished on Islam and its followers. Initially, some of the more tolerant views emerged from a limited circle of theologians and intellectuals, mostly transcendentalists and proponents of free and universal religious movements or advocates of the Enlightenment and Age of Reason. Their favourable expressions were also generally timid, often too cautious and guarded in their praise. Other views were overall more ambivalent, oscillating between condemnation and praise.

All the praiseworthy attributes were seen as derivatives or poor imitations of Christianity or Judaism. A typical example are the views of Theodore Dwight, a noted evangelist and devout Christian, who, interestingly enough, credited Muslims with elevating and 'civilizing' the blacks in Africa. But he went on to say, with respect to those Africans who had adopted Islam:

The Koran, as is well known, has copied from the Hebrew Scriptures many of the attributes of God and the doctrines of morality, with certain just views of the nature, capacities, duties, and destiny of man; and these are so faithfully taught, that they are conspicuous in the writings of many of the numerous authors in Mohammedan countries, and often displayed, in a more or less satisfactory degree, in the characters and lives of those educated in them. (Dwight, 1864)

In the same vein, L. K. Washburn, in analysing the differences between Christianity and other world religions, including Islam, maintained that all of them were based on belief in God, divine revelation and immortality of the soul. They have all, Washburn observed, been sources of inspiration and endeavoured to uphold justice, progress, freedom and other such human virtues. Of Muslims in particular, he asserted that they too have 'faith in one God, in his kindness and mercy, in his justice and love; they believe in moral and religious duty, in being upright and pure, in humanity and forgiveness, but they are not Christians.' (Washburn, 1878: 518)

Others, particularly writers like George Miles and Washington Irving, were characteristically more ambivalent in their attitudes, often oscillating between condemnation and admiration; between, as it were, Sale's 'impostor' and Carlyle's 'hero'. In prefacing his popular play on the life of Mohammed, Miles (1850) wavered between admiring the Prophet's human character and his sublime message and motives, and recognizing his potential for deceit and corruption. In another literary work, a year earlier, Irving (1849) was also puzzled by 'Mahomet's simplicity of manner, self abnegation and piety, enjoying worldly power without being vainglorious'.

> It is the perfect abnegation of self, connected with this apparently heartfelt piety, running throughout the various phases of his fortune, which perplex one in forming a just estimate of Mahomet's character. However he betrayed the alloy of earth after he had worldly power at his command, the early aspirations of his spirit continually returned and bore him above all earthly things. Prayer, that vital duty of Islamism, and that infallible purifier of the soul, was his constant practice. 'Trust in god' was his comfort and support in times of trial and despondency. (Irving, 1849: 242)

This same ambiguity had manifested itself earlier in the immensely weighty work of Gibbon, who had seen it as an embodiment of the Prophet's dual role as preacher and fighter, as 'impostor' or 'enthusiast'. The purity and sincerity of his original motives were bound, in other words, to be gradually corrupted by cruelty and justice. 'The sins of Mahomet,' Gibbon maintained, 'may be allowed as evidence of his sincerity.' (Gibbon, 1932: 377)

Carlyle's *Heroes and Hero-Worship* (1841), another influential work, also adulates Muhammad (indeed, he is the quintessential 'hero as Prophet') for his genuine sincerity and lack of affectation, the prerequisites for any heroic deed.

Of course, these and other more tolerant voices were not entirely indigenous to America. They reflected no doubt a string of sympathetic European writers such as Gibbon, Carlyle and their transcendentalist American cohorts (Emerson, Thoreau, Hawthorne, Melville, Mark Twain, Margaret Fuller, Conway and Clarke). Incidentally, by mid-century, European Christian perceptions of Islam were already becoming noticeably more favourable. (Nasr, 1976)

It is not clear, from the evidence at hand, what the seminarians at Andover and other Presbyterian colleges were exposed to. It is quite possible, given the ardent antipathies they harboured against the writings of Paine, Hume, Condorcet, Goethe, Voltaire and other deists (who, it should be recalled, were berated as 'infidels' and secularists), that they might not have received much exposure to such charitable or tolerant perceptions. Indeed, the mere attribution of such views to any of the deists or French philosophers would have invited the scorn of the evangelists.

What is unmistakable, however, is that, even if the evangelists had any familiarity with the more sympathetic images of Islam, they were unimpressed by them. Neither in the autobiographies of Fisk and Parsons nor in the 'instructions' they received from their mentors before their departure can one glean anything but the derogatory images common at the time.

In their impassioned farewell sermons in October 1819, before they sailed from Boston to Smyrna, both Fisk and Parsons displayed a rich array of such images. Fisk, reiterated all the defamatory platitudes attributed to Islam, ranging from describing Muhammad as an 'artful impostor' and Islam as a 'fortress of error and sin' to the sanctification of the 'sword, cruelty and blood' for the persecution of 'infidels, heretics and despotic governments'. To Fisk, Islam or 'Mahommedans' became

> . . . The followers of that artful impostor, who arose in Arabia, about the commencement of the seventh century. Their religion was first propagated, and is still defended, by the sword. Cruelty and blood are among its most prominent characteristics. Mahommedan piety consists very much in fasts, ablutions, and pilgrimages to Mecca, and the persecution of infidels and heretics. Mahommedans believe, that Moses and Jesus were true prophets; that Jesus was the greatest of prophets except Mahommed; that the Pentateuch, the Psalms, the Prophets, and the Gospels were revelations from God, but have been so much corrupted by Jews and Christians, as to deserve but little credit . . .
>
> They have, indeed, much of the truth in their system: but their customs, established by the usage of centuries, the despotic nature of their government, the prominent articles of their faith, and the very genius and spirit of their religion, shield the Mahommedans almost impenetrably from the influence of Christianity. To make spiritual conquests from them will require the most vigorous efforts of the Christian church. Let the Gospel prevail among them, and some of the strongest fortresses of error and sin will be taken. (Fisk, 1819)

Parsons, on the other hand, since he was destined for the Holy Land, bemoaned all the deplorable cruelties the 'Mohammedan power' had inflicted as a 'scourge' on the children of Israel.

> In the east, Divine Providence raised up the *Mohammedan power*, to be a tremendous scourge to the children of Israel. For a while, Mohammed gave them every token of friendship, and respect. But finding them inflexible, he changed his garb of friendship for the fury of a fiend. He filled his Koran with curses against them, armed his disciples, with the sabre to extirpate them, obliged parents to instil mortal enmity into the minds of their children, besieged their cities, demolished their synagogues, drove them into exile, and forbade them to return upon pain of death. (Parsons, 1819: 6–7)

The grim and desolate perceptions with which Fisk and Parsons departed the shores of America were likely consistent with those of their mentors and prominent members of the American Board of Commissions for Foreign Missions (ABCFM) and the Prudential Committee. The minutes of the Tenth Annual Meeting of the Board (September 1819), devoted to consolidating their efforts to embark on the Palestine mission, spoke more desolately about 'hundred of millions of human beings immersed in the deepest corruption and wretchedness'.

> In Palestine, Syria, the Provinces of Asia Minor, Armenia, Georgia and Persia, though Mohammedan countries, there are many thousands of Jews, and many thousands of Christians, at least in name. But the whole mingled population is in a state of deplorable ignorance and degradation, – destitute of the means of

divine knowledge, and bewildered with vain imaginations and strong delusions. (ABCFM, 1819: 230)

The solemn 'Instructions' from the Prudential Committee, designating Fisk and Parsons as emissaries to Palestine (delivered in the South Church of Boston on 31 October 1819), were equally explicit in their perceptions. The two youthful zealots were commissioned to go forth 'to the Mingled People, now sitting in darkness, in that once favoured land . . . for the recovery of the world to God, to virtue and happiness'.

Disparaging Images Reconfirmed

Once images are firmly rooted in the collective memory of a community, they die hard. The early medievalist stereotypes survived largely because there was little opportunity at the time to develop intimate knowledge of Islam and the eastern Mediterranean. Travel was strenuous and hazardous. It took months to complete the voyage across the seas. Hence many of these images, often no more than parodies and invidious caricatures, were extracted from second- or third-hand sources and impressions.

It is rather odd, as we are repeatedly reminded by a score of historians, that, despite Islam's arresting early military successes, the West did not evince any interests in seeking a closer understanding of it. The first translation of the Qur'an into French and English (particularly the widely circulated 1649 London edition of Ross) came after a lapse of an entire millennium of Islamic history. Even when contacts with the Orient and Levant became possible, the old stereotypes always resurfaced under new guises.

Whether they were labelled (depending on time and place) Saracens, Moors, Turks, Tatars or Muslims, they were always denigrated: just as the Moors were demonized during the eighth century when the Arabs brought Islam to North Africa, southern Spain and the Loire Valley in France, it was the Turks who were feared and reviled during the seventeenth century. The same ideologies of enmity transformed the 'Terrible Turks' into fierce, despotic and bloodthirsty tyrants and infidels. If they were perceived otherwise, how else could the emissaries of New England have justified and sustained their sacred errand into a region they continued to treat as a 'howling wilderness' and a 'dark' and forbidding place?

With the technological and geopolitical superiority of Europe becoming more ascendant, early in the nineteenth century, the disparaging images became more graphic and visible.

'Muslim Marauders' of the Barbary States

The ancient hostility between Christianity and Islam was reawakened during America's confrontation with despotic and adventurous rulers of the so-called Barbary States, 'the dark continent' of North Africa. For at least four decades prior to the departure of Fisk and Parsons, America was intermittently mired in often humiliating encounters with the absolute but precarious regents and overlords in that strategic region. These encounters tested the resolve, dignity and national pride of the New Republic.

At the time, the North African states – bearing titles such as the Bey of Tunis, Bey of Algiers, Emperor of Morocco and Pasha of Tripoli – were nominally provinces of the Ottoman Empire. However, by virtue of their location and arbitrary powers, they wielded considerable influence in controlling access to navigation rights, trade routes and other maritime resources in that vital stretch of the Mediterranean and Atlantic coastlines. They were, after all, the ostensible custodians of the riches of the Levant and guardians of the entrance to the Black Sea. Like other Ottoman provinces, they were caught between insurmountable internal problems (poverty, political instability, plagues, etc.) and the ruinous impositions of Ottoman sultans and pashas. Piracy, tributes levied on vessels and other arbitrary exactions became coveted sources of revenue. For years these 'Muslim marauders', as they were dubbed in the popular language of the day, had preyed upon the Mediterranean commerce of Christian nations. (Nichols, 1956: 103) Vessels that refused to defray the humiliating tribute payments were wantonly pillaged. 'Treaties' and 'pacts' safeguarding navigation rights, were wilfully violated. Hence, American ships were often seized, their cargo confiscated and the passengers taken captive and held for ransom.

The colourful history of such encounters, with their shady diplomacy, state-sponsored piracy and intrigues on the high seas, is long and tortuous. It is of no concern to us here. Interested readers can consult any of the well-documented accounts (see, for example, Irwin, 1931; Anderson, 1969; Field, 1969). Though notorious for their piracy and other flagrant exploits on the high seas, the Barbary states were clearly not alone in such misadventures. All major European powers at the time employed their own brands of pirates, corsairs and buccaneers to safeguard and extend their maritime privileges.

What needs to be underscored here is that the Barbary wars rekindled long-standing Christian–Muslim rivalry over control of the Mediterranean and the Levant. Latent symptoms of distrust, collective paranoia and misrepresentations of the 'other' resurfaced with renewed vengeance. More significant, perhaps, these unsettling events brought the United States, then a fledgling republic, in direct contact for the first time with the Muslim world. All its perceptions and images of the Orient were either formulated or reconfirmed then.

Of course, episodes of piracy had taken place earlier, during the colonial period. Diplomatic records of the last two decades of the seventeenth century reveal repeated complaints by the governor of Massachusetts about the loss of vessels and about subjects suffering the anguish and humiliation of captivity by Turkish pirates. (Sha'ban, 1991) At the time, it must be noted, American ships enjoyed the protection of Great Britain. With the astonishing growth of commerce and navigation in the subsequent century, the United States, as an independent nation, had to negotiate its own treaties with the Barbary states, particularly since diplomatic efforts to secure alternative French protection had failed. It was this period, roughly between 1780 and 1815, that witnessed a sharp upsurge in the incidence of piracy. American vessels were repeatedly captured. Numbers of captives increased. So did ransom money and annual tributes demanded by the

Barbary states and their alleged agents. Emissaries seeking diplomatic intervention – i.e. for the release of American prisoners or those negotiating peace treaties – were not spared either. Many disappeared. Others were insolently denied audience. The cumulative effects of such humiliating episodes prompted the United States to resort to military action. The ports of Tripoli and Tunis were blockaded in 1800 and those of Algiers in 1815. The United States was thereby able to conclude a peace treaty, which placed it, in the words of James Madison, 'on higher grounds than any other nation'. (Sha'ban, 1991: 72)

America's embroilment with the Barbary states attracted the concern of some of the leading public figures and intellectuals of the day. George Washington, Thomas Jefferson, James Monroe, Benjamin Franklin, John Adams and others were all directly involved in formulating and defending strategies for coping with the hazards of Mediterranean commerce and putting an end to European monopoly and intrigues. For example, in 1784 a commission composed of Franklin, Adams and Jefferson was established, with David Humphreys as secretary, to negotiate treaties of amity and commerce with the four states of Barbary. In 1790, as part of a campaign to release American hostages in Algiers, Jefferson decried the cruelty to which his compatriots were being subjected and reminded Congress of the vital connection between freeing the captives and safeguarding the freedom of Mediterranean trade.

> The liberation of our citizens has an intimate connection with the liberation of our commerce in the Mediterranean . . . The distress of both proceed from the same cause, and the measures which shall be adopted for the relief of one, may, very probably, involve the relief of the other. (Sha'ban, 1991: 78)

Likewise, George Washington was also aware of the importance of the Orient to American trade, pride and national interest. He urged the appointment of consuls in the Barbary states to ensure the successful conduct of such affairs.

Spurred by nationalist sentiments and America's awesome display of its military might and its refusal to pay tribute, men of letters were also moved to sing the virtues of a new dawn buoyed and harnessed by America's 'manifest destiny' and its enhanced splendour, glory and prestige abroad. David Humphreys, perhaps one of the most strident of his generation, was quite explicit about the role of America in 'vindicating the sea from the pirate rage of Barbary'. To him,

> The unexpected appearance of a squadron from the new world in the Mediterranean and the consequent decided measures . . . astonished the regents of Barbary . . . and operated powerfully in placing the character of the United States in a more advantageous point of view. (Humphreys, 1804: 41)

Humphreys often resorted to poetic verse to punctuate his message. Of course, 'vindicating the seas' legitimated to use of naval force. Humphreys, among others, made an eloquent plea on its behalf.

> Give me the music of the sounding axe –

Let the keen adze the stubborn live oak wood –
And anvils shrill, with stronger strokes resound.
Give me the music, where the dock equips,
With batt'ries black and strong, the battle-ships,
To whose broad decks, the hast'ning crowds repair,
And shouts, and drums, and cannon, rend the air.
Blow ye the trumpet! – sound – oh, sound th'alarms –
To arms – to arms – brave Citizens! To arms . . . (Humphreys, 1804: 20)

Even those who had been reluctant to advocate the use of the cannon were now inclined in favour. For example, Barlow's once fervent hope that 'there are persons now living who will see the day when not a cannon shall be allowed to be carried to sea . . .' gave way to the view that powder and ball might prove a civilizing agent on the maritime as on the western frontier. (Barlow, 1970: 26) So did Jefferson. While he had urged, as Secretary of State, commercial expansion as the means for increasing the happiness and improving the conditions of mankind, he too saw a link between maritime trade and maritime force. By the end of the century, it must be noted, there had been a steady increase of American commerce in the Mediterranean. Some 80 ships per year were reported passing eastward through the strait of Gibraltar. (Field, 1969: 40)

America's involvement with the Barbary states did not only test the resolve of the new republic and its founding fathers. More pertinent to our central concern, it also raised, for the first time, some crucial issues about America's relations with, and perception of, non-European societies. It is also telling that America's initiation into the Orient should be marked by so much machination, shady diplomacy, double-dealing, piracy, hostage-taking and protracted confrontation. Stereotypical views of Muslims and Turks as perpetrators of 'despotism, cruelty and barbarism' were readily reconfirmed.

Of course, this was also the period when foreign travel was becoming more accessible. Travelogues and accounts of pilgrims to the Orient and the Holy Land were capturing the public imagination. Americans were now being initiated into yet another novel form of writing: that genre of adventurous narratives chronicling the cruelties of captivity. Exaggerated tales, often as letters and diaries of interned prisoners and hostages, depicting their suffering and heartless mistreatment, compounded the popular appeal of such accounts. Indeed, by the 1820s there were special anthologies and popular periodicals devoted to highlighting the horrors of captivity. (Sha'ban, 1991: 76–81)

It was much too facile in such accounts to portray the innocent, God-fearing Christian being brutalized by 'Muslim barbarians' and bloodthirsty infidels. John Foss's (1798) journal, a widely circulated account of his captivity in Algiers, is full of such stories. In his tearful preamble to the reader he anticipated that

The tears of sympathy will flow from the humane and feeling, at the tale of the hardships and sufferings of their unfortunate fellow countrymen, who had the misfortune to fall into the hands of the Algerines – whose tenderest mercies towards Christian captivities are the most extreme cruelties. (Foss, 1798: 2)

If and when Christians were involved in such acts, they were either depicted as hapless victims or glamorized in the heroic exploits of valiant naval commanders avenging the blood of patriotic Americans. William Ray's (1821) collection of poems, another popular anthology of the period, evokes such images. In eloquent rhymed verse, he speaks of the 'unspeakable tortures' inflicted by the 'infidel' and implores the powers of justice to awaken on behalf of the valiant Westerners, scions of 'immortal Washington', and to wreak vengeance on 'Moslem despotism'. (Ray, 1821: 78–91)

The dark and damning attitudes towards Muslims were not universally held. In the case of a mild and reticent few, their first exposure prompted them to entertain more charitable views of the so-called barbarians of the Barbary Coast. Sympathetic men of letters began, at least, to suggest that certain attributes of Islam commanded respect, or, in the language of today, deserved a more even-handed treatment.

Of note here is Royall Tyler's *The Algerine Captive* (1797), a fictional portrait of the captivity of Dr Updike Underhill at the end of the eighteenth century. This is a truly remarkable and intuitive treatment of the encounter between Islam and Christianity, way ahead of its time and quite ingenious and prophetic in prefiguring a more reconciliatory and less belligerent dialogue between the two. Though Tyler's overall perspective is fundamentally supportive of American Protestantism, he was not an uncritical admirer of the Puritan zeal, fanaticism and Southern bigotry he experienced while growing up in the New World.

In the first part of the book, interlaced with snippets from his childhood, education, travels and encounters with public figures like Benjamin Franklin, we are offered lurid, satirical, often sardonic details of Southern aristocratic debauchery, anti-intellectualism, religious decadence and inhumanity towards slaves. In the second, Tyler does not fail to expose the cruelty of Dr Underhill's Muslim captors. To Dr Underhill, however (who sounds like a fictional characterization of Tyler), many aspects of Islam – its system of justice, the fundamental doctrines of faith, Muhammad's personal merits, circumstances associated with its emergence and growth – seemed admirable. Indeed, they contrasted favourably with conditions in Europe. Piracy, for example, was seen as reprehensible, but its existence was taken to be the result of unenlightened European policy.

In an emerging dialogue with the 'Mollah' (another fictional character), Tyler manages, with considerable subtlety, to highlight the traditional Western polemics with Islam. Both the protagonist, as Christian slave, and his adversary (the Mollah) debate their faiths ardently. Two excerpts, dealing with two popular misconceptions of Islam, namely its alleged belligerence and its sensuality, are worth quoting in full:

Author   Our religion was disseminated in peace; yours was promulgated by the sword.

Mollah   My friend, you surely have not read the writings of your own historians. The history of the Christian church is a detail of bloody massacre; from the institution of the Christian thundering legion under Constantine the Great, to the expulsion of the Moors out of Spain by ferocious Inquisition, or the dragooning of the Hugenots from France under Louis the Great. The Mussulmans never yet forced a man to adopt their faith. When Abubeker the caliph took a Christian city, he forbore to enter a principal church, because he would be led to pray in any temple dedicated to God; and wherever he prayed, the building would be established as a mosque by the piety of the faithful. The companions and successors of the apostle conquered cities and kingdoms, like other nations. They gave civil laws to the conquered, according the laws of nations; but they never forced the conscience to any man. It is true, they then, and we now, when a slave pronounces the ineffable creed, immediately knock off his fetters and receive him as a brother; because we read in the book of Zuni that the souls of true believers are bound up in one fragrant bundle of eternal love. We leave it to the Christians of the West Indies, and Christians of your southern plantations, to baptize the unfortunate African into your faith, and then use your brother Christians as brutes of the desert.

Here I was so abashed for my country, I could not answer him.

Author   But you hold a sensual paradise.
Mollah   So the doctors of your church tell you; but a sensual heaven is no more imputable to us than to you. When the Most Holy condescends to reveal himself to man in human language, it must be in terms commensurate with our conception. The enjoyment of the houri, those immortal virgins who will attend the beatified believer, the splendid pavilions of the heavens, are all by types and significations of holy joys too sublime for man in flesh to conceive of. In your Bible, I read, your prophet refers to the time when he should drink new wine in his father's kingdom. Now would it be candid in me to hastily brand the heaven of your prophet as sensual, and to represent your faithful in bliss as a club of wine-bibbers? (Tyler, 1797)

Alas, such redeeming views of Islam or other faiths were not very common at the time. A few other voices, particularly during America's troublesome encounters with the Barbary states, entertained equally indulgent attitudes. Joel Barlow, for example, another noted poet and essayist, admired the pirates' maritime principles of public law. They appeared to him 'more rational, and approaching nearer to civilization, than those of Europe' (as quoted by Field 1969: 39).

Tyler's views stand out because they reveal both a grounded knowledge of Islam and its basic tenets and a familiarity with the Western literature on the subject. For example, he prefaces his chapter on the Religion of the Algerine by stating that

This fortunate impostor [i.e. 'Mahommet'], like all other great characters in the drama of life, has been indignantly vilified by his opponents, and as ardently praised by his adherents. I shall endeavour to steer the middle course of impartiality; neither influenced by the bigoted aversion of Sale and Prideaux, or the specious praise of the *philosophic* Boulainvilliers. (Tyler, 1797: 129–30)

A Quintessential Protestant Orientalist: H. H. Jessup
That New England emissaries, particularly the pioneering generations, should uphold these views and invoke them so ardently in sanctifying their 'sacred errand' into the 'degenerative Orient' is not surprising, given the prevalent temper and popular misconceptions of the day. As indicated earlier, what is remarkable is the survival of such distorted views and the way in which they were sustained and reconfirmed over the years.

Henry Harris Jessup is exemplary and perhaps unrivalled in this regard. Throughout his 53 years in Syria and Lebanon (1857–1910), at a time of swift societal transformations and behavioural change, he tenaciously refused to part with or modify his first images of the Levant or his evangelistic perspective. Whether he was deploring the 'spirit of intolerance' in Islam, its 'gross immorality', the 'destruction of the family through polygamy and concubinage', 'degradation of women', etc., he invariably ended up avowing or vindicating his claims that (1) Muslims are engrossed in error and sin and destitute of any possibility of human redemption, (2) whatever virtues Islam might have are all derivatives of Christianity and Judaism, and (3) Muslims can be saved only through the Gospel. (Jessup, 1910: 768)

In 1879 in a keynote address before the General Assembly of the Presbyterian Church at Saratoga Springs, he considered the unfavourable features inherent in Islam that were bound to affect missionary ventures adversely. Despite his uninterrupted residence in Beirut, his extensive contacts and active participation in benevolent grass-roots activities, Jessup still asserted the gulf between morality and religion. 'The good works of Islam are of the lips, the hand and the outward bodily act, having no connection with holiness of life, honesty, veracity and integrity.' (Jessup, 1879: 29)

> There is no precept in the Koran enjoining love to enemies. It teaches kindness, charity and forgiveness of injuries, but only to Mohammedans. It knows nothing of universal benevolence . . . Mohammed offered to men their choice of three things – *Islam, slavery* or *death*. (Jessup, 1879: 30)

He concludes his discussion of intolerance by claiming that 'whenever Islam holds the sword it uses it for the oppression and humiliation of all infidels, but when it loses the military control it submits with fatalistic sullenness. (Jessup, 1879: 34)

When decrying the degrading, repressive measures and corporal punishments, such as wife-beating, to which women were subjected, he had this to say:

> It is asserted that the hareem of the sultan Abdu-ul-Medjid numbered not less than one thousand women and girls, who were, as all Moslem women are,

uneducated, profane, slanderous, capricious, never trained to control their tempers or their tongues for a moment. One can imagine the moral and social condition of a woman in such a home, or such a caricature of a home. The rod, the scourge, is the only instrument of discipline. Women are treated like animals, and behave like animals. (Jessup, 1879: 45)

Occasionally he provided evidence to indicate how Muslim men were beginning to relax their restrictions on and degrading treatment of women (thanks incidentally to the largesse and education offered by foreign missionaries), only to renege a few paragraphs later.

It has begun to be done in Syria. From the days of Mrs Sarah L. Smith to the present time, Moslem girls have been taught to read and write and sew, and there are many now learning in the various American, British and Prussian schools. But it will be long before any true idea of the dignity of woman enters the debased minds of Arab Mohammedans. The simple fact is that there is no moral purity or elevation among the men, and how can it be expected among the women. (Jessup, 1879: 17)

Ironically, although Jessup reviled Muslims for their 'hatred of other sects', he himself reserved his most acrimonious and wrathful sentiments to lambast the wickedness and treachery of other nominal Christians, particularly Maronites and other so-called 'black-frocked' priesthoods of the uniate churches affiliated to Rome. His rancorous prose is often shockingly vile, hardly befitting an honoured and revered clergyman.

As donkeys have a world-wide reputation for stupidity, it is eminently proper to set the Syrian priests next in order, for, with rare exceptions, they are marvels of ignorance . . . And they are not only ignorant, but many of them are very vicious men . . . Only a few out of the hundred in Syria have any education. School children in America know more of arithmetic and geography and Bible history than almost any Greek priest in Syria; for they are chosen generally, not from among the graduates of schools, but from among the lowest people. (Jessup, 1874: 136–37)

Jessup not only reviles the ignorance and treachery of priests but also berates the holy places and sacred rituals. Even the melodious calls of the *mu'adhdin* for prayer are dismissed as a form of yelling to chase evil spirits away!

The Syrian Christianity, moreover, so often alluded to in the history of the Syrian Mission, is the lowest type of the religion of the Greek and Roman churches. Saint-worship and picture-worship are universal. An ignorant priesthood, and a superstitious people, no Bibles, and no readers to read them, no schools and no teachers capable of conducting them, prayers in unknown tongues, and a bitter feeling of party spirit in all the sects, universal belief in the efficacy of fasts and vows, pilgrimages and offerings to the shrines of reputed saints, churches without a preached gospel, and prayers performed as a duty without the worship of the heart, universal Mariolatry, a Sabbath desecrated by priests and people alike, God's name everywhere profaned by men, women, and children, and truthfulness of lip almost absolutely unknown; the women and girls degraded and oppressed and left to the tender mercies of a corrupt clergy through the infamies of the confessional; all these practices and many others which space forbids us to mention, combined with the social bondage entailed upon woman by the gross code of Islam, rendered the women of the nominal Christian sects of Syria almost as hopeless subjects of missionary labour as were their less favoured Druze and Moslem sisters. (Jessup, 1873: 46).

The natives not only laugh at the priests and men who are connected with their holy places, but they ridicule and despise the holy places themselves, even though they are too superstitious to give them up. The great thing with the sheikhs who keep them is the *piastres* they make from the visitors; while the people visit them for the sake of some magic good or charm they suppose is in them. They go to them to be cured of sickness, just as they hire men to go to the mosques to sing by the hour, in a sort minor chant, the 'Praise of Mohammed's Mother', or to yell with all their lungs from the top of the mosque to drive away the evil. (Jessup, 1873: 142–43)

What is disheartening about Jessup's treatment is not only the wild dogmatic assertions he makes (mostly anecdotal and episodic in character), but also the way he collates and substantiates evidence in support of his bigoted views. For example, on an excursion to the Cedars of Lebanon, taken in September 1886, he encountered the proverbial village *natûr* (watchman to protect vineyards, orchards and estates against trespassers and wild beasts), a guide and playful village boys. This is what he recorded in the booklet commemorating the excursion.

The Syrian Nattûr is a privileged character . . . He is not only a Nattûr, but a Maronite, and not only a Maronite, but a B'sherreh Maronite. He has a powerful brawny, physical frame, carries a huge club with a double-barrelled shot-gun, and a dagger in his belt. He magnifies his office. When you ask for a favour, he is domineering and insolent. When he thinks you care nothing for him, he is cringing and suppliant . . . Lying seemed his nature. (Jessup, 1886: 78)

When the young boy who had volunteered to guide Jessup's party through the historic Cedar grove demanded reimbursement for his services, Jessup's reaction was characteristically offensive and condescending.

I then threw him a *bishlik*, which I had intended all along to give him, when they both began to curse our party, asking *Allah* to bring disaster to us all. This is a characteristic of Arab beggars. They pray for all the blessings upon you as long as they expect charity, but if disappointed, they hurl after you the vilest epithets and awful imprecations. A Maronite stands about at the bottom of the scale of Syrian moral degradation, and the Papal Confessional, an ignorant priesthood, and the destruction of moral distinctions have brought these wretched people to their present condition. The Lord have mercy on them! (Jessup, 1886: 80)

This same anecdotal style pervaded most of the portraits and inferences Jessup drew from his treatment of *Syrian Home-Life* (1874), a widely circulated monograph on socio-cultural conditions, family life and folklore, interlaced with his trite stereotypes on 'ignorance', 'lying', 'priestly craft', and 'corrupt faith' and other foibles of nominal Christians. Here as elsewhere in much of his virulent writing, Jessup is rarely nuanced or elliptic. Indeed, he introduces his chapters with unabashed, blatant assertions deduced often from no more than random encounters. Such unstructured, situational personal events, often derivative of some chance occurrence attributed to others, became the basis for reconfirming a generalized image or misrepresentation. Instances of this kind of tendentious writing are legion. A few striking examples will suffice.

As for ignorance, it is like people, like priest. It would astonish a schoolboy to hear of the blunders and lack of knowledge shown by even those who are considered learned. Comets, eclipses, meteors, and all unusual sights in the sky, are looked upon by the majority of the people as portents dire and terrible, produced by some malign spirit, who thus seeks to foretell wars, pestilence, and famine. But men and women who have been educated and instructed in the Bible, have learned to look with satisfaction and delight upon these phenomena, and by their calmness, and evident interest, disarm the fears of their less intelligent neighbours. (Jessup, 1874: 145)

Note how Jessup sneaks in one of his pet themes, namely, how those touched by the Bible become more privileged, not only by enjoying the delights of the cosmos but also by ridding themselves of the fears that plague their 'less intelligent neighbours'.

The chapter on 'the lying' also begins with another sweeping allegation.

As might be conjectured from many foregoing stories, it is a fact that all classes, Moslem, heathen, or minimal Christians are wonderfully given to lying . . . an old man in Beirut once said, in confidence to a foreigner, 'Sir, you must be careful what you believe, and whom to trust, in this country. If there are twenty-four inches of hypocrisy in the world, twenty-three are in Syria . . .' And the Syrians lie by deed as well as word. The missionaries are often greatly puzzled as to how to deal with those who come making openly most earnest professions by faith in the true religion, though, as is generally discovered, it is with a secret desire and plan to gain some selfish or wicked end, to escape from punishment for crime, or to obtain office or power, or to be married to some improper person. (Jessup, 1874: 202–4)

He applies the same rhetoric in his discussion of superstition. When he was not deriding the festive religious rites of Maronites and their monasteries as 'abodes of treachery, dark stories and scenes of the most infamous profligacy and horrible cruelty', (Jessup, 1874: 164) he was taunting the 'Bedawins' for their superstitious approach to death as manifestations of ignorance and fear.

> Among the Bedawins, when a man dies he is buried in any convenient place. The funeral service consists of a recital of the virtues of the deceased, an essential part of which is, 'He was a good man: he could steal by moonlight and in the dark'. (Jessup: 1874: 165)

His analysis of insincerity is even more bizarre and, as elsewhere, suffused with contempt and ridicule of local culture. Nothing is spared here. Nursery rhymes, love songs, popular ditties, wedding chants and eulogies are all seen as manifestations of extravagant and hypocritical sentiments. 'Very closely connected with insincerity of action', a feature that, according to Jessup, afflicted the Druzes of Mount Lebanon more than other groups, 'is the custom of using the most extravagant salutations, both in personal greetings and in letters. All Oriental salutations and protestations are valuable or valueless according to the character of the person who uses them. (Jessup 1874: 208)

The remedy to all this is the telegraph, that quintessential marvel of Yankee ingenuity.

> The use of the telegraph is teaching the Syrians brevity in their addresses. When they write letters they use long titles, and flowery salutations, so that a whole page will be taken up with these empty formalities, leaving only a few lines at the end or in a postscript, for the important business. But when they send a telegram and have to pay for every word, they leave out the flowery salutations, and send only what is necessary. (Jessup, 1874: 211)

Even the camel, the Arab's most favoured and functional beast of burden is contemptuously ridiculed:

> There is a popular fallacy in the West that camels are most patient and peaceful and gentle in their ways. And when they are tied up together in a long caravan, with a little mouse-coloured donkey leading the van, ridden by a long-legged Bedawy, who sits half-asleep smoking his pipe, one might well think them the tamest and most innocent creatures in the world; but when they fall into a panic, they are beyond all control, and then the safest place is that which is farthest off. (Jessup, 1874: 128)

In assessing the devastated state of the country after the civil strife of 1860 he attributed all that 'dark and sin' to virtually everybody but in particular to that 'atrocious and mercenary priesthood'.

> The lives of these people correspond to their corrupted faith. The monastic clergy are notoriously vile: As for the masses, a summary justice has made crimes against the law of the State less frequent, perhaps, than in some parts of

Europe. But as the power of the Sultan is weakening, crime is increasing, and in some parts of the provinces, where anarchy gives license, the condition of things is fearful; while *everywhere* theft, lying, profaneness, and sensuality prevail beyond all ordinary conception. (Jessup, 1874: 356–57)

Even the bitter enmity of the 'Mohammedans' and their unreceptivity to the disinterested benevolence of American missionaries is blamed on the 'idolatrous parodies of Christianity in the East'.

What makes it harder to work among the Moslems is, that they have seen the false, idolatrous parodies of Christianity in the East, so long, that they think one denomination claiming the name of Christ is just as bad as the rest. The Greeks and Maronites worship pictures and images, and pray to the Virgin Mary and to saints, and the Moslems think all Christians do the same. But since they have been able to look into Protestant Churches, and see there no idols, and especially since they have heard the Word of God in simplicity preached and read in their own tongue, they have begun to think there is a difference. (Jessup, 1874: 177)

Of course, on the final day of reckoning, the missionaries would carry the day.

The missionaries, by their evident disinterestedness, their fearless devotion to the good of others amid the horrors of disastrous earthquakes, or the more subtle dangers of contagion and malignant treachery, have won the entire confidence of multitudes of their professed enemies; death-bed confessions have shown this. (Jessup, 1874: 363)

By 1906, just four years before he passed away, Jessup was still upholding the same medievalist mindset, with all the unflattering images, that he had carried over with him from New England half a century earlier. The occasion this time was the first missionary conference 'on behalf of the Mohammedan World', held in Cairo. Jessup was, once again, honoured to deliver the keynote address. In reviewing the published proceedings, W. Tisdall praised the volume as a 'great step in advancing our knowledge toward the evangelization of the Mohammedan' because, as he claimed, for the first time 'we are not now dependent on the casual impressions made on the globe-trotter, but are enabled at first-hand to consult men who know these lands well, and have spent many years in close and friendly contact with the people of whom they write.' (Jessup, 1874)

Alas, one sees little auspicious evidence of such close and friendly contact. Jessup, instead, was still bemoaning, as he had done repeatedly on earlier occasions, the 'spiritual destitution of Islam', 'the evils of polygamy, the seclusion of women, facility of divorce and hatred of other sects'. (Jessup, 1874) He also reiterated his beloved theme that whatever was virtuous in Islam, insubstantial as it may be, was borrowed from Christianity. Everything else remained steeped in 'vital doctrinal error and corrupting social and moral teachings'. He then concludes that Muslims were destined to remain 'lost sinners' unless redeemed through Jesus Christ.

> In general, Mohammedans need what all men need – salvation through Jesus Christ. They need to feel their need as lost sinners. This is what they almost universally fail to experience. Their conceit, arising from the old Semitic or Judaistic idea of their essential superiority to all other men, is a serious obstacle to their acceptance of the Christian faith. (Jessup, 1874)

CHAPTER 7

On Doing Much with Little Noise

Early Encounters of Protestant Missionaries in Lebanon

On a crisp Sabbath evening in October 1819, Pliny Fisk preached his last sermon to a packed and deeply moved congregation in Old South Church in Boston. The occasion was solemn, charged with emotion. An air of excitement befitting the extraordinary circumstances surrounded the event. He and his colleague, Levi Parsons, were embarking the next day as missionaries for western Asia with the intention of establishing a permanent station at Jerusalem.

His farewell was sombre.

> The time has arrived, when we are called by the Providence of God, if its language is not altogether misunderstood, to leave the scenes of our childhood, and the country that is blessed, beyond any other country under heaven, with civil and religious privileges; not to find other privileges and friends like them in another land; but to meet the uncertainties and difficulties, attendant on a Christian mission among Turks and Jews. If any circumstances can affect the mind in health, as it is affected by a near prospect of death, it is perhaps thus affected with the prospect of leaving for life all who have ever been known, and all that has ever been seen. This prospect brings eternity near. It excites solicitude respecting that meeting, which shall be an eternal meeting, or a prelude to eternal separation. (Bond, 1828: 95–6)

A day earlier, in an equally charged encounter, he paid last tributes to his home town, Shelburne, Massachusetts. There, too, he delivered an affectionate farewell address and took leave of his aged father, family and friends, expecting to see their faces no more.

Scenes of this sort were still rare at the time. In fact, only seven years earlier, in February 1812, the seaport town of Salem, Massachusetts, witnessed the first such solemn spectacle. On that occasion, five young men were ordained as 'missionaries to the heathen in Asia'. Then, as on subsequent occasions, prominent ministers of New England churches would officiate the sacrament by laying their hands on the heads of the kneeling young recruits, who would then be given 'instructions' on behalf of the Prudential Committee of the American Board of Commissioners for Foreign Missions (ABCFM). The departing recruits would then deliver to an intent and sober audience their own justifications for embarking on such missions.

The novelty and extraordinariness of such events attracted the curiosity of large crowds. Memoirs and accounts of the day attest to this. Throngs from adjacent towns, particularly students from Andover Theological Seminary and the Philips Academy, flocked to partake in the ceremonies and bid their adventurous and heroic colleagues adieu.

Much has been written to elucidate the origin and consequences of this 'sacred errand' and how it evolved into a proselytizing ethos, particularly by way of reconfirming the connection between New England Puritanism and this longing for overseas missions.[1] Despite divergent viewpoints and perspectives, there is agreement in much of the voluminous literature regarding the nature and defining elements of this evangelistic imagination and how it served to inspire generations of young militant idealists to become envoys to so-called 'darker' and 'alien' regions of the heathen world. So impassioned were the young zealots (mostly graduates of Andover and colleges such as Amherst, Dartmouth, Yale, Princeton, Williams) that they often welcomed the prospects of breaking away from the quiet, serene provincialism of their New England towns, denying themselves the security of family and friends to risk the perilous journey into the forbidding and often unexplored regions of the world. Only a few of the early recruits, after all, made it back or survived long enough to reap the fruits of their labour. The rest perished without 'seeing the light', their lives cut short by the hazards of travel, disease or persecution. Yet this missionizing, evangelistic spirit caught on. It was fuelled among other things by the heroic tragedies of the pioneers, and evolved into 'an expansionist and proselytizing ethos', a form of 'colonial evangelism' with far-reaching consequences for the cultures it attempted to subject and transform. (Beidelman, 1982: 4–5)

The literature also reveals a few other striking features that account for the remarkable and often unintended accomplishments of New England Puritanism as a cultural transplant. The early envoys were so passionate about their 'exalted calling' that they had little or no ambivalence as to what they were to export or what was the source of their sacred errand. To them the world out there was all equally a dark and 'ruined' 'wilderness' in urgent need of moral regeneration. They

---

1.   See, among these, David Bosch, *Transforming Missions: Paradigm Shifts in Theology of Missions* (New York: Orbis Books, 1991); W. R. Hutchison, *Errand to the World: American Protestant Thought and Foreign Missions* (Chicago: University of Chicago Press, 1987); O. W. Elsbree, 'The Rise of the Missionary Spirit in New England, 1780–1815', in *The New England Quarterly*, vol. 1. (1928) pp. 296–322; R. H. Gabriel 'Evangelical Religion and Popular Romanticism in Early 19th Century America', in *Church History,* vol. XIX (March, 1950), pp. 34–37; C. J. Phillips, *Protestant America and the Pagan World* (Cambridge, MA: Harvard East Asian Monograph, 1969); T. O. Beidelman, *Colonial Evangelism* (Bloomington: Indiana University Press, 1982).

were also imbued with an abiding faith in the superiority of American Protestantism and the New World as a righteous republic. At least to them it seemed like the closest ever to a 'New Jerusalem'. As New Englanders, in particular, they thought of themselves as God's 'choicest grain' of the most 'privileged garden'.

To Fisk and Parsons, like many of the early stalwarts of New England evangelism, this moral crusade assumed at times the rhetoric of cultural penetration; an impulse to colonize and besiege so-called empires of sin. They were also far from ambivalent about their perceptions and images of Islam and the Levant. The inadequate state of knowledge of the former notwithstanding, Fisk and Parsons appear to have carried with them many of the disparaging epithets and warped stereotypes that were current at that time. Indeed, they were driven by two seemingly contradictory sets of impressions. First, they held the same contemptuous view of Islam, often defiling Muhammad as an 'artful impostor' and his creed as a 'fortress of error and sin'. They expressed equally disdainful views of all the other forces of anti-Christ and the 'deluded' emissaries of the pope. Second, they also carried with them the more charitable but romanticized and idealized images of the Orient and the Levant as exotic places of mystery and wonder.

Despite the austere, cold ferocity of New England Calvinism, it demonstrated a remarkable ability to redefine itself, appear in many guises and adapt to the exigencies of changing and divergent cultural settings. Indeed, although Puritanism had a special predilection for stable institutions and cohesive communities, it thrived best, as a score of intellectual historians have noted, as an itinerant culture. As it moved, it managed to evolve and metamorphose into a plurality of forms.[1]

Of all field stations they attempted to establish in the eastern Mediterranean (and within two decades after their entry into the region, the ABCFM had already set up missions in western Turkey, Syria and western regions of Persia), the 'Syrian' mission (roughly Lebanon today) came to occupy a special place in the hopes and aspirations of New England missionaries. Intentionally or otherwise, their inroads into Lebanon turned out to be the most seminal and far-reaching in terms of the socio-cultural transformations that they generated in the lives of the people they touched. Indeed, largely because of the formidable obstacles and promises of myriads of unforeseen opportunities they encountered, the mission to Lebanon came to acquire a mystique of its own. In the annals of world evangelism, it was referred to as the 'romance land of missions'. It was also there that the ABCFM was compelled to redefine its objectives and experiment with various 'instrumentalities' to meet the ever-changing political and socio-cultural exigencies that they faced in the Levant.

This chapter considers the salient features of New England Puritanism as a cultural transplant. By focusing on its initial encounters in Lebanon (1820–40), a period marked by chronic political unrest and hostility towards or even outright persecution of missionary incursions, it is hoped to highlight the strategies that the

---

1. Chad Powers Smith, *Yankees and God* (New York: Heritage House, 1954), p. 29. Forrest Wood, *The Arrogance of Faith* (New York: A. A. Knopf, 1990), p. 252; Winthrop Hudson, *American Protestantism* (Chicago: University of Chicago Press, 1961), p. 23.

envoys marshalled in support of unobtrusive and non-confrontational forms of cultural penetration.

I have in Chapter 5 explored the fortuitous circumstances that diverted the original Palestine mission to Lebanon and how, in the early days, the pioneers, largely by trial and error, modified and redirected their original objectives. (Khalaf, 1997) The intention here is to focus more concretely on some of their efforts, particularly those that were instrumental in reinforcing the shift in their perspectives towards the more cautionary and less intrusive measures of cultural change.

We shall focus first on some of the often inventive and canny activities with which the pioneering novices experimented, particularly through common schools and female education and outreach programmes. Secondly, we shall briefly consider some of the relentless setbacks and obstacles that they faced and how they started to adjust their strategies accordingly. Finally, we shall deal with the cultural inroads made by introducing some silent and unobtrusive forms of evangelism.

Common Schools, Female Education and Outreach

By the time the missionaries started converging on Beirut in the fall of 1823, barely three years after they had landed in Smyrna, they had already reformulated part of their initial intentions. They also began to be more certain about the direction that their labour should take and the strategies that they ought to consider.

Based on their initial explorations, Fisk and Parsons arrived at the view that the most favourable course of action lay in the distribution of tracts and books. Since so many were already literate, efforts should be directed at a general distribution of the printed word. Hence a press was urgently recommended. Deficiency in language also precluded direct preaching. The most urgent task then was to establish 'common schools' in which young people could come under their influence. This also coincided with the 'instructions' that they had received; namely, that they might engage pupils at their own residences. Such informal, unobtrusive activites were deemed desirable since they were less likely to excite jealousy or opposition.

In fact, the first such school dates back to April 1824, when Bird and Goodell, the first two married missionaries, assembled a group of seven 'Arab children' in their joint residence. They were fed, clothed and taught the alphabet, mostly by the wives, who did as best they could after their brief exposure to Arabic. Though this is often heralded as the first school established by the missionaries in the Levant, this arrangement could hardly have amounted to more than sheltering neglected children in the neighbourhood or those of the domestics and orderlies employed by the mission. By July of the same year, however, the number rose to almost 50. More promising, some of the students were advanced enough to require more proficient instruction than the missionaries could offer. A native teacher, Tannus Haddad, was hired to assist.

Within about a year, by July 1825, the number of students had increased to 80 or 90, thus requiring larger accommodation. For a 'trifling rent', a house within the city walls was secured, large enough to accommodate the school, the teacher and his family. 'Our hopes,' wrote Bird, 'were quite sanguine that this removal from the suburb to the town, would considerably increase this school.' (*Missionary Herald*, vol. XXI, 1825: 272) The instant success of the school went beyond their expectations, and it became necessary to hire a writing master. Students were all 'Arabs' ranging in age from five to 15, including two girls, one the 15–year-old wife of the teacher and the other girl aged about ten. As would be expected, the bulk of the students (about 90 per cent) were Greek Orthodox. The rest were drawn equally from other sects: three Muslims, two Maronites and two Greek Catholics.

Modest as it was, the 'school', because of its novelty, was bound to invite curiosity and, often, wild conjecture. Many were intrigued as to what these singularly odd-looking strangers from a distant and unfamiliar continent, were doing in the back alleys of their city, and why! (*Missionary Herald*, 1825: XXI, 271–72)

The background and scholastic qualifications of the students did not impress Mr Bird very much. 'These children were running about the streets in all sorts of mischief; and almost as ignorant as the beasts of the field.' In another letter, this time from Bird and Goodell, they spoke charitably of the progress that they had made, particularly in repeating the Scripture. The students were even compared favourably with their counterparts in New England, although they did not originally display the quickness characteristic of Greeks. (*Missionary Herald*, 1825: XXI, 380)

Inclined as the missionaries often were to exaggerate the success of their labour, they were this time legitimately buoyed by swift and demonstrable evidence. They used the same strategy in establishing a succession of other schools. By 1827 they had a total of thirteen with about 600 students. In fact the model of the first school in Beirut was used as a prototype to expand and multiply 'common schools' in surrounding villages. In Beirut, itself, however, they were more inventive and started to experiment with a variety of schools, almost akin to adult education, extension or outreach programmes, to meet special emergent needs.

For example, in September 1825 Fisk engaged Assad Shidiaq[1] to teach Arabic grammar. The idea for such a venture had in fact been entertained by Jonas King, who argued that proficiency in grammar, indispensable for understanding the Scriptures in Arabic, was almost a preserve of Muslims; hardly a reliable source for sharing this knowledge with or instructing native Christians. The other source, the Maronite College at Ayn Waraqa, was accessible only to those planning to enter the priesthood. Both King and Fisk also correctly anticipated that such a special school could meet the growing demand for language instruction from European travellers and traders. Unfortunately, shortly after its establishment, Shidiaq was compelled to abandon his post because of mounting pressure from the Maronite patriarch. The work was, however, continued under others.

Another novel example of an outreach activity was the school Bird operated to

---

1. Shidiaq, doubtless the most celebrated native convert and victim of Protestantism, was himself a graduate of Ayn Waraqa and had taught Arabic to King, who first discovered the precious gifts of the young scholar and must have played a role in his momentous conversion.

teach Italian to about 30 students. Italian was considered to be the lingua franca of commerce in the Levant. Already a growing number of the privileged urban bourgeoisie had displayed interest in enhancing their proficiency in this highly valued language. Bird capitalized on this need. Since the New Testament was the basic book he used, he naturally hoped to extend Christian truth to this rather unusual but influential segment of the population. Most of the young men who attended the daily two-hour sessions were either businessmen or those who served as interpreters. (Tibawi, 1963: 147) Other efforts were also made to reach presumably accessible communities such as Jews and Armenians.

A more imaginative activity, also inspired by the wish to reach unusual segments of the population, was Goodell's work with the beggars of Beirut. Writing from there (February 2, 1825) he informed the Board that he had 'recently commenced giving public religious instruction to the beggars . . . The poor, the lame, the halt and the blind . . . whose external appearance is but a faint image of their moral wretchedness'. What is astonishing was the manipulative means he chose to dispense his Christian benevolence. (*Missionary Herald*, 1825: 273)

Of all the socio-cultural transformations associated with the missionaries, they should, doubtless, be given credit for their pioneering work in women's education. The early decades of the nineteenth century in New England were characterized by the struggle for women's emancipation. The ardent missionaries must have carried over with them this consciousness of legitimate women's rights. They were also duly alarmed by what they initially saw as manifestations of women's subjugation and abuse. In fact, they reserved the greatest scorn and condemnation for those held accountable for the neglect and ill-treatment of women. No one was spared: the culture that debased women, servile men and, above all, the corrupt and contemptible priests. Women were nothing but pitiful victims; a 'disgusting compound of childish ignorance, foolish superstition, impertinence, vulgarity . . .' (*Missionary Herald*, XXX, 1834: 128) was salient in the degradation of the rest of society and the system of patriarchy that perpetuated it. Hence, it did not surprise the missionaries to encounter so much prejudice against their education. Goodell, in his characteristic sardonic and colourful style, derides the culture and the men who continue to uphold the view that it is neither possible nor desirable to educate women.

> In the first place, it was said to be an impossible thing to teach a woman to read; and it was gravely asserted, that we might as well undertake to teach the wild asses of the desert to read, as to teach a woman. And, in the next place, it was asked, with a most triumphant air, of what possible use it could be to her to learn to read, supposing any one was found capable of it? Could she light her husband's pipe any better? Could she bring his slippers with more modesty? And as to learning to write, pray what could she or would she ever think of writing but 'love letters'. (Goodell, 1853: 89)

Jonas King, in accounting for the resistance he faced in his efforts to establish a school for girls in Tyre in 1824, assigned the blame on the decadence and degradation of the local priests, who claimed that teaching them would be fruitless.

It is by no means expedient to teach women to read the word of God. It is better for them to remain in ignorance, than to know how to read and write. They are quite bad enough with what little they now know. Teach them to read and write, and there would be no living with them. (*Missionary Herald,* 1827: XXIII, 33)

Very early they recognized the urgency and need to educate women, who needed to be rescued. Since no one had deemed it vital to do anything on their behalf, the minds of the luckless native girls were 'as vacant as space . . . and as lawless as the sea'. Goodell went on to declare that 'I do not recollect to have seen a single female in this country who can read, except those instructed by us.' (Goodell, *Missionary Herald*, 1825: 271)

Given the public outcry against women's education, they also thought it was prudent to begin quietly and informally. Hence, they experimented with a two-pronged system. In addition to establishing separate schools in which girls received formal instruction, they also introduced an arrangement that allowed them to 'adopt' girls into their own families. As will be seen, this was a precursor to the establishment of special boarding schools for girls.

Here as well, the missionaries were amazed by their instant success. From two girls who were attending the common schools on an irregular basis in 1824, the number leaped to 120 by 1827; this constituted 20 per cent of a total enrolment of about 600. The instruction that they received in the new schools and the mixed background of the students were consistent with the missionary objectives. The records for 1835 of one such school, run by Mrs Smith, reveal 40 students, although only half were attending. Of those, ten were Muslim, two were Jewish, one Druze and the remainder Christian. (Hooker, 1839: 269)

The scheme for adopting girls to be brought up in American homes was also motivated by the desire to 'save the souls of such depraved and benighted creatures'. Care was taken, at least as justified by Mrs Smith, not to 'Europeanize' the girls. Otherwise they would lose their native identity and become misfits or outcasts in their own society. The adopted girls dressed in native clothes and their place in the household was 'midway in rank between a servant and daughter'. She was not allowed to associate with servants lest she be 'contaminated'. The same concern for her 'purity' restricted visits and contacts with her family. She was permitted only one night at home every year. Equally remarkable was the stern discipline that the girls were compelled to observe in fulfilling their duties and in their personal deportment and conduct. All the austere puritanical habits of work, industry, punctuality and cleanliness were strictly observed and monitored. The ultimate objectives were order, discipline and 'perfect subordination'.

Their daily routine was devoted to all kinds of domestic labour and acquisition of practical skills such as sewing, needlework and personal hygiene. Much of it, of course, went into religious instruction, reading in the Scripture and familiarity with Sunday sermons. Mrs Smith was, after all, an ardent believer in education as 'the incipient step to enlighten females . . . and to transform the Levant from the government of Satan to that of Christ'. (Hooker, 1839: 279)

The adopted girls were also expected to assist their surrogate mothers with their day schools. This activity became ultimately vital in training the core of 'native helpers' who provided the much-needed assistance in running the proliferating number of boarding schools, which were the outgrowth of this venture. Of course all the missionary wives had volunteered their services: Eliza Thomson, Martha Dodge, Salome Carabet (Mrs Wortabet), Hanne Wortabet (Mrs Richards) and Mrs Whiting were soon supplemented by special recruits such as Rebecca Williams (1835), Betsey Tilden (1839) and Ann Whittlesey (1851) who were among the first single women to join the mission in Syria. Their contribution allowed a lengthening and broadening of the curriculum.

In both types of schools the underlying religious character of education was pronounced. Indeed, in 1836 the missionary wives launched another outreach programme to supplement their proselytizing, which involved making repeated selective visits to mothers in their own homes. According to Mrs Smith, such visits also became colourful spectacles, attracting the curiosity of neighbourhood crowds. Her account also reveals how determined and instrumental she was in delivering the message of the Scriptures. Just as Goodell enticed his beggars with a loaf of bread, Mrs Smith gave each of her visitors a piece of cloth to make an infant's dress! (Hooker, 1839: 327–29)

In no time the demand for schools caught on like wildfire. The missionaries were hard pressed to meet this growing interest. One strategy they resorted to, especially in remote villages, was to engage a teacher to open a school and then arrange to pay him a monthly salary based on average attendance. Such arrangements inevitably invited some abuses, since it was not always possible to ascertain the actual number of students who appeared regularly, let alone the quality of instruction or education they were receiving.[1] On the whole, however, the standards of the schools and their accomplishments drew envious praise. They became models eagerly requested and emulated elsewhere. For example, at Hasbaya both the Greek and Druze princes so rejoiced at the prospect of having such a school in their domain that they offered to defray the cost of the house in which the school was established. (ABCFM, 1827: 46)

The assistance of the missionaries was often sought out by other provinces of the Ottoman Empire. They always obliged. The sultan, as early as 1832, had solicited the help of William Goodell in the formation of special academies for soldiers. Goodell formulated the curriculum and advised on the books and instruments to be used. Commodore Porter, who had occasion to visit the schools, expressed astonishment at the equipment, which included globes, a planetarium and models of spheres and cubes and cones for teaching solid geometry. He was also amazed at the progress made by the students in reading. (Daniel, 1964: 80)

Such auspicious beginnings were, alas, shortlived. Benign and well-meaning as some of their ventures were, they were destined to arouse the hostility of rival groups or those threatened by the rapid incursions that they were making. In fact, as early as 1824 the missionaries were already becoming restive about a mood of 'apprehension, disputation, and disturbance'. From then on their fortitude was

---

1. This arrangement also invited unavoidable disputes between the missionaries and their local agents or teachers, who, it seems, always inflated the figures. In some instances the conflict was so intense that the British consul was prevailed upon to mediate (*Missionary Herald*, XXIV (1828), p. 305).

acutely tested as they were compelled to weather a succession of unsettling obstacles and setbacks.

Obstacles and Setbacks

The year 1824 ushered in two milestones in the history of the mission. In Beirut, missionary wives opened a class for six children. In Jerusalem, the itinerant missionaries faced their first censor. The two events were not unrelated.

Until then the bulk of missionary labour had been peripatetic. Much like the classic prototype of the roving emissary, they had made exploratory trips as itinerant travellers, visitors or pilgrims. Their work consisted mainly of learning languages and distributing tracts and testaments. Indeed as 'visitors' they were received with hospitality, often mixed with wonder and amazement at these novel creatures with their strange customs, demeanour and messages. Even leaders and prominent Eastern ecclesiastics at first gave them a friendly reception. Amir Bashir, in exile in Alexandria, had urged them to visit Lebanon. A few weeks before they held their first conference at 'Ayn Turah, in the autumn of 1823, Fisk, King and Wolff called upon the Maronite Patriarch at Qannubin. There, too, they were 'civilly' received. At least this was how their reception was perceived by Fisk and Wolff in their journals. (London Jews Society, Annual Report, 1825: 79)

By then a mood of optimism had overwhelmed many of the early reports from Beirut. Some spoke of 'a wide and effectual door opening to us . . .' Others were cheered by how their 'prospects daily brighten'. These optimistic reactions soon subsided as the missionaries faced a relentless series of adversities.

The first episode, in which Bird and Fisk were arrested in February 1824 while distributing the Scriptures to Armenian pilgrims in Jerusalem, was received with shock by the Board. Their rooms were searched. Their papers were seized and they were brought before Muslim judges on the strange charge of distributing books that were neither Mohammedan, Jewish nor Christian. Like many subsequent incidents, it became the subject of incriminating accusations. Such episodes were also often exaggerated, a ploy that the missionaries put to good use to overstate the hardships that they suffered at the hands of their many 'enemies'.

In that particular instance, because it involved the two most inveterate 'antichrist' forces, namely the Ottomans and the Pope, the episode was dramatized. The Board perceived it as part of the paranoia and hostility that the papal church bore towards American Protestants and other 'Bible' people.

The arrest was just one of many forms of repressions and persecutions to which the missionaries were subjected. In Mount Lebanon the first such episode provoked a more aggressive outcry. The confluence of so many 'Bible-men' on, of all places, the heartland of Maronite land (particularly after the 'Ayn Turah conference in autumn 1823), reawakened the bitter polemics with the Eastern churches over the questionable version of the Bible, replete with errors, that was being circulated by a band of heretics and atheists. Even Amir Bashir was persuaded to issue an order evicting the missionaries from their premises at 'Ayn Turah.

The instant success of their common schools in Beirut must also have irked seemingly friendlier groups. This time it was the Greek Orthodox Patriarch of Antioch who took offence. In their report to the Board (January 11, 1825), Goodell aand Bird made reference to circulars issued by the Orthodox hierarchies against the schools and other missionary activities. The threatening tone of the circulars must have 'intimidated many parents to remove their children'.

These and other recurrent episodes of repression and persecution were chronicled in the monthly columns of the *Missionary Herald* or the Board's *Annual Reports*, not without undue and often deliberate exaggeration. In a sense, the initial hostile reaction of Eastern ecclesiastics is understandable. Few native Christians at the time, if measured by the feeble trickle of conversions, were immediately convinced of the innate superiority of Calvinistic Christianity. The patriarchs, archbishops and priests understandably regarded the American teachings as a threat to their own hegemony and a hostile invasion of their constituencies.

In some respects, though, the intimidations and outright persecutions the missionaries suffered were real enough and could not have been exaggerated. The sharpest, of course, came from the Maronite clergy. Repeated edicts pronounced 'anathema' on the missionaries and their potential converts. Maronites were not to visit or employ them, do them favours or give them salutation, nor converse with them in any form or manner. Native Christians suspected of consorting or having any dealings with the missionaries were persecuted. Their shops were boycotted. Native teachers and helpers were banished. The few women who married recent converts were excommunicated along with their families. Others were stoned in the streets, hung up by the thumbs, spat upon and struck in the face, tortured with the bastinado or imprisoned without charge or trial. (Bartlett, 1872: 104–06)

The most notorious case was the story of Assad Shidiaq, the first native martyr, who had dared to display an inclination for Protestanism. He paid dearly for it. The story of his conversion, imprisonment and ultimate death in a dungeon of a Maronite monastery has been told and retold, often in epic form. In the most commonly repeated version we are told how he was brought before the Maronite Patriarch, 'loaded with chains, cast into a dark, filthy room, and bastinadoed every day for eight days, sometimes fainting under the operation . . . He was then left in misery, his bed a thin flat mat, his covering his common clothes. The door of his prison was filled up with stones and mortar, and his food was six thin cakes of bread a day, and a cup of water . . .' (Anderson, 1872: 69)

Shidiaq's martyrdom was used by the missionaries not only to highlight the depth of their enemies' wickedness but also the fear and anxiety it had provoked. It was this fear, they argued, that prevented others favourably inclined towards Protestanism from publicly recognizing Christ. Indeed, one effusive report in the *Missionary Herald* went so far as to maintain that had Shidiaq not been imprisoned 'half of Mount Lebanon could have become Protestants'. (XXIV, 1828: 16)

The missionaries, of course, were not spared the belligerent reactions. Fisk was himself a victim of one such episode. On his way back to Beirut from Jerusalem in the spring of 1825 with a group of pilgrims, they were set upon by highwaymen. In the tumult Fisk suffered a heavy blow from a bludgeon, from which he never fully recovered. The assault must have aggravated his already enfeebled physical condition and he passed away in Beirut in October 1825. Like his departed companion, Levi Parsons, Fisk had his life cut short before he had 'seen the light'.

Although clerical opposition and other repressions were their first obstacles, in the long run the missionaries suffered setbacks of a more debilitating nature. At least three such sources can be identified: epidemics and plagues, illness and civil disturbances Lebanon's agreeable and temperate climate and its relatively healthy conditions had enhanced its appeal as a field station. The missionaries fully recognized these blissful attributes and considered themselves fortunate to have been sent there. Yet as time went on they became chronically uneasy about the poor sanitary conditions, the blustering and tempestuous elements and the prospects of illness, disease and pestilence. They wrote special detailed reports monitoring changes in weather and climatic conditions. They were naturally most apprehensive about the recurring onslaught of epidemics and plagues.

They had every reason to be concerned. In less than two decades in the field nine of their colleagues had died abroad (30 per cent) and four had given up for reasons of health. Indeed, the life span of the average missionary was comparatively short. With the exception of Fisk, who survived for nearly five years, many of the pioneers (Asa Dodge, Mrs Thompson, Mrs Smith) never made it to their third year in the field. Because of the recurrence of pestilences, scourges and less treacherous epidemics, many missionary stations were quarantined between three and six months a year. (Daniel, 1964: 82) Much of the missionaries' energies and resources were drained in efforts to protect themselves against such threats. Their circulation and daily routines were curtailed. Absenteeism among their staff and native helpers and irregular and diminished school attendance also took their toll. In a culture not too receptive to the demands of structured and disciplined activity, this could be doubly damaging. Little wonder that, no sooner had the missionaries arrived, than they started imploring, often earnestly beseeching the Board to recruit medical missionaries. A decade elapsed before their appeals were answered. Asa Dodge, the first medical missionary, arrived in Beirut in February 1833, only to die in January 1835 in Jerusalem from an unidentified disease, a victim of the perils from which he had come to protect his colleagues. His brief life was even shorter than those of Parsons and Fisk.

Perhaps the most worrying events were the local disturbances generated or provoked by international and regional rivalries. Initially, they were mostly associated with the Greek war of independence, which unleashed 'a season of war, tumult, oppression and robbery'. (Goodell, 1826: 354) In March 1828 several Greek vessels entered the port of Beirut and landed 500 men. Unable to scale the city's walls, they plundered the houses outside. The Bedouin, sent down by the Pasha of Acre to repel the attackers were 'wilder than the Greeks. They plundered within without making any distinctions . . .' (Anderson 1872: 45) All the American schools were disrupted and the missionaries took refuge in the mountains. Within a year or so, most of the schools were reopened only to suffer the setbacks of virulent clerical opposition and a renewed wave of persecutions. The ecclesiastical denunciations this time were in reaction to the admission of 16 'hopefully pious natives' into the church.[1] Maronite and Greek Catholic churches were so roused by the spectacle that they issued their 'accursed anathemas' against the missionaries and all who tried to render them any service.

Incidentally, only a few months earlier they were still writing their usual letters to the Secretary of the Board regarding their relentless yet fruitless labour. On rare occasions they were heartened when a native displayed 'an interesting state of mind' or when three of their school teachers 'acknowledged themselves to be in a state of sin'. (*Missionary Herald*, 1827: XXIII, 20) Hence they must have been much encouraged by this seeming surge of enthusiasm and were more than eager to play the occasion to the full. This only provoked the wrath and vengeance of the local clergy who renewed their 'most violent and cruel measures' to censor their activities. The repressions must have worked. Writing in 1827, the missionaries complained that 'there is no hiding place in Syria for those who are guilty of reading God's blessed book' (*Missionary Herald*, 1827: XXIII, 109) It was more poignant that Goodell was forced to go about the neighbourhood furtively and ultimately was trapped at home, rarely venturing outside. He was reluctant to appear by a window or the open doorway of his residence. Even his sleep became restless.

> During the last two years of our stay in Beirut I seldom closed my eyes in sleep without first thinking over ways and means of escape, if our slumbers should be disturbed by enemies . . . for several months before we left Beirut I had many of my things packed up, and my money so separated and disposed of that I might not even be hurried off to prison penniless. (Riggs, 1964: 22)

By the spring of 1827, still struggling to recover from the tumultuous Greek invasion, Beirut was visited by the plague. In October of the same year, the destruction of the Turkish fleet at Navarino generated considerable apprehension among the foreigners of Beirut, particularly when some English and Irish consuls and merchants were arrested. The missionaries first took shelter in the mountains, where Goodell could only occasionally, and by stealth, visit his family, while he continued his efforts in the city. Conditions, however, deteriorated further. With no source of protection, no foreseeable visits from British or American warships and depletion of funds because of breakdown in trade, the future seemed bleak to the stranded missionaries. It was made bleaker by the fear of Muslim hostility towards Christians from countries with whom the Ottomans might be at war.

The crestfallen missionaries had no choice but to turn their backs on the scene of their labours. On May 2, 1828 the entire station – the Birds, Goodells with their families, Smith and Nicolayson and his family along with the two recent Armenian converts (Wartabet and Carabet) – departed to Malta. The parting scene was more 'tender and affecting' than they had expected. 'Droves of natives' came, despite the menaces of the plague, to bid them farewell. Some were tearful and prayed for

---

1. Among those considered 'pious natives' were: Assad and Phares Shidiaq, from the Maronite Church; a lady from the Latin Church; Dionysius, Gregory Wortabet, Jacob, and the wife of Dionysius, of the Armenian Church; the wife of Wortabet and Yooseph Leflufy, of the Greek Catholic Church; and Asaad Jacob and Tannus el-Haddad, of the Greek Church.

their protection. Downcast, they parted with a 'comforting evidence that, whatever may be the impression we have left on the general population, there are some hearts in Syria, which are sincerely attached to us'. (Anderson, 1872: 51)

Strategies Reconsidered

Retreats are never a cause of cheer, but the missionaries in exile at Malta turned theirs into a sobering experience. They started to reconsider their strategies in light of the resistance and obstacles they faced and the inroads they had made.

Indeed, their accomplishments should not be underestimated. Partly serendipitous, partly by trial and error, but mostly because of their dogged determination and zealotry, they were able to lay some remarkable foundations. These young New England apostles did not flinch in the face of obstacles. They managed to penetrate a complex and extremely hostile milieu. Despite all the repressions to which they were subjected, they were able to preach and win 'a few hearts'. This is no mean accomplishment. The ethnic and linguistic diversity of the Levant demanded, above all, a virtuosity in foreign tongues. And one can only marvel at the gifts they displayed and deployed in so short a life span. Fisk was able to preach in Arabic, French, Italian and Greek. Bird was so accomplished in Arabic that he could write a series of scholarly and polemical treatises amounting to more than 500 pages. Goodell was fluent in both Armenian and Turkish and completed a translation of the entire Bible into Armeno-Turkish.

There was, clearly, something in the character of these zealots that gave them the fortitude to endure adversity to a much greater extent than other American compatriots, particularly merchants, travellers and diplomats. Indeed, they gloried in hardships. They sought damnation to safeguard their redemption in the eyes of their gracious Saviour. They were also far better educated than most other Americans, having had on average at least five to seven years of university education at a time when only two per cent of the Americans went to college. Moreover, they were also willing to go without any remuneration until 1843. The adventurous surveys and exploratory trips they took bore no comparison with the carefree excursions that their self-indulgent, travel-minded contemporaries were enjoying at the time. Theirs were hardship posts, treacherous and risky. They also went about their labour in frequent scorching heat, whiskered and dressed in no-nonsense black, humourless, stern, stiff almost to a fault. They acted as they looked; fearsome, ascetic and daunting.

By far their most significant accomplishment was the schools that they launched. Little as they may seem, they stand out as tangible proof of the role that education (especially boarding and girls schools) came to assume in their efforts. The die was cast. From these modest beginnings great things grew. The generative forces they unleashed cannot and should not be belittled.

First and foremost, it was the swift and unanticipated willingness of the natives to be engaged that impressed the ardent missionaries the most. Beirut, beyond any doubt, revealed a thirst for learning. It was as if they had tapped a potential source of longing for enlightenment. Within a few months of their arrival at what they presumed would be a temporary station, they found a promising response, and after they had had long periods of failing to make any headway with their preaching. Secondly, with hardly any resources or preparation, they managed to meet the demand for qualified instructors. The native teachers they hired, beginning with Butrus Bustani, Asaad Shidiaq, Joseph Laflufy and Gregory Wartabet, became their first converts. This pattern was successfully applied in all their common schools and other related activities. Thirdly, the missionaries were also pleasantly surprised by the receptiveness of students and their parents. Though initially confined to a handful of children and descendants of employees of the mission, they managed to keep schools open to others who desired to attend. The fact that tuition was free and students were furnished with books and other supplies was naturally an inducement. The schools also afforded the missionaries legitimate pretexts to introduce and sanction their evangelism. Since at the time there were no printed texts in Arabic other than the Scriptures, they were able to inject their intended evangelistic leaven under seemingly right and natural conditions.

Finally, and most important perhaps, they began to realize that they had been a bit too impetuous, aggressive and confrontational in the way that they were prosecuting their work. Instructed to show concern for local customs, traditions and rituals, they were instead critical and disdainful. New England Puritanism, with its zealous commitment to a 'city built on a hill' for all to see, inevitably meant that at times they were bound to offend local mores or be contested by competing ideas and lifestyles. The outcries of native groups, often from those deemed accessible to their message, were largely a reaction to vehement denunciation of local culture. It is these reactions that prompted New Englanders to reconsider some of their strategies.

As early as 1827 they evinced concern over the methods that they were employing, particularly in their preaching and operations of the press. There were, of course, differences among them in this regard. Goodell, for example, was reluctant to resort to confrontational and polemical preaching. Missionaries, he maintained, must avoid 'agitation' and 'meddling'. He went further in 'Hints and Cautions to Missionaries' – a series of letters that he wrote collectively with his colleagues at Constantinople – to caution against 'pity' or 'patronizing' attitudes towards the 'heathen'. He also warned against 'impetuosity'. What was wanted, he declared, 'was not a headful of romantic notions but a willingness to work . . . and settle for gradual results . . .' (Field, 1991: 265–66)

In much the same spirit Goodell was also arguing that Eastern Christians need not leave their churches or rebel against their churches' doctrines and rituals; not at this juncture anyway. Interestingly, Goodell was not shunning controversy as such. Rather, he was advocating a delay until native Christians display enough religious enlightenment and consciousness to partake in this process themselves.

I do not think that this is the time for controversy in these countries. There is, so to speak, no foundation. There is no knowledge enough. There is no conscience enough. There is no religion enough. We must labour to give the people knowledge, an enlightened conscience, and pure and undefiled religion, and controversy will then commence of course; but it will commence among themselves, and be carried on between themselves, and not between them and us who are strangers and foreigners. (*Missionary Herald,* 1830: XXVI, 18)

Eli Smith, as well, inclined towards a more cautious and milder approach, particularly with regard to the policy of the press. The object, he declared, is not to 'pull down' but to revive and reform. Solicitous efforts must be made to win them over by 'love', not by disputation and public polemics. Like Goodell, he also believed that, once a revival of religion had taken root (particularly among the Eastern churches, as opposed to the 'Romish' Catholics), they would develop a 'natural appetite' to read the publications of the press. (*Missionary Herald,* 1830, XXXVI, 177)

The views of Goodell and Smith in favour of non-confrontational and non-controversial strategies did not remain unchallenged. The challenge came from a rather unusual source, clearly not mainstream nor part of the circle of New England emissaries, graduates of Amherst and Andover and heirs to Jonathan Edwards and Samuel Hopkins. Instead, it came from a Presbyterian pastor (John Paxton) who had served in Virginia and Kentucky and was already over 50 when he secured the reluctant permission of the Board to join the Beirut mission.[1] While there, he managed to provoke a contentious dialogue over questions of missionary policy. Fundamentalist in his leanings, he advocated a more forthright and aggressive approach to missionary labours among nominal Christians. Indeed, he was quite explicit and complained indignantly that there were few converts in Beirut precisely because the missionaries there were very tentative in their evangelizing. Not only were the missionaries too timid, but they were, in his view, placing too much emphasis on education and the press.

Smith responded promptly. He also did not mince words. The thrust of his reply focused on issues regarding the substance and magnitude of change; how much to 'pull down', when and by whom? 'Rather than disputation,' he told Paxton, 'love, real Christian love, ought to be the leading characteristic of a missionary.' A reckless course of 'pulling down' the corrupt Eastern churches was bound to be rash, foolhardy and ill-advised. Smith reminded Paxton that native churches were not likely to declare the obsolescence of their doctrines and rituals, debased as they were, simply because Protestant missionaries disclosed their foibles and errors. The soul-searching and questioning must be initiated by the natives themselves. When there were enough pious believers among them, 'convulsion' would eventually come. 'And yet,' he cautioned, 'I have deemed it of the least importance, that we take no necessary steps to hasten the crisis.' In fact, Smith was apprehensive that the crisis might surface soon, when 'not enough preparation has been made and the truth will be overthrown . . .'. 'Our strength,' he repeated, '*lies in doing much with little noise.*'

---

1.   The Board considered Paxton too controversial a figure and too advanced in age to begin missionary work under its auspices. Nonetheless he appeared in Beirut some time in 1836 and engaged the missionaries there in dialogue, not always friendly, over questions of missionary policy. Strangely, neither the *Missionary Herald* nor the official chronology of Rev. Thomas Laurie makes any reference to his presence there between 1836 and 1838 (for these and other details see Badr, 1992: 149–55).

Smith concluded his rebuttal by reminding Paxton that their ultimate goal as evangelists was 'higher than ecclesiastical: it was the salvation of souls. Whether men belonged to one church or another, was a matter of very little consequence.' He went on to anticipate, however, that the Eastern churches were not likely to tolerate evangelically minded members in their midst for too long; they would eventually compel all of them either to recant or to suffer excommunication (for more on the Smith–Paxton controversy see Badr, 1992: 149–57).

Most probably it was these unsettling circumstances that prodded the Prudential Committee to take remedial action while the missionaries were still stranded in Malta. Rufus Anderson, the Assistant Secretary of the Board, was delegated on a special mission to explore the directions that their work could take in the entire eastern Mediterranean. Anderson was expected to confer with the stranded evangelists. Perhaps he had Greece in mind when he wrote his instructions, which contained a rather curious set of inquiries regarding the moral and spiritual conditions in the country.

> What is the state of morals among the people? How far truth and integrity prevail? What is the state of things, in regard to industry, temperance, chastity? How the female sex is treated? What is the state of morals among women? Whether the people are desirous of having their daughters well educated?
>
> How far there is a distinction of ranks among the people? What are the claims of birth? What the influence of wealth? . . . How far there is such a thing as political integrity among leaders? How far there is such a thing as moral integrity among eminent merchants? What is thought by people of such vices as lying, cheating, lewdness, and drunkenness? (Phillips, 1969: 142)

Anderson's first exploratory visit to the region in 1830 turned him into a staunch supporter of the mission to the Eastern churches in the Ottoman Empire and Greece. More important, the Board now was in a position to advance a set of strategies establishing the parameters to direct their operations in the field.

First, as soon as practicable the missionaries on Malta were to seek access to the unsettled regions in the eastern Mediterranean. Particularly favourable centres marked for 'occupation' were, once again, Constantinople, Smyrna, Malta, Beirut and Jerusalem. Second, further explorations were urged to find appropriate mission fields. Third, the immediate policy of Mediterranean missions should be directed by three underlying principles or perspectives: 1) preference for 'conversational' rather than formal preaching, 2) the extensive employment of educational techniques, 3) cautious advances to 'nominal' Christians rather than a direct assault on 'Mohammedanism'.

Altogether the two-year interlude in Malta was a mellowing and instructive experience. It allowed the exiled missionaries to indulge in some soul-searching and to reconsider more judicious strategies that were not offensive to local mores and hence not prone to provoking clerical opposition. They emerged from the retreat with a more accommodating frame of mind and a clearer view of the communities that were more receptive or accessible to their brand of Evangelism.

Upon their return to Beirut in 1830, circumstances, both internal and regional, seemed to augur well for the missionaries. The threat of war had become remote. Relations between England and Turkey had improved sufficiently to permit the return of the British consul and hence protection to American subjects. During that year, the United States, which had, since the turn of the century, been eager to conclude a commercial treaty with Turkey, managed to do so. Most encouraging, however, was Muhammad Ali's invasion of Syria in 1831. He launched extensive development schemes, stamped out lawlessness, reformed the administration and, most pertinent from the evangelists' perspective, adopted an agreeable attitude towards foreign enterprise, commercial and missionary alike.

It was within this seemingly promising context that the missionaries returned. Bird, however, was the only person who made it back to Beirut. Soon he was joined by George Whiting, William Thomson, Eli Smith and Asa Dodge. Given the new policy of branching out and exploring other prospects, Goodell went to Constantantinople, Smith and Dwight went out on a most ambitious and exacting exploratory survey of Persia, Russia and northern Turkey,[1] and Jonas King re-entered Greece.

The ebullient optimism that accompanied their return to Beirut quickly slipped away. No sooner had Bird started reopening the schools than the usual burst of repressions was renewed, notwithstanding his cautious attitude. Romish clerics (both Maronite and Greek Catholics) issued their excommunicating edicts against any member of their churches who evinced any interest in such activities. Even the Greek Orthodox, normally sympathetic to the missionaries, took offence this time. In 1837 the Patriarchs of Constantinople and Antioch, together with 16 metropolitans and bishops, issued a pronouncement denouncing 'the Americans in very bitter terms, and directed the formation of a watch committee to protect the community against the mission's heretical books and to prevent the missionaries from pouring the poison of heresy in the ears of children'. (Tibawi, 1966: 79) Orthodox children were withdrawn from missionary schools. Teachers belonging to the Orthodox community were prohibited from serving in mission-run institutions. Books, tracts and Bibles were destroyed. A new Orthodox school was established, in fact, in an effort to stall missionary influence.

The annual reports of the period also complained about shortages of qualified instructors and the debilitating effects of recurrent waves of epidemics. These setbacks, however, were altogether brief and benign.

The more significant changes were largely exogenous in character. Just as the Greek revolt had earlier obstructed the labours of Bird and Goodell in Beirut, so anti-Western reaction at Constantinople and the ensuing rivalries with Egypt over the control of Syria left their mark on the missionaries. The consequences, though, were more auspicious. The success of the Egyptians in safeguarding public security opened up the country further to merchants and travellers. The missionaries took full advantage of this situation.

---

1. The exploring tour, commissioned by the Prudential Committee took them, for the first time, into the interior of Asia Minor and as far as northern Persia and Russian Georgia. They were instructed to secure information about the various Christian subjects – races of Anatolia and the Armenians and Nestorians in particular (for further details, see Phillips, 1969; Grabill, 1971).

Silent and Unobtrusive Evangelism

It was during the decade of the 1830s, which coincided roughly with the Egyptian occupation, that the missionaries managed to expand and consolidate some of their activities. By 1835 they had a total of 11 schools with considerable diversity: one was the 'Frank' school, conducted by the missionary wives, which provided instruction in Arabic, Italian and arithmetic for Europeans. In another, the 'English' school, so called because it used English as the medium of instruction, was established in 1833 to train native helpers for mission schools. Here English, Arabic and geography were taught. There were two 'female' schools, opened about the same time, in which girls were taught reading, sewing and knitting. There was another 'Greek' school and the remaining six were 'native' schools, under native teachers, where the emphasis was on reading through the use of Bible stories, the Psalter and the New Testament (see Lindsay, 1965: 100–1; Tibawi, 1963: 156).

Perhaps the most favourable diplomatic event, and one that had far-reaching consequences, was the appointment of the first American consul in Beirut in 1836. For some time the missionaries and their Boston mentors had been lobbying to secure the appointment of a 'prudent and pious' consul predisposed to bolster the activities of the mission. They were, of course, delighted when this came to pass; particularly since this meant that they would enjoy the security of their own consular protection and need not be at the mercy of British goodwill.

The good fortune of the missionaries was also enhanced by their adoption of a modfied strategy that called for a more conciliatory, less confrontational approach and less debasement of local mores and religious rituals. The new policy also called for less obtrusive forms of evangelizing; a kind of silent penetration. Their judicious efforts paid off. At least for a while, clerical opposition was restrained. They were, in the words of Smith's epigram, *doing much with little noise!*

What were some of the salient forms of 'silent' penetration, particularly those that evolved into identifiable strategies associated with New England Puritanism as an agency of cultural change? Such forms of silent penetration epitomized the American ideals of cultural expansion. For a young nation, without as yet any imperial ambitions, the transfer of spiritual and civil values could have been realized only through such non-aggressive and unobtrusive measures.

'Lancastrian' Schooling

The most obvious and central measure, of course, was education. The ABCFM, as evident in the 'instructions' Fisk and Parsons received, had expected that educational activities would engage their attention. They were not, obviously, expecting much initially. Their instructions stated that they might receive pupils at their house for tutoring, either in a regular course or in one limited to only some of the branches of learning. Possibly a few gifted young people could receive their attention, particularly in view of the 'services they may eventually render to the cause'. (ABCFM, 1819: 50) The method proposed in establishing the schools was 'engagedness', namely the engaging of a teacher or 'native helper' to collect children into a school and then instruct them.

Naturally the interest in education among the pioneering envoys was not merely the by-product of official instructions or avowed expectations of the Board. This longing to impart 'holy truth' to benighted children had early inspired their enthusiasm for the foreign mission. In fact, Parsons, as a young impressionable student at Andover, while still agonizing over the prospects of his career as a missionary, had recorded in his journal that 'to spend my life in inculcating the first principles of our religion, in teaching children the way of life, in establishing schools, societies, religious meetings, and many such things would be peculiarly pleasant and comforting' (Morton, 1830: 97)

In spite of the instructions and their own intentions, Fisk and Parsons did not operate schools themselves! As we have seen, the initial contacts of the missionaries, particularly during their first two years in the field, were mostly with Europeans or Western-oriented individuals. It was only after they had opportunities to travel, explore and, on occasion, live and interact with natives that they began to realize the kind of education that they should be engaged in. In fact, on their exploratory surveys they deliberately sought out leading religious and political figures to solicit their reactions. From these expectations came Fisk's preference for the native, indigenous approach using the vernacular as a language for instruction and in distributed tracts and books.

Despite all the obstacles (clerical opposition, epidemics, wars, pestilence, shortage of qualified teachers, etc.), the schools were an instant success. By 1826 average attendance in Beirut and vicinity was already 300. In the following year it was more than double that number and nearly 20 per cent were females, thanks especially to the existence of boarding and female schools, which allowed them maximum access with minimum intrusion.

The reformulated policy of the Board, as propounded by Anderson after his first visit to the field in 1829, reconfirmed these trends. Indeed, the Prudential Committee's instructions of 1832 urged the missionaries in the Levant to adopt the 'Lancastrian' system of education, under which, among other things, qualified native teachers would be involved in the propagation of vernacular textbooks of an evangelical character.

More important, the duration of evangelism was meant to be brief. As in the 'Lancastrian' schools popular in New England at the time, the function of the teacher was to plant a mustard seed to initiate growth. This concept has been traced back to the efforts of Hopkins, who recommended the speedy establishment of 'self-governing, self-supporting and self-propagating' native churches and institutions.

During the retreat in Malta, some of the natives assumed leadership in running the schools. Incidentally, such involuntary exiles and withdrawals from field stations became recurrent events during successive episodes of political strife. In all these instances, natives rose to the occasion and displayed leadership qualities. Yet the missionaries always found reasons not to stand by their obligations. They never acted on their good intentions. The enabling foresight for self-government remained, at best, a faint hope; a metaphor for an aborted mindset. Indeed, over the years they found it even harder to let go. They never went home again. Nor did they, even when circumstances called for it, encourage natives to assume the leadership that they were articulating conceptually.

At any rate, this early shift in perspective towards more cautionary and less intrusive measures is one indication of recognition on their part that the confrontational methods that they had initially employed were perhaps responsible for the adverse prohibitive and reactionary responses that their zealotry had provoked among local ecclesiastical and Ottoman officials.

Native Preachers

While education was recognized as an expedient method of inculcating knowledge of the Scriptures, preaching assumed a primary role in the order of priorities. From its inception, in fact, the mission had constituted itself as a church into which converts were inducted. By 1839 a chapel for preaching in Arabic had been opened in Beirut. The missionaries themselves had, of course, been repeatedly imploring the Board for reinforcements if they were to attend adequately to this basic but exacting function. By the late 1830s there were not more than 12 or 15 missionaries for a population of one and a half million (see Laurie, 1866 for further details).

Partly because of such shortages, they turned almost exclusively to non-Muslims, with the exception of some initial flirtation with the Druze. It must be remarked that the exclusion of Muslims was not necessarily predicated on the belief that nominal Christians displayed more religious or moral superiority than followers of the prophet. Indeed, Goodell admitted that the Muslim Osmanlis he met in Turkey exhibited 'in some respects better traits of character, than do the various sects of nominal Christians'. (*Missionary Herald*, 1826: 126) By uplifting the moral and spiritual level of Eastern Christians, it was hoped that they would serve as better examples to the infidels who surrounded and despised them. Many missionaries laboured under the belief that, had Muslims and Jews been exposed to a better or more genuine form of Christianity, they might have been more receptive to Christ's undiluted message.

The new policy of the Board, as articulated by Secretary Anderson, re-emphasized the primary task of the mission, namely, 'preaching the Word through the living voice'. Given clerical opposition, however, preaching in public was, at best, dubious and cumbersome. Their only safe and expedient strategy was to bring under their direct influence adults and children who could be taught and exposed to the Protestant faith and Puritan life styles.

Missionaries, in the field, in other words, had to accommodate the expectations of their mentors, who were, after all, providing the necessary funds and backing. Hence, a compromise became imperative: the Beirut Boarding School was regarded as a 'seminary', a future theological school with the objective of producing native ministers, preachers and teachers. Even the Female School was perceived in a similar vein, its purpose being to produce 'pious wives' for the native helpers.

The 'Gutenberg' Mentality

Another 'mustard seed' they planted was the press. This was inevitable, given the primacy of the written word to the evangelists. Protestantism is, after all, a scriptural religion. Hence, a literate audience is vital for its propagation. Groups deemed accessible to their message in the Levant were not, or so it was thought, particularly receptive to reading and reflection. Very early in their labour the missionaries came to realize that before the 'Gospel candle' could be lit, the candle of education had to 'burn in the wilderness'. This is why they were stunned but delighted by the thirst for learning that the Lebanese displayed. With the shift in emphasis from 'tracts for adults to primers for abecedarians' (Fields, 1969: 102), education and the press were destined to become the most potent regenerative sources of cultural change and societal transformations.

Once again, the same unusual combination of serendipity, ingenuity and laborious diligence on the part of the missionaries largely explain why this particular 'mustard seed' ended up in Beirut and turned out to be so prolific and generative.

The eagerness of the missionaries to establish a press was also prompted by their conviction that the version of the Bible in circulation at the time was 'a servile imitation of the vulgate'. (Laurie, 1866: 19) It was a reprint of the ancient translated edition of 1671 revised by a Maronite bishop of Damascus. According to the missionaries, there was not much in it worth preserving: ' . . .The Epistles are often obscure, and their doctrinal arguments robbed of almost all their force . . . Many of the prophetical and practical parts of the Old Testament are in bad taste, and the whole version is neither classical nor grammatical.' (Laurie, n.d.: 19)

Much of the credit for the establishment and initial growth of the press in Beirut goes to Eli Smith.[1] Pliny Fisk had, of course, recognized the need and urgency for printing tracts and testaments in the vernacular shortly after he arrived. He was relentless in his appeals for an 'able, faithful and pious missionary printer'. The Board responded in 1826 by dispatching Mr Homan Hallock, a competent lay journeyman with remarkable mechanical ingenuity, along with two more presses, to boost the modest operation in Malta. In December 1833 Daniel Temple and Hallock moved the press to Smyrna and in the following year the Arabic section was transferred to Beirut. Until then, the output of the press consisted mostly of tracts published in Greek, Italian and Armeno-Turkish. It was not until 1836 that efforts were launched to create a new Arabic typography.

The story of the creation of the press, almost epic in dimensions, has been told and retold by a score of historians. It need not detain us here. Assembling its components physically, given the primitive state of technology at the time, was a feat. Mr Smith took pains to collect models of the characters in the best manuscripts. Unfortunately, the archetype of the font he had assiduously assembled was lost when his ship was wrecked on his way to Smyrna in June 1836. In the shipwreck he also lost his wife. His steely determination, however, was undiminished. Mr Hallock, the printer in Smyrna, cut the punches, drove the matrices and a leading German firm in Leipzig cast the type under Smith's personal supervision. Incidentally, it is this topography, closely modelled on classical calligraphy, which remained for years the standard form of Arabic printing (for

---

1. Parsons, of course, never had the chance. His life was cut short. Fisk gave some private instruction to the six children of the Swiss family he roomed with while at Smyrna. Just a few days before his death in 1825 he assisted in the establishment of an Arabic grammar school at Beirut.

further details see Anderson, 1872: 233–35; Phillips, 1969: 149–50; Laurie, 1866: 18–19). The original one-hand press and two-fonts Arabic type, with a foundry and bindery, were later modernized by adding a power cylinder-press and more refined fonts. The final product is a form of 'American Arabic', which provided the Arab world stretching from Morocco to the Philippines with an aesthetically pleasing and orthographically correct typeface. (Daniel, 1964: 81) Like the reactions to common schools, the press was also an instant success. By 1836, 381,000 pages were printed; six years later the figure had leapt to 1,708,000. (Field, 1969: 180) More significant perhaps, was the 'Gutenberg mentality', which, as a cultural transplant, became one of the most powerful vectors of liberal and secular change and the dissemination of popular culture. The type-set page, in the privacy of a reader's home or the classroom, began to expose inquiring minds to novel ideas and lifestyles and spur others to challenge or depart from archaic forms of behaviour and traditional modes of thought.

Of course the missionaries wished to expedite the propagation of God's word, in Gospel and tract. They had no inkling that they were also laying the foundations for some of the most profound socio-cultural transformations and secular changes beyond their control. Much of the output of the press was, of course, avowedly religious. Secular publications, however, were not insignificant in number. Many of the missionaries wrote books on geography, spelling, grammar, arithmetic and moral science. Two of the missionaries' most gifted 'native helpers', outstanding scholars in their own right, were also among the early contributors. Butrus al-Bustani's two editions on arithmetic and Nasif al-Yazji's on Arabic grammar remained standard texts until the end of the century. It was also these 'secular' texts that managed to transcend communal readership. They appear, judging by their sustained popularity, to have been circulated across all sectarian boundaries.

Often moralistic tales like Leigh Richmond's *Dairyman's Daughter,* Hannah Moore's *The Shepherd of Salisbury Plain* and Young's *Night Thoughts* were becoming very popular. Indeed, it is said that converts to Protestantism attributed to such books their intelligent familiarity with Gospel truth. (Field, 1969: 178) These and other popular reading material – spelling cards, hymn books, the Sermon on the Mount, tracts on cholera and temperance – generated a spirit of inquiry among the populace.

Nor was the traffic in words, as James Field rightly points out, a one-way traffic only. In this literary exchange, it is not always easy to ascertain the balance of imports and exports. While the Scriptures flowed eastward to the so-called heathen and infidels, the words of the American envoys flowed back to their New England constituencies and beyond. (Fields, 1969: 102) The riveting narrations of Parsons and Fisk, the erudite journals of Jonas King and William Thomson and the scholarly surveys and field reports of Eli Smith, H. G. O. Dwight and William Goodell were eagerly read as they appeared in the monthly columns of the *Missionary Herald.* They stimulated interest in the Levant and Orient, inspired further enthusiasm and donations for overseas missions and brought forth what Anderson termed the 'sinews of spiritual war'.

Missionaries as Scholars

Closely related to the establishment of the press was the emergence of many missionaries as scholars capable of undertaking original and stimulating work of the highest quality. Many of the ground-breaking empirical surveys and methodical studies they had launched, often under exacting conditions, became models for others. For decades to come they remained the chief source of information and knowledge of the regions that they explored. They were also the chief force behind the appearance of successive generations of archaeologists, biblical scholars, comparative historians, ethnographers and social scientists.

As pioneers, the missionaries did not just drift aimlessly into scholarly ventures. Their 'instructions' exhorted them not to be totally consumed by their evangelistic purpose 'as ministers of Christ commissioned to testify the Gospel to the infidels . . .' They were also expected to attend to the 'task of procuring and communicating information':

> The fruits of your researches, consisting of facts, descriptions, notices, reflections, comparative views and suggestions of methods and means of usefulness . . . you will regularly enter in your journals and transmit to us as opportunities are afforded. Possibly also you may be able to send home some books or ancient manuscripts . . . In all your communications, it will be of high importance that your statements and representations be correct and exact. (ABCFM, 1819: 7)

There was an exuberant literary imagination in New England at the time, inspired by curiosity about the physical environment of the Christian Scriptures and the *Arabian Nights*. John Stephen's two volumes on the Near East were already bestsellers by 1835. Edward Robinson, another Andover graduate, laboured with the collaboration of Eli Smith to produce two monumental works: the standardized system for the romanization of Arabic names and *Biblical Researches in Palestine, Mount Sinai, and Arabia,* the outcome of their extended travels in the area. The latter volume, published in 1841, has been hailed as surpassing 'the total of all previous contributions to Palestinian geography from the time of Eusebius and Jerome'. (Field, 1969: 181) More important, like other classic tomes, it provided the scholarly foundation for subsequent nineteenth-century explorations. These impressive contributions of New England emissaries had a decisive impact on the quality of international research that they spawned. By the time the influential American Oriental Society was established in London in 1842, 16 of its 68 chartered members were affiliates of the ABCFM. (Grabill, 1971: 38)

Even the less scholarly products broke new ground. The missionaries' penchant for writing biographies, memoirs, letters and personal journal – often using pietistic and evocative prose – stimulated public interest in literary works and travelogues. William Thomson's two-volume *The Land and the Book* (1859), a conversational but dignified narrative, animated with warmth and humanity, apparently sold more copies than any other American title save *Uncle Tom's Cabin*. (Grabill, 1971: 39)

Outstanding among such works were the seminal contributions of Eli Smith and Cornelius Van Dyck, particularly in connection with the prodigious project of translating and printing the Bible. Through this sustained venture, spanning the best part of 16 years, a gifted circle of native scholars and budding intellectuals were drawn into this collaborative enterprise. The central figures – Butrus al-Bustani, Nassif Yaziji, Yusuf al-Asir, Jurji Zaidan, Faris Shidiaq – spearheaded the cultural awakening and became, along with their scions and disciples, the prime movers in kindling the Arab literary renaissance during the nineteenth century.

It was out of this circle that some of the most vibrant forces of intellectual and ideological change were generated. Many of the region's public intellectuals, journalists, teachers, scholars, heads of voluntary associations, even dissident and opposition groups and political activists who sparked off emancipatory movements and nationalist struggles may be traced back to such networks.

Grief and 'Gentle Death'

As teachers, preachers, scholars and writers, missionaries were able to reinforce and legitimize much of their sacred errand. They and their mentors in Boston never lost a moment to prosecute these activities as vectors for the propagation of their view of the Scriptures. Their efforts were not confined to these visible forms of cultural penetration. Other subtler, often strictly private encounters, personal trials and anguishing visitations, were also wilfully exploited for such purposes.

Here, as well, they were not only opening wedges in the local culture to create favourable predispositions towards their own beliefs and practices. They also took pains to reveal the 'folly, cruelty, avarice and amazing selfishness' of native groups.

Whereas the missionaries were outraged by the excessive manifestations of grief the natives displayed during their mourning rituals and funerals, they were eager to share their own private afflictions to illustrate the composure, serenity and calm dignity with which they prepared for and faced such misfortunes and tragedies. Indeed, missionaries often used their own experiences to beseech sinners to be reconciled to their precious Saviour. They never lost an opportunity. The dying scenes of their beloved companions, often their own wives and children, were transformed into occasions for delivering their evangelical message, showing how they 'part in glorious hope of meeting their ultimate Redeemer and be freed from all sin'.

The first such occasion was the death of Pliny Fisk. Goodell, in a poignant piece of writing, described how that affecting moment was used to inform the natives of their view of Christ and heaven. It was prosecuted, he told his mentors in Boston, 'to deepen the solemn impression and improve the event in our public discourses with the natives'.

Some of the Arabs were deeply affected, as they stood around his dying bed. They were amazed at his peace of mind, and could not conceive it possible how any one could be so willing to die. They wept. We explained to them the cause of his tranquillity and joy, related to them much of his religious views and experience, and told them of Christ and heaven. Indeed we sometimes felt, that Christ and heaven were present. It seemed but one step 'to Him that sitteth upon the throne, and to the Lamb', where God himself wipes away all tears. (*Missionary Herald*, 1826: XX, 132)

They had many 'seasons to celebrate the joyous parting' of their colleagues and they always used such occasions to exhort the natives to live closer to their Saviour. Mr Hebard gives the following account of the parting scene of his own wife who died in Beirut in February 1840:

A few days before her death, the native brethren assembled at her request to hear her last words. Among this little band, were our friends, bishops Carabet and Jacob Aga. All hung in breathless silence upon her lips as she exhorted them to live near to the Saviour, to let their light shine, to love one another, to do good to all around them, and to be faithful even unto death. They kneeled around her dying bed, while one of them led in prayer, after which they extended to her the parting hand and received her dying benediction. It was a solemn, a precious season. All were bathed in tears and all wept aloud. (*Missionary Herald,* 1840: XXXVI, 314)

The closing scene of Mrs Smith's 'gentle death' (she died in 1836 at the age of 34) was also affectionately narrated by her husband. The stormy shipwreck, which extended for some 28 days, must have aggravated her consumptive tendencies and hastened her premature passage to the grave. As the bereaved friends and neighbours gathered, Mr Smith describes how her 'involuntary groans melted into musical notes . . . and how their ears were charmed with the tones of the sweetest melody . . .' (Anderson, 1872: 234)

Mrs Smith herself never lost a moment to display her faith. During her last few months, her frail body became feeble and was 'fast ripening for heaven, nothing was lost. She redeemed the time . . . by winning others to the skies . . .' (*Missionary Herald*, 1837: XXXIII, 444)

The missionaries were also equally adept at transforming other times of disquiet, 'seasons of affliction, tumult, war, pestilence and disorder' into beneficent moments, or what they termed 'vantage grounds'. Very early during their exploratory travels, they realized how much more effective evangelization would be if they sent colporteurs not only as agents of wisdom and piety, but also bearing simple remedies for bodily diseases and, aiming, as they put it, to 'heal the deeper maladies of the soul'. (Dennis, 1872: 31) In fact, they had been in Beirut hardly a year when they expressed the urgent need for a 'pious and skilful physician . . . not only as it respects the life and health of our own families, but as it respects the temporal and spiritual good which he might be the means of doing in all this country'. Their appeal to the Board claimed that 'He would be literally followed by "the lame, the halt, and the blind"' – a reference to the biblical injunction – and went on that he

would have more influence in the character of a physician than in any other character. The Arabs have several times brought their sick to us to be healed, and have some times hailed us as we passed their dwellings, to know if we understood anything of medicine. It is matter of grief to us, that we can do so little for their souls or for their bodies. But we endeavour in our prayers to commend them to the Great Physician. May we be more and more like him 'who went about doing good'. (*Missionary Herald,* 1824: XX, 216)

A few years later this solicitous appeal for 'pious and skilful' physicians became more pressing. This is apparent not only in their repeated requests but in their justifications as well. They were, of course, anxious about their own state of health and physical well-being and hence the prospect of prolonging their own life and attending to their labours without fear of disease or infirmity or early death. They also explicitly noted the instrumental character of such Christian benevolence, particularly since it gave them direct inroads into groups otherwise inaccessible to them. Above all, as Mr Bird observed (in a letter from Beirut on April 3, 1832), it availed to the physician an 'unostentatious, inoffensive way in which he may drop his remarks on religious subjects, answer inquiries, remove prejudices in bigoted families or companies, where a missionary would not be heard'. (*Missionary Herald*, 1832: XXVIII, 288)

The Board, incidentally, was not oblivious to the poor living and sanitary conditions that were depleting the precious lives of their young envoys. Nothing much could have been done beyond the efforts they made to assign a medical doctor to each station. The first such missionary doctor, assigned to Beirut, did not, however, survive for long. Asa Dodge arrived there in February 1833, only to pass away early in 1835. The mission remained without a doctor until Cornelius Van Dyck joined it in April 1840; followed by Dr Henry DeForest in 1842.

After the premature departure, in quick succession, of three of their colleagues (Mrs Thomson, Mrs Smith and Dr Dodge), none of whom completed three years in the field, the missionaries once again implored the Board to replenish the supply of physicians. As before, they were quick to stress the importance of the physicians as agents not only for the preservation of the lives and health of the mission but also for 'preparing the way for the gospel, which could not in many instances be otherwise opened'. (*Missionary Herald*, 1837: XXXIII, 493)

At any rate, the standards of American medicine at the time left much to be desired. They did not, in fact, have much of an edge over native practitioners. Doctors bled patients for all the manner of ailments. They excelled, it seems, in setting fractures and removing external tumors and cataracts. (Daniel, 1964: 82) Occasionally a missionary wrote a pamphlet on public health. Yet, even if the missionary doctors had been more 'scientific' or proficient in their skills, they would still have been inhibited by the 'instructions' and conceptual baggage they carried over with them. When he left Dr Dodge had been reminded by the Board of the ultimate purpose of his medical skill and practice: he was to use them 'only as a means of furthering the spiritual objects of the mission'. (ABCFM, 1832: 156)

Shelter in Dark Times
This proclivity on the part of the physicians to 'spiritualize' their interest in public welfare was also visible in the way they dispensed relief and shelter in hard times or 'seasons of affliction'. Their benevolence, much like their seemingly ardent

longing to 'heal the halt and lame', was rarely disinterested. Here, as well, they were particularly adept at transforming disaster and public despair into vantage grounds.

While offering relief and shelter in times of war, communal violence, epidemics or natural disaster, they never refrained from exhorting stricken and anxious natives to trust in God. During the Greek assault on Beirut in April 1826, terrified citizens took refuge in Goodell's residence. Goodell responded without missing a beat.

> My house has been filled with the poor Christians, who were preparing to escape to the mountain. Twenty-seven slept in the room of my house one night, and the other rooms were equally well filled . . . Some were so terrified, they crept under the bed, some concealed themselves in various parts of the house, and others let themselves down by a rope from the window and escape . . . To those who stayed I daily read the scriptures, and exhorted them to trust in God. (*Missionary Herald*, 1826: XXII, 354)

Thomson, only days after the earthquake of January 1837 that devastated the south all the way to Safet and Tiberias (6,000 out of a population of 10,000 instantly perished), organized rescue operations, perhaps the first of their kind. Accompanied by Mr Calman and whatever articles and supplies they could collect, they left their families and set off for the scene, a journey of several days, 'with much anxiety, my health doubtful, while the season promised nothing but bad roads, storms of rain and snow, and on the mountain fierce cold'. Thomson added that his 'only ardent desire' was to

> render our journey prosperous and profitable and to promote the glory of God and honor the gospel amongst the Jews and Moslems of that region, by alleviating the sufferings of the poor, the sick, the wounded, and orphan; and this will be cheaply purchased at any expense of time, toil, and danger. (*Missionary Herald*, 1837: XXXIII, 434)

At Safet, where the devastations were most alarming, Thomson and Calman risked danger to give heavily of their time and toil. They managed miraculously to assemble, from salvaged boards, broken doors and timber, a makeshift 'hospital' and hired a native physician to attend to the maimed and wounded. Upon their return to Beirut, Thomson, always keen to extract moral precepts from such calamities, highlighted the selfless sacrifices and perils that they had had to endure but went on to berate others for their cold-hearted villainy. (*Missionary Herald*, 1837: XXXIII, 443)

Times of quarantine, normally imposed during epidemics, scourges and other recurring hazards to public health, were also converted into good omens. Writing on August 7, 1837, during a strict quarantine in the wake of a plague that had broken out in Beirut, Mr Thomson revealed how the distress felt by the 'throng of ignorant mountaineers' who had taken shelter in his residence was pleasantly consumed by reading and expounding the Scriptures.

After we broke up quarantine, I prepared the only spare room in my house for Arabic prayers, and invited the neighbours to attend. At first but few came, but for some time past the room has been full every night. To this audience, varying in number from twenty to forty, I preach the gospel with all the plainness I can. Thus an hour passes pleasantly away every evening in reading and expounding the scriptures and prayer. Always more or less remain to converse after prayer, with whom the whole evening is generally consumed. We have never had our houses so thronged before. May the Lord bless our unworthy labours, and his holy name be honoured in the salvation of these ignorant mountaineers. (*Missionary Herald*, 1837: XIV, 300)

'Ungodly Puritans'

Judging by the initial reactions of native groups to New England puritans, they seemed at times more struck, often amazed, by their unfamiliar and eccentric manners and customs than by the religious message they were preaching. In some respects this was to be expected. Inhabitants of the region were fairly acquainted with Europeans by a long association dating back to the Crusades, but American missionaries, as emissaries of the New World, were bound to appear peculiar, even a bit outlandish. Indeed, they and their products and customs became objects of curiosity, mixed with wonder and relish. The missionaries again cleverly turned this curiosity to their advantage; part of their silent strategy to open a wedge in the Levant.

Incidentally, some American 'products' clearly not to the liking of the ascetic Puritans, had already predated their entry. When Smith and Dwight made an exploratory field survey into Turkey, they came across, in far-off Tiflis, Georgia, barrels of New England rum! Not only was this 'particularly Boston' product coveted but the prefix 'American' was added to an assortment of local products to enhance their market value.

It is amusing to see how our country, on account of its being the *New World*, its distance from Turkey, and the general ignorance prevailing in respect to it, has the honour of giving name to whatever is curious, or particularly good. During the late festivities, the water-carriers would cry out among the people, '*American water*!' meaning good fresh water. The seller of cakes would call out as wonderful recommendation, '*Made of American butter*!' while a man who kept an ostrich for shew, stood at the door of his stall, calling out from morning till night, '*An American bird*!' Even on ordinary occasions, the Jew is met at the corners of the streets, calling out at the top of his voice, '*American cotton*!' And it is a singular coincidence, that the American built frigate is now the flag-ship of the capudan pasha. (*Missionary Herald*, 1837: XXXIII, 156)

It must be recalled that the 'Puritan ethics' as a collective mentality embodied two seemingly discordant elements. There was first a spiritual and divine heritage, which found expression in such notions as 'disinterested benevolence', and other theological reformulations of Edwards and Hopkins, which sparked off New England evangelism and much of the enthusiasm for foreign missions. Secondly,

Puritanism also involved some utilitarian, pragmatic and secular precepts and patterns of behaviour, particularly those 'ungodly' instrumental virtues brought to popular attention by Benjamin Franklin. As a cultural transplant, it was the diffusion of such practical precepts – temperance, moderation, sobriety, frugality, industry, silence, cleanliness – which were less obtrusive and hence more penetrating in their impact.

Initially, it was the novelty and curiosity of these attributes that was most appealing. Eventually, however, the demonstrable and sustained effectiveness of these practical, prosaic edicts persuaded native groups of the relevance and utility of Puritanism as a cultural transplant. Early on, the missionaries became cognizant of such realities and made judicious use of them in extending and deepening their entry into the Levant. Even those who were hostile to the spiritual or evangelistic message of Puritanism were drawn to its so-called 'ungodly' features.

There was much in the outward behaviour, mannerisms, fashions, etiquettes and conventions of the missionaries that stimulated curiosity. Equally intriguing were the products that they used: wooden floors, glass windows, wagons, clocks, sewing machines, organs, the cotton gin, telegraphs, even tomatoes and potatoes (see Grabill, 1971: 19). It was these seemingly mundane items and cultural artifacts, along with the more significant American innovations such as boarding schools, female education, philanthropy, volunteerism and outreach programmes, that laid the foundation for some of the liberal and progressive transformations that they generated.

PART III

The Spaces of War in Lebanon

CHAPTER 8

The Scares and Scars of War

Violence, unlike Achilles' lance, does not heal the
wounds that it inflicts.

John Keane, *Reflections on Violence* (1996)

The animus was always the same: Whether nation,
province, or city, whether religion, class or culture –
the more one loved one's own, the more one was
entitled to hate the other . . . Through the centuries
politicians had exploited this human trait. In the
knowledge that hatred can be cultivated with a purpose,
they constructed enemies in order to bolster domestic
concord.

Peter Gay, *The Cultivation of Hatred* (1993)

For almost two decades, Lebanon was besieged and beleaguered by every possible
form of brutality and collective terror known to humankind. From the cruelties of
factional and religious bigotry to the massive devastations wrought by private
militias and state-sponsored armies, all generated an endless carnage of innocent
victims and immeasurable toll in human suffering. Even by the most moderate of
estimates, the magnitude of such damage to human life and property is staggering.
About 170,000 people have perished, twice as many were wounded or disabled;
close to two-thirds of the population experienced some form of dislocation or
uprootedness from their homes and communities. By the autumn of 1982, UN
experts estimated that the country had sustained US$12 billion to $15 billion in
damages, i.e. $2 billion per year. Today, more than one-third of the population is
considered to be below the poverty line as a result of war and displacement (for

these and other related estimates, see Hanf, 1993: 339–57; Labaki and Abu Rjeily, 1993).

For a small, dense, closely-knit society of about 3.5 million, such devastations are, understandably, very menacing. More damaging, perhaps, are some of the socio-psychological and moral concomitants of protracted hostility. The scars and scares of war and manifested in pervasive post-stress symptoms and nagging feelings of despair and hopelessness. In a culture generally averse to psychoanalytic counselling and therapy, these and other psychic disorders and fears are particularly debilitating as they are bound to remain masked and unrecognized and, hence, unattended to.

The demoralizing consequences of the war are also visible in the vulgarization and impoverishment of public life and the erosion of civility. The routinization of violence, chaos and fear only compound the frayed fabric of the social order. It draws seemingly pacific and non-violent groups into the vortex of conflict and sow a legacy of hate and bitterness. Thus Lebanon's pluralism, radicalization of its communities and consequent collective violence have become pathological and uncivil. Rather than being a source of enrichment, variety and cultural diversity, the modicum of pluralism the country once enjoyed is now generating paranoia, hostility and differential bonding.

Moreover, although the outward manifestations of violence have ceased, enmity today assumes different forms and is deeper and more pervasive than it used to be at the initial stages of hostility.

Unfortunately, much of the literature on civil strife continues to be concerned with its etiology, a preoccupation that is not just short-sighted but has become counterproductive. Consistent with the overwhelming bias inherent in most of the leading perspectives on collective violence, explorations of episodes of political unrest in Lebanon, as elsewhere, have also been skewed in that direction. Hence we know too much already about the preconditions, changing political settings (both regional and global), economic disparities, cultural and psychological circumstances that motivated and predisposed groups to resort to collective protest.

Instructive as such analyses have been, they tell us little about the forces that sustained violence and escalated its brutality. Nor do they expose or explore the changing forms of violence. More striking, perhaps, they do not help in understanding how seemingly ordinary citizens get entrapped in it and how traumatized groups come to cope with chronic hostility and fear. Likewise, this obsession with the origin of violence tells us comparatively little about the impact of war on collective memory, on changes in group loyalties, collective psychology, perceptions and changing attitudes towards the 'other'.

At least in the case of Lebanon this exercise has become rather futile, at best a laborious elaboration of the obvious. For example, it is not very uncommon for a fragile, pluralistic society, caught up in regional and superpower rivalries, to display a high propensity for violence. The lack of political integration in such fragmented political cultures has been cited over and over again as a major cause, indeed a prerequisite for political unrest. One could, likewise, write volumes about the destabilizing impact of internal socio-economic disparities, the presence of Syrians, Palestinians and Israelis or the unresolved regional and global rivalries, without adding much to what we know already. The existence of extensive distant and recent evidence may obviate the need for further substantiation of the realities.

What is, however, in need of elucidation is the persistence and growing intensity of violence, its shifting targets and the way in which it acquired a momentum and a life of its own unrelated to the initial sources of conflict. Most atrocious in the case of Lebanon was the way violence splintered further as intercommunal rivalries degenerated into fratricidal bloodletting. The ecology of violence, reinforced by the demonization of the 'other', led to heightened vengeance and entrapment in relentless cycles of retributive in-fighting. Hence, much of the conventional characterization of the initial stages of civil unrest (i.e. 'Christian versus Muslim', 'right versus left') became outmoded as internecine and inter–factional violence became more rampant and bloodier.

First and foremost we must elucidate how some of the worst cruelties of the war were normalized and domesticated. I shall argue here that by 'sanitizing' the war and transforming it into an ordinary routine, terrorized groups were able to survive its ravages. By doing so, however, they also allowed it to become more protracted and diffused.

Secondly, we consider how the war managed to reshuffle the country's social geography and impose its grotesque and ferocious logic on private and public space. Here again, by seeking shelter in communal solidarities, traumatized groups were able to find temporary relief. What enabled them to survive its immediate horrors, however, rendered them more vulnerable to other, more menacing, long-term consequences. By distancing themselves from the demonized 'other', they could of course release their guilt-free aggression with impunity, but they also made themselves easier and more accessible targets to focused acts of hostility. Casualties on both sides mounted and at the same time the prospects for reconciliation and peaceful co-existence became more formidable, if not unlikely.

Finally, we look at the intriguing way in which various communities displayed strikingly different predispositions and evolved different adaptive strategies to cope with the cruelties of protracted strife. This gave rise to an anomaly: communities that were victims of a larger magnitude of trauma were not necessarily those that displayed greater stress and post-traumatic symptoms. An effort will be made to account for this disparity. How is it, in other words, that some of the more traumatized groups were able to put up with the adversities of war without the accompanying syndromes of distress and demoralization? Such resilience, incidentally, may also give us a clue about the persistence of violence. This is another seemingly anomalous situation in which the Lebanese were trapped. The more adept they became at adjusting to or coping with the cruelties of strife, the more opportunities the war had to reproduce and sustain itself. Once again, the enabling and disabling features became inexorably locked together.

The Domestication of Violence

One may well argue that wars in Lebanon, despite some of their appalling manifestations, displayed comparatively little of the bizarre and grotesque cruelties associated with so-called 'primitive' and/or 'modern' forms of extreme violence, namely, the systematic rape of women by militias, the ritual torture and mutilation of victims, the practice of forcing members of a family at knife-point or gunpoint to kill each other (for further such details see Wilson, 1992). Other than episodic massacres and vengeful acts of collective retribution (Sabra and Chatila, Tal-el-Za'tar, Damour, etc.), there was little to compare to the planned and organized cruelty on a mass scale typical of extermination campaigns and pogroms.

The incivility of collective violence in Lebanon was, nonetheless, visible in some equally grotesque pathologies, particularly those that domesticated killing by rendering it a normal, everyday routine; sanitized *ahdath* (events) bereft of any remorse or moral calculation. A few of these pathologies merit highlighting here. Collective violence assumed all the aberrant manifestations and cruelties of relentless hostility. Unlike the other comparable encounters with civil strife, which are often swift, decisive and localized, and in which a sizeable part of the population remain sheltered from its traumatizing impact, the Lebanese experience has been much more protracted and diffuse. The savagery of violence was also compounded by its randomness. There is therefore hardly a Lebanese today who was exempt from experiencing these atrocities either directly or vicariously. Violence and terror touched virtually everyone.

Fear, the rage to survive and instinct for self-protection from random violence had a levelling, almost homogenizing, impact throughout the social fabric. Status, class differences and all other manifestations of privilege, prestige and social distinctions, which once stratified and differentiated groups and hierarchies in society, somehow melted away. At least momentarily, as people fell hostage to the same contingent but enveloping forces of terror and cruelty, they became oblivious to all distinctions, class or otherwise. Other than those who had access to instruments of violence, no one could claim any special privilege or regard. Mai Ghoussoub has expressed it poignantly.

> The civil war that sprang upon the country very soon engulfed the neighbourhood in which Farid's second home was located. The stagnant, cozy routines of its inhabitants were so abruptly disrupted, and their streets turned so easily into an apocalyptic battlefield, that it was as if it had all happened under the spell of some magician's wand. The settled little hierarchies of these petty bourgeois clerks, these shopkeepers and their families, were suddenly huddled into anguished corridors and damp cellars, in which their status was squeezed as well as their bodies. The powerful and the less powerful, the compassionate and the unfeeling, the arrogant and the timid were brought to one same, common level in their struggle for survival. Nothing of what had once been mattered any longer, in the apocalyptic fires that governed their fate at this moment. They all feared the streets, and submitted willingly to the chaos of control by trigger-happy fighters. (Ghoussoub, 1998: 66)

Another aspect was that the war had no predictable or coherent logic to it. It was everywhere and nowhere. It was everywhere because it could not be confined to one specific area or a few combatants. It was nowhere because it was not identified with or linked to one concrete cause. Recurring cycles or episodes of violence erupted, faded and resurfaced for no recognized or coherent reason.

The warring communities had also locked themselves into a dependent relationship with violence and chronic conflict, with the result that violence became both protracted and insoluble. It was a form of self-entrapment that blocked all avenues of creative peaceful change. It was also sustained by a pervasive feeling of helplessness, demoralization and an obsessive dependence on external patrons and foreign brokers. It was then that violence started to create a 'tunnel vision' effect, i.e. a tendency to focus, almost obsessively, on one's involvement in the conflict to the exclusion of any other relevant course of action. In acute cases, every action, every statement and every institution acquired value and meaning in relation to the conflict itself. So much so, in fact, that some observers at the time went as far as to suggest that in Lebanon violence and chronic fear had become an intrinsic part of society's ethos and mythology. It became an absorbing and full-time concern, overshadowing many other societal, communal and individual interests (Azar, 1984: 4). It may sound like a cliché, but violence became a way of life; the only way the Lebanese could make a statement or assert their beings or damaged identities. Without access to instruments of violence, one ran the risk of being voiceless and powerless. Literally, the meek inherited nothing. This is perhaps one of the most anguishing legacies of the arrogance and incivility of violence.

Abhorrent as it was, the fighting went on largely because it was, in a sense, normalized and routinized. In the words of Judith Shklar (1982), it was transformed into an 'ordinary vice', something that, although horrible, was to be expected. The grotesque became mundane, a recurrent everyday routine. The dreadful and outrageous were no longer dreaded. Ordinary and otherwise God-fearing citizens could easily find themselves engaged in events or condoning acts that once provoked their scorn and disgust. In effect, an atrocious raging war became, innocuously, *ahdath* (literally, 'events'). This 'sanitized' label was used casually and with cold indifference; a true wimp of a word to describe such a dreadful and menacing pathology. But then it also permitted its hapless victims to survive its ravages.

This is precisely what had transpired in Lebanon: a gradual pernicious process in which some of the appalling features of protracted violence were normalized and domesticated. Killing became, in a word, inconsequential. Indeed, groups engaged in such cruelties felt that they had received permission, some kind of cultural sanction or moral legitimization for their grotesque deeds. Those who witnessed the horrors were also able, by distancing themselves from their gruesome manifestations, to immune themselves against them. Witnessing and coping with the dreaded daily routines of war became also remorseless and guilt-free.

The manifestations of such normalization are legion. In the early stages of the war, when bearing arms and combat assumed redemptive and purgative features, any identification with the garb, demeanour or lifestyle of fighters and militia groups became almost chic; a fashionable mode of empowerment and enhancing one's machismo. Belligerency, in fact, was so stylized that groups literally disfigured themselves to ape such identities. Bit by bit, even the most grotesque attributes of the war became accepted as normal appendages to rampant chaos and fear. Literary accounts and personal diaries recorded such events and circumstances with abandon, often in highly evocative tones. The daily body count was greeted with almost the same matter-of-factness as the weather forecast. Fallen bodies, kidnapped victims and other casualties of indiscriminate violence became, as it were, the barometer by which a besieged society measured its daily cycles.

The most dismaying development, no doubt, is when those grotesque features of war begin to envelop the lives of innocent children. All their daily routines and conventional modes of behaviour – their schooling, eating and sleeping habits, playgrounds, encounters with others, perceptions, daydreams and nightmares, their heroes and role models – were inexorably wrapped up in the omnipresence of death, terror and trauma. Even their games, their language and their cognitive and playful interests became warlike in tone and substance. Their makeshift toys, much like their fairly tales and legends, mimicked the cruelties of war. They collected cartridges, empty shells and bullets. They played war games by simulating their own gang fights. They acquired sophisticated knowledge of the artifacts of destruction just as earlier generations took delight in identifying wild flowers, birds and butterflies.

There is hardly an aspect of Lebanese children's lives, and this is certainly true for adolescents who were involuntarily drawn into the fray of battle, that is exempt from such harrowing experiences. They have all been homogenized by the cruelties of indiscriminate killing and perpetual anxieties over the loss of parents and family members. These and other such threats, deprivations and indignities continue to consume their psychic energies and traumatize their daily life. Successive generations of adolescents have, in fact, known little else.

Norbert Elias's notion of the 'sanitization of violence' is relevant here. It most certainly helps us in understanding not only how violence is camouflaged, even stylized so that it no longer seems offensive, but how in the process it becomes protracted and insoluble. (Elias, 1988) During certain interludes, these same horrors were not only bereft of any moral outrage, they managed to become sources of fascination and venues for public amusement and entertainment. The war, in other words, began to acquire some of the trappings of a spectacle, not unlike the morbid fascination frenzied spectators feel for the stylized rituals of a Spanish bullfight! (Marvin, 1986: 133–34) In his recent book *On Killing* Dave Grossman argues that a continuous presence of images of violence threatens to blur the line between entertainment and the conditioning of fighters and soldiers. He refers to a 'stage of desensitization at which the infliction of pain and suffering has become a source of entertainment . . . we are learning to kill and we are learning to like it.' (Grossman, 1997: 311)

Mai Ghoussoub (1998) recounts the transformation of Said, a cheerful, gentle and spirited grocer's son, the neighbourhood's most beloved boy, who was metamorphosed overnight into a callous and heartless killer. Said, the pride of his doting parents, was destined to fulfil his father's ambitions by pursuing his studies at the Ecole Hôtelière. Instead, he was so entranced, almost bewitched, by the machismo and charisma of the militiamen that he could not resist the temptation to become one himself, to the chagrin of his dismayed parents. This is how Ghoussoub depicts the episode signalling this anguishing transformation:

> . . . despite his mother's warnings and lamentations, he watches the groups of militiamen who have settled in at the entrance of the building facing his. They have all that he does not. And they are free of all that he has. The sad, heavy, constant presence of his parents worrying about him. Asking him to hide and keep a low profile, to smile, like his father, at every potential customer on the street. The militiamen are dressed in a relaxed but manly way. They sit on their chairs with their heads slightly tilted back, their feet stretched way in front; cigarettes hanging constantly from the corners of their mouths, they smoke and laugh and play cards just there on the pavement, next to the door of the building. When a jeep stops with a great sudden screech of its brakes, two lithe and powerful young men jump out of it, adjust the position of their kalashnikovs on their shoulder and give big, generous handshakes to each one of the militiamen that Said sees from his balcony. To Said these men are beautiful. The glamour that emanates from them fills his heart with dreams. He would like to belong to these men, to be as attractive as they are, to feel as young and powerful as they feel, instead of rotting in his miserable little apartment. (Ghoussoub, 1998: 81)

This almost effortless and light-hearted socialization of innocent adolescents into militancy is another disheartening function of the arrogance and incivility of collective violence. Said's case is far from exceptional. Legions of such recruits, often from privileged families, stable and entrenched middle-class groups, became willing volunteers to join the ranks of militias as regular fighters or subsidiary recruits. If one were to believe autobiographical accounts and obituaries of fallen fighters (often doctored to heighten notions of self-sacrifice, daring and fearless courage), they were all lionized into exemplary and mythical heroes. On the whole, though, particularly during the early rounds of fighting, one saw evidence of over-zealous fighters buoyed by the bravado of their savagery and warmongering. This is again a reminder that killing does not emanate from some crazed, deranged, monster-like creatures driven by atavistic frenzy or an irresistible compulsion for aggression. Rather, it more often originates with ordinary people who have been induced into this culture by their peers or by the aura of bearing arms in defence of threatened values.

This is precisely what Primo Levi had in mind when he cautioned: 'Monsters exist, but there are very few of them to present any real danger. Those who are dangerous are the ordinary men.' (Levi, 1960) More anguishing is to observe how ties of trust, intimacy, benevolence and caring among neighbours were readily deflected and deformed into enmity. Once embroiled in such structured and heightened enmity, a person is compelled to take revenge on behalf of his group, even though he may bear no particular grudge against those he has to kill. Here too, combatants flung themselves, often irrationally, into a relentless series of gangfights linked to one concrete cause. Recurring cycles or episodes of violence erupted, faded and resurfaced for no apparent, coherent reason.

Multiple and Shifting Targets of Hostility

Unlike other comparable experiences with protracted collective violence, hostility was not confined to a limited and well-defined number of combatants and adversaries. At last count (by the spring of 1984), it had already involved no fewer than 186 warring factions, splinter groups with different backgrounds, ideologies, sponsors, grievances, visions and justifications for their resort to armed struggle.

It was this bewildering plurality of adversaries and shifting targets of hostility that made the Lebanese experience particularly dreadful. For example, from 1978 to 1982, the interlude between the two Israeli invasions, the country was besieged and beleaguered by every conceivable form of collective violence and terror. The sheer volume and magnitude of such incidents reached a higher point than during any other 'round' or phase of the war. Keeping track of who was fighting whom, the swift oscillation in proxies and sponsors, the targets of hostility and the motives propelling and sustaining the violence is a dizzying and perplexing task.

Virtually no area in the country was spared the ravages of war. All traditional battlegrounds were ablaze. East Beirut was still under siege from relentless Syrian bombardments. Many residents had no choice but to seek shelter, much as they resented it, in West Beirut. Though at the time the neighbourhoods of West Beirut were still riven by turf battles between the Mourabitoun and other Sunni Muslim rivals, the area was considerably safer than Achrafieh, on which the Syrian army was lobbing devastating artillery attacks. Both suburbs of Beirut were embroiled in intra-communal turf wars. After Bashir Gemayyel had, in the spring of 1977, gained effective control of the Lebanese forces (a coalition of all Maronite militias comprising the Phalange, Tanzim, Tigers and Guardina of the Cedars), he proceeded to consolidate his powers by subduing his potential rivals. Hence there were repeated incursions into the strategic coastal enclaves of Dany Chamoun's Tigers, particularly the military installations at Safra and Amsheit. These were finally overrun (on July 7, 1980), after bloody and fierce assaults, which wiped out over 150 innocent civilians. Christian militias were also engaged in intermittent clashes with Armenian leftists and the Syrian National Party (PPS).

On the southern fringe, confrontations between Amal and the Communist Action group were already breaking into open shoot-outs, a preamble to the more contentious struggles between Amal (Syrian proxy) and Hizbollah (Iran proxy). Further north, Franjieh militias were still trying to thwart the encroachment of Gemayyel's Lebanese forces into their traditional fiefdom. In June 1978 Bashir's commandos made that fateful crossover, which ended in the tragic massacre at Ihden where over 40 members of the Franjieh clan were murdered, including Tony (the heir apparent to the clan's leadership), his wife and child.

In Tripoli, Sunni centrists and Sunni radicals were engaged in pitched battles. The former were supported by the Syrians, the latter by the PLO and Muslim fundamentalists. In the Beqà, particularly Zahlé, Ba'albek and Chtoura, Bashir Gemayyel had hoped to link up with Zahlé, the largest Christian enclave in the central Beqà. Being armed and assisted openly by the Israelis, he was over-confident and audacious. The Syrians, of course, were not likely to accept such an affront to their hegemony in so strategic a region. They besieged the town for three months and drove Bashir out of the Beqà.

The Palestinians and Shi'ites were also embroiled in their own pernicious strife between and among their various factions. In addition to the continuing rivalry between pro-Syrian Amal and pro-Iranian Hizbollah, the latter were split further between those loyal to indigenous leaders like Sheikh Fadlallah and those affiliated to Iranian clerics in the Beqà. The in-fighting within the various Palestinian factions was also unabated. Pro-Iraqi and pro-Syrian groups sought to resolve their regional and ideological rivalries in Lebanon. So did Arafat loyalists and those opposed to him.

This became much more pronounced in the wake of mounting public discontent with the PLO's splintering and in-fighting among the various factions, and then its lack of resistance to the Israeli invasion of 1982. Syria deployed several of its local proxies to undermine Arafat. It bolstered the 'Palestine Salvation Front' with the military units of Abu Musa, the dissident Fatah rebel. Along with Syria's Sa'iqa and the Yarmouk brigade, they battled against Arafat's forces from mid-1983 onwards. In Tripoli they were joined by the local 'Alawi militias and other Syrian client groups such as the Ba'th and the Syrian Nationalists (SSNP).

Marginal ethnic groups such as Armenians and Kurds, as if drawn into the vortex of belligerency by contagion, also found excuses to redress their differences by resorting to arms.

The most beleaguered region was, of course, the south. Added to the long-standing splits between the traditional *zu'ama* and scions of feudal and neo-feudal families, the south was splintered further by the volatile and vacillating hostility between and among the various Shi'ite and Palestinian factions, exacerbated by the presence of the Israeli-backed Saad Haddad's South Lebanese Army (SLA). The major breach between Amal and Hizbollah, fuelled by their Syrian/Iranian patronage, was also compounded by the emergent hostility between Palestinians and Shi'ite villagers. Embittered by the havoc and terror Palestinians were spawning in the south, some of the Shi'ite of Jabal Amil were drawn into the SLA.

So multiple, so various and so explosive are the sources of belligerency that south Lebanon is doubtless today the world's most perennial war zone and killing field, a peerless example of 'low-intensity conflict' that never goes away. Given the mounting casualties, the prefix 'low' does not do justice to the magnitude of the cruelties to which the southerners are subjected. Its hapless victims live in constant fear of being killed or displaced without anticipating or recognizing the identity of their assailants. Villagers are not only terrorized by the turf wars of warring factions, they are also the surrogate victims of state-sponsored armies. Indeed, villagers in the south could well be bombarded from at least six different sources: Israelis, Syrians, Palestinians, the so-called Republic of Free Lebanon (SAL), UNIFEL and the Lebanese Army, if and when it ventured south.

Is this not the ultimate in incivility, which compounds the futility of violence? Innocent people suffer without knowing who is attacking them or why. In this regard it might be argued that Palestinians, Jews, Armenians, Kurds, Corsicans, Ulster Catholics, Basques, Bosnians, Serbs, Croats and other victims of collective suffering are, perhaps, more privileged. They can at least identify and mobilize their outrage against those who might be held accountable for their suffering. The Lebanese are still unable to vindicate their collective grievance. They have been homogenized by fear, terror and grief, but remain divided, powerless and gripped by a crushing sense of impotence and entropy. They are bitter but cannot direct their fury towards recognized targets.

The Reterritorialization of Identities

Another striking and disturbing feature of protracted and displaced hostility is the way the Lebanese were caught up, since the outbreak of fighting in 1975, in an unrelenting process of redefining their territorial identities. Indeed, as the fighting blanketed virtually all regions in the country, few were spared the anguish of being cast adrift from their spatial moorings. The magnitude of such displacement is greater than commonly recognized. Recent estimates suggest that more than half, possibly two-thirds, of the population have been subjected to some transient or permanent form of uprootedness from their homes and communities (see Labaki and Abou Rjeily, 1993).

Throughout the war, in other words, the majority of the Lebanese were caught in a painful sequence of negotiating, constructing and reconfirming a fluid pattern of spatial identities. No sooner had they suffered the travails of dislocation by taking refuge in one community, than they were again uprooted and compelled to negotiate yet another spatial identity or face the humiliation of re-entry into their profoundly transformed original communities. They became homeless, so to speak, in their own homes, or furtive fugitives and outcasts in their own communities.

The socio-psychological consequences of being dislodged from the familiar and reliable landmarks of home and neighbourhood can be quite shattering. Like other displaced groups, the Lebanese became disoriented and distressed because the terrain had changed and because there was no longer a neighbourhood for them to live in and rely upon. 'When the landscape goes, says Erikson, 'it destroys the past for those who are left: people have no sense of belonging anywhere.' (Erikson, 1976) They lose the sense of control over their lives, their freedom and independence, their moorings to place and locality and, more damaging, a sense of who they are.

They become homeless in at least three existential senses. First, they do so in the literal sense of being physically dislodged from enduring attachments and familiar places. Secondly, they suffer the stigma of being outcasts in their neighbourhoods and homes. Finally, like true exiles, they are impelled by an urge to reassemble a damaged identity and a broken history. Imagining the old places, with all their nostalgic longings, serves as their only reprieve from the uncertainties and anxieties of the present.

The prolific war literature, particularly the output of a generation of so-called 'Decentrist' woman writers and other disinherited liberals, is clearly symptomatic of efforts to grapple with such damaged identities. Much like the earlier generation of exiled Lebanese and Syrian poets (e.g. Gibran and Rihani), who had transformed the anguish of their uprootedness into inventive literary movements (the Pen Bond and the Andalusian Group), they too found shelter in a 'poetics of disaster' (see Alcalay, 1993: 99) But this brief, blissful interlude came to an end as the tensions between the vibrant Beirut of old and the city descending into anomie became more flagrant. Khalil Hawi's suicide on the eve of the Israeli invasion is seen now as a grim icon, a requiem for that dark abyss in Arab cultural history (see Ajami, 1998; Alcalay, 1993).

Curiously, Beirut Decentrist women found some redemption in the war. The chaos, anarchy, meaninglessness and the ultimate collapse of society gave women, paradoxically, a liberating place and a new voice (for an elaboration of these see Cooke, 1988; Alcalay, 1993; Manganaro, 1998). As society was unravelling itself and the country was being stripped of its identity, women were discovering arenas for validating and asserting their own identities. Incidentally, this transformative, redemptive role did not mean that women were in effect challenging patriarchy or that they were partaking in efforts to restore civility in society. Miriam Cooke has described the situation well.

> Their concern was not to gain acceptance into a predominantly male preserve but rather to register a voice. These voices were rarely heard in what has been termed the public domain. Their content was deemed irrelevant. How could the expression of private experience become acceptable outside its immediate confines? How could the apparently mutually exclusive domains of private and public, of self and other, be reconciled? Boundaries had to be challenged and shown to be fluid, elusive. Such a radical reassessment and construction of social and literary order could not be achieved spontaneously . . . The Lebanese war provided the context. Violence in this case represented universal loss of power, but it also undermined the private/public dichotomy, revealing the private to be public, and the personal to be universal. Private space became everyone's space and it was appropriated literarily in a collective endeavor to express and thereby understand the reign of unreason. (Cooke, 1988: 87)

But even as 'voice' or mere writing, the works of women remained marginal and frivolous. The writers themselves harboured few illusions in this regard other than seeing their personal struggles to forge new identities or reconstruct more coherent selves linked with the enveloping malaise surrounding them. Cooke provides evidence from the works of Ghada Al-Samman, Etél Adnan, Claire Gebeyli, Hoda el-Námani and Hanan al-Shaykh in support of this.

> By the late 1970s, the Beirut Decentrists were using language to create a new reality. Their writings were becoming transformative, even prescriptive. As self-censorship gave way to uninhibited expressions of self-assertion, the hold of the oppressive male critic was shaken. It was only with the breakdown of Lebanon's identity as an independent patriarchal polity that women began to assert their female identity publicly . . . As the violence persisted and men fought senseless battles or fled, women came to realize that the society of which they were also members was collapsing; unravelling seams revealed the need for collective responsibility, but also for responsibility for the self. The

individual had to become aware to survive. The time that was right for assertion of female identity coincided with the disintegration of the country's identity. (Cooke, 1988: 11–12)

This poignant predicament, in which the horrors of war are transformed into redemptive features, is most eloquently expressed in Hanan al-Shaykh's novel, *The Story of Zahra*. The torments of war do not only render all conventions irrelevant and sweep away the hollowness of daily routine and restore normality; they also became sources of illumination and self-discovery. Indeed, given the catalogue of horrors to which Zahra has been subjected to in her 'normal' life (domestic violence, incest, rape, arranged marriage, divorce), the war seems more than just a blissful antidote and return to normality. In her own words, it makes her 'more alive and more tranquil'.

> This war has made beauty, money, terror and convention all equally irrelevant. It begins to occur to me that the war, with its miseries and destructiveness, has been necessary for me to start to return to being normal and human.
> The war, which makes one expect the worst at any moment, has led me into accepting this new element in my life. Let it happen, let us witness it, let us open ourselves to accept the unknown, no matter what it may bring, disasters or surprises. The war has been essential. It has swept away the hollowness concealed by routines. It has made me ever more alive, ever more tranquil. (al-Shaykh, 1986: 138)

Equally devastating has been the gradual destruction of common spaces in Beirut and many other parts of the country. The first to go was Beirut's Central Business District, which had served historically as the undisputed focal point and meeting place. Beirut without its 'Burj,' as the city centre is popularly known, was unimaginable. Virtually all the vital public functions were centralized there: the parliament, municipal headquarters, financial and banking institutions, religious buildings, transport terminals, traditional souks, shopping malls, places of entertainment, etc., all kept the pre-war 'Burj' in a sustained state of day- and night-time animation. There, people of every walk of life and social standing came together.

With decentralization, other urban districts and regions in the country served as supplementary meeting grounds for common activities. They too drew together, albeit on a seasonal and interim basis, groups from a wide cross-section of society, thereby nurturing outlets conducive to coexistence and plural lifestyles. Altogether, there were very few exclusive spaces beyond the reach of others. The social tissue, like all seemingly localized spaces, was fluid and permeable.

Alas, the war destroyed virtually all such common and porous spaces, just as it dismantled many of the intermediary and peripheral heterogeneous neighbourhoods that had mushroomed with increasing urbanization in cities like Tripoli, Sidon and Zahleh. The war not only destroyed common spaces but also encouraged the formation of separate, exclusive and self-sufficient spaces. Hence, the Christians of East Beirut had no compelling urge to cross over to West Beirut for its cultural and popular entertainment. Likewise, the Muslims and other residents of West Beirut were understandably reluctant to visit the resorts and similarly alluring spots of the Christian suburbs. With internecine conflict, quarters within urban districts, just like towns and villages, were often splintered into smaller and more compact enclosures. Spaces within which people circulated and interacted shrank still further. The socio-psychological predispositions underlying this urge to huddle in insulated spaces is not too difficult to trace or account for. Its consequence was a further 'Balkanization' of Lebanon's social geography. There is a curious and painful irony here. Despite the many differences that divide the Lebanese, they are all in a sense homogenized by fear, grief and trauma. Primal fear is the tie that binds them together – three fears, in fact – the fear of being marginalized, assimilated or exiled. But it is also those fears that keep the Lebanese apart. This 'geography of fear' is not sustained by walls or artificial barriers, as one observes in other comparable instances of ghettoization of minorities and ethnic groups. Rather, it is sustained by the psychology of dread, hostile bonding and ideologies of enmity. Massive population shifts, particularly since they are accompanied by the reintegration of displaced groups into more homogeneous, self-contained and exclusive spaces, have also reinforced communal solidarity. Consequently, territorial and confessional identities are beginning to converge, more so perhaps than at any other time. For example, 44 per cent of all villages and towns before the outbreaks of hostilities included inhabitants of more than one sect. The sharp sectarian redistribution, as Salim Nasr (1993) has shown, has reshuffled this mixed composition. While the proportion of Christians living in the southern regions of Mount Lebanon (i.e. Shouf, Aley, Upper Metn) was 55 per cent in 1975, it shrank to about 5 per cent by the late 1980s. The same is true of West Beirut and its suburbs. Likewise, the proportion of Muslims living in the eastern suburbs of Beirut has also been reduced from 40 per cent to about 5 per cent over the same period. (Nasr, 1993)

Within urban areas, such territorial solidarities assume all the trappings and mythology of aggressive and defensive 'urban *'asabiyyas'* (a feeling of communal or tribal solidarity), which exist, Seurat (1985) tells us, only through their opposition to other quarters. The stronger the identification with one's quarter, the deeper the enmity and rejection of the other. Seurat's study also suggests that, once such a process is under way, a mythology of the quarter can develop. In it, the quarter is seen not only as the place where a beleaguered community fights for its survival, but also as a territorial base from which the community may set out to create a utopia, a world where one may live a 'pure' and 'authentic' life, in conformity with the community's traditions and values. The neighbourhood community may even be invested with a redemptive role and mission (such as the defence of Sunni Islam in the case of Bab Tebbane in Tripoli which Seurat was studying). Hence, the dialectics between identity and politics may be better appreciated. Politics implies negotiation, compromise and living side by side with 'the other'. Heightened feelings of identity, however, may lead one to a refusal to compromise, if negotiation comes to be perceived as containing the seeds of treachery that may undermine the traditions, values and 'honour' of one's community. In such a context, violence and polarization become inevitable: precisely the phenomena that have plagued Lebanon for so long.

The Spaces of War

Another graphic and poignant consequence of protracted strife is the way the spaces of war and their concomitant geographies of fear started to assert their ferocious logic in virtually every nook and cranny of public and private spaces. Much of Lebanon's geography and landscape in fact took on the grotesque nomenclature of the war. The besieged inhabitants showed much ingenuity in accommodating this change in their spatial surroundings.

Public thoroughfares, crossroads, bridges, hilltops and strategic intersections that served as links between communities were the first to be converted. They became 'Green Lines', barriers preventing any cross-over. Incidentally, the infamous 'Green Line' acquired its notorious label when shrubs and bushes sprouted from its tarmac after years of neglect. It is ironic that this great divide, which ripped the city in two, was none other than the major throughway (i.e. the old Damascus Road), which connected Beirut to its hinterland and beyond. Likewise, major squares, traffic terminals and pedestrian shopping arcades, once the hub of gregarious activity and dense interaction, became a desolate 'no man's land', *al-mahawir al-taqlidiyya* (traditional lines of confrontation) or *khutut al-tamas* (lines of confrontation).

While prominent public spaces lost their identity, other rather ordinary places, such as crossings, junctions, even shops, became landmarks of dread. The war produced its own lexicon and iconography of places. In an evocative, often searing memoir of her encounters with civil strife in Beirut, Jean Said Makdisi (1990) provides an amusing but instructive 'Glossary of Terms Used in Times of Crisis'. Schoolboys, oblivious to the location of some of their country's national treasures, were more impressed by *Galerie Sim'an, Sodeco, al-Matahen, Hayy al-Buseinat, al-Laylaki, Barbir, Bourj al-Murr, Fattal, Mar Mikhail, Khaldeh triangle*, etc. These and other such inconsequential places and spaces became points of references and demarcation lines, part of the deadly logistics of contested space.

When the hostility shifted into internecine confrontations, as it repeatedly did, it took the form of factional, localized 'turf wars' between militias vying to eliminate adversaries or extend the basis of their operations. Negotiating safe havens within this labyrinthine maze of embattled quarters and dense pockets of shifting allegiances became more cumbersome. Here as well, little-known passageways and winding alleys, because they provided relatively safe access to rerouted roads, acquired a new image and notoriety. Overnight, a road became a barricade or a 'flying roadblock'; a walled garden became a blockaded stronghold; a street corner turned into a checkpoint.

Private space was not spared these radical changes in land use. Indeed, the distinctions between private and public space were blurred and lost much of their conventional usage. Just as basements, rooftops and strategic openings in private homes became part of the logistics of combat, roadways were also 'domesticated' as family possessions, and discarded furniture and bulky items spilled into the public domain to improvise barricades. Balconies, verandahs, walk-ups, doorways and all the other open airy and buoyant places the Lebanese craved and exploited with such ingenuity became spaces to be avoided. Conversely, dingy basements, tightly sealed corridors, attics and other normally neglected spaces became more coveted simply because they were out of the trajectory of snipers and shellfire. They became places of refuge. (For further details see Sarkis, 1993; Yahya, 1993; Khalaf, 1995.)

The symbolic meanings and uses of a 'house', 'home' or 'dwelling' space, as Maha Yahya (1993) has demonstrated, were also overhauled, most strikingly in the way the family unit and its private space were broadened to accommodate other functions, as disengaged and unemployed household members converted or relocated their business premises to their homes. The thriving informal war economy reinforced such efforts and rendered them more effective.

As land turns over, so do our perceptions and commitments to it. Such changes are not only visible in the way the Lebanese are confirming their spatial moorings and the language they employ in asserting their retribalized identities. Their images of the 'other', those who intrude on their spaces and beyond, have also been profoundly transformed.

Such transformations are, doubtless, a reflection of their attachments and devotions to the places they occupy. The war has had in this regard two diametrically opposed reactions. On the one hand, displaced Christians who have been relocated among their co-religionists in integrated communities have become more spatially anchored. On the other hand, uprooted refugees, largely Shi'ites and other disenfranchised groups, have had a markedly tenuous attachment to the spaces they are compelled to occupy. At both ends, the environment suffers. As we have seen, the exodus of Christians has been disproportionately higher than that of other groups. It is estimated that today they make up not more than 35–38 per cent of the total Lebanese population. They have not only shrunk demographically, they have also contracted spatially. Salim Nasr (1993) suggests that by the mid-1980s more than 80 per cent of the Christians were concentrated in a surface area of only about 17 per cent of the country. Such a contraction was bound to change their perception and uses of space dramatically. Feeling more hemmed in within compressed areas, they have become predisposed toward more intensive forms of land utilization. Hence, the eastern suburbs and the lush slopes of the northern mountain ridge are now dense with high-rises and other strictly city-like constructions.

While the countryside is being urbanized, the cities and sprawling suburbs are being ruralized. Both are perverse. Dislocated groups that converge on squatted settlements in the city centre and urban fringe are generally strangers to city life. On the whole, they are dislodged, dispossessed and unanchored groups, traumatized by fear and raging with feelings of bitterness and betrayal. They are, so to speak, *in* but not *of* the city. Hence, they have no attachments to or appreciation of the areas in which they find themselves and are not likely to display any interest in safeguarding or enriching its character. To many, in fact, their makeshift settlements are merely places to occupy with amenities to exploit.

Perhaps the most negative aspect of this whole development is the way in which the tempo of war has imposed its own perilous time frames, dictating traffic flows and spaces to be used or avoided. Time, space, movement and interaction all became enveloped with contingency and uncertainty. Nothing is taken for granted any more. People live, so to speak, situationally. Short-term expediency has replaced long-term planning. Everything has had to be negotiated on the spur of the moment. The day-to-day routines, which once structured the use of space and time, played havoc with their lives. Deficient communication and irregular and congested traffic rendered all forms of social interaction fortuitous and unpredictable. One was expected to accomplish one's daily activities at unexpected hours, depending on the merciless whims of fighters and the capricious cycles of violence. Beirutis became, as a result, astonishingly adept at making instant adaptations to such jarring modulations and precipitous shifts in the use of time and space.

> The street was suddenly deserted. Beirutis have broken all records for getting out of the way on time. It is incredible to see how quickly a street swarming with people can be transformed into ghostly emptiness. Shopkeepers close their doors and pull down their iron shutters, mothers scoop up their children and run, vendors scuttle away with their carts, and after an even more than usually furious beeping of horns, the traffic jam evaporates in no time at all.
>
> As suddenly as the commotion started, it stopped, and as suddenly as Hamra was emptied, it filled up again; within a few minutes life went on as though nothing had happened. (Makdisi, 1990: 86)

A War System

The resilience of the Lebanese and their adaptive strategies to cope with the cruelties of war would not alone have reproduced the circumstances to allow the war to go on for so long. What abetted and reinforced its continuation was that the war itself evolved an elaborate sub-culture of its own and became something akin to a 'war system'. Foremost, the void created by the collapse of state authority (particularly between 1975 and 1990) enabled the war to generate and institutionalize its own groups and networks with its particular structures and an interrelated web of rules and obligations. Individuals and agencies, who provided access to amenities, vital resources, information, smuggled goods, black markets and war booty, found new shortcuts and other venues for empowerment and enhanced status. Some became folk heroes. Others, almost overnight, became acclaimed public figures with no legitimate claims to prominence other than the access they provided for such ephemeral but coveted goods and services. These and the burgeoning informal, parallel or war economy, with its extortionism and protection rackets, its under-class of new warlords and war profiteers and other well-placed individuals, were, understandably, reluctant to put an end to a situation that had become their route to power and privilege. They all had a vested interest in maintaining the status quo of belligerency.

The 'war booty' was a bountiful windfall to large segments of society and not restricted to those directly involved in combat. Given its disguised and clandestine character, it is extremely difficult to ascertain its full magnitude, but by any criteria it was immense. Nor was it an ephemeral or transient feature. It served as a major vector in reshuffling the conventional socio-economic strata in society. Indeed, during the first two years of the war the fighting for control of Beirut's Central Business District must have precipitated what some claim to be 'the greatest redistribution of wealth in modern Lebanon's history'. (Hanf, 1993: 329)

Like other nefarious exploits, this 'war system' was not entirely indigenous. Regional and global sponsors of local militias funnelled in inordinate sums of money. Foreign sources also poured in large reserves to bolster the war efforts of their respective communities. Most dramatic, however, was the new social stratum of war profiteers, contraband traders and large-scale looters, who flaunted their new wealth and privileges with unrestrained exuberance and abandon.

There is also evidence that the looting of souks, vandalizing of private estates and residential quarters and the extensive bank robberies were not all the work of amateurs. Much of these were accomplished with the technical assistance of professional pillagers and safecrackers from Europe, possibly supplied by the Mafia (see, for further details, Randal, 1984: 98–100; Petran, 1987: 231–32; Winslow, 1996: 212–29). Zuhair Muhsin, leader of Sa'iqa (the Syrian-sponsored Palestinian militia), was derisively nicknamed 'the Persian' for the quantities of valuable Persian carpets that his men looted as they vandalized privileged residential quarters in Beirut.

The string of clandestine and makeshift ports stretching from Junieh to Tripoli, in addition to those appropriated from the state, generated untold revenue to the Lebanese forces. The Gemayyel militias alone, by barring the government from levying custom duties from Pier Five at Beirut's port, managed to siphon off, it is estimated, over 5 billion LP ($1.4 billion) during the first seven to eight years of the war. (Winslow, 1996: 217) Traffic in hashish and other drugs through the Biqa Valley was also heavy during this period. The Syrian-Franjieh coalition walked away with the lion's share of such nefarious but lucrative ventures. The Syrian army in Shtura and Akkar was also involved in protection rackets for the trafficking of consumer durables and other products. (Harris, 1997: 212) Indeed, the scandalous and extensive corruption and involvement of Syrian soldiers and officers in unscrupulous and self-aggrandizing schemes and activities were a source of embarrassment to the Syrian regime. Efforts were made in fact to rotate office-holders or to restrict their term, to foil or curtail such opportunities. The magnitude of such complicity was still immense: bribery, sale of arms to local Lebanese militias, cultivation, drug smuggling and drug trafficking and widespread smuggling of other goods from Lebanon to Syria. Rifat Assad alone, the President's notorious brother, was reportedly involved in deals worth billions of Syrian pounds (see *Le Monde,* 1984; Avi-Ran, 1991: 195, 207).

Incidentally, the Israeli Army did not fare any better in this regard. They too displayed many of the symptoms of wanton greed, arrogance and profligacy of any conquering army. Ironically, they came in as peace-keepers. Their 1982 invasion, an operation they dubbed 'Peace for Galilee', had little to do with peace-keeping or peace-making. They besieged and bombarded the residential quarters of West Beirut and its dense suburbs, destroyed its infrastructure and generated the heaviest toll of casualties of the entire war. An estimated 17,000 were killed and about 30,000 wounded, mostly innocent citizens (see Labaki and Abou Rjeili, 1993: 27; Hanf, 1993: 341). As if the massive destruction and its legacy of hate and bitterness were not enough, they also carried off a substantial haul. Not only did the army seize 520 tonnes of arms and material, but ordinary Israeli soldiers were evidently taken by the wealth and lifestyle of the Lebanese bourgeoisie and freely looted the quarters that were under their control. Nothing was spared: private cars, telephones, telex machines, gadgets and appliances, even wooden school benches! (For further substantiation see Randal, 1984: 266–67.)

The Magnitude of Trauma and Stress

Since Lebanon was, for nearly two decades, subjected to every conceivable form of collective terror, it is pertinent to assess its impact on the victims. As we have already seen, the damage to human life and property and the psychological and moral consequences of relentless violence have been, by any measure, immense, the more so since the society in question was comparatively small and fractured with a bewildering plurality and shifting targets of hostility.

An empirical survey conducted in 1983 to probe some of the salient socio-psychological effects of the war provided a few explicit and systematic measures of these effects. The sample was extracted from a universe of mostly middle- and upper-middle-class professionals, semi-professionals, businessmen, bankers, university and college professors and instructors, government employees, journalists and the like, residing in three different communities in Beirut. Close to 900 heads of households responded to the questionnaire. Matters such as the changing attitudes and perceptions of the respondents, their everyday experiences during the war and their experiences of traumatization, deprivation and displacement were explored. The survey also permitted assessment of the symptoms of stress, particularly some of the psychological and behavioural disorders induced by the traumas of war.

As Table 1 shows, close to 75 per cent of the respondents had experienced some form of deprivation and 66 per cent were compelled to take refuge in shelters. By 'deprivation' is meant being denied water, electricity, power and other basic amenities. A fairly large portion, about 55 per cent, also suffered property damage and over 40 per cent were displaced from their homes or communities. More traumatizing, 36 per cent indicated that they had lost a family member or close relative and slightly more (38%) a close friend or acquaintance. Worse still, a quarter of the sample reported that they had directly witnessed a war-induced death.

The incidence of humiliation, insult, intimidation or harassment by armed men at checkpoints or street crossings was also fairly high. Nearly one-third of respondents suffered such indignities. Also a fairly large portion (21%) had their houses broken into or occupied (19%). While only 5 per cent of the respondents reported being kidnapped, the proportion leapt to 21 per cent among other family members and 30 per cent among friends. A slightly higher number suffered injury that required hospitalization: 26 per cent among family and relatives and 32 per cent among friends. Also 10 per cent of the respondent's family and relatives and 21 per cent of their friends suffered a permanent disability.

Table 1
Magnitude of Traumatization (% of total respondents)

	Respondent	Family/relatives	Close friend	Witnessed	Average
Deprivation	74	53	58	36	55
Refuge in shelter	66	50	59	34	52
Property damage	54	42	51	27	43
Displacement	41	37	42	22	35
Death	0	36	38	25	33
Humiliation	33	27	29	26	29
Injury	8	26	32	23	22
House broken into	21	24	22	9	19
House/property occupied	19	23	23	12	19
Insult/harassment	19	18	20	20	19
Impostoring	17	20	19	11	17
Car stolen	12	26	20	7	16
Kidnapped	5	21	30	10	16
Assault	4	14	21	22	15
Threats	14	16	18	12	15
Disability	3	10	21	16	12
Detention	6	13	19	7	11

Though not directly related to the conduct of fighting, car thefts, like other symptoms of the breakdown in law and order and public security, became rampant, affecting 12 per cent of respondents. It was considerably higher for other family members (26%) and friends (20%). About the same number were victims of psychological and moral hostility such as impostoring, detention and threats.

The psychological concomitants of trauma, particularly as they manifest themselves in emotional and psychosomatic disorders and in behavioural and associational problems, were also quite pervasive. As Table 2 shows, no one was spared these stresses and strains. This is, after all, another poignant attribute of all 'uncivil' wars; violence and destruction leave repressed feelings of guilt, shame, trauma and fear in their train. The scars and scares of war have a way of resurfacing, often with greater intensity and trauma. They rarely go away. The violated are doomed to be haunted by the ghosts of violence. The most stressful consequences, as the respondents reported, were symptoms of restlessness and instability, inability to concentrate, sleep disorders, depression and other behavioural problems such as a tendency to overreact and excessive smoking. About 49 to 54 per cent of the respondents suffered these symptoms from time to time.

Table 2
Induced Stress and Psychological Disorder (% of total respondents)

	Never	From time to time	Often	Index
Psychological disorders				
Restlessness/instability	18.6	52.0	14.7	81.4
Sleep disorders	20.2	54.0	10.0	74.0
Depression	21.6	47.0	9.0	65.0
Desperation	32.3	37.6	8.6	54.8
Worry, unjustified fears	28.0	39.0	7.6	54.2
Psychosomatic problems	34.7	30.2	7.8	45.8
Loss of will	39.4	30.7	4.6	40.0
Thoughts of death	45.2	23.6	3.4	30.4
Self-blame	53.0	17.3	2.3	22.0
Behavioural changes				
Overreacting	22.6	44.0	14.2	72.4
Smoking too much	38.0	24.8	19.0	62.8
Inability to concentrate	26.2	49.0	5.0	59.0
Overeating	38.5	30.8	7.0	44.8
Drinking too much	49.5	20.6	4.0	28.6
Unlawful predispositions	53.2	17.0	2.5	22.0
Aggressive tendencies	56.3	13.2	2.6	18.4
Problem in interacting with others				
Problems with friends	35.7	38.6	2.7	44.0
Problems with family	30.7	35.5	3.2	42.0
Problems with colleagues	34.8	36.5	4.2	35.0
Problems with spouse	33.9	20.0	2.2	24.6
Sexual problems	54.5	16.7	1.1	19.0

The moderate symptoms of stress centred on problems such as feelings of desperation, obsessive worry, eating and psychosomatic disorders. The quality of people's social relations, particularly their interactions with family, friends and colleagues at work, was also adversely affected. More than 38 per cent cited these as sources of unnecessary tension and friction. The family in particular, especially since it is embedded in a kinship culture sustained by a network of close and intimate ties and obligations, was a surrogate victim of such displaced tension. Much of the unappeased hostility and daily frustrations induced by protracted violence is apt to be released in such settings on vulnerable and accessible family members.

Table 3
Magnitude of Stress-related Disorders (% of total respondents)

Acute problems (%)	Moderate stress (%)	Mild stress (%)
Restlessness (81)	Desperation (55)	Drinking too much (27)
Sleep disorders (74)	Excessive worry (52)	Problems with spouse (24)
Overreaction (72)	Psychosomatic (46)	Self-blame (22)
Depression (65)	Overeating (45)	Unlawful predispositions (22)
Smoking too much (63)	Problems with friends (44)	Sexual problems (19)
Lack of concentration (59)	Problems with family (42)	Aggression (18)
	Problems with colleagues (40)	Suicidal tendencies (5)
	Preoccupation with death (30)	

Tension within the family was compounded by two seemingly divergent sources of strain. Heads of households and other adult members of the family (particularly males), who had to interrupt their employment, were compelled to become housebound. Hence they were 'wasting' inordinate chunks of idle and uncommitted time at home. Such involuntary confinement at home, let alone the demoralization that accompanies such symptoms of disengagement and entropy, became an inescapable source of family discord. Conversely, families suffered from the other extreme: the involuntary absence of men from home. In addition to those involved in the war, many had to seek employment opportunities outside Lebanon and hence suffer the difficulties of living in the diaspora and extended periods away from home. Both the lack of intimacy within and the distance from the family were excessive and unwanted. The former exacerbated the intensity of family squabbles and rendered the already beleaguered family more vulnerable and testy. The latter did much to 'feminize' the household. The absence of men and heads of household for extended interludes undermined patriarchal authority and, more damaging, denied children their conventional male role models. Defective socialization of this sort may have grievous socio-psychological implications.

The results of the survey disclose another seemingly anomalous feature. There was no direct relationship between the magnitude of traumatization and symptoms of stress and psychological disorder. In other words, groups who had suffered a larger share of trauma were not necessarily those who also displayed greater symptoms of stress. Two factors could readily account for this disparity. First, at the time the survey was conducted, shortly after the Israeli invasion of 1982, Christian respondents and residents of the eastern suburbs of Beirut, who had exhibited such tendencies, were inclined then to view the conduct of the war in more positive terms. Since they felt that the fortunes of war were still in their favour, the trials that they had suffered were partly assuaged or redeemed. Christians were not as yet afflicted with feelings of *ihbat* (a sense of being defeated or demoralized): that happened later.

Second, Christian groups had also displayed greater readiness for communal solidarity and mobilization in hard times. Voluntary groups, church and neighbourhood associations were active in providing the needed services and support for welfare and relief. Such mobilization might have redressed some of the sources of tension.

Post-war Barbarism

Post-war interludes, particularly those marked by diffuse and protracted civil strife, anarchy and disorder, normally generate moods of restraint. People are more inclined to curb their conventional impulses and become more self-controlled in the interest of reappraising and redirecting their future options. Rather than freeing them from their pre-war excesses, the war in Lebanon paradoxically induced the opposite reactions. It unleashed appetites and created insatiable desires for acquisitiveness, lawlessness and unearned privileges.

Some of these excesses are so egregious that they become the not-so-moral equivalents of war. In such circumstances the tendency to aggression may break free from ordinary civilized constraints. In Lebanon most of the conventional restraints that normally moderate people's rapacious and impulsive behaviour were neutralized. Boisterous and disorderly behaviour became routine. Some elements of this behaviour, such as ravaging the country's natural habitat, violating zoning and building ordinances, embezzlement, fraud, corruption, deficient civic and public consciousness – most visible in the preponderance of low crimes and misdemeanours – are all deeply embedded in the cultural ethos of laissez faire, excessive economic liberalism and political clientelism.

For example, mercantilism and its concomitant bourgeois values were always given a free reign in Lebanon. The outcome of such excessive commercialization was already painfully obvious in the pre-war years. With staggering increases in land values, commercial traffic in real estate (particularly during the 1960s, when urbanization and construction industry were at their peak) became one of the most lucrative sources of private wealth – hence the ruthless plundering of the country's scenic habitat and the dehumanization of its living space. In the late 1960s, at the height of Beirut's splendour and golden age, the seasoned world traveller John Gunther was so dismayed by what he saw that he prefaced his chapter on the 'Pearl of the Middle East', with the following:

> Beirut commits treason against itself. This ancient city, the capital of Lebanon, blessed with a sublime physical location and endowed with a beauty of surroundings unmatched in the world, is a dog-eared shambles – dirtier, just plain dirtier, than any other city of consequence I have ever seen.
>
> In the best quarter of the town, directly adjacent to a brand-new hotel gleaming with lacy marble, there exists a network of grisly small alleys which, so far as I could tell, are never swept at all. Day after day I would see – and learned to know – the same debris: bent chunks of corrugated iron, broken boulders or cement, rags, rotten vegetables, and paper cartons bursting with decayed merchandise. Much of the detritus seems to be of a kind that goes with a rich community, not a poor one. The cool and sparkling Mediterranean across the boulevard looks enticing for a swim, until you see that the water is full of

orange peel, oil slick, blobs of toilet paper, and assorted slimy objects. (Gunther, 1969: 281)

In the absence of government authority, such excesses became more rampant. What had not been ravaged by war was eaten up by greedy developers and impetuous consumers. Hardly anything was spared. The once pristine coastline was littered with tawdry tourist attractions, kitsch resorts and private marinas, as well as by a proliferation of slums and other illegal makeshift, shoddy tenements. The same blight afflicted the already shrinking green belts, public parks and terraced orchards. Even pavements and private backyards were stripped and defiled. As a result, Beirut today suffers, perhaps, from one of the lowest rates of open space per capita in the world. The entire metropolitan area of the city claims no more than 600,000 square meters of open space. A United Nations report stipulates that a healthy environment requires about 40 square metres of open space for each person. In Beirut the figure is as low as 0.8 square metres per person (for these and other estimates see Safe, 2000).

Rampant commercialism, greed and weakened state authority could not, on their own, have produced so much damage. These are now being exacerbated by a ravenous post-war mentality. People subjected for so long to such atrocious human suffering become insensitive to what seem like benign and inconsequential transgressions. It is understandable that, in the wake of an ugly and unfinished war, moral and aesthetic restraints that normally control public behaviour become dispensable virtues. Victims of collective suffering normally have other rudimentary things on their mind. They rage with bitterness and long to make up for lost time and opportunity. The environment becomes an accessible target on which to vent their wrath. Moreover, violating the habitat is also very lucrative. Both greed and hostility find an expedient proxy victim here. The abandon with which ordinary citizens litter and defile the environment and the total disregard they evince for safeguarding its ecological well-being are extremely alarming. Their attitude is compounded by a notoriously high incidence of quarrying, deforestation, traffic congestion, reckless driving, air and noise pollution and hazardous motorways, which violate minimum safety requirements, not to mention the disregard for the rules and manners of the road.

The sharp increase in traffic violations and fatal car accidents in recent years attests to this. As Table 4 shows, both the incidence of traffic violations and the impounding or seizing of cars for legal custody – because of forged papers or licence plates, or a lack of inspection or proper registration – have been persistently increasing. From 21,692 seized cars and 192,487 violations in 1993, the number almost doubled by 1999.

Traffic accidents were naturally few during the war years. Records of the Information Division of the Internal Security Forces registered no more than six injuries and 20 deaths caused by collisions and car accidents in 1987. The figures increased to 21 and 56 respectively in 1988. From 1993 onwards, however, and with the cessation of hostilities, the number of such casualties increased sharply and persistently. From 274 deaths and 2,042 injuries in 1993, the numbers increased to 331 and 4,210 respectively in 1999.

Perhaps access to new highways and the recent introduction of radar and new technologies for monitoring roadways may, in part, account for this increase, clearly not all of it, however, particularly since the increase in violations and other manifestation of reckless driving were visible before such facilities became readily available.

Table 4
Car and Traffic Violations

Year	Traffic violations	Impounded cars
1993	192,487	21,692
1994	334,536	32,637
1995	412,867	45,667
1996	239,910	33,280
1997	258,981	30,531
1998	262,031	38,845
1999	303,455	42,561

Source: Information Division, Internal Security Forces.

Table 5
Traffic Casualties

	1987	1988	1993	1994	1995	1996	1997	1998	1999
Injuries	6	21	2,042	3,017	3,422	3,215	3,465	3,445	4,210
Deaths	20	56	274	328	355	327	357	325	331

Source: Information Division, Internal Security Forces.

Table 6
Ordinary Violations (excluding traffic)

	1993	1994	1995	1996	1997	1998	1999
Violations	10,954	10,813	15,511	14,051	14,023	15,465	18,335

Source: Information Division, Internal Security Forces.

This almost innate cultural disposition to break the rules and contravene expectations is apparent in the preponderance of ordinary infractions, misdemeanours and other breaches of public ordinances. As shown in Table 5, these too have been persistently increasing: from about 10,000 in 1993 to 14,000 in 1996 and 18,000 in 1999. Under the rubric of 'ordinary violations', the Internal Security normally includes offences such as the infringement of protective regulations safeguarding forests, public gardens, sand dunes, archaeological and tourist sites and building and zoning ordinances, as well as transgressions of the rules governing hunting, fishing, quarrying and municipal and public health requirements. Similarly, public utilities, particularly water, electricity and telephones, are readily abused as people project their rage and hostility on to them.

Recently the press is beginning to devote some attention to such violations, particularly flagrant instances of environmental abuse, corruption and misuse of public funds in high office. Much of the other 'ordinary' violations, however, remain undetected and when they are discovered the fines are so meagre that violators usually pay them without demur.

If smoking in public spaces were ever to be prohibited by decree, the Lebanese would most certainly ignore the ban, just as they brush aside all other restrictions on their impulses and extravagant appetites. Lebanon today is a haven for smokers. Anyone can indulge, virtually anywhere and to their lungs' delight, unhampered by any prohibition or public conscience. Indeed, the incidence of smoking is perhaps one of the highest in the world. Studies conducted by WHO and the Ministry of Health reveal that 68 per cent of the adult male population are smokers and a notoriously high 47 per cent of women. In developing countries the percentage of women smokers almost never exceeds single digits, for example it is not more than 2.3 per cent in Egypt and 7.1 per cent in Jordan.

The incidence of smoking is bad enough. Worse still is the bravado with which smokers flaunt their addiction, exhibiting total disregard for its public health menaces or the rights of non-smokers to fresh air.

For a country committed to the need to spend huge amounts on rehabilitation and reconstruction, the waste of money on cigarettes and their effects of smoking is staggering and disgraceful. According to the Ministry of Health, a total of $400 million a year is spent on healthcare for those suffering from smoking-related illness. Another $100 million is spent every year on cigarette promotion. The most witty and seductive advertisements are for tobacco. Liquor, lingerie and cellular telephones run it a poor second. Public highways and desolate country roads alike are decked with imposing billboards beckoning travellers to 'Malboro' country'!! Even politicians and public figures (who should be the country's most illustrious role models) fail to put their cigarettes aside when they appear on talk shows and other television programmes.

Smoking is so entrenched in everyday life and personal conduct that it would be almost impossible to deracinate it. To date, all attempts to launch a comprehensive, countrywide strategy to curb the use of tobacco have been abortive. Even the laws passed in 1995 banning smoking in hospitals, infirmaries, pharmacies, theatres, public transportat terminals, health clubs, schools, universities, elevators, etc., are not observed or implemented. A proposal for a law banning all tobacco advertisements on television, radio and print media failed to be endorsed by the Council of Ministers. In this and other regards, Lebanon is today where the United States used to be more than 50 years ago. Given the mood of popular intransigence, the public is not likely to accept any restrictions on their self-indulgent licence to pollute their surroundings.

In such a free-for-all context, any concern for the aesthetic, human or cultural dimensions of living space is bound to be dismissed as superfluous or guileless. It is of little concern whether our public spaces are ugly, whether they debase their inhabitants, whether they are aesthetically, spiritually or physically tolerable, or whether they provide people with opportunities for authentic individuality, privacy and edifying human encounters. What counts is that the unconditional access to land must satisfy two overriding claims: the insatiable appetite for profit among the bourgeoisie and the vengeful feeling of entitlements to unearned privileges among the disenfranchised. By the time authorities stepped in to restrain or recover such violations, as they did repeatedly in the pre-war years, the efforts were always too little, too late. By then, officials could only confirm the infringements and incorporate them into the legitimate zoning ordinances.

Retribalization

As the scares and the scars of war became more savage and cruel, it is understandable that traumatized groups should seek refuge in their most trusted and deeply embedded primordial ties and loyalties, particularly those that coalesce around the family, sect and community. Even in times of relative harmony and stability, kinship and communal groupings were always effective as mediating sources of socio-psychological support and political mobilization.

As we have seen, however, the hostilities drastically rearranged the country's social geography. Massive population shifts, particularly since they involved the reintegration of displaced groups into homogeneous and exclusive communities, rendered territorial identities sharper and more spatially anchored. Thus 'retribalization' became more pervasive. The term is employed here loosely to refer to the reinforcement of kinship and confessional and communal loyalties, which were especially significant as they converged on tightly-knit spatial enclosures. Lebanon is, in other words, being retribalized precisely because in all three most elemental groupings (family, community and sect), loyalties and obligations and the density of social interaction that binds groups together are becoming sources of intense solidarity. A word about each is in order.

Familism

The Lebanese family has always been a resilient institution. Despite the inevitable decline in the sense of kinship that the family experienced in the pre-war years – caused by increasing urbanization, mobility and secularization – it continued to have a social and psychological reality, which pervaded virtually all aspects of society. As many studies demonstrated, there was hardly a dimension of a person's life that was untouched by the survival of family loyalty and its associated norms and agencies. To a considerable extent, a person's status, occupation, political behaviour, personal values, spatial and residential patterns, visiting habits and associational behaviour, lifestyle and milestones in life were defined by kinship affiliation. These attachments were intense and all-embracing and the average Lebanese continued to seek and find refuge and identity within close family circles. The emergence and survival of family associations was perhaps unique to Lebanon. Even when other secular and civic voluntary associations were available, recourse was always had to the family as a means of access to a variety of welfare and socio-economic services. (Khalaf, 1971)

The war years have shored up the family's prominence. A significantly larger number found themselves, willingly or otherwise, drawn closer to members of their immediate and extended family than they had been before the war. They were also expending more effort, resources and sentiments on family obligations and interests. As a result, the traditional boundaries of the family expanded even further to assume added economic, social and recreational functions.

For example, the concept of kin, *ahl* or *'ayleh*, spread to extend beyond the confines of the nuclear family. Only 12 per cent of the respondents perceived the boundaries of their family to be limited to spouses and children. Almost 40 per cent extended their definition to include both parents. Another 22 per cent stretched it further to include paternal and maternal uncles. The remaining 27 per cent extended the boundaries even further to encompass all relatives. The family was not only becoming more encompassing. It was also becoming more intimate and affectionate, reinforced by repeated visits and mutual help. Close to 60 per cent evaluated their family relations in such highly positive terms. The remaining 38 per cent considered them moderately so. Only 2 per cent admitted that their family relations were distant, cold and incapable of giving mutual help or support.

As Table 7 shows, over 58 per cent of the respondents reported that their ties and relationships with their immediate families were strengthened by the war. The incidence fell to about 23 per cent for relatives and dropped to as low as 18.8 per cent for colleagues. The respondents were also asked to indicate, on the conventional five-point scale, the degree of their involvement in domestic and family affairs. More concretely, an effort was made to assess the extent to which such family concerns were becoming more important, remained the same or were less important since the outbreak of civil hostilities. Here as well, and for understandable reasons, over 60 per cent of the respondents indicated that they had become more preoccupied with domestic and family affairs. Thirty-eight per cent felt that there was no change in such relations during the war, and only 2 per cent reported that domestic and family-centred interests became less important for them.

Table 7
Impact of the War on Social Relations (% of total respondents)

Special Relations	Immediate family	Relatives	Friends	Colleagues
Strengthened	58.2	22.9	27.6	18.8
About the same	39.4	65.4	57.5	68.6
Weakened	2.4	11.7	14.9	12.6
Total	**100.0**	**100.0**	**100.0**	**100.0**

Given the large-scale devastation of state and other secular agencies and institutions, the family was one of the few remaining social edifices in which people could seek and find refuge in its reassuring domesticity and privacy. It became, in Christopher Lasch's apt term, a 'haven in a heartless world.' (Lasch, 1977) Whether the family will be able to withstand such mounting pressure remains to be seen. What is clear, however, is that during the war it had to reinvent and extend itself to assume added functions. For example, beyond absorbing a larger share of the leisure, recreational, welfare and benevolent needs of its members, it also served as an economic and commercial base. Many, particularly lawyers, craftsmen, retailers and agents, were forced to convert their homes into offices for business operations. Housewives, too, were known to have used their homes to conduct various transactions and to sell apparel, clothing and other such items.

Communalism

The manifestations of 'retribalization' were also resurfacing at the communal level with, perhaps, greater intensity. Since the boundaries within which groups circulated were becoming more constricted, these tightly knit localities naturally became the source of heightened communal and territorial identities. Inevitably, such bonding in exclusive spaces was bound to generate deeper commitments towards one's community and corresponding distance from others. In-group/out-group sentiments became sharper. Segmental and parochial loyalties also became more pronounced. So did the socio-cultural, psychological and ideological cleavages. In this sense the community, locality, neighbourhood or quarter was no longer simply a space to occupy or a place to live in and identify with. It became an ideology, an orientation or a frame of reference through which groups interacted and perceived others. At this point the community becomes a form of communalism.

Two disturbing features of such retribalization are worth highlighting again. More and more communities began to assume attributes of 'closed' and 'total' entities. The two are naturally related. Comparatively mixed, hybrid and open communities were becoming more homogeneous and closed to outsiders. Such polarization was bound to engender and sustain the growth of self-sufficient, almost 'total' communities and neighbourhoods.

From early in the initial stages of the war the traditional city centre and its adjoining residential quarters had witnessed some of the fiercest rounds of fighting and destruction, the episodes accompanied by a quickening succession of massive population shifts and decentralization. In no time, business establishments and virtually all the major public and private institutions – including universities, schools, banks, embassies, travel agencies – took measures to establish headquarters or branch offices in more than one district. This clearly facilitated the proliferation of self-sufficient urban enclaves. Before the war, people by necessity were compelled to traverse communal boundaries to visit some of their public services and amenities. Gradually the urge to cross over became undesirable. The result was that a quite substantial number of Lebanese were living, working, shopping and meeting their recreational, cultural, medical and educational needs within constricted communal circles. Generations of children and adolescents grew up thinking that their social world could not extend beyond the confines of the ever smaller communities within which they were trapped.

Some of the socio-psychological and political implications of such reversion to 'enclosed' communities are grievous. The psychological barriers and accompanying socio-cultural differences are getting deeper and more ingrown. More and more Lebanese have been forced, over the past two decades, to restructure and redefine their lives into smaller circles. Strangely, they do not seem particularly to resent such restrictions. A few results of our empirical survey, particularly those that highlight the proclivity of groups to seek shelter in cloistered spatial enclosures and their corresponding inclination to maintain distance from other communities, are worth noting. Around 70 per cent of the respondents indicated that their daily movements were restricted to the area or neighbourhood in which they live. Surprisingly, a slightly larger number actually wished to live and work and confine their movements to such restricted areas. Only 22 per cent were moving at the time, albeit furtively, between different sectors of the city.

No doubt the religious composition of the three broad communities from which our samples were drawn (Ras Beirut, Basta and Achrafieh) made them more likely to harbour feelings of solidarity with their own kind and unfriendly, even hostile feelings towards other groups. The sectarian composition of our respondents corresponds to the religious profile that we generally associate with those urban districts. As Table 8 shows, Ras Beirut is the only fairly mixed district. The majority (40%) are Orthodox, followed by Sunnis and Protestants. The rest are almost equally distributed among Maronites, Catholics, Shi'ites and Druze, along with a few Armenians and other Christian minorities. On the whole, however, Ras Beirut is more than two-thirds Christian and around 27 per cent Muslim. On the other hand, Basta is almost exclusively Muslim in composition, just as Achrafieh is almost exclusively Christian. The proportion of Maronites, Catholics and Protestants is as negligible in Basta, as is the proportion of Sunnis, Shi'ites and Druze in Achrafieh. The only exception is perhaps the Orthodox. It is the only sect that is represented in the three communities, although to a much lesser degree in Basta.

Table 8
Religious Composition of the Three Communities (% of total respondents)

Communities	Ras Beirut	Basta	Achrafieh	Total
Maronites	9.1	2.0	40.0	17.2
Catholics	7.3	2.0	13.5	7.6
Orthodox	40.0	7.8	30.8	26.2
Protestants	15.4	0.0	1.9	5.8
Armenians	1.8	2.0	5.7	3.2
Sunnis	17.3	60.8	3.8	27.3
Shi'ites	5.5	15.6	3.8	8.3
Druze	3.6	9.8	0.0	4.4
Per cent	**100.0**	**100.0**	**100.0**	**100.0**
Number	**110**	**51**	**52**	**213**

It is natural that residents of such closely knit and homogenous communities should begin to display particular attitudes towards other sectarian groups. The war, judging by some of our preliminary results, has sharpened such sentiments. The respondents were asked, 'How do you evaluate your present feelings and opinions towards the groups listed below? Do you feel closer to them now than before the war, are your feelings unchanged, or do you feel more distant?'

The results, as summarized in Table 9, reveal some obvious and expected tendencies, which reflect the roles that the various communities played during the war at the time of the survey and the consequent social distance between them. If we take the sample as a whole, 39 per cent and 38 per cent respectively have grown more distant from the Kurds and Druze and harbour hostility towards them. Next come Maronites (29%), Shi'ites (26%) and Sunnites (23%), followed by Syriacs (18%) and Armenians (17%). The rest, namely Catholics, Christian minorities, Orthodox and Protestants, evoke little or no hostility or negative feelings. Conversely, the respondents feel closer to Maronites (22%), Orthodox (19%) and Sunnites and Shi'ites (15%). Groups that elicit least sympathy are Druze (8%), Syriacs (8%), Armenians (5%) and Kurds (1.6%).

It is interesting to note that, with the exception of the Druze, attitudes towards belligerent sects (Maronites, Sunnis, Shi'ites) invite both extremes. The proportions of those who indicate that they have grown closer to a particular sect and of those who display enmity or detachment in their regard are nearly the same. They are equally admired and shunned. It is also interesting to observe that attitudes towards non-belligerent groups or those who were not directly involved in the fighting (i.e. Protestants, Christian minorities, Catholics and Greek Orthodox) remained largely unchanged.

Table 9
Enmity and Social Distance (% of total respondents)

Communities	Closer	Unchanged	More distant
Maronites	22	40	29
Orthodox	19	62	8
Catholics	10	71	7
Protestants	7	73	8
Xian minorities	8	72	7
Sunnites	15	50	23
Shi'ites	15	47	26
Druze	8	44	38
Kurds	1.6	45	39
Armenians	5	64	17
Syriacs	8	60	18

Distant from (%)		*Closer to (%)*	
Kurds	39	Maronites	22
Druze	38	Orthodox	19
Maronites	29	Shi'ites/Sunnites	15
Shi'ites	26		
Sunnites	23		

A few other, albeit self-evident, variations are also worth noting. Ras Beirutis on the whole feel much closer towards Maronites (32%) and Orthodox (23%) than they do towards Sunnis (16%) and Shi'ites (15%). The Druze received the lowest score (5%). They have grown most distant from the Druze (56%) and then almost equally from Shi'ites (30%), Sunnis (26%) and Maronites (24%).

The Basta residents feel closer towards Shiʻites (27%) and, to a slightly lesser degree, to Sunnis, Druze and Orthodox (23%). The bulk of their resentment is directed towards the Maronites.

The Achrafieh residents are naturally closest to Maronites (51%), followed by Orthodox (35%) and Catholics (27%). Their resentment is directed towards the Druze (57%) and, to a much lesser degree, towards the Shiʻites (30%) and Sunnis (22%).

Communites in Lebanon were becoming more 'closed' in yet another, and perhaps, more vital and disturbing sense. A few of them were beginning to evince features that were 'total', even 'totalitarian', in several significant respects. I borrow the term here employed by Erving Goffman (1961) in his analysis of 'total' institutions such as prisons, hospitals, monasteries and mental asylums.

1. First, as we have seen, because of the massive population shifts and decentralization, accompanied by the fear and terror of intercommunal hostilities, communities became increasingly self-sufficient. A full range of human activities have developed within each of those communities.

2. As a result, even where entry and exit into and from these communities remained largely voluntary, an increasing number of people were reluctant to cross over. The boundaries, incidentally, are not merely spatial. Sometimes an imaginary 'green line', a bridge or a road may serve as a border. More important, the barriers became psychological, cultural and ideological. Hence, there emerged within each of those communities a distinct atmosphere of a cultural, social and intellectual world closed to 'outsiders'. It is for this reason that the social distance and the barriers between the various communities grew. The barriers are often dramatized by deliberately exaggerated differences. Such dramatization serves to rationalize and justify the maintenance of distance. It also mitigates some of the residents' feelings of guilt for indulging in avoidance.

   The same kinds of barriers that have polarized Beirut into East and 'West' started to appear elsewhere. As we have seen, residents of East Beirut depict the western suburbs as an insecure, chaotic, disorderly mass of alien, unattached and unanchored groups, stirred up by borrowed ideologies and with an insatiable appetite for lawlessness and boorish decadence. In turn, residents of West Beirut portray the eastern suburbs as a self-enclosed 'ghetto' dominated by the overpowering control and hegemony of a one-party system where strangers are suspect and treated with contempt. In short, both communites are cordoned off and viewed with considerable fear and foreboding. Each has vowed to liberate society from the despicable evil inherent in the other!

3. A total institution, often in subtle and unobtrusive ways, tends to remake or resocialize individuals and groups within it. This, by necessity, requires that prior values, ideas and patterns of behaviour be dislodged and replaced by new ones. To varying degrees, such manifestations of resocialization became visible in the early stages of the war. The various communities and warring factions,

supported by an extremely developed and sophisticated media – with their own broadcasting stations, newspapers, periodicals, pamphlets, slogans, symbols and motifs – competed in gaining access to potential recruits, clients and converts. Each developed its own ethnocentric interpretation of the war, its own version of the social and political history of Lebanon, and proposed diametrically opposed views and programmes for the socio-economic and political reconstruction of the country. The differences do not stop here. They have pervaded virtually every dimension of everyday life: the national figures and popular heroes they identify with, their lifestyle, public and private concerns and their perceptions of the basic issues in society are being drastically reshaped and redefined.

As a result, there are very few national symbols or fundamental issues with which all Lebanese can identify. Such facts prompt me to argue that Lebanon's pluralism, particularly if those same parochial loyalties and sentiments are maintained, remains more of a divisive force than a viable source of organic solidarity and national unity.

4. Finally, one can also discern signs of total control. Individuals and groups, particularly in areas where private militias and political groups enjoy a large measure of hegemony, are subjected to increasing forms of social controls – ranging from direct measures such as conscription, taxation, impositions and censure to the more subtle forms of intervention in individual freedom and modes of expression and mobility. So pervasive did some of these measures become at different interludes of the war that it seemed that nothing was morally or legally exempt from the scope and grasp of the group in power.

Confessionalism
Finally, symptoms of retribalization were doubtless most visible in the reassertion of religious and confessional consciousness. What makes this particularly interesting is that religious and confessional loyalties manifest a few paradoxical and seemingly inconsistent features, which reveal the sharp distinctions between them. Clearly religiosity and confessionalism are not and need not be coterminous. Indeed, results of the 1982–83 empirical survey revealed some sharp distinctions between the two.

Curiously, respondents indicated that, as their religiosity was declining (as measured by the degree of changes in the intensity of their spiritual beliefs, religious commitments and observation of rituals, practices and duties of their faith), their confessional and sectarian identities were becoming sharper. When the respondents were asked whether the war had had an impact on their religious practices and activities, the majority (85%) admitted that they had not changed in this regard.

One could infer from such findings that the Lebanese are not having recourse to religion in an effort to find some spiritual comfort or solace from their fear and anxiety. To a large extent, this kind of refuge is better sought and served in the family and community. Evidently, then, religion is serving some other secular – indeed socio-economic and ideological – function.

Some of the results clearly support such an inference. It is, in a way, revealing that when it comes to matters that reflect their religious tolerance and their willingness to associate and live with other sectarian or religious groups – such as the schooling of their children, their attitudes towards inter-confessional marriages and their residential preferences – confessional considerations begin to assume prominence.

When asked, for example, whether they would agree to send their children to a school affiliated to a sect other than their own, close to 30 per cent of the respondents answered in the negative. Their attitudes towards mixed sectarian or religious marriages – for both males and females – reveal similar sentiments. Close to 28 per cent disapprove of such religiously mixed marriages for males and 32 per cent for females. Similarly, around 21 per cent expressed a preference to live in a locality that has a majority of people from their own sect.

Altogether, a surprisingly large proportion of what presumably is a literate, cosmopolitan and sophisticated sample of professionals, university and college teachers, intellectuals, journalists and the like displayed strong confessional biases, distance from and intolerance towards other groups. This was apparent not only in their disapproval of inter-confessional marriages, preference for parochial schooling for their children and reluctance to associate and live with other sectarian and religious groups. More poignant, perhaps, it was also becoming increasingly visible in a rather 'narcissistic' preoccupation with one's own community and a corresponding wish to exclude, even to feel phobic towards others. This heightened confessional consciousness, understandable in times of sectarian hostility and fear, started to assume fanatic and militant expressions of devotion to and glorification of one's group. The relative ease with which the various communities were politically resocialized into militancy was largely an expression of such aroused sectarian consciousness.

CHAPTER 9

The Radicalization of Communal Identities

A defining element in Lebanon's chequered socio-political history, one that has had substantive implications for the character and magnitude of collective strife, is the survival and reassertion of communal solidarities. In fact, the three over-arching and persistent features of 1) foreign intervention, 2) the reawakening of primordial identities and 3) the escalation of protracted violence – are all intimately related. This is the main theme of this chapter. Elsewhere I have made an effort to explore how unresolved regional and global rivalries have contributed to the protraction and escalation of conflict and the reassertion of communal solidarities (Khalaf, 2001). The aim here is to document a few of the persistent features underlying the survival of communal loyalties, particularly those aspects of Lebanon's 'retribalization' exacerbated by the inside–outside dialectics. How and under what circumstances, to be more precise, are communal loyalties radicalized?

By focusing on different episodes – ranging from peasant uprisings, factional feuds, 'class' and ideological struggles to other intermittent incidents of civil strife – it is possible to elucidate how, regardless of their origins and overt manifestations, they are all transformed (or deformed) into sectarian hostility.

I am suggesting here that it is possible to identify three different layers or magnitudes of violence. There is first social strife, the product largely of socio-economic disparities, asymmetrical development, ideological rivalries, relative deprivation and feelings of neglect and dispossession. These are normally non-militant in character and express themselves in contentious but non-belligerent forms of social protest and political mobilization. Secondly, if the socio-economic disparities persist and the resulting hostilities are unappeased, particularly if they are accompanied by anxiety about threats to communal legacy and confessional loyalties, conflict and discord are inclined to become more militant and bellicose. It is at this point that social discord is transformed into communal violence, or, in the words of Bouyer-Bell, that *civil strife* passes the point of no return into *civil war* (1987). Finally, civil violence is not, or does not always remain, 'civil'. When inflamed by the atavism of reawakened tribalism, enmity and deep-seated suspicion of the 'other', internecine feuds and unresolved regional and global conflicts, collective violence can readily degenerate further into the incivility of proxy wars and surrogate victimization. Violence then acquires its own inherent self-destructive logic and spirals into an atrocious cycle of unrelenting cruelties.

Within this context, it is worth trying to identify and account for some of the circumstances associated with the tenacity of communalism and its various manifestations. I shall also attempt to discover how social strife is deflected into communal violence and ultimately descends into further barbarism and incivility. Questions of this sort are not only of historical significance. There has recently been renewed theoretical interest in the nature, manifestations and consequences of renewed 'tribalism' and reassertion of local and communal identities, particularly as they relate to the forces of globalization and post-modernity.[1]

The Resilience of Communalism

For some time mainstream theoretical paradigms – i.e. those associated with modernization and Marxism and their offshoots – represented unchallenged analyses of the erosion of primordial ties and loyalties. Despite the striking ideological differences underlying the two meta theories – Modernization and Marxism – they shared the conviction that ties of fealty, religion and community – which cemented societies together and accounted for social and political distinctions – were beginning to lose their grip and would, ultimately, become irrelevant. Indeed, to proponents of modernization theory, notions like familism, tribalism and confessionalism were not only pejoratively dismissed and trivialized, but were also seen as obstacles to modernity. So-called 'traditional' societies were expected to disengage themselves from such relics of pre-modern times if they were to enjoy the presumed fruits of modernity or to become full-fledged nation-states. Given the resilience of traditional loyalties, some proponents made allowances for interim periods during which 'transitional' societies might linger

1. There has been a profusion of writing recently exploring various dimensions of the globalization of ethnic and communal violence. Interested readers may wish to consult the following: Benjamin R. Barber, *Jihad vs. McWorld* (New York: Ballantine, 1996); Zbigniew Brzezinski, *Out of Control: Global Turmoil on the Eve of the Twenty-first Century* (New York and Toronto: Scribner, Maxwell Macmillan, 1993); Thomas Friedman, *Lexus and the Olive Tree* (New York: Anchor Books, 2000); Michael Ignatieff, *Blood and Belonging: Journeys into the New Nationalism* (New York: Farrar, Straus and Giroux, 1994); Theodor Hanf, *Coexistence in Wartime Lebanon: Decline of a State and Rise of a Nation* [1990] (London: I. B. Tauris, 1993); Sudhir Kakar, *The Colors of Violence* (Chicago and London: University of Chicago Press, 1996); Daniel Patrick Moynihan, *Pandaemonium: Ethnicity in International Politics* (Oxford: Oxford University Press, 1993); Walter B. Wriston, *The Twilight of Sovereignty: How the Information Revolution is Transforming our World* (New York and Toronto: Scribner, Maxwell Macmillan, 1992); Milton J. Esman and Itamar Rabinovich, eds, *Ethnicity, Pluralism and the State in the Middle East* (Ithaca and London: Cornell University Press, 1988); Milton J. Esman, *Ethnic Politics* (Ithaca, NY: Cornell University Press, 1994).

for a while. Eventually, however, all such precarious hybrids would have to disappear. A generation of social scientists in the 1960s and 1970s argued that they could not and would not be able to resist the overpowering forces of industrialization, urbanization and secularization.[1]

Likewise, to Marxists, communist and socialist regimes were perceived as 'giant brooms', expected to sweep away pre-existing loyalties. If non-class attachments and interests survived or resurfaced, they would be treated as forms of 'false consciousness' to mask or veil fundamental economic and social contradictions. In short, ethnic and primordial loyalties were treated, as Theodor Hanf put it, as a transitory phenomenon by modernization theorists and as an epiphenomenon by Marxists. (Hanf, 1999) Both agreed, however, that primordialism was destined to disappear. Both, of course, have been wrong. It is a blatant misreading, if not distortion, of history in both advanced and developing societies. It is a marvel, in fact, that such misrepresentations could have persisted given persuasive evidence to the contrary.[2]

Ernest Gellner provides such evidence while exploring the nature of nationalism and cohesion in complex societies. He finds it conceptually fitting to re-examine the role of collective forgetfulness and anonymity in the emergence of nation-states. Among other things, he argues that the presumed erosion of primordial allegiances is not a prerequisite to the formation of cohesive nation-states. Likewise, the formation of strong, ruthless, centralizing regimes is not the monopoly of any particular state or culture. Seemingly cohesive and integrated old states are not as culturally unified and homogeneous. (Gellner, 1988)

One might argue that Lebanon has not been detribalized sufficiently to be experiencing retribalization. The term, nonetheless, is being employed here rather loosely to refer to the resurgence of communal loyalties, particularly the convergence of confessional and territorial identities. As has been demonstrated by a score of socio-economic and political historians, the sweeping changes to which Lebanon has been subjected, from internal insurrections to centralized and direct rule by foreign powers or the more gradual and spontaneous changes associated with rapid urbanization, spread of the market economy and the exposure of a growing portion of the population to secular, liberal and radical ideologies, etc., did little to weaken or erode the intensity of confessional or sectarian loyalties. Indeed,

---

1. As early as 1960 scholars were already challenging such false dichotomies and neo-evolutionary views of social change and modernization. See, among others, Rupert Emerson, *From Empire to Nation: The Rise of Self-Assertion of Asian and African Peoples* (Boston: Beacon Press, 1960).

2. For a representative cross-section of the literature, see Daniel Lerner, *The Passing of Traditional Society: Modernizing the Middle East* (New York: The Free Press, 1958); Gabriel A. Almond and James S. Coleman, eds, *The Politics of The Developing Areas* (Princeton, NJ: Princeton University Press, 1960; Gabriel A. Almond and G. Bingham Powell, Jr, *Comparative Politics: A Developmental Approach* (Boston: Little, Brown, 1966); David Apter, *The Politics of Modernization* (Chicago and London: University of Chicago Press, 1965); S. N. Eisenstadt, *Modernization, Protest and Change* (Englewood Cliffs, NJ: Prentice-Hall, 1966); Edward A. Shils, *Political Development in the New States* (S. Gravenhage: Mouton, 1965); Lucian W. Pye, *Aspects of Political Development. An Analytical Study* (Boston: Little, Brown, 1966).

in times of social unrest and political turmoil such loyalties became sharper and often superseded other ties and allegiances.[1]

As the cruelty and violence became more threatening, traumatized and fearful groups understandably sought shelter in their communal solidarities and cloistered spaces. Confessional sentiments and their supportive loyalties, even in times of relative peace and stability, have always been effective sources of social support and political mobilization.

As will be demonstrated in the next essay, the massive population shifts generated by protracted strife, particularly since they are accompanied by the reintegration of displaced groups into more homogeneous, self-contained and exclusive communities, have also reinforced communal solidarity. Consequently, territorial and confessional identities, more so perhaps than at any other time in Lebanon's history, are beginning to converge. Thus 'retribalization' is becoming sharper and more assertive.

Some of its subtle, implicit and nuanced earlier manifestations have become much more explicit. Political leaders, spokesmen of various communities, opinion makers and ordinary citizens are not as reticent in recognizing and incorporating such features into their daily behaviour or in bargaining for rights and privileges and validating their identities. Even normally less self-conscious and more open communities, such as Greek Orthodox, Catholics and Sunni Muslims, are beginning to experiment with measures for enhancing and reinventing their special heritage and particular identity.

Recently such symptoms of 'retribalization' have become more pronounced. Ironically, during the pre-war and pre-Taif periods when confessionalism was recognized, its manifestations and outward expression were often subtle and attenuated. Groups seemed shy, as it were, to be identified by such labels, especially during the decades of the 1950s and 1960s, when nationalism and often secular and so-called progressive and ideological venues for group affiliation had special appeal. (Melikian and Diab, 1974).

Today, as deconfessionalization is consecrated by Taif and, to the same extent, by public opinion, the overt expression of communal and sectarian identities has become much more assertive. Political leaders and spokesmen of various communities, of all persuasions, are not at all reticent or shy in invoking such parochial claims. Indeed, dormant and quiescent communal identities are being reawakened, often reinvented, to validate claims for special privileges. Universities, colleges, research foundations, voluntary associations, special advocacy groups, radio and TV stations are all being established with explicit and

---

1. Substantive and persuasive evidence can be extracted from a score of studies in support of such views. See, among others, Dominique Chevalier, *La Société du Mont Liban à l'époque de la révolution industrielle en Europe* (Paris: Librairie Orientaliste, 1971); Ilya F. Harik, *Politics and Change in a Traditional Society: Lebanon, 1711–1845* (Princeton, NJ: Princeton University Press, 1968); Samir Khalaf, *Persistence and Change in 19th Century Lebanon: A Sociological Essay* (Beirut: American University of Beirut and Syracuse University Press, 1979); Elizabeth Picard, *Lebanon, A Shattered Country: Myths and Realities of the Wars in Lebanon* [1988] (New York: Holmes and Meier, 1996); Kamal Salibi, *The Modern History of Lebanon* (London: Weidenfeld and Nicolson, 1965); Ussama Makdisi, *The Culture of Sectarianism* (2000).

well-defined communal identities. So are cultural and popular recreational events and awards to recognize excellence and encourage creative and intellectual output. Even competitive sports, normally the most transcending and neutral of all human encounters, have been factionalized by sectarian rivalries.

These and other such efforts can no longer be wished away or mystified. They must be recognized for what they are: strategies for the empowerment of threatened groups and their incorporation into the torrent of public life. The coalition of confessional and territorial entities, since it draws upon a potentially much larger base of support, is doubtless a more viable vector for political mobilization than kinship, fealty or sectarian loyalties. Hence, it is not surprising that protest movements and other forms of collective mobilization of social unrest, sparked by genuine grievances and unresolved public issues, were often deflected into confessional or communal rivalries.

Theodor Hanf (1995) coins the term 'ethnurgy' to highlight such conscious invention and politicization of ethnic identity. (Hanf, 1999) Circumstances associated with the emergence and mobilization of such identities are instrumental in accounting for the pattern and intensity of intra- and interstate conflict. Since all societies are, to varying degrees, horizontally stratified with vertical cultural cleavages, conflict is bound to reflect both the horizontal socio-economic disparities and the deep cultural divisions. By themselves, however, the strata and cleavages will not become sources of political mobilization unless groups are also made conscious of their distinctive identities. Differences in themselves, horizontal or vertical, become politicized only when those who share common distinctive attributes also share awareness of their distinctiveness. Analogically Hanf translates Marx's 'class-by-itself' *(Klasse an sich)* and 'class-for-itself' *(Klasse für sich)* into ethnic group loyalties. Hence, only an ethnic group 'for itself' can become a source of political mobilization.

It is interesting to consider the circumstances in Lebanon's socio-political and cultural history that heighten and mobilize the political and radical consciousness of communal and confessional identities. Of course, technically speaking, communal and confessional attachments are not strictly 'ethnic' in character, if by that is meant that the assignment of status within a culture or social system is arrived at on the basis of purely racial or physical characteristics. But if 'ethnicity' is broadened to incorporate traits associated with religion, communal, ancestral affiliations, dialect and other behavioural and sub-cultural distinctions, then confessional and sectarian identities may well assume some ethnic attributes. (Horowitz, 1985) It is also then that these identities become sharper and more militant. They acquire a density of their own and coalesce around sentiments of solidarity and collective self-consciousness.

As was mentioned in the previous chapter, religiosity and confessionalism are not coterminous. A survey carried out in 1982–83, on a random sample of households in selected urban districts and neighbourhoods of Beirut, revealed some sharp distinctions between the two. Many respondents indicated that, while their religiosity had been declining, their confessional and sectarian identities and prejudices were becoming sharper.[1] Many educated people displayed strong confessional biases and distance from and intolerance towards other groups, preferring to send their children to parochial schools and their sons and daughters to marry within their confession or sectarian group.[2] The relative ease with which the various communities were politically resocialized into militancy was largely an expression of their aroused communal consciousness.[3] Popular accounts of events noted with amazement the eagerness with which impressionable teenagers flocked to the barricades, just as their older brothers earlier had taken to frivolous pastimes, such as nightclubbing, driving fast cars and playing on pinball machines (Randal, 1984) This is all the more remarkable since we are dealing with a fairly quiescent political culture, one without much background or tradition in military service, conscription or membership of paramilitary organizations.

What these and other manifestations imply is that people do not resort to religion as a spiritual or ecclesiastical force. It is not a matter of communing with the divine as evidence of a redemptive longing to restore one's sense of well-being. Rather, religion is pursued largely as a form of ideological and communal mobilization. Indeed, it is often people's only means of asserting their threatened identities. Without it, groups are literally rootless, nameless and voiceless.

Such realities, incidentally, are certainly not unique to Lebanon. In an insightful and thoroughly documented study of Hindu–Muslim rioting and violence in India, Sudhir Kakar reaches essentially the same conclusion. (Kakar, 1996) The author also draws on other historical events – such as the anti-Semitic pogroms in Spain in the fourteenth century, sixteenth-century Catholic–Protestant violence in France and anti-Catholic riots in eighteenth-century London – to validate the inference that all such instances of collective mobilization were more a by-product of cultural identities and communalism rather than a reflection of religiosity or revitalization of religious zeal as such.

> ... if we look closely at individual cases around the world, we will find that the much-touted revival is less of religiosity than of cultural identities based on religious affiliation. In other words, there may not be any great ferment taking place in the world of religious ideas, beliefs, rituals, or any marked increase in the sum of human spirituality. Where the resurgence is most visible is in the organization of collective identities around religion, in the formation and strengthening of communities of believers. What we are witnessing today is less the resurgence of religion than (in the felicitous Indian usage) of communalism where a community of believers not only has religious affiliation but also

---

1. Unpublished survey conducted by Samir Khalaf and Salim Nasr in 1983–84 on the impact of civil unrest on socio-cultural transformations and the adaptation of various communities to chronic and protracted strife (Department of Social and Behavioural Studies, American University of Beirut).

2. See results of survey published in successive issues of *an-Nahar* (January, 14 and 24, 1997; February, 4 and 19, 1997).

3. Observers and commentators at the time uniformly noted how puzzled they were by the readiness that seemingly quietist, self-indulgent and carefree youth displayed for political mobilization and militancy.

social, economic, and political interests in common which may conflict with the corresponding interests of another community of believers sharing the same geographical space. (Kakar, 1996: 166–67)

To Kakar, communalism is a state of mind elicited by the individual's assertion of being part of a religious community, preceded by the awareness of belonging to such a community. He goes further to maintain that only when what he terms the 'We-ness of the community' is transformed into the 'We are of communalism' can we better understand the circumstances that translate or deflect the potential or predispositions for intolerance, enmity and hostility and how these are ultimately released into outward violence. (Kakar, 1996: 192) Enmity, after all, can remain latent. Hostility between the various communities in Lebanon did not always erupt in bloody confrontations. Rather, it managed, and for comparatively long stretches, to express itself in a wide gamut of non-violent outlets and arrangements ranging from mild contempt, indifference, guarded contacts and distancing to consociational political strategies and territorial bonding in exclusive spaces.

This is why it is instructive to identify those interludes in Lebanon's history – the critical watersheds, so to speak – during which feelings of communal identity have been undermined and when the vague, undefined threats and fears became sharper and more focused. At such times communities made efforts to revive and reconnect with communal solidarity and mobilization. Identifying with and glorifying the threatened virtues of one's own group is heightened and rendered more righteous – as the psychology of in-group/out-group conflict reveals – if it is reinforced by enmity towards the out-group. (Kelman, 1987) If uncontained, especially when amplified by rumours and stoked by religious demagogues, the hostility can easily erupt into open violence. By then only the slightest spark is needed for a violent explosion.

A drop of blood here and there, in moments of aroused communal passions, always begets carnage. Put more crudely, there is a relationship between hot-headedness and cold-blooded violence. The more impassioned and impetuous groups are, the more likely they are to be merciless and untroubled by guilt in their brutality. Hot-headedness should not be mistaken for mindlessness. Hard-core fighters, by virtue both of their youth and their effective resocialization, are normally impelled by an ardent, often sacrificial commitment to the cause and strategies of combat. Hostility is thus made more legitimate by dehumanizing, depersonalizing and reducing the enemy into a mere category; a target to be acted upon or eliminated. The 'other' becomes no more than an object whose body can be carelessly dispensed with.[1] Assailants can commit their cruelties with abandon

---

1. For further details, see V. D. Volkan, *Cyprus: War and Adaptation: A Psychoanalytic History of Two Ethnic Groups in Conflict* (Charlottesville: University Press of Virginia, 1979); V. D. Volkan, 'The Need to Have Enemies and Allies: A Developmental Approach', *Political Psychology*, 6 (1979) 2; Sam Keen, *Faces of Enemy: Reflections on the Hostile Imagination* (New York: Harper and Row, 1986); O. Zur, 'The Psychohistory of Warfare: The Co-Evolution of Culture-Psyche and Enemy', *The* (continued...)

and without shame or guilt. And collective violence can degenerate into barbarism and incivility.

Social Strife and Communal Violence

By drawing on the rather prosaic distinctions we employed earlier between 'horizontal' and 'vertical' divisions, we can begin to isolate the circumstances that radicalize communal loyalties. At least, we can better gauge the magnitude and direction conflict is likely to assume as ordinary social strife is deflected into communal and factional violence and then escalates into barbarism and incivility.

Horizontal socio-economic disputes, at least as far as the experience of Lebanon is concerned, are more likely to remain comparatively mild. The strata affected are prone to experience various degrees of deprivation and neglect. Their social standing is undermined. They become less privileged. Like other impoverished, aggrieved and dispossessed groups, they resort to collective protest to dramatize and thereby correct the injustice and inequities. Such mobilization, however, unless it is deflected into confessional and communal hostility, rarely escalates into violent confrontation.

Communal and sectarian rivalries are of a different magnitude. While social strata are embittered by loss of status, material advantage and privilege, 'ethnic' groups (in these confessional and communal formations) are threatened by the loss of freedom, identity, heritage and even their very national existence. As Hanf aptly puts it, 'politicizing ethnic distinctions shifts the struggle from divisible goods to indivisible principles'. (Hanf, 1995: 45)

At precisely such junctures, as socio-economic and political rivalries in Lebanon are transformed into confessional or sectarian conflict, the issues underlying the hostilities become 'indivisible'. Violence is bound to become more savage and merciless. At the same time, prospects for resolving the conflict non-belligerently become all the more unlikely.

In his probing analysis of civil strife in Ireland, Bouyer-Bell (1987) expresses this poignant dilemma in terms that are quite applicable to Lebanon.

A prolonged civil war is the most overt indication of an attenuated societal schism. In the preliminary civil discord – no matter how divisive and mutually contradictory are the elements involved, no matter how long-standing the opposing values or how deep-seated the distrust – a society, however strained or artificial, continues to exist. Once civil strife has passed the point of no return into civil war, however, the prewar society has, for better or worse, committed suicide. There can be no restoration of the uncomfortable but familiar past, for civil war can lead only to the ultimate triumph and imposition of a new society, cherished by the victors, inconceivable to the vanquished. (Bouyer-Bell, 1987: 76)

(...continued)

Journal of Peace Research, 24 (1987) 2, pp. 125–34.

Alas, this is a lesson that the Lebanese have yet to learn, despite their repeated experiences of both civil strife and civil wars. Prolonged or recurrent wars are the most overt indication that something is not changing. The *belligerent equality* has never transformed itself into the *peaceful inequality* that entails the designation of one as victor and the other as vanquished. Despite the intensity and scale of damage and injury, the wars went on. They imperilled and demoralized everyday life. There was perpetual hurt and grief with no hope for deliverance or even temporary reprieve. Like a malignant cancer, hostility grows, refusing all the while to deliver its victim from the anguish of his pain. The enfeebled patient lives on, doomed, as it were, to be rejuvenated by the very sources of his affliction.

Lebanon's experience in this regard, both past and more recent, is not very encouraging. In fact, it is quite dismal. Throughout the hostilities of 1975–90, cycles of violence were interspersed with efforts of foreign emissaries interceding on behalf of their shifting client groups to broker a short-lived ceasefire or an abortive political settlement. Lebanon's political landscape is strewn with the wreckage of such failed efforts. Ceasefires, in fact, became the butt of political humour and popular derision. As soon as one was declared, it was summarily violated. These were more ploys to win respites from the cruelties of war and recoup losses than genuine efforts to arrest the fighting and consider less belligerent strategies for resolving conflict.

Incidentally, comparative evidence on the relationship between civil violence and conflict resolution is very instructive. Unfortunately, much of this evidence tends to reinforce Lebanon's bleak prospects. At least, a recent analysis of the ways in which six other instances of civil unrest have ended – Colombia, Zimbabwe, Greece, Yemen, Sudan, Nigeria and the American Civil War – suggest that in cases where conflict is primarily of an ethnic, communal character, rather than provoked by economic and/or political issues, the likelihood of a negotiated non-belligerent resolution becomes very slim. (Rutgers, 1990) Indeed, all communal wars seem to end in blood. There must be a victor and a vanquished before combatants begin to consider negotiation. (Kaplan, 1980)

Frek Ikle arrives at the same conclusion, particularly when he distinguishes civil conflict from international wars. 'Outcomes intermediate between victory and defeat are difficult to construct. If partition is not a feasible outcome because belligerents are not geographically separable, one side has to get all, or nearly so, since there cannot be two governments . . . and since the passions aroused and the political cleavages opened render a sharing of power unworkable.' (Ikle, 1971) More interestingly, even if any of the major adversaries is defeated, they may not admit to or recognize that reality. This, too, is a phenomenon that has plagued Lebanon for so long. Defeat is a state of mind; everyone decides for themselves when they are defeated. (Carroll, 1980: 56)

Being trapped in such a setting of unresolved and protracted hostility is inflammable. The most trivial slight or petty personal feud can become, as was to happen time and time again, an occasion for the shedding of blood. Hypersensitivity to insult or violation, nurtured by muted enmity, almost always provoked a retaliation out of proportion to the initial offence. This was clearly the case in the massacres of 1860, less so in 1958, but much more pronounced in 1975–90.

Quickly during the early rounds of the war of 1975–76, the conflict started to display many of the features of confessional struggle. The two major combatants – the Christian Phalange and their allies and the Palestinians and the Muslim–Left Coalition – behaved as if their very existence was at stake. Little wonder that the fighting quickly descended into the abyss of a zero-sum deadly rivalry, where the perceived victory of one group could be realized only by annihilating the other. Spurred on by the fear of being marginalized or subsumed into an Arab–Muslim mass, the Kata'ib reacted with phobic fanaticism to what seemed to them at the time an ominous threat. They felt that they were defending not only the violated authority of state sovereignty but also their way of life, unique heritage and national existence. Often the threat was wilfully dramatized to incite and awaken communal solidarity and, thereby, mobilize reticent Christians to the cause of militancy.

Moderation is hard to sustain in the midst of distrust and fear. Progressively the Kata'ib, more so perhaps than other Christian communities, departed from their earlier support of pluralist social arrangements and their preference for a democratic dialogue for progressive reform. They reverted, instead, to a more fanatical anti-Islamic rhetoric. Such awakened parochialism associated with sectarian hostility provided an added stimulus to hatred.

Palestinians were likewise threatened by the fear of being liquidated. By the mid-1970s, Lebanon was, so to speak, their last abode. It had become at the least their most strategic stronghold. After the loss of its Jordan base, the PLO was more entrenched in Lebanon. It also jealously guarded the political and strategic gains it had managed to carve out there. The 1969 Cairo Accord, by ceding Palestinian refugee camps under PLO control and making them virtually inaccessible to Lebanese authorities, was tantamount to an act of national liberation. The logistical and ideological support that they were receiving from Arab radical and rejectionist regimes, particularly after the Egyptian-Israeli peace accord, made their presence in Lebanon all the more vital for their survival. Hence, they were protecting not merely the privileges and freedoms that they had acquired in recent years but also the political setting that had nurtured and safeguarded their very existence.

So both major combatants were locked into that deadly duel. As the sectarian fighting became bloodier, so the vengeance and enmity intensified. In his book *Human Aggression* Anthony Storr warned that 'it is more difficult to quell an impulse towards violence than to arouse it'. (Storr, 1968) Once aroused it acquires a logic of its own. It feeds on itself and becomes self-propagating. Again and again, the binary categories of the diabolic 'them' and the virtuous 'us' resurface with sharper and more deadly intensity. The enemy is demonized further and the conflict is seen as a war between light and darkness, between the virtuous and the damned. As ordinary, quiescent citizens are drawn into the vortex of such hostility, they become engulfed in enmity. Communities, aroused to action, buzz with pejorative anecdotes. Adversaries compete in assigning blame and trading invectives. Indeed, especially in the early rounds of fighting in Lebanon, rancorous political discourse was elevated to a high art. All the repressed antagonisms of the past came to the surface. Adversaries, once perceived as rigid, became hopelessly intransigent. 'Isolationists' degenerated into bigots and traitors. Disenfranchised and unanchored masses became aliens with 'green faces'. 'Borrowed ideologies' became repressive, chaotic and obfuscating. In short, the bad became worse; the unsavoury and undesirable degenerated into the repulsive and the demonic.

One has only to read a sampling of the war diaries and accounts of combatants, even of dispassionate observers or neutral bystanders, to understand the impulses to war so generated. Fanaticism is naturally more visible in the polemical platforms of warring factions, militias and their affiliated political pressure groups and parties, but it also permeated the rest of society. Pamphleteering, local historiographies, position papers and public pronouncements became ever more divisive in tone and substance, as did even church sermons and Friday mosque *khoutbas*. Colourful wall graffiti, expressive sheet displays, propaganda campaigns, elaborate obituaries of fallen fighters also evolved their own popular images and art forms.

Such manifestations, though largely symbolic, in that they may not inflict direct and immediate damage, are nonetheless responsible for preparing the psychological and moral justifications for aggression. Violence is thus rendered socially acceptable and tolerable. Even wanton and gratuitous violence becomes, in the words of Robin Williams, 'virtuous action in the name of applauded values'. (Williams, 1981)

The 'ideologies of enmity', as John Mack (1988) calls them, converge on three overriding but related objectives. First, the glorification of one's community and the ominous threats to it. Communalism in this regard becomes a rapacious scavenger. It feeds upon the awakened sense of a privileged but threatened territorial identity. Secondly, the proliferation of mutual vilification campaigns, in which each group depicts the 'other' as the repository of all the ills and pathologies of society. Ironically, the 'other', as John Keane aptly puts it, is treated 'simultaneously as everything and nothing'. (Keane, 1996) The enemy is dreaded and feared, but it is also arrogantly dismissed as inferior and worthless, finally, the legitimization of violence against the defiled other. (Mack, 1988; Pinderhughes, 1979)

The moral and psychological implications of such strategies, though perhaps self-evident, should not be overlooked. By evoking such imagery, the 'other' is transformed into a public menace, a threat to security and national sovereignty. Hence it becomes easier to inflict violence on him. At least the moral inhibitions associated with such acts of aggression are suspended or removed. Indeed, aggression against the 'other' acquires a purgative value. It becomes an act of liberation, the only way to preserve or restore national dignity and integrity. More, it obviates much of the guilt of having blood on one's hands. And this is not necessarily the blood of strangers and distant enemies. As the hostilities descend into the atrocities of internecine and intra-communal warfare (as it did when Christian militias were eliminating their Christian rivals, the in-fighting between Palestinian factions or between Amal and Hizbullah), the blood is quite often the blood of brothers and kinsmen.

Alas, as the recent history of other episodes of 'ethnic cleansing' tells us, the alleviation of guilt in the frenzy of battle is only momentary. When wars are nurtured by religious passions and the visceral hatreds that go with them, they acquire a self-destructive momentum of their own and they spiral, inexorably, out of control. Altogether they become harder to forget and even more difficult to resolve. Lodged in such an unremitting and atrocious cycle of vengeance and reprisal, fighting in Lebanon started to display many of the pathologies of barbarism.

PART IV

The Restoration of Civility in Lebanon

CHAPTER 10

From a Geography of Fear to a Culture of Tolerance

Reflections on Protracted Strife and the Restoration of Civility in Lebanon

> When unappeased, violence seeks and always finds a surrogate victim. The creature that excited its fury is abruptly replaced by another, chosen only because it is vulnerable and close at hand.
> René Girard, *Violence and the Sacred* (1977)

> Most societies seem allergic to internal anonymity, homogeneity, and amnesia.
> Ernest Gellner, *Culture, Identity and Politics* (1987)

> The point is not to learn to live with the demons, but to take away their powers.
> R. Collins, 'The Three Faces of Cruelty' (1974)

In recent studies of the changing incidence and character of armed conflict, there has been renewed interest in mapping out the interplay between internal and external sources of political unrest. This chapter considers three interrelated dimensions of this interplay to explore the impact of protracted strife on the resurgence of communal and territorial identities and prospects for the restoration of civility in fragmented political cultures like Lebanon.

First, an effort is made to extract from Lebanon's long and chequered experience of civil strife a few recurrent patterns or features that can elucidate the nature and magnitude of such protracted conflict. Secondly, two rather unusual consequences of prolonged and unresolved strife, namely symptoms of 'retribalization' and 'collective amnesia', are exposed in an attempt to consider how they could become the bases for articulating a political culture of tolerance.

Finally, under the rubric of the 'technologies of social pacification', I will advance a few alternative options (thus far overlooked in much of the literature on post-war reconstruction) for enhancing Lebanon's internal immunity or reducing its vulnerability to external sources of unrest.

Let me first place the discussion within a broader theoretical context, particularly as it relates to changing perspectives and trends associated with recent global transformations. The demise of the cold war and the disintegration of the Soviet empire and the tumultuous reverberations of these events throughout the world have, among other things, brought about a perceptible decline in major wars between nation-states. These and associated global events – particularly reform and liberalizing movements in the former USSR and eastern Europe and the presumed homogenizing impact of Western consumerism and popular culture – have reawakened the polemics over the nature and consequences of such transformations.

Some, often in apocalyptic terms, herald these epochal transformations as blissful signs of the 'end of history', 'the universalization of Western liberal democracy', the 'retreat from doomsday', or at least as manifestations of the longest stretch of peace in recent history (among others, Fukuyama, 1989; Mueller, 1989; Melko, 1990).

These and other celebrated world views have not, of course, gone unchallenged. Rebuttals abound. Some critique the unilinear vision of the uninterrupted progress of capitalism into an idyllic facsimile of a conflict-free liberal democracy. They contend that, while the world is moving away from bipolarity, it is being beset by new tensions and the reawakening of dormant primitive hostilities. Competition for world markets is likely to generate trade wars, marginalization of growing segments of intinerant labour and other grievous dislocations. New forms of East/West, North/South and inter-state conflict and conflicts provoked by environmental degradations are bound to exacerbate human-rights abuses. Nor are the alleged allures of cultural modernity likely to be accepted without resistance. Sharp increases in reactionary movements, fundamentalist militancy and so-called identity conflicts concerned with the preservation of cultural authenticity and ethnic and tribal purity attest to this. (Moynihan, 1993)

Controversy over these and related issues notwithstanding, one can discern a convergence of views on a few realities. Three overriding features stand out.

First, while these changes are associated with the decline of major wars between nation-states, they have left in their wake a trail of bewildering and destabilizing transformations. In some instances this has led to the consolidation of larger entities (longing for a 'European homeland') and the burgeoning interest in global issues that transcend state boundaries (i.e. environment, human rights, labour migration, world terrorism, epidemics, drug and trade wars, etc.). In others, we see unmistakable evidence of a sharp increase in the incidence of so-called low-intensity conflict (LIC), mostly internal and communal forms of strife fuelled by ideological, ethnic, racial, sectarian and tribal tensions and solidarities. More important, most of these internal wars are sustained with outside assistance and patronage, thereby reconfirming the complexities of the interplay between local, national, regional and international rivalries. They then often degenerate into 'dirty wars', involving proxy battlegrounds for other peoples' wars and surrogate victims of unresolved regional and global tensions. One prime characteristic of all such wars, of which Lebanon and the former Yugoslavia are poignant examples, is the deliberate targeting of innocent civilian groups and the mood of unrelenting terror and fear that blankets the entire population.

Secondly, and as a consequence, the conventional boundaries between seemingly internal and external conflicts are blurred or are no longer tenable. State boundaries, at least, can no longer be an adequate gauge or measure of the structure of conflicts. (Boulding, 1992, xiii; Rupesinghe, 1992, 1–23)

Finally, there is considerable agreement that these tumultuous changes disclose once again the inadequacy of the state and the international system in coping with the mounting tensions beleaguering the world and hence demand alternative and more innovative strategies for redressing some of their devastating consequences. We already see some promising efforts in that direction, mostly NGO-supported grass-roots movements and the resurgence of the voluntary sector as an intermediary between states and markets. (Wuthnow, 1991) Such strategies seem effective in circumventing the ideologies of enmity and cycles of vengeance rooted in cultures of violence, or the pitfalls of international organizations. Recent documentation of both successful and failed instances, gleaned from African, Asian and Latin American countries, provide some telling case histories (see Midlarsky, 1992; Rupesinghe, 1992). What is particularly instructive about such cases is that they also focus on concrete examples that fall outside the scope of official or deliberate processes of political reconciliation.

Lebanon's sanguine history epitomizes the predicament of other small, plural fragmented political cultures, caught up in turbulent regional and superpower rivalries. Indeed, 'Lebanization' has not only become an ugly metaphor indiscriminately employed in media soundbites to conjure up images of random and reckless violence elsewhere in the world, it has now even entered the regular lexicon of social science terminology. Rupesinghe in fact employs it to describe 'situations where the state has lost control of law and order where many armed groups are contending for power'. (Rupesinghe, 1992: 26)

Such characterization is, in all fairness, too benign and generic to capture or do justice to some of the particular pathologies and circumstances associated with Lebanon's entrapment in that ravaging spiral of protracted hostility, which has beleaguered its strife-torn history. Nor is the blurring of boundaries between internal and external conflict of recent vintage, a portent, as some claim, of the new world order or precursor of what is to become the dominant unfolding pattern. Virtually all episodes of collective strife during the first half of the nineteenth century – recurrent peasant uprisings, sectarian rivalries, even petty factional feuds – were predisposed to being manipulated by external circumstances. Such internationalization of the conflict almost always contributed to the protraction of hostility. In earlier and more recent conflicts, as the country became increasingly embroiled in regional and superpower rivalries, it could not be sheltered from the destabilizing consequences of such struggles. As this occurred, the original issues provoking the conflict receded. Threatened and marginalized groups, victims of internal socio-economic disparities or political neglect, sought external protection and patronage. Foreign powers, keen on gaining inroads into the region, were always too eager to rush into the fray. Such intervention, solicited or otherwise, almost always served to polarize the factions and deepen sources of hostility. In short, Lebanon was again an object and victim of this 'inside–outside' dialectic.

To assert that Lebanon's entrapment in protracted strife is largely a by-product of the interplay between internal dislocations and external pressures is, in many respects, a statement of the obvious. Yet it is a statement worth making, given some of its persistent complexities and disruptive consequences. The catalogue of horrors of nearly two decades of bloody strife makes it abundantly clear that unless we consider alternative strategies for neutralizing external sources of instability and pacifying internal conflict, Lebanon's precarious polity will always be vulnerable.

Unfortunately, conflict resolution and post-war rehabilitation programmes have, with rare exceptions, been almost exclusively focused (often to the point of obsession) on matters like institutional and administrative reforms, demilitarization, bilateral agreements with neighbouring states, the involvement of the UN and the international community, economic and infrastructure reconstruction. Vital as these deliberate activities are, they must be supplemented by considering the role of voluntary, indigenous and grass-roots efforts, particularly programmes that are effective in mobilizing otherwise disengaged, isolated and indifferent groups to participate in public ventures.

Much can still be done in this regard to experiment with types of post-war agencies and reconstruction programmes more conducive to a greater degree of involvement in the voluntary sector. The voluntary sector is appropriately perceived here as an intermediary between the rather coercive, bureaucratic, clientelistic state agencies and those of the instrumentality, gaudy commercialism, profiteering and greed so typical of the marketplace. By providing greater access to avenues of sociability, conviviality, camaraderie and other activities free of obligation or remuneration, ideally the voluntary sector (in the words of Habermas, 1989), can do much to allay fears of being colonized by the state or the marketplace. More important, it can facilitate participation in open associations more receptive to the diffusion and discussion of critical social agendas (i.e. collective values, visions of the future, human rights, urban and town planning, environmental issues, etc.).

This is of particular relevance to Lebanon because its voluntary sector, comparatively lively in the pre-war period, has been either devastated or rendered more parochial. Thus there is an urgent need to reform and revitalize these agencies in such a way as to render them more effective in transcending their insular and localized attributes. Given their hybrid character, they can at least introduce groups to broader forms of associations without threatening their communal or segmental loyalties. In this sense they are better equipped than purely secular or parochial agencies to consolidate patterns of reconciliatory pluralism and tolerable diversity, and thereby help in mitigating distance and hostility between the various communities.

This is, admittedly, a difficult but not insurmountable task. Since all forms of primordial loyalties, even the most proscribed and inviolable, are cultural constructs subject to being patterned in many ways, I will consider how they could be restructured to become vectors for the articulation of a political culture of tolerance. The role of urban planning, landscape design, popular culture and performing arts, sports and other civic-centred activities, as well as efforts to reconnect with the maligned symbols and edifices of Lebanon's national heritage, should not be dismissed or trivialized. If imaginatively pursued, they can do much in creating opportunities for lethargic and demoralized groups to associate together in open and common spaces. Hence they are vital for articulating and healing Lebanon's conflicting perceptions of itself and its past and in reshaping the country's damaged collective identity.

The voluntary sector, it must be noted, even in vibrant liberal democracies, is always an endangered zone. As Robert Wuthnow put it, it is like a 'treasure trove of our most cherished possessions, surrounded by the marauding forces of state bureaucracy and rampant capitalism'. (Wuthnow 1991, 25) At least such programmes can protect these imperilled associations and restore their ability to safeguard the instruments of civil society.

The Dynamics of Protracted Strife

Typical of small, communal and highly factionalized societies, the history of Lebanon has been characterized by intermittent outbursts of political violence. Dramatic episodes such as the peasant uprisings of 1820, 1840 and 1857; the repeated outbreaks of sectarian hostilities in 1841, 1845, 1860 and 1958; and the latest prolonged hostilities (1975–90) reveal, despite their diversity, the fragility of Lebanon's precarious democracy and the perpetual grievances of dominant groups within society and their vulnerability to external pressures.

Much of the early violence assumed the form of internal strife between factions and feuding families vying for a greater share of power and privilege. Little of it, at least until 1840, took on the character of open confessional conflict. Nineteenth-century travellers and local chroniclers all uniformly commented on the spirit of amity that had characterized confessional relations at the time.

There is no need here to review the circumstances associated with the outbreak of such protracted conflict. They are complex and varied and have been amply and ably explored elsewhere (see Salibi, 1965; Harik, 1968; Kerr, 1959; Polk, 1963; Porath, 1966; Khalaf, 1979; Chevallier, 1971). What I wish to do, instead, is to extract a few broad recurrent features that elucidate characteristics of Lebanon's political legacy. Others share much with instances of collective violence in comparable historical settings. A caveat is in order: since I am dealing with events and episodes spanning nearly two centuries, the discussion will inevitably be sweeping and eclectic.

The circumstances that impelled groups to resort to political violence were not necessarily those that sustained their mobilization and informed the direction and outcome of conflict. For example, all the peasant uprisings were initially sparked by a sense of collective consciousness and a concern for public welfare. Yet all were deflected, at one point or another, into confessional hostility. Likewise, episodes of communal conflict originally provoked by socio-economic disparities and legitimate grievances were transformed (or deformed) into factional rivalry. The enthusiasm for 'class' struggle and collective mobilization among Christian peasants in the north found little appeal among their counterparts in the Druze districts. By arousing latent confessional enmity, traditional Druze leaders could easily manipulate such sentiments to turn their people against involvement. The lapse of nearly 40 years, from 1820 to 1860, had done little to transform the loyalties and attachments of peasants. Confessional, local and feudal allegiances continued to predominate over other public and collective interests. A Druze remained a Druze first, a Junblatti second and a Shufi third, and then a *fellah* or part of the *'ammah* (common people).

Much the same patterns were still in evidence a century later during the civil disturbances of 1958. Here too, the resort to collective violence was initially rooted in legitimate socio-economic and political grievances. The issues underlying the conflict were non-sectarian. So were the composition and motives of the main adversaries. Both insurgents and loyalists were broad and loose coalitions of religiously minded groups. Yet fighting in urban and rural areas assumed a religious character. Indeed, leaders on both sides incited religious sentiments to reawaken communal solidarities and extend the basis of their mobilization.

The protracted strife of 1975–90 provides much to support such patterns; namely, that forms of political unrest sparked by genuine socio-economic disparities or legitimate grievances are often transformed into sectarian rivalry. Thus, in order to understand and in future to control such phenomena, we need to extend our analysis to consider those circumstances that *sustain* violence, as distinct from those that caused it. Unfortunately, our knowledge remains lopsided. We know much more of the latter (i.e. the etiology, origin and predispositions for violent politics) but not as much about the socio-cultural and psychological forces sustain and reinforce belligerency.

Initially, nineteenth-century uprisings employed non-confrontational strategies of collective protest. Rallies, gatherings, petitions, mass agitation were very common. In some instances, particularly in 1858 when peasants felt strong enough to resist impositions of their feudal lords, they often ceased payments of rent they owed their Khazin sheikhs. When these methods failed, rebels had no compunction about experimenting with other more contentious strategies.

Indeed, in all three uprisings (1820, 1840 and 1858), conflict spiralled into violent scuffles, armed hostilities and frontal clashes between masses of armed peasants and state-sponsored armies. In some instances, particularly in 1840, peasants employed the conventional logistics of guerrilla warfare, such as ambushing and attacking Egyptian convoys transporting ammunition and supplies. (Smilianskaya 1972, 81; al-Shidiaq, 1954, II: 226) On the whole, however, the instruments of violence involved little more than the ordinary rifles and hatchets common at the time in factional combat and local rivalries. As regional and European powers were drawn into the conflict, violence in most instances escalated into full-blown warfare, with regular armies reinforced by the technologies of mass destruction such as massive troop movements, naval blockades, bombardment, heavy artillery and the like. At that point damage to life and property became more devastating.

The internationalization of the conflict in 1958 also contributed to the protraction and escalation of hostility. Events outside Lebanon (i.e. the Suez Crisis of 1957, the formation of the UAR in February 1958 and the Iraqi revolution in July 1958) threatened Western interests in the region, raised the spectre of growing Soviet influence and legitimized the internationalization of Lebanese politics. Heated debates in the Arab League and the Security Council riveted world attention, and the ultimate landing of US troops did little to assuage the internal sources of discontent. As was the case in earlier and subsequent instances, the intervention only polarized the factions and deepened paranoia and hostility. Needless to say, one can point to much in the bloody confrontations touched off in 1975 to reconfirm such views.

As violence unfolded in the twentieth century, 1958 and 1975, it acquired its own momentum and began to proliferate. Embattled groups were trapped in an escalating spiral of vengeance and retribution, a feature that clearly became much more pronounced in 1975. Leaders themselves often helplessly admitted that, once incited, violent episodes tended to skim out of control and that there was little they could do to quell the fury of aroused passions. This supports another basic premise of this chapter, namely, that the origin of violence is not necessarily located in enduring structural and attitudinal conditions but in the flux of events associated with the outbreak of hostility. It also accounts for another seeming paradox inherent in collective violence: that of leaders who are initially reluctant to entertain belligerency but, once it erupts, are inclined to romanticize its redemptive and regenerative attributes.

Inevitably, strife generated by the episodes in all three epochs assumed a vast array of forms. There was much, however, in their underlying pattern and character to support René Girard's (1977) insight regarding the nature of 'surrogate victims'. Given the multi-layered hierarchical structure of feudal society, compounded by regional and global rivalries, all the protagonists – powerful and weak, rooted and marginal, internal and external – were equally embroiled in juxtapositions of competing interests and shifting loyalties. Hence, many of the episodes of strife created unlikely and ironic coalitions of awkward political bedfellows. European powers and their proteges and agents, Ottoman sultans with their *walis* and *pashas*, feudal sheikhs, *ayan* clerics, *wakils* (agents), *shuyukh al-shabab* (leaders) and an undifferentiated mass of commoners were all caught up in an intricate hierarchy of contentious relationships.

In such a milieu, to paraphrase Girard, when hostility is unappeased, it seeks and always finds surrogate victims. Groups and individuals responsible for its original fury are promptly replaced by others. Such proxy targets of renewed hostility are victimized only because they happen to be vulnerable and accessible. (Girard 1977) Examples of such displaced victimization are legion. A sultan, eager to ingratiate himself with a given Western power, spares his local proteges or protected communities but oppresses others. An *amir*, unable or unwilling to defy the rapacious executions of a *pasha* turns to leaderless *muqataas*. Rebellious peasants, not powerful enough to confront their main adversaries (the central government), vent their vengeance on weaker groups (Khazin sheikhs).

Another pertinent conceptual element can be inferred from the manifestations and consequences of communal conflict, which provide vivid evidence in support of two broad perspectives on the dynamics of civil strife elucidated by James Rule (1988). On the one hand, one encounters much to substantiate the 'consummatory' or expressive character of collective strife, the kind that is incited and sustained by group solidarity, the sharing of revolutionary excitement engendered by the insurrections. Here, the flux of events themselves – the unfolding episodes associated with the outbreak of hostilities – serves to draw insurgents together. Conflict and the threat of violence become, in the words of Alain Touraine (1981), the 'glue' that cements groups together. Mass rallies, animated gatherings, collective agitation, the resourcefulness of *wakils*, the camaraderie of *shuyukh al-shabab* and the exhilaration of combat all contribute to this. In short, the appeals of expressing solidarity with one's group, assailing one's enemy and destroying hated symbols provides the catalyst for collective violence, which then spreads by contagion and manifests itself in looting, plunder and physical assaults.

On the other hand, there is also evidence of the 'instrumental' character of collective strife, the type that bears a closer affinity to protest movements, with their rational calculation of costs and benefits. In such cases rebels are driven not only by an impulse to correct injustices and seek reprieve from feudal abuse but also by a desire to secure basic necessities and material benefits. For example, looting the Khazin's property and confiscating his crops were more parts of organized operations designed to place expropriated property at the disposal of the rebels. These were not random, unrestrained acts of marauding and pillaging nor were they driven by a compulsion to wreak vengeance for its own sake. Indeed, particularly in 1858, the expulsion of the Khazins lasted long enough to be accompanied by their *de facto* expropriation and, hence, a substantial redistribution of property in favour of commoners. (Baer 1982, 200–301) Mount Lebanon's geography, the density of village settlements and the personal allegiance and loyalty inherent in the system of *iqta* (tax farms) must have inhibited the emergence of peasant brigandage typical of 'primitive rebels' and wanton banditry. (Hobsbawm 1972)

Insurgents, peasants and rebels rarely acted alone. In all episodes of peasant uprising, for example, organizational and ideological leadership was assumed by Maronite clerics. It was they who first articulated the peasants' revolutionary attitude towards the feudal system. They organized them into village communes and appointed *wakils* as spokesmen for the *ammiyyah* (commoners' uprising).

In addition to ecclesiastical intervention, the peasants almost always received either the direct or moral support of Ottoman authorities and foreign consuls who manipulated the uprisings for purposes unrelated to the of the *ammiyyah* genuine protest movement or any of the commoners' grievances or interests. The Ottomans were eager to undermine the privileged status of Mount Lebanon and the local authority of feudal chiefs. Indeed, pitting one group against another, through alternating strategies of ingratiation and manipulation, became a popular shorthand for Ottoman barbarity and repression.

Foreign powers, eager to gain inroads into the Middle East and win protegés, also reverted to the same divisive strategies. This was poignantly apparent in 1840. While the European powers, France, Britain, Russia, Austria and Prussia, were all acting in concert to rescue Syria from its Egyptian occupiers, each had its own diplomatic agenda. Sometimes, discord within a country (e.g. the conflict in France between the prime minister, Louis-Adolphe Thiers, and the king, Louis-Philippe) left its reverberations on the course and outcome of the rebellion. Consequently, a genuine local uprising was, literally, appropriated and deflected into a global crisis. Indignant peasants, already violated by the adverse effect of European economic transformations, were victimized further. Kisirwan, in the process, was turned into a proxy killing field for other peoples' wars.

Another disconcerting but explicable inference stands out, one with prophetic implications for the course and magnitude of the violence that was to ensue. As long as the conflict remained a 'class' rivalry, exacerbated by fiscal pressures, socio-economic disparities, political coercion and the like, it was comparatively bloodless. If and when, however, it was transformed or deflected into confessional or communal hostility, the violence increased greatly in extent and intensity.

This, as René Girard reminds us, carries even more ominous implications. 'Religion shelters us from violence just as violence seeks shelter in religion.' As this happens, communities become trapped in a vicious circle of vengeance and reprisal. 'The mimetic character of violence is so intense it cannot burn itself out . . . Only violence can put an end to violence and that is why violence is self-propagating.' (Girard, 1977: 24–26)

Finally, the events of 1958 reconfirmed another curious attribute of collective strife in Lebanon, namely, the ethos of 'no victor, no vanquished', which also characterized many of the earlier episodes of communal conflict in the nineteenth century. Somehow, violent confrontations never ended, or were never permitted to end, by the unequivocal defeat or victory of one group over the other. From one perspective, this might be taken to mean that, disruptive as the events were, they did not dispel the hope for reconciliation and compromise between the warring communities. Or, to put it another way, the differences and grievances that led to armed struggle had perhaps not quite reached the point where they could not be reconciled. Leaders of the major factions in the conflict were still able to take part in the same coalition government.

But the 'no victor, no vanquished' formula also carried less auspicious implications: that the Lebanese have not as yet heeded the lessons of their troubled history with its recrudescent civil strife. Had any of the earlier episodes of political violence been more definitively concluded, by designating a winner and a loser and thereby resolving the issues associated with each, then perhaps the country might have been spared many of the cruelties of subsequent strife.

On Retribalization and Collective Amnesia

Among all the disheartening consequences of Lebanon's encounters with collective violence, two are particularly relevant to the central concern of this chapter: first, symptoms of 'retribalization' apparent in re-awakened communal identities and the urge to huddle in cloistered spatial communities; and second, a pervasive mood of lethargy, indifference and weariness, which borders, at times, on 'collective amnesia'.

Both are understandable reactions, which enabled traumatized groups to survive the cruelties of protracted strife. Both, however, could be disabling as the Lebanese contemplate less belligerent strategies for peaceful coexistence. The questions underlying these problems can be restated in explicit terms. Through what vectors and mediating agencies can the resurgent parochialized identities become the bases for the articulation of a political culture of tolerance? And who is to mobilize and speak on behalf of those who are numbed and bereft of speech?

Let me pose the questions more graphically still. Suppose we were to establish a war museum in Lebanon or erect a score of national monuments, what messages, artifacts, symbols, if any, could crystallize events associated with the war or the new socio-cultural realities and unite the society around them? How is one to write or rewrite a coherent and unifying history of the war? How, in the words of Wagner-Pacifici and Schwartz (1991, 379), 'is commemoration without consensus, or without pride, possible?'

Discussing and analyzing such processes can tell us much about how culture and cultural meanings are produced, how they lodge and are assimilated into the collective memory of society. In the case of Lebanon, they also tell us how a society comes to terms with troubled events in its past and how the process of 'celebrating' and memorializing these divisive and futile events can become a source of moral unity and collective rejuvenation.

The recent experience of Israel, particularly how those involved in the war have come to rationalize their misadventure in Lebanon, is instructive. When Israeli officials speak publicly about their war in Lebanon, they extol their soldiers in vivid and inspiring words. Their remarks about the war itself, however, are vague and pointless. They affirm the war as historical entity but 'deny it an elevated place in the national experience. The event is swallowed, as it were, but never assimilated. Such is the memory of "Israel's Vietnam": a misbegotten cause nobly pursued.' (Wagner-Pacifici and Schwartz, 1991: 380)

Clearly there is nothing 'noble' about Israel's Lebanon war. It was a misbegotten experience in all its despicable dimensions. Yet, for us Lebanese, it is an experience that must be assimilated into our collective consciousness and transformed into an instrument for recovery and national solidarity. I have elsewhere (Khalaf, 1993b) explored these issues as they relate to the impact of protracted strife on collective memory and the prospects for restoration of civility. I will here focus only briefly on retribalization and collective amnesia before I move on to consider how such symptoms can be mitigated and transformed into rehabilitative strategies.

Retribalization

In exploring the nature of nationalism and social cohesion in complex societies, Ernest Gellner (1988, 6–28) finds it conceptually fitting to re-examine the role of shared amnesia, collective forgetfulness and anonymity in the emergence of nation-states. Among other things, he argues that the presumed erosion of primordial allegiances is not a prerequisite to the formation of cohesive nation-states.

Likewise, the formation of strong, ruthless, centralizing regimes is not the monopoly of any particular state or culture. Seemingly cohesive and integrated old states are not always culturally unified and homogenous.

Of course Ottoman Turkey became the prototype of the 'mosaic', where ethnic and religious groups not only retained much of their so-called primordial and archaic identities, but were positively instructed, through edicts, centralization, fiat, etc., never to forget. The Ottomans were tolerant of other religions but they were strictly segregated from the Muslims. In other words, the various 'millets' were mixed together but were never truly combined into a homogeneous and unified society. Today a similar dread of collective amnesia is amply visible in the dramatic events surrounding the collapse of the USSR and the disintegration of Eastern Europe.

Nor are the nascent nations today bereft of the loyalties and institutions often attributed exclusively to civil and secular nation-states. Perhaps conditions of anonymity pertain in times of swift or revolutionary social change and turmoil. But after the upheavals, when the deluge subsides, when social order is restored, internal cleavages and continuities resurface. New memories are invested when the old ones are destroyed. Indeed, 'most societies,' Gellner reiterates, 'seem allergic to internal anonymity, homogeneity and amnesia.' (Gellner, 1987: 9)

Lebanon's political history, both in good and bad times, reinforces this self-evident but often overlooked or misconstrued reality. Throughout its epochal transformation – the emergence of the 'principality' in the seventeenth and eighteenth centuries, the upheavals of the mid-nineteenth century and the consequent creation of the *Mutasarrifiyyeh* of Mount Lebanon (1860–1920), down to the creation of Greater Lebanon in 1920, the National Pact of 1943, the restoration of unity and stability after the civil war of 1958 and the aftermath of fifteen years of violence – a few abiding realities about the ubiquity of 'retribalization' are reconfirmed.

I am employing the term 'retribalization' to refer to the resurgence of communal loyalties, particularly the convergence of confessional and territorial identities.

As I have noted in the previous chapter, the sweeping changes that occurred in Lebanon scarcely weakened or eroded the intensity of confessional or sectarian loyalties. Indeed, in times of social unrest and political turmoil, such loyalties became sharper and often superseded other ties and allegiances.

Confessional loyalties have not only survived and retained their primacy; they continue to serve as viable sources of communal solidarity. They inspire local and personal initiative and account for much of the resourcefulness and cultural diversity and vitality of the Lebanese. But they also undermine civic consciousness and commitment to Lebanon as a nation-state. Indeed, the forces that motivate and sustain harmony, balance and prosperity are also the very forces that can pull the society apart and contribute to conflict, tension and civil disorder. The ties that bind, in other words, also unbind. (For further details see Khalaf, 1991.)

As the violence went on, it is understandable why traumatized and threatened groups should seek shelter in their communal solidarities and cloistered spaces. Confessional sentiments and their supportive loyalties, even in times of relative peace and stability, have always been effective sources of social support and political mobilization. But these are not, as Lebanon's fractured history amply demonstrates, unmixed blessings. While they cushion individuals and groups against the anomie and alienation of public life, they also heighten the density of communal hostility and enmity. Such processes have been particularly acute largely because class and ideological and other secular forms of group affiliation have been comparatively more distant and abstract and, consequently, of less relevance to the psychic and social needs of the uprooted and traumatized. Hence, more and more Lebanese today are metaphorically brandishing their confessionalism as both emblem and armour.

Confessional identity is used as an emblem in the sense that it has become the most viable medium for asserting presence and securing vital needs and benefits. Without it, groups are literally rootless, nameless and voiceless, unable to organize or to be heard. It is only when an individual is placed within a confessional context that his ideas and assertions are rendered meaningful or worthwhile. Confessionalism is also being used as armour, in that it has become a shield against real or imagined threats. The more vulnerable the emblem, the thicker the armour.

Conversely, however, the thicker the armour, the more vulnerable and paranoid other communities become. It is precisely this dialectic between threatened communities and the urge to seek shelter in cloistered worlds that has plagued Lebanon for so long.

There is a curious and painful irony here. Despite the many differences that divide the Lebanese, they are all in a sense homogenized by fear, grief and trauma. Three primal fears bind them together: of being marginalized, assimilated or exiled. But it is also those fears that keep the Lebanese apart. This 'geography of fear' is not sustained by walls or artificial barriers of the kind one observes in other comparable instances of ghettoization of minorities and ethnic groups. Rather, it is sustained by the psychology of dread, hostile bonding and ideologies of enmity.

As we have seen (Chapter 8) massive population shifts, particularly since they are accompanied by the reintegration of displaced groups into more homogeneous, self-contained and exclusive spaces, have also reinforced communal solidarity. Consequently, territorial and confessional identities, more so perhaps than at any other time, are beginning to converge. Expressed in more spatial terms, if urbanization normally stands for variety, diversity, mix and openness, then what has been happening in Lebanon, at least in a majority of areas, is ghettoization. In this sense the Lebanese are inverting what might be assumed to be the most typical course of evolution in social systems.

As has often been pointed out, a fascinating historical development in most societies involves their passage from a relatively 'closed' to a more 'open' system: membership, exit or entry, access to privileges and benefits are no longer denied by virtue of limitations of religion, kinship or race. Such openness accounts for much of the spectacular growth in the philosophical, artistic and political emancipation of contemporary societies. In this sense, Lebanon is now at the critical threshold, since it is about to invert and reverse this natural course of history. Indeed, what we may be witnessing is the substitution of one form of pluralism, imperfect as it has been, for a more regressive and pathological kind. We are destroying a society that by and large permitted groups with divergent backgrounds and expectations to live side by side. What is emerging is a monolithic archetype that is hostile to any such co-existence or free experimentation.

Such realities can no longer be wished away or mystified. They must be recognized for what they are: strategies for the empowerment of threatened groups and their incorporation into the torrent of public life. The coalition of confessional and territorial entities, since it draws upon a potentially larger base of support, is particularly potent in Lebanon. It is clearly a more viable vector for political mobilization than kinship, fealty or sectarian loyalties.

Collective Amnesia

The war in Lebanon has not only destroyed common spaces and reinforced proclivities to exclusive and reclusive spatial arrangements; it has also generated a pervasive mood of what has been labelled, for want of a better term, collective amnesia. To survive the cruelties of war, the Lebanese became deadened and numbed, overwhelmed by muted anguish and pain.

During the war, this apparent callousness (often masquerading as resilience) served them well. It allowed them to survive but also to inflict and rationalize cruelties on the 'other'. By distancing themselves or cutting themselves off from the 'other', the brutality of embattled communities was routinized. Violence became morally indifferent. People could engage in guilt-free violence and kill with impunity precisely because they had restricted contacts with their defiled victims. To a large extent, it is 'the group boundaries,' as Randall Collins says, 'that determine the extent of human sympathy; within these boundaries, humanity prevails; outside them torture is inflicted without qualm'. (Collins, 1974: 417)

The phenomenon that enabled the Lebanese to survive the cruelties of civil strife is clearly disabling them now that they are considering options for peaceful coexistence. In this context, Collins usefully reminds us that 'the point is not to learn to live with the demons, but to take away their power.' (Collins, 1974: 416) The issue, here as well, converges on who is to mobilize or speak on behalf of those who are numbed and bereft of speech.

There is something in the character of intense pain, according to Elaine Scarry, that is 'language-destroying'. 'As the content of one's world disintegrates, so the content of one's language disintegrates . . . world, self, and voice are lost, or nearly lost, through the intense pain.' (Scarry, 1985: 35) This is also a reflection of the fact that people in pain are ordinarily deprived of the resources of speech. The language about pain is often evoked by those who are not themselves in pain but by those who speak on behalf of those who are. Richard Rorty expresses the same thought. He too suggests that people who are suffering do not have much access to language. That is why there is no such thing as the 'voice of the oppressed' or the 'language of the victims'. 'The language the victims once used is not working any more and they are suffering too much to put new words together. So the job of putting their situation into language is going to have to be done for them by somebody else'. (Rorty, 1989)

What groups are most qualified to play such roles? Where, when and with what does one begin processes of healing and rehabilitation? A critical question in this regard asserts itself. To what extent is it possible to reverse deeply embedded cultural attributes or geo-political realities rendered all the more incompliant by retribalization and protracted hostility? The Lebanese have been predisposed, for understandable reasons, to retribalize their communal and spatial identities. In unsettled times, even in cultures averse to propinquity, traumatized groups are inclined to reconnect with family, home and community for security and shelter.

The point I wish to advance is that, pathological as they may seem at times, such communal solidarities need not continue to be sources of paranoia and hostility. They could be extended and enriched to incorporate other more secular and civic identities. If stripped of their bigotry and intolerance, they could also become the bases for more equitable and judicious forms of power-sharing and the articulation of new cultural identities. Here lies the hope, the only hope perhaps, for an optimal restructuring of Lebanon's pluralism.

This not another elusive pipe dream. Just as enmity has been socially constructed and culturally sanctioned, it can also be unlearned. Group loyalties can, after all, be restructured. Under the spur of visionary and enlightened leadership, groups can, through a revitalized voluntary sector, at least be resocialized to perceive differences as manifestations of cultural diversity and enrichment; not as dreaded symptoms of distrust, fear and exclusion.

The Social Technologies of Pacification

Lebanon's troubled history with pluralism leaves little room for further experimentation. Of all its experiences with pluralism in its varied forms – co-existence, guarded contact, compromise and integration – the political management of separate, exclusive and self-contained entities has always been the most costly and short-lived. If it has been difficult for the Lebanese to live together, it is extremely unlikely that they can live apart. The calls for cantonization, federalism or other partitioning and dismantlement schemes, like earlier such experiments, stem from xenophobic fears and vengeful impulses. Their motives are the merging of parochial interests and short-term political expediency, not genuine coalescing of identities.

None of these appeals, though understandable in the aftermath of widespread fear and distrust, is or can become viable sources of socio-economic and political mobilization. Nor can they inspire any cultural rejuvenation. Like other monolithic and cloistered communities, they can only inculcate further dogmatism and intolerance. They are inclined to stifle cultural and intellectual experimentation and generate obfuscating milieux conducive to the spiritless, joyless lifestyles symptomatic of all closed and homogenized societies. Pluralism is, after all, an antidote to collective amnesia.

Another veritable reality also affirms itself. As a fragmented, diminutive state entrapped in a turbulent region, Lebanon will always be made more vulnerable by forces beyond its borders. This is the fate of many tiny republics. Hence, Lebanon is destined to remain at the mercy of its neighbours' goodwill and the compassion of international organizations. Much can be done, however, by the Lebanese themselves to merit and consolidate such redemptive concerns. Furthermore, tasks of reconstituting or reconstructing a society are much too vital to be left to embattled local and political groups or to the imperious whims of international organizations. The former are too vengeful and the latter are too distant and often obsessed with intricate diplomatic haggling over matters such as bilateral or multilateral agreements, constitutional reforms, demilitarization, peacekeeping, border controls and the like.

The Lebanese can at least begin by putting their internal house in order. There are measures and programmes, already proved effective elsewhere, that can be experimented with to fortify their immunity against disruption by external destabilizing forces. Such efforts can do much to reduce the country's chronic vulnerability to these pressures, particularly if directed towards two basic objectives: to broaden and incorporate the participation of seemingly indifferent and lethargic groups in society and to consider alternative dimensions thus far overlooked or dismissed as irrelevant.

I take my cue here from two seemingly incongruent sources: a classic nineteenth-century liberalist (Spencer, 1874) and a post-modernist (Rabinow, 1989). In addressing exigent public issues, Herbert Spencer implored us to recall the analogy of the bent iron plate. In trying to flatten the wrought-iron plate, it is futile, Spencer pointed out, to hammer directly on the buckled area; we only make matters worse. To be effective, our hammering must be around, not directly on, the projecting part.

The implications are obvious. Rather than focusing almost obsessively on issues such as peace accords, conflict resolution, political and constitutional reforms and the like, we could reach out to other seemingly irrelevant components or areas. For example, urban planning, architectural design, the rejuvenation of popular culture and the performing arts, curricular reform, competitive sports and the wider participation of indigenous groups in local rehabilitation projects – thus far overlooked because of excessive reliance on regional and international initiatives for conflict resolution – can do much to pacify and heal sources of division and thereby speed the transformation of the geography of fear into a culture of tolerance (see Khalaf, 1993; Khalaf and Khoury, 1993).

Paul Rabinow's (1989) analysis of the socio-cultural history of France between 1830 and 1930 offers equally instructive hints. He delineates the constellation of thought, action and passion underlying what he terms the 'social technologies of pacification', the tools for reforming and controlling the inherent antagonisms between space and society and between forms and norms current in France during that eventful century. Rabinow identifies a set of actors – ranging from architects and intellectuals to urban reformers – who were all infused with this passion to 'pacify the pathos' and, consequently, articulated a set of pragmatic solutions to public problems in times of crisis (e.g. wars, epidemics, strikes, etc.). Despite their divergent backgrounds, they shared two common perspectives: bitterness about the institutional and cultural crisis of their society and an unshaken faith in the production and regulation of a peaceful and productive social order.

One can easily glean from Rabinow's analysis several persuasive examples of such successful consolidation. Urban designers, architects, intellectuals, humanists of all shades and persuasions, along with other outraged but muted groups, are particularly qualified to play this role in Lebanon. Wilfully or otherwise, they have thus far been shunted aside and trivialized. They have to shed their timidity and reclaim the credibility of their professions and legitimate interests. By mobilizing aesthetic sensibilities and other artistic energies and popular cultural expressions in everyday life, they can do much to arouse the public to redeem its maligned heritage. More important, they can prod the Lebanese to turn outwards and transcend their parochial identities to connect with others. City life, after all, is an ideal environment for working out personal and social conflicts. Competitive sports, the performing arts, a revival of interest in national theatres and museums and efforts to rehabilitate the country's neglected landmarks and historic sites can do much in this regard.

There are three further reasons why such groups are ideally suited today to articulate this new language and vision on behalf of their besieged compatriots. First, a disproportionate number of such groups have been, for much of the duration of the war, in diaspora. Every culture has its own diaspora. Lebanon's trials with exile and dispersal have been quite acute. They were, however, also enabling. Mavericks, as histories of itinerant populations tell us, rarely stay at home. Just like the traditional Lebanese *mkari* (peddler), who always wandered beyond the narrow confines of his village and came back with tales, goods and titbits from the world beyond, there exists today a growing generation of global multiculturalists. Both established and younger cohorts of gifted professionals and entrepreneurs have been deepening and extending their skills and experiences abroad. Many are rightly disillusioned, perhaps bitter, but have not been rendered speechless by the harrowing events. They experienced the war only vicariously, from a distance. Hence, they have not become as numbed or cynical. Nor do they harbour deep-seated hostility towards other groups. Secondly, though exiled, they have not severed their ties to nor abandoned their nostalgia for their native culture. They bring in comparative vision, not the alien constructs of 'foreign experts' imposed on unfamiliar and unreceptive milieux. Finally, by virtue of such multicultural sympathies, they are less likely to perceive their projects as efforts for privileging or empowering one group or community in opposition to another. Hence, they are more predisposed to transcend their parochialism and use their broader view as a means of doing away with the geography of fear and its demarcating lines and enclosures.

Pacifying Lebanon's pathos, though intricate, is not insurmountable. Much can be done to prepare for this blissful eventuality. First and foremost, the Lebanese must be made to realize that massive post-war reconstruction and development can and must be accomplished without added damage to the environment. Given its size, Lebanon clearly can ill afford any further environmental abuse. Spare and menaced, the country's dazzling landscape is, after all, its distinctive legacy, a source of national pride and resourcefulness. Indeed, other than the ingenuity of its human resources, the goodwill of its neighbours and gratuitous guarantees of geo-politics, the country has little else to sustain its vulnerable existence.

In an existential sense, there are two inescapable realities that homogenize the

Lebanese today: geography and fear. We have no choice but to invoke the captivating beauty of the country's habitat as an antidote to fear. Much can be done to stop the defoliation of open spaces and reconnect disinherited and denationalized groups with their county's national treasures and collective memory. Likewise, fearful people can be assured that they need not be fully appreciative of the 'others' to be able to live with them. Some of the liveliest cities in the world, after all, have managed to live with tolerable conflict among their diverse communities. Many in such places express violent aversion towards those with whom they do not identify. Yet they recognize such differences as a given, something they must live with. (Fischer, 1982: 206) Louis Wirth, in his classic essay 'Urbanism as a Way of Life', expressed this same reality when he declared that 'the juxtaposition of divergent personalities and modes of life tends to produce a relativistic perspective and a sense of toleration of differences'. (Wirth, 1938: 155)

Likewise, the Lebanese must also be reassured that their territorial commitments are understandable and legitimate under the circumstances. But so is their need to break away. Being spatially anchored reinforces their need for shelter, security and solidarity. Like other territorialized groups, they become obsessed with boundary delineation and safeguarding their community against trespassers and interlopers. The need for wonder, exhilaration, exposure to new sensations, world views and the elevation of our appreciative sympathies – which are all enhanced by connectedness with strangers – are also equally vital for our sustenance. Witness the euphoria of kids in an urban playground as they cut themselves off in play from the ties of family and home, or the excitement of tourists in a bustling city street. The village *mkari*, in admittedly a different time and place, played much the same role. He, too, broke away, crossed barriers and was a cultural broker of sorts, precisely because he exposed himself to new sensations and contacts. He had no aversion to strangers. He wandered away but always returned home again. We need to revive and extend the ethos of the *mkari* as the prototype of an idyllic national character. With all his folk eccentricities, he epitomizes some of the enabling virtues of a 'traveller' and not a 'potentate'.

Edward Said employs this polar imagery to construct two archetypes for elucidating the interplay between identity, authority and freedom in an academic environment. In the ideal academy, Said tells us, 'we should regard knowledge as something for which to risk identity, and we should think of academic freedom as an invitation to give up one identity in the hope of understanding and perhaps even assuming more than one. We must always view the academy as a place to voyage in, owning none of it but at home everywhere in it.' (Said, 1991: 81) Are these not also the attributes or paradigms we should seek in restoring a city or the places and institutions within it to render them more conducive to this kind of voyaging?

The image of traveler depends not on power, but on motion, on a willingness to go into different worlds, use different idioms, and understand a variety of disguises, masks, and rhetorics. Travelers must suspend the claim of customary routine in order to live in new rhythms and rituals. Most of all, most unlike the potentate who must guard only one place and defend its frontiers, the traveller *crosses over*, traverses territory, and abandons fixed positions, all the time. (Said, 1991: 81)

Ideally, this could well serve as the leitmotif of those entrusted with educational reform, cultural rehabilitation and political resocialization, i.e. to create the conditions that will encourage the transformation of 'potentates' into 'travellers'. When people plead with us to find some way of making 'ghettos' and all other cloistered spaces more respectable, they are in effect asking that they be kept open to facilitate the voyaging, traversing and crossing over. Places should, in other words, be designed in such a way that people can move on when the need for communal support and shelter is no longer essential. Any form of confinement, in the long run, becomes a deprivation. Conversely, open urban spaces can also be rendered more congenial to cushion groups against the tempestuousness of city life.

The image of the Lebanese as a spatially anchored creature, compulsively huddling together with his family and defending his domains (i.e. the compact enclosures of family and neighbourhood) against potential trespassers, needs to be modified. He is also (or at least was until the war terrorized his public spaces) a creature of the outdoors. Design can do much to restore the conviviality of such open spaces. Street life is emblematic of urban provocation and arousal precisely because that is the setting in which people let go, so to speak, dropping their conventional reserves towards others. As Richard Senett puts it, as 'one goes to the edge of oneself, he sees, talks and thinks about what is outside . . . By turning outward, he is aroused by the presence of strangers and arouses them.' Sympathy in such instances becomes a condition of 'mutual concern and arousal as one loses the power of self-definition'. In such instances 'differences' are reinforced without sustaining 'indifference' to others (Sennett, 1990: 149).

Prospects for the Restoration of Civility

The Lebanese seem at the moment, for understandable reasons, bent on 'retribalizing' their communal and spatial identities. As we have seen, this is not unusual. In times of disaster people have a propensity to seek territorial solidarities. These need not, however, continue to be a source of paranoia and hostility; stripped of their bigotry, they can instead be extended and enriched to incorporate more secular and plural identities. There is still a faint hope, given the tenacious survival of religiously mixed communities, that the country may evade this fateful crossover into the barbarous logic of enclosure and partition.

Even in times of fierce fighting, when all crossings between the two halves of Beirut were either cut off or hazardous, people continued to defy the risks and cross over. Hence, differences between the two sides were 'staved off,' as Jean Makdisi put it, 'by those sullen people who stubbornly cross over, day after day by the thousands, some to go to work, others to visit friends and relatives, and *many just to make a point.*' (Makdisi, 1990: 77; the italics are mine) A more telling indicator of the refusal to succumb to pressures of partition is the marked difference in real-estate prices. Land values in religiously mixed areas, regardless of their aesthetic or urban quality, continue to be higher than in exclusive or homogeneous areas. So is the volume of construction activity and other manifestations of economic enterprise.

Lebanon's experience, treacherous and perplexing as it has been, is not unique. Michael Walzer, contemplating the most supportive environment for what he calls the 'good life', arrives (after reviewing predominant socialist and capitalist ideologies in the nineteenth and twentieth centuries) at a similar conclusion. To 'live well,' he concludes, 'is to participate with other men and women in remembering, cultivating and passing on a national heritage.' Such a 'good life' can be realized only in a civil society, 'the realm of fragmentation and struggle but also of concrete and authentic solidarities where we fulfill E.M. Forster's injunction of *only connect*, and become social or communal men and women.' (Walzer, 1991: 298)

Walzer goes on to assert:

The picture here is of people freely associating and communicating with one another, forming and reforming groups of all sorts, not for the sake of any particular formation – family, tribe, nation, religion, commune, brotherhood or sisterhood, interest group or ideological movement – but for the sake of sociability itself. For we are by nature social, before we are political or economic beings . . . What is true is that the quality of our political and economic activity and of our national culture is intimately connected to the strength and vitality of our associations. Ideally, civil society is a setting of settings: all are included, none is preferred. (Walzer, 1991: 298)

Other equally sobering voices (e.g. Dahrendorf, 1990; Konrad, 1984; Havel, 1985) have also been making similar appeals for the restoration of civil society. All remind us that the task of reconstruction will require more than political reform, physical rehabilitation and economic development. More vital and more difficult is the need to restructure basic loyalties. By its very nature, this is bound to be a long and delicate process. Dahrendorf is, perhaps, most assertive: 'It takes six months to create new political institutions; to write a constitution and electoral laws. It may take six years to create a half-way viable economy. It will probably take sixty years to create a civil society. Autonomous institutions are the hardest things to bring about.' (Dahrendorf, 1990: 42) In almost identical terms, all three of these cited authors caution that the reproduction of loyalty, civility, political competence and trust in authority are never the work of the state alone, and the effort to go it alone – one meaning of totalitarianism – is doomed to failure.

Two parting thoughts: now that the prospects for an imminent recovery of Beirut seem favourable (indeed it is heralded as a momentous milestone presaging the new order), we must bear in mind, lest we get disillusioned again, that cities, civilizations, and citizenship share a linguistic and historical root. Where cities, great or small, are not hospitable to the multiplicity of groups, voices and the interplay of viewpoints, civil society will always suffer. Secondly, creating such a political culture of tolerance demands, among other things, that every Lebanese today should change his perception of the 'other'. Only by doing so can we begin to transform the geography of fear into genuine but guarded forms of co-existence.

CHAPTER 11

Contested Space and the Forging of New Cultural Identities

Lebanon today is at a fateful crossroads in its political and socio-cultural history. At the risk of some oversimplification, the country continues to be imperilled by a set of overwhelming predicaments and unsettling transformations. At least three stand out, by virtue of the ominous implications they have for the massive reconstruction underway and the prospects for forging a viable political culture of tolerance and peaceful coexistence.

First, Lebanon is in the throes of post-war reconstruction and rehabilitation. Given the magnitude and scale of devastation, the country will almost certainly require massive efforts in virtually all dimensions of society to spearhead its swift recovery and sustained development. Processes of post-war reconstruction, even under normal circumstances, are usually cumbersome. In Lebanon, they are bound to be more difficult because of the distinctive character of the traces left by the collective terror and strife that afflicted the country and that set it apart from other instances of post-war reconstruction. Among such disheartening consequences, two are particularly poignant and of relevance to the concerns of this essay. They are the tendency towards 'retribalization' apparent in reawakened communal identities and the urge to seek shelter in cloistered spatial communities; and a pervasive mood of lethargy, indifference and weariness, which borders, at times, on 'collective amnesia'. Both are understandable reactions, which enable traumatized groups to survive the cruelties of protracted strife. Both, however, could be disabling, as the Lebanese are now considering less belligerent strategies for peaceful coexistence.

Secondly, Lebanon is not only grappling with all the short-term imperatives of reconstruction and the long-term need for sustainable development and security, but it has had to do so in a turbulent region with a multitude of unresolved conflicts. Impotent as the country may seem at the moment to neutralize or ward off such external pressures, there are measures and programmes, already proved effective elsewhere, that can be tried to fortify Lebanon's immunity to such destabilizing forces. Urban planning and design, architecture, landscaping, among other often overlooked forms of public intervention, can offer effective strategies for healing symptoms of fear and paranoia and transcending parochialism.

Finally, Lebanon as of late is also embroiled, willingly or otherwise, in all the unsettling forces of 'postmodernity' and 'globalism': the magnified importance of mass media, popular arts and entertainment in the framing of everyday life, an intensification of consumerism, the demise of political participation and collective consciousness for public issues and their replacement by local and parochial concerns for nostalgia and heritage.

Unfortunately, many of the public manifestations of nostalgia so rampant today in Lebanon have scant, if any, concern with what Christopher Lasch (1988: 178) has called a 'conversational relationship with the past'. Instead, they take the form either of the construction and embellishment of grandiose and monumental national symbols or of a search for roots, a longing to preserve or invent often contrived and apocryphal forms of local and communal identities. More disheartening, this valorization of or escape into the past, particularly at the popular cultural level, has taken on some of the garish symptoms of commodification of heritage into kitsch and the vulgarization of traditional folklore and indigenous artifacts.

Within this context, issues of collective memory, contested space and efforts to forge new cultural identities begin to assume critical dimensions. How much and which aspects of the past need to be retained or restored? By whom and for whom? Commonplace as these questions may seem, they have elicited little agreement among scholars. Indeed, the views and perspectives of those who have recently addressed them vary markedly.

To Ernest Gellner, collective forgetfulness, anonymity and shared amnesia are dreaded conditions resisted in all social orders. (Gellner, 1988) Perhaps, he argues, conditions of anonymity are inevitable in times of turmoil and upheaval. Once the unrest subsides, internal cleavages and segmental loyalties resurface.

D. MacCannell goes further, to assert that the ultimate triumph of modernity over other socio-cultural arrangements is epitomized not by the disappearance of premodern elements but by their reconstruction and artificial preservation in modern society. (MacCannell, 1989) Similarly, Jedlowski also maintains that a sense of personal identity can be achieved only on the basis of personal memory. (Jedlowski, 1990)

Benjamin Barber, however, argues that successful civic nations always entail a certain amount of 'studied historical absentmindedness . . . Injuries too well remembered,' he tells us, 'cannot heal'. (Barber, 1996: 167) What Barber is implying here, of course, is that if the memories of the war and its atrocities are kept alive, they will continue to reawaken fear and paranoia, particularly among those embittered by it. Without an opportunity to forget, there can never be a chance for harmony and genuine coexistence.

Both manifestations – the longing to obliterate, mystify and distance oneself from the fearsome recollections of an ugly and unfinished war and the efforts to preserve or commemorate them – coexist today in Lebanon. Retribalization and the reassertion of communal and territorial identities, as perhaps the most prevalent and defining elements in post-war Lebanon, incorporate in fact both these features. The convergence of spatial and communal identities serves, in other words, both the need to search for roots and the desire to rediscover, or invent, a state of bliss that has been lost; it also serves as a means of escape from the trials and tribulations of war.

Expressed more concretely, this reflex or impulse for seeking refuge in cloistered spatial communities is sustained by two seemingly opposed forms of self-preservation: to remember and to forget. The former is increasingly sought in efforts to anchor oneself in one's community or in reviving and reinventing its communal solidarities and threatened heritage. The latter is more likely to assume escapist and nostalgic predispositions to return to a past imbued with questionable authenticity.

Either way, concerted efforts need to be made to reinvigorate or generate meaningful public spaces in order to diminish fear and transcend parochialism and the compulsion to withdraw into the compact enclosures of family and community. If this essay has a plea, it is a call to go beyond what Nan Ellin terms 'defensive urbanism' and to generate conditions germane to the articulation of a more 'offensive urbanism'. (Ellin, 1997)

More than in any other time in recent history, architects and urban planners in Lebanon now have a rare opportunity to step in and assert the radical visions of their profession. With the manifestations of war still present, we catch Lebanon at a critical and propitious threshold in its urban history. The massive reconstruction underway, particularly the historic core of Beirut's Central Business District, has provoked a rare mood of nascent and growing public awareness of spatial and environmental issues. Perhaps for the first time growing segments of the Lebanese are becoming increasingly conscious and verbal about what is being done to the spaces around them.'[1]

If there are visible symptoms of a 'culture of disappearance', evident in the growing encroachment of global capital and state authority into the private realm and heedless reconstruction schemes, elements that are destroying or defacing the country's distinctive architectural landscape and urban heritage, there is also a burgeoning 'culture of resistance'. It is this that is contesting and repelling such encroachment and dreaded annihilation, or the fear of being engulfed by the overwhelming forces of globalization. (Alger, 1988)

Within this setting, urbanists have considerable latitude for advancing strategies

---

1. A critical core of established architects and urbanists, particularly those who had taken part in pre-war construction (Assem Salam, Henri Eddeh, Pierre el-Khoury, Jad Tabet), have been very active in launching campaigns to disclose the foibles and shortcomings of SOLIDERE (*Société Libanaise pour le Développement et la Reconstruction du Centre-Ville de Beyrouth*, SAL [The Lebanese Company for the development and Reconstruction of Beirut Central District, PLC]) and associated projects and schemes. These critical mentors have been recently joined by a growing number of a fairly young, mostly Western-trained architects and urbanists. On their own or through APSAD (Association for the Protection of Sites and Ancient Dwellings) and the revived Order of Engineers and Architects, they too have added their dissenting voices and proposed more viable alternatives. Hashim Sarkis, Habib Debs, Joe Nasr, Maha Yahya, Joumana Ghandour Atallah and Oussama Kabbani come to mind.

to awaken and mobilize silenced, lethargic and disengaged segments of the society to become more vigilant and actively engaged in controlling some of the forces ravaging their habitat and living space. It is my view that in this ameliorative interlude of post-war reconstruction, such involvement can do much in healing and transcending sources of fear and division in society. Also through such involvement, an aroused public can begin to assist in transforming 'spaces' into 'places'. After all, the way spaces are used is a reflection of people's identities and commitments to them. The more we live in a particular place – as we become part of it, so to speak – the more inclined we are to care for it.

As concerned citizens, it is vital for us to be involved in safeguarding, repairing and enriching our experience of space. Indeed, these are basic human rights, almost universal needs. If they are abused, we all are diminished. Consider what happens when a country's most precious heritage is maligned or becomes beyond the reach of its citizens. This is precisely what has been happening to many Lebanese. Their country's scenic geography, its pluralistic and open institutions, which were once sources of national pride and inspiration, things around which they wove dreams and that made them a bit different from others, have either become inaccessible to them or, worse, are being redefined as worthless. At best, they have been reduced to mere 'spaces' for commercial speculation.

To understand better the nature and character of this interplay between collective memory or obsession with 'heritage', the reassertion of space and the forging of new cultural identities, this essay discusses three related themes. First, it highlights briefly a few of the most striking spatial transformations associated with the war, particularly those that have some bearing on the relationships between space, memory and collective identity. All three are in flux and are being contested today. How they will be resolved will prefigure much of the emerging contours and future image of Beirut. Secondly, an attempt will be made to identify and account for a few of the responses communities are having in resisting or accommodating some of the global forces presumed to undermine their local heritage and identities.

Finally, it will consider what role urban planning and design can play in recovering or reclaiming Beirut. Who is to reclaim? Which area and how much of the old heritage should be restored and rehabilitated?

The Spaces of War

For almost two decades, Lebanon was besieged and beleaguered by every possible form of brutality and collective terror known to human history: from the cruelties of factional and religious bigotry to the massive devastations wrought by private militias and state-sponsored armies. They have all generated an endless carnage of innocent victims and an immeasurable toll in human suffering. Even by the most moderate of estimates, the magnitude of such damage to human life and property is staggering. About 170,000 people perished, twice as many were wounded or disabled; close to two-thirds of the population experienced some form of dislocation or uprootedness from their homes and communities. By the fall of

1982, UN experts estimated that the country had sustained $12–15 billion in damage, i.e. $2 billion per year. Today more than one-third of the population is considered to be below the poverty line as a result of war and displacement.

For a small, dense, closely-knit society of about 3.5 million, such devastations are, understandably, very menacing. More damaging, perhaps, are some of the socio-psychological and moral concomitants of protracted hostility. The scars and scares of war have left a heavy psychic toll, which displays itself in pervasive post-stress symptoms and nagging feelings of despair and hopelessness. In a culture generally averse to psychoanalytic counselling and therapy, these and other psychic disorders and fears are more debilitating. They are bound to remain masked and unrecognized and, hence, unattended to.

The demoralizing consequences of the war are also visible in symptoms of vulgarization and impoverishment of public life and erosion of civility. The routinization of violence, chaos and fear only compounded the frayed fabrics of the social order. It drew groups into the vortex of bellicose conflict and sowed a legacy of hate and bitterness. It is in this fundamental sense that Lebanon's pluralism, radicalization of its communities and consequent collective violence have become pathological and uncivil. Rather than being a source of enrichment, variety and cultural diversity, the modicum of pluralism that the country once enjoyed is now generating paranoia, hostility and differential bonding.

The first striking and, perhaps, unsettling feature is the way in which, since the outbreak of the war in 1975, the Lebanese have been caught up in an unrelenting process of redefining their territorial identities. Throughout the war, the majority of the Lebanese were trapped in a curious predicament, the painful task of *negotiating*, *constructing* and *reconfirming* a fluid and unsettled pattern of spatial identities. No sooner had they suffered the travails of dislocation by taking refuge in one community than they were again uprooted and compelled to negotiate yet another spatial identity or face the added humiliation of re-entry into their profoundly transformed communities. They became homeless, so to speak, in their own homes, or furtive fugitives and outcasts in their own communities.

The socio-psychological consequences of being dislodged from one's familiar and reliable landmarks, those of home and neighbourhood, can be quite shattering. Like other displaced groups, the Lebanese become disoriented and distressed because the terrain had changed and because there was no longer a neighbourhood for them to live in and rely upon. 'When the landscape goes,' says Erikson, 'it destroys the past for those who are left: people have no sense of belonging anywhere.' (Erikson, 1976) They lose the sense of control over their lives, their freedom and independence, their moorings to place and locality and, more damaging, a sense of who they are.

Bereft of place, they become homeless in at least three existential senses. First, they suffer the angst of being dislodged from their most enduring attachments and familiar places. Secondly, they also suffer banishment and the stigma of being outcasts in their neighbourhoods and homes. Finally, much like the truly exiled, they are impelled by an urge to reassemble a damaged identity and broken history. Imagining the old places, with all their nostalgic longings, serves as their only reprieve from the uncertainties and anxieties of the present.

Equally devastating has been the gradual destruction of Beirut's and, to a large extent, the country's common spaces. The first to go was Beirut's Central Business District, which had served historically as the undisputed focal meeting place. Beirut without its 'Burj', as the city centre is popularly labelled, was unimaginable. Virtually all the vital public functions were centralized there; the parliament, municipal headquarters, financial and banking institutions, religious edifices, transport terminals, traditional souks, shopping malls, entertainment, etc., kept the pre-war 'Burj' in a sustained state of day- and night-time animation. There, people of every walk of life and social standing came together.

With decentralization, other urban districts and regions in the country served as supplementary meeting grounds for common activities. They too drew together, albeit on seasonal and interim bases, groups from a wide cross-section of society, thereby nurturing outlets germane for coexistence and plural lifestyles. Altogether, there were very few exclusive spaces beyond the reach of others. The social tissue, like all seemingly localized spaces, was fluid and permeable.

Alas, the war destroyed virtually all such common and porous spaces, just as it dismantled many of the intermediate and peripheral heterogeneous neighbour-hoods that had mushroomed with increasing urbanization, in cities like Tripoli, Sidon and Zahleh. The war did not only destroy common spaces. It also encouraged the formation of separate, exclusive and self-sufficient spaces. Hence, the Christians of East Beirut need not now frequent West Beirut for its cultural and popular entertainment. Likewise, one can understand the reluctance of Muslims and other residents of West Beirut to visit resorts and similar alluring spots of the Christian suburbs. With internecine conflict, quarters within urban districts, just like towns and villages, were often splintered into smaller and more compact enclosures. Spaces within which people circulated and interacted shrank still further. The socio-psychological predispositions underlying this urge to huddle in insulated spaces are not too difficult to trace or account for.

The war has also transformed the perception and use of space in a more compelling sense. When a 'playground' (as pre-war Lebanon was legitimately labelled), turns into a 'battleground' inevitably this is accompanied by a dramatic change in land use. Hashim Sarkis has demonstrated how space during episodes of civil strife develops its own logic and propels its own inhabitation. (Sarkis, 1993) He tells that 'it precedes, resists, yields to and survives those who assume it to be a neutral site for their control'. He also advances the view that 'inhabitants are more elusive in their relationships with places they inhabit. They move across given boundaries, negotiate and renegotiate their spatial identities.' Much can be added to substantiate both of these seemingly antithetical viewpoints.

The spaces of war have manifestly asserted their ferocious logic on virtually every part of public and private space. Equally telling is the ingenuity of its besieged hostages in accommodating this menacing shift in their spatial surroundings.

The Cultures of Disappearance and Resistance

All wars, civil or otherwise, are atrocious. Lebanon's encounters with civil strife, it may be suggested, are particularly galling because their horrors were not anchored in any recognizable or coherent set of causes. Nor did they resolve the issues that had sparked the initial hostilities. It is a poignant fact that the war was altogether a wasteful and futile encounter with collective violence.

The muted anguish and unresolved hostilities of the war are now being compounded by all the ambivalences of post-war reconstruction and the way in which conglomerate global capital challenges the efforts of indigenous groups to reclaim and reinvent their threatened spatial identities. What we are witnessing at the moment, in fact, is a multi-layered negotiation or competition for the representation and ultimate control of Beirut's future image. The contesting groups (i.e. funding and state agencies, planners', property owners' and shareholders' advocacy groups, voluntary associations and the concerned public), by virtue of their distinct composition and objectives, vary markedly in their proposed visions and strategies.

The ongoing competition and the public debate it has incited have also served to accentuate the fears of the public, particularly since the struggle is now intimately aligned with the intrusions of global capital, mass culture and consumerism. Hence fears of disappearance, erasure, marginalization and displacement are becoming acute. The overriding reactions have much in common, in fact, with the three neurophysiological responses to fear and anxiety, namely, 'freeze', 'flight' and 'fight'. While the first two normally involve efforts to disengage and distance oneself from the sources of fear, the third involves a measure of direct involvement, negotiation and/or resisting the threats of erasure.[1] All three, in varying proportions, are visible today in Lebanon.

The first, and perhaps the most common, is a relic of the war. To survive all its cruelties, the Lebanese became deadened and numbed. Like other victims of collective suffering, they became desensitized and overwhelmed by muted anguish and pain. During the war, such callousness (often masquerading as resilience) served them well. It allowed them to survive but also to inflict and rationalize cruelties on the 'other'. Once they distanced themselves from the 'other', the brutality of embattled communities was routinized. Violence became morally indifferent.

There is a painful irony in this mode of response. As we have seen, the qualities that enabled embattled groups and communities to survive the atrocities of strife are clearly disabling them now as they consider options for rearranging and sharing common spaces and forging unified national identities.

A second more interesting and complex response is not purely one of 'flight', but an effort to distance oneself from the atrocious residues of protracted strife and the disenchanting barbarism of post-war times. This nostalgic retreat is a search for

---

1. A recent volume edited by Nan Ellin contains meaningful theoretical and empirical evidence and instructive case studies substantiating the interplay between architecture, urban design and fear.

're-enchantment' evident in the revival of heritage or the imagined nirvana of an idyllic past. Three manifestations of such escapist venues are becoming increasingly visible in various dimensions of daily life and popular culture: 1) the reassertion of communal solidarities, 2) nostalgic longings, and 3) the proliferation of kitsch.

As mentioned earlier, it is understandable why traumatized and threatened groups should seek shelter in their communal solidarities and cloistered spaces. Confessional sentiments and their supportive loyalties, even in times of relative peace and stability, have always been effective sources of social support and political mobilization. But these are not, as Lebanon's factious history amply demonstrates, unmixed blessings. While they cushion individuals and groups against anomie and the alienation of public life, they also heighten the density of communal hostility and enmity. Hence, more and more Lebanese are today brandishing their confessionalism, if we may invoke a dual metaphor, as both emblem and armour: emblem, because confessional identity has become the most viable medium for asserting presence and securing vital needs and benefits. Without it groups are literally rootless, nameless and voiceless. One is not heard or recognized unless confessional allegiance is first disclosed. It is only when an individual is placed within a confessional context that ideas and assertions are rendered meaningful or worthwhile. Confessionalism is also being used as armour, because it has become a shield against real or imagined threats. The more vulnerable the emblem, the thicker the armour. Conversely, the thicker the armour, the more vulnerable and paranoid other communities become. It is precisely this dialectic between threatened communities and the urge to seek shelter in cloistered worlds that has plagued Lebanon for so long.

There is a curious irony here. Despite the many differences that divide the Lebanese, they are all in a sense homogenized by fear, grief and bafflement. Fear is the tie that binds them together. But it is also fear that keeps them apart. This 'geography of fear' is not sustained by walls or artificial barriers, as one observes in other comparable instances of ghettoization of minorities and ethnic groups. Rather, it is sustained by the psychology of dread, hostile bonding and ideologies of enmity.

The implications of such heightened forms of spatial and communal solidarities for urban planning are clear. Expressed in more concrete terms, if urbanization normally stands for variety, diversity, mix and openness, then what has been happening in Lebanon, at least in a majority of areas, is ghettoization. In this sense, the Lebanese are inverting what might be assumed to be the most typical course of evolution in social systems. How, where and when can such fairly 'closed' spaces become more 'open'? At least, how can public spaces be made more malleable and accessible to divergent groups, which continue to harbour indifference or latent hostility towards each other? Clearly, any premature or imposed schemes that attempt to open up spaces for groups reluctant to mix and interact with others might be counterproductive.

A nostalgic escape into a re-enchanted past is not the same as pathological retreat into a delusionary past. As Bryan Turner has argued, it could represent a redemptive form of heightened sensitivity, sympathetic awareness of human problems and, hence, it could be 'ethically uplifting'. In this sense, it is less a 'flight' and more of a catharsis for human suffering. (Turner, 1987: 149)

In the vulgarization of traditional forms of cultural expression and the commodification of kitsch and sleazy consumerism, so rampant in post-war Lebanon, there is much that needs to be curtailed and challenged. This nostalgic longing, among a growing segment of disenchanted intellectuals, is at least a form of resistance or refusal to partake in the process of debasement of aesthetic standards or the erosion of *bona fide* and veritable items of cultural heritage. Impotent as such efforts may seem, they express a profound disgust with the trivialization of culture so visible in the emptiness of consumerism and the nihilism of the popular cultural industry. They are also an outcry against the loss of personal autonomy and authenticity. Even the little commonplace things and daily routines – street smells and sounds and other familiar icons and landmarks of place – let alone historic sites and architectural edifices, are allowed to atrophy or be effaced.

Here again a nostalgic impulse is beginning to assume some redemptive and engaging expressions. A variety of grassroots movements, citizen and advocacy groups and voluntary associations have been established recently to address problems related to the preservation and protection of the built environment. Existing special-interest groups have had to redefine their objectives and mandates to legitimize and formalize their new interests. A succession of workshops, seminars and international conferences has been hosted to draw on the experience of other comparable instances of post-war reconstruction. Periodicals and special issues of noted journals, most prominently perhaps the feature page on 'heritage' by the Beirut daily *an-Nahar*, are devoting increasing coverage to matters related to space, environment and architectural legacy.

At the popular cultural level, this resistance to the threat of disappearance is seen in the revival of folk arts, music and lore, flea markets, artisan shops and other such exhibits and galleries. Personal memoirs, autobiographies, nostalgic recollections of early childhood and life in gregarious and convivial quarters and neighbourhoods of old Beirut are now popular narrative genres. So are glossy illustrated anthologies of Beirut's urban history, old postcards, maps and other such collectibles. They are all a thriving business. Even the media and advertising industry are exploiting such imagery and nostalgic longing to market their products.

Finally, another mode of retreat or escape from the ugly memories of the war and the drabness or anxieties of the post-war era is the proliferation of kitsch. While kitsch, as an expression of the appeal of popular arts and entertainment whose objective is to 'astonish, scintillate, arouse and stir the passions', is not normally perceived as a mode of escape, its rampant allure in Lebanon is symptomatic of the need to forget and, hence, it feeds on collective amnesia and the pervasive desire for popular distractions. (Calinescu, 1987: 238) It is clearly not as benign or frivolous as it may appear. At least it should not be dismissed lightly. It has implications for the readiness of the public to become actively and creatively engaged in the processes of reconstructing and safeguarding the edifying beauty of their natural habitat and built environment.

It is not difficult to account for the allure of kitsch in post-war Lebanon: the need to forget and escape the atrocities and futility of a senseless war; the mindless hedonism and narcissism associated with an urge to make up for lost time; the dullness and trivialization of everyday life; the cultural predispositions of the Lebanese for gregariousness, conviviality and fun-loving amusement. All of these have contributed to its appeal. So has the ready access to the vectors of high technology and 'infotainment'. Lebanon is not spared the scintillations of such postmodern and global incursions. Indeed, bourgeois decadence, mediocrity and conspicuous consumption have compounded the public seductions of kitsch.

Kitsch offers effortless and easy access to the distractions of global entertainment and it is compatible with the public mood of lethargy, disengagement and disinterest. Thus it becomes a form of 'false consciousness' and ideological diversion; a novel opiate for aroused and unanchored masses. To the rest, particularly the large segments who have been uprooted from their familiar moorings, kitsch feeds their hunger for nostalgia. Altogether, it is a form of collective deception since it is sustained by the demand for spurious replicas or the reproduction of objects and art forms whose original aesthetic meanings have been compromised. As Calinescu puts it, kitsch becomes 'the aesthetics of deception; for it centres on such questions as imitation, forgery, counterfeit. It is basically a form of lying. Beauty turns out to be easy to fabricate.' (Calinescu, 1987: 228)

In Lebanon, the pathologies of kitsch display more ominous by-products. They not only debase the aesthetic quality of high culture. Folk arts and vernacular architecture are also vulgarized. National symbols, historic and other cherished monuments become expendable trophies or vacuous media images. This frenzy for the prostitution of cherished cultural artefacts and the consumption of pseudo-art cannot be attributed merely to the impulse for status seeking and conspicuous consumption, potent as these predispositions are in Lebanon today. What constitutes the essence of kitsch, as Adorno among others reminds us, is its promise of 'easy catharsis'. (Adorno, 1973) The object of kitsch, after all, is not to please, charm or refine our tastes and sensibilities. Rather, it promises easy and effortless access to cheap entertainment and scintillating distractions.

Here again the implications for urbanists, architects and other cultural producers are vital. How far can they go in restraining the distractions of kitsch or redirecting them into more redemptive and creative venues? This is not an easy task. Above all, it involves the incorporation or reconciliation of two seemingly opposing options: to tame and restrain the excessive manifestations of kitsch, while acting as sentinels who arouse the disengaged and disinterested by infusing their world with some rejuvenated concern for the aesthetic quality of their built environment.

Providing outlets for the release of such creative energies should not be belittled or trivialized. As Nietzsche was keen on reminding us, an aesthetic solution through artistic creation can well serve as a powerful expression for releasing individuals from the constraints of nihilism and resentment. 'It is in art that we appear to realize fully our abilities and potential to break through the limitations of our own circumstances'. (Stauth and Turner, 1988: 517)

By far the most promising signs in this regard are the strategies to which various communities have been recently resorting in order to resist threats to their local heritage and identity. Here responses to fear and uncertainty – whether generated by internal displacement, global capital or mass culture and consumerism – have reawakened and mobilized local groups to reclaim their contested spaces and eroded cultural identities. The emergent spaces reveal more than just residues or pockets of resistance. There are encouraging signs of so-called 'third spaces' on in-between cultures of hybridity, mixture and tolerance.

This is, after all, what Bennett implied by 'cultures of resistance', i.e. how a 'local spatial system retains many of its traditional institutions and utilizes these to manipulate and control the extreme forces'. (Bennett, 1996: 80) Hence, many of the public spaces, more the work of spontaneity than design, are in fact spaces of bargaining and negotiation for national memory and indigenous re-emergence. More so than in other such instances of 'glocalization', what we are witnessing in Lebanon today are manifestations of local groups becoming increasingly globalized and, conversely, global incursions being increasingly localized. In other words, we see symptoms of 'inward shifts', where loyalties are redirected towards renewed localism and subnational groups and institutions. We also see 'outward shifts', where loyalties and interests are being extended to transnational entities. (DiMuccio and Rosenau, 1996:62)

This is, incidentally, a far cry from the portraits one can extract from recent writings on the spatial and cultural implications of this global/local dialectics. For example, in his polemical but engaging work on the interplay between 'jihad' and 'McWorld', Benjamin Barber pits McWorld, as the universe of manufactured needs, mass consumption and mass infotainment against *jihad,* the Arabic word meaning holy war, as a shorthand for the belligerent politics of religious, tribal and other forms of bigotry. (Barber, 1996) The former is driven by the cash nexus of greedy capitalists and the bland preferences of mass consumers. The latter is propelled by fierce tribal loyalties, rooted in exclusionary and parochial hatreds. McWorld, with all its promises of a world homogenized by global consumerism, is rapidly dissolving local cultural identities. Jihad, by recreating parochial loyalties, is fragmenting the world into tighter and smaller enclosures. Both are a threat to civil liberties, tolerance and genuine coexistence. 'Jihad pursues a bloody politics of identity, McWorld a bloodless economics of profit. Belonging by default to McWorld, everyone is a consumer; seeking a repository for identity, everyone belongs to some tribe. But no one is a citizen.' (Barber, 1996:8)

We see little of such sharp dichotomies and diametrical representations in post-war Lebanon. While many of the emergent spatial enclaves are cognizant and jealous of their indigenous identities, they are not averse to experimenting with more global and ephemeral encounters and cultural products. Likewise, global expectations are being reshaped and rearranged to accommodate local needs and preferences. Expressed in the language of globalization and post-modernity, the so-called 'world without borders' is not a prerequisite for global encounters. At least this is not what has been transpiring in Lebanon. Indeed, as Martin Albrow argues, one of the key effects of globalization on locality is that people 'can reside in one place and have their meaningful social relations almost entirely outside it and across the globe'. This, Albrow goes on to say, 'means that people use the locality as site and resource for social activities in widely different ways according to the extension of their sociosphere'. (Albrow, 1997: 53)

Recent case studies of three distinct sites in Beirut (Ain al-Mryseh, Gemmayzeh, and the 'Elisar' project in Beirut's southern suburb) provide instructive and vivid evidence of the way in which local groups and communities have been able to resist, avert and rearrange the powers of global agendas. Indeed, in all three instances, globalization has contributed to the strengthening and consolidation of local ties and, thereby, has reinforced what Persky and Weiwel call the 'growing localness of the global city'.

Ayn al-Mryseh, arguably one of the oldest neighbourhoods of Beirut, huddles on a picturesque cove on the waterfront of the western flank of the city centre. It adjoins the hotel district devastated during the war. In the pre-war period, Ayn al-Mryseh, like the rest of Ras Beirut, was a mixed neighbourhood with fairly open and liberal lifestyles. Indigenous groups, mostly Sunni, Druze, Shi'a and Greek Orthodox, along with Armenians and Kurds, lived side by side. The location of the American Embassy and the American University of Beirut also drew a rather large number of foreign residents – diplomats, freelance intellectuals, journalists, artists and other itinerant groups. The neighbourhood's politics were progressive; its culture cosmopolitan and pluralistic. By virtue of its proximity to the city centre and seaport, many inhabitants were merchants, retailers and clerks in the burgeoning tourist sector of hotels, nightclubs, bars and pavement cafes. The bulk of its indigenous population worked at the port or were fishermen, serving as the mainstay of the neighbourhood and its defining character.

More than in other neighbourhoods of Beirut, the war profoundly changed its character. Because of heavy internecine fighting, Christians and Sunnis were compelled to leave, along with, of course, most of the foreign residents. These were replaced by displaced Shi'a, mostly from the south and Beirut's suburbs.

The massive reconstruction of Beirut's centre and adjoining hotel and resort district has enhanced the economic prospects of the neighbourhood. Real estate and land values have increased sharply. Traditional property holders and homeowners could not resist the tempting offers of conglomerate capital in collusion with local entrepreneurs. Hence, many of the edifying suburban villas and red-tiled roofs that once graced the shoreline have given way to high-rise office buildings and smart, exclusive resorts. Foreign capital is not only transforming its skyline. It is also undermining the moral character and public image of the community. The social fabric is becoming more fragmented, its culture more raucous, strident and kitschy. Shi'ite squatters, awaiting gentrification and other speculative projects, resist eviction from the premises they unlawfully occupy. Hence, fashionable hotels and global resorts stand next to dilapidated homes and squalid backyards. The most jarring event, perhaps, was the invasion of the Hard Rock Café, less than fifty metres away from two of the neighbourhood's most imposing landmarks: the mosque and Gamal Abdul-Nasser's monument.

Armed with a city zoning law that outlaws the location of entertainment functions too close to religious establishments, the neighbourhood association organized a protest movement to resist such intrusion. Its mobilization, however, failed to relocate the 'offensive' café. Now, the *muezzin*'s righteous calls to prayer are competing with the impertinent din of loud music just one block away.

The fishermen did not fare any better in their opposition to the construction of

Ahlam, a towering, forty-floor high-rise comprising an upscale residential complex with a direct underground passage to the Mediterranean and private landings for yachts and speedboats. Ahlam's site is none other than the traditional cove, a miniature harbour, that the fishermen of Ayn al-Mryseh have used for centuries to tend to their time-honoured trade and only source of livelihood.

The Mosque Association and that of the Revival of Heritage of Ayn al-Mryseh came to the assistance of the fishermen by lobbying the authorities and mobilizing the support of local politicians to thwart the project. The outcome, after nearly three years of embittered negotiation, was naturally in favour of *Ahlam*. As compensation, the fishermen have been offered an alternative site as a fishing harbour (five kilometres further south), which they refuse to recognize or use.

As this local-global tug-of-war has continued, two rather interesting strategies for coping with global intrusions have recently emerged within the neighbourhood. Both seem likely to prefigure the direction Ayn al-Mryseh is bound to take in the future. First, a growing number of young fishermen, enticed by the new and appealing jobs the global-resort sector is generating, no longer seem as virulent in their opposition. Indeed, quite a few, to the chagrin of the older generation, are beginning to break away and accept new jobs. A second group, largely members of the Association for the Revival of Heritage, have opted for a more nostalgic and retreatist response. Recognizing that they can do little to contain or tame the forces of global capital, they have taken shelter in preserving and rediscovering the threatened legacy of their history and culture. This is evident in a couple of makeshift 'museums' and galleries established to collect and display items emblematic of its colourful past. (For further details, see Swalha, 1997)

Gemmayzeh, at least spatially, is Ayn al-Mryseh's counterpart on the eastern flank of Beirut's city centre. It also adjoins the port with its outlying resort attractions, warehouses and traffic terminals. Much like Ayn al-Mryseh, the neighbourhood emerged as the city's population started to spill beyond the confines of its medieval walls during the second half of the nineteenth century. Both also harbour strong communal loyalties and pride in their unique history and collective identity.

But this is where all similarities end. While Ayn al-Mryseh was confessionally mixed and socially heterogeneous, Gemmayzeh was predominantly an enclave of the Greek Orthodox and Maronite communities. It also remained so: fairly prosperous Greek Orthodox propertied families were 'invaded' by successive inflows of more modest Maronite craftsmen, retailers and small-scale merchants. This symbiotic association between the two rather distinct socio-economic strata has been one of the defining elements of the neighbourhood.

Although located on the demarcating lines separating East and West Beirut, Gemmayzeh was spared the devastations other comparable communities witnessed during repeated rounds of civil strife. Nor was it beleaguered by any dislocations or permanent displacements of its indigenous inhabitants. Except for two moderate high-rise apartments, at its remote eastern limits, its skyline has remained largely intact.

As the city centre is being virtually reconstructed from scratch, Gemmayzeh is simply remaking and embellishing its original identity. Through APSAD

(Association for the Protection of Sites and Ancient Dwellings) and other voluntary associations, efforts are being made to preserve the architectural character of the neighbourhood. Plans are being finalized for a joint project with the European Commission to paint and beautify the facades of all buildings originally earmarked for restoration.

The neighbourhood is experiencing more than just a cosmetic facelift. Voluntary associations, youth clubs and local businessmen are collaborating in efforts to revitalize its image and cultural identity as the 'Montmartre' of Beirut. This is in fact how some of the young generation speak of Gemmayzeh. A seasonal festival, *Daraj al-Fann* (Stairway of the Arts), now attracts a devoted following. So do the rehabilitated craft shops, sidewalk cafés and up-market boutiques.

The neighbourhood, finally, does not seem reticent or furtive about pronouncing its Christian character. Festive decorations during Christmas, festoons of crosses and other religious emblems, adorn walls and windows. During the Pope's historic visit (May 1997), posters depicting him were decked with white and yellow ribbons. His only competitor was the equally imposing portrait of the late Bashir Gemayel, the neighbourhood's deceased leader.

Altogether, post-war Gemmayzeh does not feel any threat to its identity or future prospects. In fact, the destruction and long-term reconstruction of the city centre are largely viewed with indifference and disregard, mixed with some derision and sarcasm, and Beirut's centre is often contemptuously dismissed as 'Solidere'. (For further elaboration, see Genberg, 1997)

While Ayn al-Mryseh and Gemmayzeh are neighbourhoods rich in history and uncontested collective memory, the Elisar Project is an attempt to forge an identity for a suburban slum with no history to speak of, other than the besmirched and defiled image of a squalid space. It is, to borrow Benjamin's apt label, Beirut's 'site of dereliction', an eyesore defamed with every slur possible. Indeed, the neutral expression, *al-dahiya al-janubiyya* (literally, 'the southern suburb') has been debased to become a synonym for degradation, squalor, anarchy, squatters, illegality and aberrant behaviour.

Late in the 1960s, as successive waves of displaced Shi'ite refugees were fleeing the chronically embattled villages in southern Lebanon, the *dahiya* quickly acquired the label of Lebanon's 'misery belt': a ghetto seething with feelings of neglect and abandonment and, hence, accessible to political dissent, mobilization and violence. This constructed global image, spawned and reinforced by the international media, belies, of course, much of the reality of the suburb. It is not so monolithic in its composition or misery. Nor is it a hotbed of dissidents and marginalized groups eager to wreak vengeance on a neglectful government and an indifferent public. As an open, coveted space, though, it has always managed to attract a much larger share of the dispossessed than other marginal and impoverished suburbs. During the war, its demographic and sectarian composition was sharply altered as other displaced groups – predominantly from the Beqà and the south – sought it for shelter. Initially, for example, the Shi'ite–Maronite balance was slightly tilted in favour of the latter. Today, approximately 80 per cent of the southern suburb's inhabitants are Shi'ites. (Harb el-Kak, 1998: 173–80)

The political mobilization of the *dahiya* began before the war. First, the relatively moderate Amal Movement, inspired by the late Imam Musa al-Sadr, gained considerable popularity. Early in 1980s it was joined by Hizbullah and other more radical 'Islamic' factions. Hizbullah, by virtue of its aggressive outreach programmes of social, educational and medical welfare, has been able to make great inroads and consolidate its virtual hegemony over the area. It is, however, still rivalled by other, lesser political factions in the production and management of urban services. Today, this plethora of political actors has to reckon with the growing efforts of the government to regain its legitimate presence.

It was largely part of such efforts, and to allay Prime Minister Rafik Hariri's public image as someone obsessively and exclusively interested in the rehabilitation of downtown Beirut, that the Elisar Project was launched in 1992.[1] Conceived as an infrastructure rehabilitation works, it evolved by 1994 into a real-estate company legitimized by the same law that established SOLIDERE. Amal and Hizbullah immediately contested its formation as a private company. The ensuing power struggle resulted in some significant modification, whereby the company was transformed into a public establishment, the state becoming, in effect, the major actor in the reorganization of the project. More important, perhaps, Amal and Hizbullah gained their own representatives on Elisar's board.

Despite the sharp antagonisms between the three major rivals (Hariri, Amal and Hizbullah), the project was uniformly conceived and perceived as a scheme for development and modernization. The vision and underlying ideology of the overall design comply with other such urban 'utopias' intended to introduce a hygienic element of 'cleansing' and relocation through social housing and supportive rehabilitative strategies.

Prospects for Urbanists

Paul Rabinow, in his analysis of the socio-cultural history of France between 1830 and 1930, describes a constellation of thought, action and passion underlying what he terms the 'social technologies of pacification'. These might well be considered appropriate tools for reforming and controlling the inherent antagonisms between space and society and between the forms and norms that characterized France during that eventful century (Rabinow, 1989).

Hard-nosed positivism may have fallen on hard times. One can, however, still glean several persuasive examples of such successful consolidation from Rabinow's analysis. The recent experience of the Lebanese themselves has also been reassuring in this regard. It is at least proof that, as intricate as the problems are, pacifying Lebanon's pathos is not insurmountable. Much can and has already been done to prepare for this blissful eventuality.

In my view, urban designers, architects, intellectuals, humanists of all types,

---

1. Incidentally, Elisar derives its name from an ancient legend of a Phoenician queen who escaped Tyre to establish the city of Carthage. Prime Minister Hariri, a Sunni form Saida, suggested the name to commemorate this prehistoric myth. Nabih Berei, leaders of Hizbullah, and other Shi'ite notables were of course delighted to adopt the name, which allowed them to reassert Shi'ite control over the southern suburb.

along with other outraged but muted groups, are particularly qualified to play this role. Until recently, they had been shunted aside and trivialized. They now have to shed their timidity and reclaim the redemptive promises of their professions. By mobilizing aesthetic sensibilities, other artistic energies and popular cultural expressions in everyday life, they can do much to arouse the public to redeem its maligned heritage. More important, they can prod the Lebanese to turn outwards and transcend their parochial identities to connect with others.

There are three further reasons why today such groups are ideally suited to articulate this new language and vision on behalf of their besieged compatriots. First, disproportionate numbers of their members have been, for much of the duration of the war, in diaspora. Lebanon's trials with exile and dispersal have been quite acute. They were, however, also enabling. Mavericks, as histories of itinerant populations tell us, rarely stay at home. Just as the traditional Lebanese *mkari* (peddler) always wandered beyond the narrow confines of his village and came back with tales, goods and titbits from the world beyond, so too today we have the makings of a growing generation of global multiculturalists. Both established and young cohorts of gifted professionals and entrepreneurs have been expanding their skills and experiences abroad. Many are rightfully disillusioned, perhaps bitter, but nonetheless have not been frozen into inaction or insensibility by the harrowing events. They experienced the war only vicariously, from a distance. Hence, they have not become as numbed or cynical as others. Nor do they harbour deep-seated hostility towards other groups. Secondly, though exiled, they have not severed their ties with nor lost their nostalgia for their native culture. They bring in comparative visions, not the alien constructs of 'foreign experts' imposed on unfamiliar and unreceptive milieux. Finally, by virtue of such multicultural and global sympathies, they are less likely to perceive their projects as efforts for privileging or empowering one group or community over another. Hence, they are predisposed to transcend their parochialism and offer an antidote to fear and its demarcating lines and enclosures.

The first and most vital task confronting architects and planners is to arouse among the Lebanese a few cardinal but overlooked realities about the interplay between space and well-being. Self-evident as it may be, they must be made to realize that the quality of the environment has an impact on their lives, in the sense of who they are and their attitudes toward others. Indeed, repeated research findings in fields such as photobiology, colour therapy and other fairly novel areas of exploration all substantiate the extent to which physical and emotional well-being, even creativity, are intimately associated with the aesthetic and enriching attributes of the environment (Hiss, 1990: 23). Put simply, the places where we spend our time affect the people we are and can become. Hence, as the places around us change – whether fortuitously or by design, carelessly or in good faith – we too are bound to change. Thus, despoiling our natural habitat not only damages our cities and living spaces, it can also damage the quality of our lives.

Secondly, this image of the Lebanese as spatially anchored people, compulsively defending the compact enclosures of family and neighbourhood, needs to be altered. The same goes for the phobic and nostalgic drive for heritage and the longing to reclaim seemingly unique communal legacies, something that today borders on becoming a national pastime. The Lebanese once longed for the outdoors, at least until the war terrorized their public spaces. Here again, urban design can do much to restore the conviviality of such open spaces.

This impulse to venture beyond familiar enclaves is always driven by mixed emotions. There is the exuberance of strange places, the pleasure and excitement of being drawn out of one's secure routines to encounter the novel and surprising. This induces an element of anxiety and fearfulness. But we also take pleasure in being open to and interested in people we experience as 'different'. Both these impulses, the need for intimacy and the need for distance; the urge to break away and the equally trenchant urge to reconnect with one's original moorings are essential for human sustenance. They also account for much of the vitality of open and permeable spaces. To borrow a trite but apt metaphor, we need at different interludes in our lives, both 'roots' and 'wings'. Roots nourish our need for security, solidarity, commitment and heritage. Wings express our longing for movement, breaking away and taking occasional flights of fancy. We have a duty to heed and incorporate both impulses in strategies for spatial rearrangement.

The urbanist, in other words, has to design weak borders rather than strong walls. This means spaces constructed malleably enough to permit constant alterations and shifts. There is still much to commend in Robert Frost's adage that 'good fences make good neighbours'. Fences are not, after all, impregnable barriers. They merely delineate borders, often through hedges, shrubs, and other demarcating but scaleable objects. Indeed, fences are borders and not boundaries. Borders are usually more porous and malleable; hence they are less likely to serve as partitions between one area and another. Boundaries, on the other hand, conjure up images of confinement and exclusion.

Finally, urbanists must not shy away from another redemptive role not conventionally linked to their constructive or reconstructive ventures. Whatever strategies they propose, they must bear in mind that the mere involvement of the Lebanese in such common and shared interests (i.e. recovering their country's maligned heritage) could bring them closer together and help in transcending their parochial identities. By doing so, they are also creating opportunities for disengaged groups to reclaim their right to be engaged in redefining their collective memory and stewardship over the spaces they inhabit and bequeath to future generations.

PART V

Reflexive Essays

CHAPTER 12

From Aley to Ras-Beirut: A Memoir

> ... In the good city a person crosses from one distinct
> neighbourhood to another without knowing precisely
> where one ended and the other began.
>
> Iris Young, *Justice and the Politics*
> *of Difference* (1990)

I cannot refrain from prefacing this essay with a personal confession and a few
pertinent autobiographical remarks. Let me dispense with the confession first: I
have always had, as Robert Frost would put it, a 'lover's quarrel' with urban
planners and architects! As I think back, with some detachment, I must have all
along harboured an unfulfilled longing to be an urban planner or architect.

While still in high school I was inspired by Ayn Rand's *The Fountainhead*,
which I devotedly read and reread one summer. The film version with Gary Cooper
playing Howard Roark, the unyielding, idealistic architect, made the fancy still
more attractive. Early in college, I recall struggling through the tomes of Max
Weber, Lewis Mumford, Jane Jacobs, Kevin Lynch, Louis Wirth and other classics
on the city and urban history. The first term paper I wrote, one that must have
prefigured much of my proclivity for empirical research in later years, was an
ecological study of my home town, Aley.

Incidentally, my academic interest in Aley and Ras Beirut was far from
fortuitous. Since I was virtually confined to one or other of these two settings for
much of my adolescent and college years, it was natural that they should also
become the formative sites of my early research experience. In both places I acted
as a prudent and unobtrusive participant observer in pursuit of a mundane and
reflective sociology of everyday life. Both places were microcosms of the interplay

between local and broader structural forces underlying the ruptures that were later to afflict Lebanon.

Aley, this once-quaint, salubrious resort town in the resplendent hills overlooking Beirut, epitomized many of the same forces that had formed and deformed the impetuous, haphazard and rapacious growth of other villages and towns. In less than a decade, beginning in the late 1950s, the town's spatial and social structures were defaced by the irresistible incursion of petro-dollars, land speculation, gaudy commercialism and the massive inflow of itinerant resort visitors. The old souks, village squares and courtyards, suburban red-tiled villas and terraced orchards that had once graced its lush habitat gave way to more intensive forms of land use. By the early 1970s few of the old edifying structures remained intact. Even its main streets and more rural side roads, lined with eucalyptus, acacia and sycamore (remnants of Ottoman and French landscaping), succumbed.

Not everything, however, was swept away by these seemingly irresistible and merciless forces. Its indigenous population, roughly two-third Druze and one-third Christian, co-existed peacefully. So did its multi-ethnic, multi-confessional and cross-cultural resort-goers (close to 200,000, ten times the number of permanent residents) who thronged its amusement parks, exclusive casinos, nightclubs and other attractions during the cool summer months.

Within a two-kilometre radius of our house, all four Christian churches (Maronite, Greek Orthodox, Catholic and Protestant) adjoined the mosque, synagogue, Druze retreats and meeting places. Groups from all parts of the town mixed freely without fear or paranoia. They participated collectively in each others' ceremonies, their occasions of mourning, joy or achievement. The renowned National College drew students from other parts of Lebanon and the Arab world. A 'cultural circle' mobilized a cross-section of spirited, civic-minded young people in support of artistic and intellectual activities that transcended their sectarian allegiances.

As the president's summer residence, the town attracted a flow of regional and world dignitaries. Its stylish hotels and locandas, some in kitsch imitation of mansions on the French and Italian Rivieras, hosted international fairs and exhibitions. I recall, as an adolescent in the 1950s (also the heyday of the town's fame as a resort centre for the rich and famous), the elan that celebrities and world-class entertainers generated. Maurice Chevalier, Edith Piaf and other European stars appealed to the Francophiles, just as Umm-Kulthum, Abdul Wahab, Farid Atrash and other Egyptian crooners and belly dancers dazzled and entranced local and Arab devotees.

I was privileged to serve, early in the 1970s, on the town's Municipal Council and tried, with like-minded colleagues, to resist the reckless deformation Aley was undergoing. We imposed more restrictions on exploitation and stricter zoning ordinances, but our efforts came too little and too late to curb the insatiable impulse to 'modernize' the town.

Modernity then, to both Aley's native residents and visitors, was sought in wide boulevards, high-rise apartments and shopping arcades decked with glittering neon lights. Traffic congestion, like the reckless construction the town was attracting, was seen as an emblem of vitality and growth. My last contribution as a Council member was a project to restore the town's historic water fountains (relics of its feudal and Ottoman past) and to landscape its bare pavements and public squares. I helped to secure the necessary funds and solicit the gratuitous services of landscapers and architects. In autumn 1972 I took a sabbatical to Harvard and was dismayed to learn when I returned two years later that nothing had been done.

Divisions within the town were largely factional and personal; rival clans or kinship groups vied for a greater share of power and privilege. Such rivalry, however, rarely assumed direct confessional manifestations. Indeed, Aley was spared the successive waves of communal strife that devastated neighbouring regions in the nineteenth century. The town was not, however, exempt from the ravages of the past two decades of civil strife. Willingly or otherwise, it was embroiled in the so-called 'mountain war' in the wake of the Israeli invasion of 1982. The ensuing deadly fighting pulverized its Christian quarters and displaced its inhabitants. Aley now, perhaps more so than adjoining towns and villages, is a deserted and forsaken place. Calls for the rehabilitation of its uprooted residents remain unheeded to date. While Christians are still reluctant to return to their homes, the Druze are apprehensive about the prospects of having other, possibly less desirable elements replace their traditional partners. This same impasse continues to delay the reintegration of other displaced communities and threatens to redraw Lebanon's political geography.

Urban sociology was one of my major areas of concentration in my graduate studies at Princeton in 1958. Upon my return to the American University of Beirut (AUB), much of my teaching, research and involvement in public projects converged on problems of urbanization and efforts to curtail the aesthetic defoliation of the habitat and the dehumanization of living space. In 1964 I was part of a Presidential Commission to explore the urban renewal of Beirut's Central Business District. My study of legalized prostitution, the *maisons de tolérance* of the city's notorious red-light district, was largely an offshoot of that project. The brothels were perceived as an eyesore and government authorities were keen to relocate them to other less visible locations in the suburbs. The concern was not to rescue the prostitutes from the evils of confinement and abuse, but to cleanse and thereby release prime urban space for more intensive forms of capital exploitation. The study, widely circulated at the time, dismissed some popular misconceptions about the world's oldest profession and offered a few insights about the role of commercial sex in a changing urban environment, but it had no impact on restructuring the damaged lives of its trapped victims or in rehabilitating the blighted urban centre within which they were plying their trade. Recommendations of the survey, like those of the broader project of which it was part, were not implemented.

One of the proposals of the survey, given the relaxation of sexual and moral standards in other sectors of the society, was to refrain from taking any measures that could impede the inevitable attrition of legal prostitution or its confinement to licensed brothels. Instead, it was recommended to permit, with some measure of public health control, the process of permeation of prostitution into society. Unfortunately these and other proposals were deemed too liberal by government authorities at the time. Of course the war has demolished the area and no plans are being considered for relocating licensed brothels to the suburbs.

In 1972, in collaboration with Per Kongstad, a Danish human geographer, I made a study of Hamra of Ras Beirut. Ras Beirut (literally the 'head' or 'tip' of Beirut) was not an ordinary urban district. A set of unusual historical circumstances and fortuitous urban developments had swiftly transformed it into one of the most dominant urban centres in the Arab world.

With the beginning of civil unrest in 1975, it had become journalistically expedient and fashionable to refer to 'East' and 'West' Beirut and the so-called 'green line' (the old Damascus Road extending southwards from the centre of the old city) demarcating the two distinct parts of the city. Ras Beirut, spatially and otherwise, lies within the greater agglomeration of West Beirut. Yet Ras Beirut has always been a community of its own with distinct spatial and socio-cultural features that distinguish it from surrounding areas.

In the short span of about two decades – roughly between 1950 and 1970 – this once secluded and sparsely settled garden-farming area evolved into a truly unique cultural experiment. It became, arguably, the closest the Arab world ever come to a liberal and open community, where pluralistic groups could co-exist in relative harmony and peace.

In the early 1950s, as young adolescents, we felt that the entire neighbourhood, lined with cactus hedges and red sand dunes, was still entirely ours. Its unpaved streets and alleyways, walled garden plots and well-tended patios were our playgrounds. We flew kites, played soccer, improvised track and field events. We had few competitors. Cars were still very rare sights at the time. Even human traffic was sparse, save for colourful street vendors and occasional shepherds herding their stray cattle by the shrubby pavements. Rarely did we stop our games to make room for the intrusion of strangers.

In no time this enchanting world swiftly slipped away. Empty lots and backyards were the first to be filled in. When they were eaten up, existing structures, including the neighbourhood's most beautiful landmarks – its flat-roofed farmhouses, suburban tiled villas and walk-ups with elaborate facades, decorative railed stairways and balconies – were converted or demolished. Sharp rises in land values and speculation in real estate ushered in corporate financing. Plots were split into yet smaller parcels. Ras Beirut lost its 'horizontal' skyline and acquired the look of an exploding 'vertical' metropolis with its inevitable massive towering structures in reinforced concrete with glittering but faceless glass facades and prefabricated aluminium frames. Ras Beirut and its suburban open expanses, sooner than other districts in the city, began to display some of the universal symptoms of large-scale urbanization, which can proceed only by eating up breathing space.

The spatial metamorphosis of Ras Beirut and the demise of its well-knit neighbourhoods, with all their felicitous features, was not wholly deplorable. The inevitable loss of inwardness, intimacy and tranquillity was to some extent compensated by the vibrancy of the cosmopolitan and plural lifestyles it nurtured.

By virtue of its mixed ethnic and religious composition and permissive political atmosphere, Ras Beirut became remarkably innovative and venturesome, serving as a safe refuge for the dispossessed and marginal groups that were periodically out of favour with the political regimes in the adjacent Arab states. More important, perhaps, it evolved as an intellectual sanctuary, a pace-setter for new trends, from serious ideological doctrines and political platforms to the more frivolous fads and fashions. Also, because of the presence of AUB, it displayed some of the typical features of a university town. It produced and attracted a relatively young, literate and highly professional and mobile population, unmistakably middle class in its occupations and lifestyles. It fostered, indeed licensed, experimentation in nearly all domains of public and private life.

In a more fundamental sense, by acting in turns as a critical gadfly and a safety valve, it was also instrumental in shaping some of the most significant ideological movements in the entire region. Many of the crucial political and socio-cultural changes in the Arab world were, to a large extent, initiated and nurtured in its pavement cafés, bistros, open forums and clubs. It was by virtue of its openness that Ras Beirut evolved into such a 'melting pot' of diverse religious, ethnic and ideological groups and was able to engender sentiments of trust, mutual respect and deference to pluralistic lifestyles.

As in my hometown, Aley, a remarkable spirit of tolerance pervaded all social contacts in Ras Beirut until the advent of mass modernization. Here as well intimacy, caring for others and respect for difference were characteristic features of community life. Such sentiments were visible in the pluralistic composition of the community just as much as in the bewildering variety of urban settlements, mixed land-use patterns and curious blend of architectural styles and house types, ranging from squat farmhouses and red-tiled suburban villas to walk-up apartments and skyscrapers.

More important, no one tried to oppress, tyrannize or malign anyone else. Just as the Sunni Muslim and Greek Orthodox, the Druze and Protestant lived together, so did groups drawn from discrepant socio-economic backgrounds or those who professed divergent ideologies or led different lifestyles. Wadad Qurtas (1983) recalls that when she was growing up in Ras Beirut in the 1930s, the family's Sunni Muslim landlord used to instruct the drummer who roused the believers before dawn during the month of Ramadan to muffle his drum lest he disturb his Christian neighbours. A touching gesture! A Muslim believer could observe his religious duties without offending his Protestant neighbour.

There was room for everyone: devout and heathen, pious Puritans and graceless hedonists, left-wing radicals and ardent conservatives, footloose and self-centred Bohemians, steadfast chauvinists and conventional patriots. They all had a stake in preserving its amorphous and permeable character. Diversity animated and enriched life in the community. It was a source of vitality, not a cause for paranoia and hostility.

During the war, particularly at times when hostility was being fuelled by religious bigotry, one saw very little of that blissful world depicted by Wadad Qurtas. Indeed, the exact opposite was taking its place. As Muslim calls for prayer were getting louder and religious festivities more vociferous, Christians became furtive about decorating their Christmas trees. The assault has been extended to include other symbols and manifestations of liberalism and permissive lifestyles.

Foreign subjects and institutions – university presidents, diplomats, journalists, professors, priests – have been indiscriminately eliminated, kidnapped or blown up. Stereo-clubs, bars, supermarkets and liquor stores have likewise become symbols of blasphemous and satanic decadence.

The same minds, academic institutions, cultural centres, spiritually enriching urban landscape that once animated the world around the city became targets of contemptuous hostility or were allowed to waste and atrophy.

Like Aley, and, arguably, because of its plural and open character, Ras Beirut was also able – at least initially – to stave off the havoc of civil strife. But not for long. It, too, became the surrogate victim of cruelties unleashed elsewhere. Alas, this legacy, with all its enriching heritage, is today in the throes of transformations that may deface its character, obstruct its liberalizing role and disfigure its image as a paragon of peaceful co-existence. It is in this sense that Ras Beirut, more so than Lebanon, stands today at a historic watershed. The harbingers of these disquieting transformations have become especially prominent in the past few years.

For example, when I was growing up in pre-war years of the 1950s and 1960s communal tolerance and genuine appreciation of cultural differences were the order of the day. Religious holidays were muted or moderately observed in the exclusive domain of private homes. Different communities, in fact, participated voluntarily in these joint celebrations. Today *iftars*[1] during the holy month of Ramadan has become much too assertive and pronounced; celebrated more as a statement or public demonstration than a quiet and reflective family reunion.

If these and other symptoms of communal assertiveness and narcissism are not restrained, there is a danger that they will become dominant and even irreversible. The entire plural and cosmopolitan character of the community could well be in jeopardy.

Such an eclipse of the old society would be, to say the least, grievous and lamentable. It is bound to have ominous consequences for both Lebanon and the rest of the Arab world. Lebanon will lose its one and only viable example of successful pluralism. The Arab world will also have to live without its precious safety valve.

Our study of Hamra was supposed to have other sequels: complementary explorations of the other two distinct urban communities within Beirut, namely Basta and Achrafieh, the former being predominantly Sunni Muslim and the latter a Christian neighbourhood. The outbreak of civil strife and the dizzying speed with which it engulfed other regions compelled us to suspend our efforts. Conducting fieldwork in an urban war zone that teemed with random and savage hostility became a perilous venture. It was also useless, given the disarray and despair that were pervading the entire social fabric.

Bearing witness to Lebanon's agony and the relentless anguish of its distraught and innocent citizens only compounded one's sense of impotence. Our scholarly research and writing, even the most cogent, seemed like an exercise in futility. We only added insight to injury, so to speak. As our understanding of the harrowing

---

1. Daily banquets held at dusk to break the fast during the holy month of Ramadan.

events and unfolding darker forces became more lucid and profound, the pathology devouring our society became graver and more intractable. Like other entrapped compatriots, I found myself drawn into efforts at least to decry, if we could not ward off, the forces exacerbating my country's descent into anomie. Ignoring some of the principles of my own academic discipline, particularly those that constrain us to maintain value neutrality, I wrote a series of impassioned essays disparaging symptoms of demoralization in public life (see, for example, Khalaf, 1987: 238–92; Khalaf, 1989).

During this same disheartening period I was privileged to serve (some of these efforts date back to at least a decade prior to the outbreak of civil unrest) on a score of national, municipal and voluntary councils and organizations concerned with problems of urban planning and the preservation of architectural sites and monuments. Here as well, I became aware of a nagging tension between the country's natural endowments and captivating landscape and its squalid urban milieu and treacherous political culture. This same tension appeared in the disharmony between official codes, the credo that articulated visions and defined tasks, and the powerlessness of those entrusted to enact them; between playful, audacious planning and parasitic, inept bureaucracy.

One cannot but lament all the wasted efforts spent on commissions, exuberant schemes, lavish projects and master plans, which were aborted or remained unrealized blueprints. Worse still is to witness how the implemented schemes were violated by political clientelism, self-serving officialdom or unreceptive local traditions. Episodes of abuse and malpractice, which normally would provoke alarm and outrage elsewhere, became institutionalized as ordinary occurrences; at best they were dismissed as part of the mercantile ethos of shrewd and cunning business dealing.

For example, instances of collusion between private entrepreneurs and the political establishment in land speculation were legion. Favoured businessmen, with political connections, often in scandalous cases, were always in a position to benefit from unfettered land-speculation ventures. They were frequently privy to inside information on the areas about to be subjected to zoning and would exploit their knowledge to make strategic purchases of such land accordingly. Such speculation was highly profitable, since it almost always generated a sharp increase in land values. Within such a context, virtually everyone within the government bureaucracy – from the ordinary municipal clerk who overlooked a minor transgression to a high government official who intervened on behalf of a client or a patron to reroute a road network or rezone a certain area – was placed in a strategic position to affect the redistribution of rewards and privileges. Deals of this sort generated instant and immense profits.

As we have seen (Chapter 3), one of many amendments to the building code of 1932 was passed by Parliament in 1954, allowing a maximum of nine floors per building. But, like almost all other zoning regulations, this was virtually ignored by landowners. Additional floors were built on top of converted houses whose ground floors were normally used as retail and shopping outlets, and courtyards were filled in by new constructions. Since high-rise apartments had frontages directly on the street, pavements were eaten up and the possibilities of street widening became almost nil. Beirut as a result has become one of the few treeless modern cities. Its stifled pedestrians are denied access to shaded and secure pavements, let alone the lush beauty of foliage.

These and other flagrant instances of mismanagement of Lebanon's already imperilled spatial and ecological resources are galling precisely because of their dire implications for the country's ability to reclaim or reconstitute its legacy. We are, after all, dealing with one of the smallest sovereign nations in the world, already burdened by high densities, massive population shifts and overurbanization. Yet, this threatened heritage has never become a public issue; it has never invited, let alone mobilized, collective concerns or national debate. The average citizen remains, to this day, unaware that his informed attention or consciousness could make a difference.

Let me express this in more personal terms. Perhaps because I grew up in places like Aley and Ras Beirut I became fascinated but also troubled by this underlying dualism between the integrated and vibrant communities and the forces of disorder, corruption and greed that were deforming them. I also started to realize that these spatial and social deformations were a reflection of some basic values rooted in society. Short of a fundamental restructuring of such values, which could help transform Lebanon into a more civil society, little can be done to protect or salvage its imperilled natural habitat and dehumanized living space from further abuse.

Therein lies the origin of my 'lover's quarrel' with architects. Perhaps I was expecting that their idealistic and aesthetic professional sensibilities would act as a counterbalance to those destructive forces. They could, I thought, inject some reasoned calculation, control and forecasting into our flawed and lethargic planning process. Instead, many of the gifted young architects and builders of the day became wilful participants in or accessories to the very processes despoiling our living space.

But then, in all fairness, the disruptive transformations were much too strong to be repelled or chastened by the activities or principles of a few idealistic architects. Even a generation of unyielding Howard Roarks would have failed to resist the regional and international forces or the corporate financiers that were besieging Beirut. But I still harboured the hope that architects could become the cautionary voices, the gatekeepers, so to speak, warning of any further onslaughts and arousing the public in defence of their rightful interests.

A few courageous prominent architects and urbanists have indeed been uncharacteristically vigilant and strident recently in expressing dissent against what they perceive as flawed and inappropriate schemes for redevelopment. They are predisposed to favour open, fluid, flexible master plans and counsel against the premature adoption of colossal and rigid ventures in which the state abdicates its role of monitoring and regulating sensitive projects, such as the massive reconstruction of Beirut's Central Business District by SOLIDERE. Objectors are particularly alarmed by the impact such projects could have in terms of defacing the city's collective memory and distinctive heritage. They call instead for the preservation and remaking of the capital, with the energetic participation of a hitherto docile and silent public.

While the protestors are sympathetic to the need for massive post-war development, particularly the rehabilitation and modernization of the country's devastated infrastructure, they are keen not to undermine attributes of private property and individual initiative, those inveterate hallmarks of liberal economic enterprise in Lebanon. They are also wary about any measures to manipulate the public into accepting giant transnational corporate real-estate ventures that are fated to undermine their legitimate interests and welfare.

A group of concerned architects, archaeologists, urbanists and social scientists have recently issued a trenchant critique castigating the overall vision of the CBD Master Plan and its likely contravention of some of the salient juristic, constitutional, socio-economic and architectural dimensions. They also propose alternative options and models (see Nabil Beyhum et al., 1992).

In this and other contexts, prominent architects and town planners (e.g. Assem Salam, Pierre El-Khoury, Jad Tabet, Hashim Sarkis, Rodolphe el-Khoury) have expressed their criticisms of various aspects of SOLIDERE's schemes. For example, Ghassan Tueni, as early as 1992, was already making ardent pleas to preserve the collective memory of Beirut by sanctioning its plural history and cultural diversity. He suggests that we incorporate a few of its imposing archaeological emblems, such as the columns of the Roman School of Law, Fakhriddine Gate or even some of the poignant devastations of the war, into the envisioned future space. (Tueni, 1992)

In response to these objections, SOLIDERE has already introduced a score of restorative modifications and additions to the original plans. To its credit, it has also incorporated a few bold and enlightened schemes and projects, which preserve and enrich some of the distinctive architectural and urban features of the city's historic core. The decisions to pedestrianize almost 75 per cent of the preservation zone and to introduce a 'heritage trail' to display and promote Beirut's rich and diverse archaeological legacy are, clearly, judicious moves in that direction. So is the 'Garden of Forgiveness', the project to turn the excavated ruins of the Roman Cardo Maximus and adjacent areas into a public park.

Other commendable projects are the plans to downsize the original massive transport schemes by reconverting the proposed major highway system into tree-lined roadways. Similar modifications were made to the loop around the waterfront. It is more accessible now and hence more welcoming to pedestrians and leisure seekers. These measures will do much to reshape the city's skyline and energize desolate and open spaces.

CHAPTER 13

The Americanization of George

America is coming between me and my twelve-year-old son. Actually, it started earlier when George was hardly ten. Since then, I have helplessly watched this incursion, often with dismay and growing alarm.

Over two years ago we escaped the horrors of Lebanon, chose quaint and quiet Princeton over the vibrancy of Harvard because we thought, and correctly so, that the relatively more tranquil milieu of the Garden State would be more supportive and calming for children traumatized by the havoc and anguish of a decade of protracted violence and random terror! George, I used to say to myself, was as old as the civil war. He deserved better.

But little did I know that he was to face, at an impressionable and vulnerable age, the more subtle 'terror' of American peer pressure, the tantalizing media and the unsettling dissonance of conflicting norms and expectations.

The family system in Lebanon is, on the whole, intimate, warm and affectionate. This claim may seem incredible for a country that has lately been reduced to an ugly and accursed metaphor. Yet it is largely true. A child grows up in a nurturing atmosphere of extended kinship networks sustained by filial piety and mutual obligations. Arguably, such primordial ties and loyalties are often overwhelming. An inventive and resourceful child, however, can always manage some elbow room to preserve some personal freedom and autonomy. Indeed, children are known to manipulate filial piety to secure privileged treatment and personal benefits not available to them elsewhere. The more canny of them even go further and substitute ritual for righteousness and get away with it.

The Lebanese, much like people in adjacent Mediterranean cultures, are very tactile. Touching, kissing, hugging and outward displays of emotion – regardless of gender – are generously and spontaneously expressed. At least, children of George's age indulge in these expressions with little self-consciousness or feelings of shame and guilt. Rather, they are natural and spontaneous aspects of daily human contact and playfulness. Ritualized as they often are, they remain nonetheless tokens of goodwill and camaraderie and serve to allay many of the fears and anxieties experienced by pre-adolescents.

I feel resentful that George should be disarmed of such harmless but reassuring expressions. So, it seems, does he. Otherwise, he wouldn't be so furtive and listless when either avoiding or indulging in them.

I first noticed this transformation (or deformation) when I returned from a brief trip a few months after we had settled in Princeton. This shows, among other things, how swiftly boys begin to take on cues from their peer sub-culture. I arrived from the airport one evening after an absence of five or six days. Normally, when I returned home even after an ordinary day's work, George would interrupt his play and rush across the driveway to greet me, often literally, hurling himself into my open arms. If I happened to be carrying books or a briefcase, he would whisk them away, accompany me to the doorway and regale me with an account of the highlights of his day at school. He was also keen to inquire about mine, but more eager to see if I could spare time for horseplay or for watching his favourite TV programme in the evening. Altogether these acts were gestures of affection and mutual respect, which rendered the homecoming a tender encounter fondly anticipated by both.

On that day, however, just as he was yield to his normal impulse to rush across the driveway, he suddenly 'froze' in mid-passage, looked in the direction of his watchful playmates and, with obvious hesitation and embarrassment, walked leisurely over to greet me with a cold handshake and a casual 'Hi, Dad'. Now even this gesture has now been abandoned. On a lucky day, the most I can expect is a disengaged and distant nod.

Such 'frozen' moments have recurred and spilled over to other daily encounters with members of the family and in particular acquaintances from Lebanon. I could see him fretting as relatives and friends he had not seen for two years tried in vain to solicit a hug or a kiss on the forehead. The brush-off has been transformed into a boast, a statement to inform his fellow Lebanese that he is now an 'American boy', not to be touched or fondled!

His 'Americanization' was most forcefully conveyed to me by a recent incident on the tennis court. George is a versatile, gifted athlete and a superb tennis player for his age. It is a pleasure to witness his natural talents unfold by leaps and bounds. We were struggling in a doubles game against two other more seasoned partners who normally beat us. After a long and heated game we won the set, partly because of two exquisite passing shots by George. He was ecstatic. As he rushed across to share his exuberance with me Lebanese-style, he 'froze' once again and treated me to a tame version of the American 'high five'.

These are benign symptoms of George's 'Americanization'. They seem, in fact, trivial, compared with the more reckless barrage of messages and scripts he is bombarded with: not only the hints and precepts of his persuasive peers and the unrelenting media, but also by the more authoritative voices of school officials armed with the therapeutic rhetoric of counsellors and social workers. When George was still in 5th grade, a social worker was brought to his class – part of a concerted state-wide effort at the time – to caution and enlighten students about child sex abuse. According to George, whose evidence was later corroborated, the social worker had instructed them that if any member of their family touched them anywhere on their body, making them feel awkward as a result, they should promptly report the incident to their school!

As George progressed to the 6th and 7th grade, such instruction extended to include sessions on more depressing problems: illegitimate birth, teenage pregnancy, child abuse, divorce, alcoholism, drugs, AIDS and other symptoms of the frayed fabric of the American family.

Given the public outcry over such problems, the concern of school officials is certainly timely and legitimate. I cannot help but feel, however, that George has been needlessly damaged and disturbed by this premature exposure to threats too far removed from his interests and passions of the moment.

Last week as he was preparing a list of the friends he wished to invite to his twelfth birthday, I noticed that he did not include any girls. When I inquired why, he answered without hesitation, 'It is too early. Perhaps when I become a teenager.'

There is a painful irony here. At the same time as George thinks he is uninterested in and unprepared for the pleasures of love and sex, he is being instructed and warned about their dangers. More worrying, perhaps, is the fact that he is being denied the warmth and shelter of his family to soften the anguish of such awakenings. The loss of innocence, if this is what he is going through, has been, as a result, an abrupt, jarring and dislocating experience. Alas, as crude and jarring as America is at times.

Richard Rodriguez, the Mexican-American scholar, in a gripping autobiographical essay he wrote in 1974, explained how, in order for him to become an 'American scholarship boy', he was compelled to sever his psychological ties with his family. He described how the solitude, silence and rationality of the Oxford library clashed with the intimacy, gregariousness and rambunctiousness of his family culture. Losing touch with his past and becoming alien to his family were, to Rodriguez, the inevitable and legitimate price of becoming an 'American scholarship boy'. Incidentally, Rodriguez has subsequently employed the same reasoning to argue against some of the excesses and abuses of bilingualism.

Is George doomed, I wonder, to suffer the same fate? He has had to be uprooted from his true home and suffer the anguish of exile at a very tender age. Is this to be compounded now by a more baffling and painful form of homelessness? On balance, America has thus far been good to him. In fact, any respite from Lebanon these days must be, in and of itself, a liberating and reassuring experience. His peer-mediated encounters have been sources of exuberance and enrichment and have enhanced his sense of self-worth and autonomy. He is much more independent and self-sufficient, and he has had valuable experiences that are clearly not available to him in Lebanon.

Can he not continue to enjoy this exuberance and freedom without breaking away from the reassuring and familiar intimacies of his family? He certainly needs both if he is to be the wholesome and loveable kid he has been so far. Am I asking too much? Is this not, after all, one of the redeeming virtues or promises of American pluralism?

CHAPTER 14

On Madonna and Mount Sannin

A Boy's Rediscovery of His Lebanese Identity

When we left Lebanon in the summer of 1984 our youngest son, Ramzi, was barely two years old. Even then, one was aware of his fondness, almost an inborn talent, for music and dance. Rhythmic movement, miming, even a bit of burlesque were unmistakably his favourite form of self-expression. He indulged his passions with the abandon and exuberance of a gifted child, oblivious to the havoc of deadly strife raging outside his own enchanted world. Like whistling in the dark, dance was perhaps his own beguiling respite from the scares and scars of war.

The enchantment was not, though, a mere flight of fancy. Over the past seven years, he has pursued his flair for dance and other artistic pursuits with added fervour. Thanks to the supportive milieu of Princeton, the allures of Broadway, HBO, MTV, the Disney Channel and Princeton Ballet, he has had ample opportunity to cultivate his talents. He is, as a result, an avid reader and listener. For a child of nine, he has developed a rather critical and discriminating taste for the performing arts. He choreographs his own dance routines, writes school sketches and lyrics and acts out their parts. He scans daily, much like an ardent connoisseur, the news and reviews of new releases and events.

He longs to entertain and be entertained and seems, while doing so, buoyed by a blissful mood of intense rapture. No wonder he greets his day, often at the break of dawn, with spirited bouts of dancing! Whatever oracles he is responding to, they are clearly voices within, demons beckoning him to heed his unabashed impulses. As a doting but baffled father there is little I can do, I have come to realize, to mute or redirect such impulses.

His world is largely a fantasy world of 'secret gardens', witches, ghosts, animated cartoons, superstars and entertainers. His room is cluttered with posters and mementos of his idols: Roald Dahl, C. S. Lewis, Anjelica Huston, Mikhail Baryshnikov, Fred Astaire, the Bangles, Expose, Debbie Gibson, Andrew Lloyd Webber, Belinda Carlisle and, off and on, Madonna. As of late, in fact, Madonna has been more off than on. Somehow, the notoriety over her shows 'Blonde Ambition' and 'Truth or Dare' has cooled Ramzi off. When I inquired about the soured relations with his one-time idol, he replied that he is now 'old enough to understand what she is all about'!

With or without Madonna, Ramzi's fanciful world, a figment of his own imagination, remained until recently largely intact. Scarcely little has happened since his exile from Lebanon to challenge the props and symbols that endeared and sustained his attachments to its wonders.

An episode a few days ago signalled the first symptoms of a change in his self-image, with portents perhaps of a more felicitous reshaping of his interests and loyalties. We had gone to the Lebanese Consulate in New York to renew our expired passports in anticipation of our trip to Lebanon in August. The encouraging upturn in security conditions after 17 years of turmoil prompted us, like throngs of other expatriates, to revisit our beleaguered country. We harboured no illusions other than the faint hope that, by exposing our two boys to the few as yet unravaged features of their country – its captivating scenic beauty and geography, the warmth and compassion of family and friends, its prehistoric sites, colourful folklore, delicious produce and cuisine – we might rekindle their longing for Lebanon's threatened and defiled legacy. Alas, to them Lebanon has been reduced to an ugly metaphor, a mere figure of speech applied to the most threatening situations elsewhere in the world. The mere word 'Lebanon' or the term 'Lebanonized' is invoked by the media to conjure up images of the grotesque and deadly.

It is immensely sad that the Lebanese have been maligned and humiliated by words and deeds that make the things that were once sources of national pride and resourcefulness seem futile, trivial and pathological. Consider what happens when a child's most precious possessions – things around which he weaves fantasies and that make him a bit different from all others – are redefined as worthless. In a sense, this is what has been happening to the Lebanese. Their country's geography, its plural and open institutions, which, as sources of tolerance and co-existence, had once set it apart, for better or worse, from its adjoining repressive and monolithic political cultures, are now dismissed as aberrant.

We didn't have to wait too long for Lebanon's image to be partly redeemed, at least in Ramzi's eyes. The moment he walked into the Consulate and saw posters of Lebanon – the usual glossy mounted portraits one sees in tourist offices and travel agencies – he was overwhelmed with amazement and wonder. There was a sudden sparkle in his eyes, as dazzling as when he is dancing or simulating the fantasy world of his favourite fairy tales.

The scenes from Lebanon, juxtaposed against the ordered, flat, dull, antiseptic milestones of America (at least the America most familiar to him: the America of suburbia, manicured lawns and parks, shopping malls, mega-highways, etc.) seemed out of this world and much closer to Ramzi's world of make-believe. The ancient Roman monuments of Baalbek, Byblos, Tyre, Sidon, Anjar; Phoenician mosaics and amphitheatres, Crusaders' castles; Ottoman souks and bazaars; feudal estates; fortresses, caverns, tombs and quaint villages with their picturesque red-tiled roofs huddled in deep gorges, on hilltops or coastal towns hugging the

Mediterranean shore . . . all seemed like idyllic backdrops to the fantasy world he conjures up and plays out in the backyard of our Princeton home.

He was captivated and awe-struck. The Lebanese Consul, touched by Ramzi's reaction, graciously volunteered to give him a poster. He picked the compelling view of Sannin, with the highest snow-capped peaks and ridges of Mount Lebanon standing out in splendour against the blue skies. It is incidentally this same view that captivated generations of Orientalist painters and engravers (e.g. Roberts, Taylor, Bartlett, Wilson, Van de Velde, Harper, Woodward) and inspired native poets and writers. It is also this view that is etched vividly in the memory of emigrants and speaks to their longing for the old country.

When Ramzi got home he furtively dismounted one of Madonna's portraits and replaced it with his new acquisition, which represented his reawakened longings to reconnect with his disinherited past. He now counts the days to the moment he will behold the same riveting view from the window of the plane taking him back home.

Ramzi's rediscovery of his country's natural and historic endowments should not be dismissed as an infantile gesture. It carries an instructive message. Just as an intuitive young boy is willing to part with his ephemeral symbols to embrace those of a higher and more enduring order, so his besieged compatriots in Lebanon (young and old) can do likewise. Now that many are in fact revisiting parts of their country previously inaccessible to them, they too have the chance to renounce all the alien and borrowed ideologies they embraced to sustain their belligerency. They could at least begin by disarming themselves of the instruments of collective violence.

Lebanon has long been plagued by disharmony between the beauty of its natural endowments and its boisterous political culture. An awakened sense of geography, sustained by an ethos for preserving and enriching the edifying features of their habitat, could be life-enhancing, enriching and, especially in the post-war period, a means of bringing tranquillity and vitality. Ecological and environmental concerns, for legitimate reasons, are also becoming generational issues. It is the so-called 'eco-smart' children who are today most incensed by the damage done to their environment. It is, after all, their future abode that is being violated. For the disinherited children of Lebanon, almost half the victimized society, such concerns could well serve as the rallying call for their active reintegration and involvement in pacifying and healing their damaged environment.

Other than being homogenized by fear and grief, little else today holds the Lebanese together. But geography can be an antidote to fear. Stripped of their bigotry and intolerance, territorial entities could become the bases for the articulation of new cultural identities. With visionary leadership and enlightened spatial planning, communities can be resocialized to perceive differences as symbols not of distrust, fear and exclusion but of cultural diversity and enrichment.

Herein lies the hope, the only hope, for transforming the geography of fear, which has beleaguered Lebanon for so long, into a new political culture of tolerance.

CHAPTER 15

Lebanon as a Playground

All metaphors, like any other figures of speech, involve some inevitable distortions of reality. They rarely tell the whole truth. Labelling Lebanon as a 'playground' is still, in my judgement, more relevant and informative than some of the other hackneyed labels that have been attached to it over the years: both the redeeming ones, which make it seem like an ultra-desirable place, such as the 'Switzerland' or 'Paris' of the Middle East, or the more pejorative, almost epitaph-like, slurs, which suggest congenitally flawed, an artificial entity bent on self-destruction, deranged, beyond understanding and beyond cure. Like a diseased organism, the most one can do is to 'quarantine' or contain it lest it contaminate others.

The word 'playground' conjures up images of an open, gregarious, accommodating space, conducive to happy invention and experimentation but also vulnerable to all the vicissitudes of excessive passion, careless narcissism, complacency and indulgent egoism. In this sense it is a more neutral metaphor. It neither adulates nor abnegates. It allows us, instead, to allude to and illuminate certain realities that cannot be wished away, whitewashed or mystified. It is also a more inclusive metaphor, incorporating everyday discursive and reflective manifestations, which pervade virtually all dimensions of society.

A 'playground', incidentally, is more than just a heuristic and analytical tool. It has also cathartic and redemptive features. By eliciting latent and hidden longings for play, conviviality and adventure, a 'playground' may serve as an expressive and transcending outlet. It brings out all the 'Homo Ludden' virtues of fair play, the exuberance of self-fulfilling and competitive sports and differential rewards for tried and accomplished feats of excellence.[1] Thus a 'playground' becomes an ideal site for cultivating the virtues of civility and commitment to the courtesies of the rules of the game. The very survival of a playground, particularly

---

1. For further elaboration, the interested reader may consult the following: Huizinga (1949), Illich (1980) and Peattie (1998).

since it is associated with spaces where children can indulge in play, is predicated on the premise of monitoring and controlling the hazards of reckless, rash and foolhardy impulse. When uncontained, a 'playground' could easily slip into a free-for-all, raucous, rough-and-tumble public ground. At that point the lines demarcating civil and uncivil, vulgar and refined behaviour and foul and fair play are blurred. Indeed, fair becomes foul and foul fair.

The curative and healing aspects of a playground are naturally more pertinent in times of collective unrest and post-war stress and uncertainties. A boisterous political culture suffused with factional and contentious rivalries can find more than just momentary release in such outlets. Some of the enabling features of a playground – i.e. those of fair play, teamwork, equal recognition and the sheer exuberance of doing one's thing without encroaching on the rights and spaces of others – can all become vectors for the restoration of civility. At least they need not be dismissed and trivialized. Inordinate effort and resources have been squandered on strategies of political and administrative reform and the broader issues of regional conflict and infrastructural reconstruction. Important as these are, they overlook some of the more human and socio-cultural issues of coping with pervasive fear and damaged national identities. It is also these areas that are amenable to individual intervention. Ordinary, otherwise passive and lethargic, citizens are given opportunities to participate and become actively and meaningfully engaged in processes of reconstruction and rehabilitation.

Within this context, at least five features of a playground stand out, particularly those that have some bearing on Lebanon's seemingly lopsided character. In all those features we find many of the enabling and disabling sources of the 'playground', those that account for Lebanon's 'success story' and those that render it more vulnerable to internal and external contradictions.

1. By virtue of its location, composition and its historical role as a place of refuge for dissidents or a gateway for itinerant groups, Lebanon has always been a fairly open and free space. Exit from and entry into society has been relatively easy. Indeed, some argue that Lebanon became much too open, too hospitable and, hence, too vulnerable to the vicissitudes of internal and regional disturbances. It laid itself open to abuse by the very forces that sought it as a haven from repression or homelessness. A free press, uncensored media, absence of exchange controls, a 'free zone' in Beirut's port, secret bank accounts, liberal migration laws, receptivity to novelties and fads, progressive and permissive lifestyles, all reinforced the discordant dualism inherent in its character as a free and open society. Hence its generative and positive attributes were often undermined by subversive and negative elements. Lebanon became all too often no more than an expedient conduit, a transit point, for the trafficking and recycling of displaced groups, goods, capital and ideas.

   Naturally, such trafficking was not always of a desirable and lawful character. Inevitably, Lebanon became notorious for smuggling, arms-running, trading in drugs, black-marketing of illicit contraband products and other nefarious activities. Perhaps more damaging was the abandon with which dissident groups exploited this freedom to launch vilifying press campaigns and plots against repressive regimes in the region. This only served to arouse suspicion and retributive acts by the targeted states or groups against Lebanon. On both counts Lebanon became unjustly victimized.

2. As in a playground, the Lebanese displayed a proclivity for playfulness, a carefree, uncommitted, almost sportive attitude, with a special fondness for jocular and humorous experiences. But this playfulness too is double-edged. It is a source of unflagging resourcefulness, sustained by a sense of experimentation and adventure. When unrestrained, however, it can quickly degenerate into restlessness, mischievousness or even anarchy. A thread of careless play and spontaneous activity ran through society. The laissez-faire ethos, in such a free-for-all milieu, is clearly a relief to an inept government and a welcome feature to those adept at exploiting it. Even the corrupt civil servant 'became increasingly appreciated by the national and international business communities, since bribes now served to circumvent red tape and to effect short-cuts; which made conduct of business, in many ways, more "efficient" in Lebanon than in even the most advanced countries'. (Tabbarah, 1977: 22)

    There are other more grievous manifestations of this predisposition for unrestrained play. It is evident in the wasteful discrepancy between audacious and playful planning on the one hand and executive ineffectiveness on the other. This has plagued government bureaucracy for too long and has been a blatant source of administrative inefficiency and misuse of resources. Some of the schemes for development are often so adventurous in their vision that they must necessarily remain unrealized blueprints, victims of reckless planning or short-sighted expediency. Examples are legion.

    The Litani River Authority of 1954 was supposed to irrigate, once completed, 32,000 hectares in the south-western regions of the Beqà valley. By 1975, twenty years after the establishment of the project and despite the expenditure of hundreds of millions of pounds, the precious waters of the Litani are still draining to the Mediterranean. (Nasr, 1978: 8) The Green Plan of 1964, successive urban planning schemes and comprehensive master plans, rent and zoning laws, educational and civil services reforms, to mention a few, are all regrettable by-products of this dissonance between exuberant planning and flawed implementation.

    This is also apparent, as we have seen, in the political process, particularly electoral campaigns and contests for public office, which were suffused with playful and festive elements. The whole style of daily politics is typified by political manoeuvrings and animated exchanges bordering on public entertainment. Indeed, as one of the smallest nation-states in the world, Lebanon has always suffered from the inordinate number of people who expend their energies and derive their sense of esteem from 'playing' politics. This is, in itself, another reflection of the difficult, even ungovernable character of the Lebanese polity. To many of these political actors, prominent and not-so-prominent figures who meddle in the political affairs of their society, the art of politics is often reduced to a self-indulgent game, a morbid form of public amusement and exhibitionism. So alluring is the game that successive generations of politicians find it extremely difficult to redirect their energies into less self-flattering but more demanding and creative pastimes. Many have what amounts to an addiction to playing politics. Just as actors, like others engaged in any addictive or habit-forming activity, suffer withdrawal symptoms if they are compelled to 'rest', so too it is difficult for political actors in Lebanon to retire from politics.

Even the character of fighting was not entirely free from elements of play. Combatants, during the early stages of the 1975 war, when the bearing of arms and combat were still regarded as redemptive and purgative activities, acted out their roles with considerable aplomb and savoir faire. Indeed, identification with the garb, demeanour or lifestyles of fighters and militia groups became almost chic; machismo was fashionable. Belligerency, in fact, became so stylized that groups literally disfigured themselves to simulate such playful and attractive identities. As fighting escalated into massive bombardment, random shelling, car bombs, ground troop movement and aerial attacks . . . it acquired all the trappings of a colourful and dazzling spectacle, a 'danse macabre', and was often viewed as such by the non-belligerent population.[1]

3. A playground is, above all, a place that thrives on gamesmanship. In an open, free and competitive milieu, one sustained by the maximization of private initiative and free enterprise, there is a correspondingly high premium placed on individual success and socio-economic mobility. Ruthless competition may propel the Lebanese into new heights, stretch their abilities to new thresholds. Yet it also generates a form of 'social Darwinism' and heedless individualism impervious to any controls or ethical restraints. Symptoms of anomie become rampant. Everything and anything become accessible or feasible, by fair means if possible or foul means if necessary. Benign play could then readily degenerate into malevolent and foul play.

At the height of Lebanon's golden age (mid- and late 1960s), there was already a growing chorus of dissenting voices decrying the abuses and the desecration of the country's potential. To René Habachi, there was nothing new about the crisis.

> The present crisis is a quarter of a century old. It is as old as independence, that is one generation. It is a chronic, latent, disease which has suddenly burst out from under the embers of people's souls. The old style Lebanese, those who wore Ottoman boots, took over a country which had entered the modern age, but they ruled it with the mentality of the Sultan. The level of development of the country, its openness to civilization and its geographic, economic and human resources fitted it to live within the democracy of science and knowledge. Instead they ruled it like someone exploiting a farm he had inherited from his father, with the right to bequeath it in turn to his

---

1. I borrow the expression from Miriam Cooke (1988: 15) who, in exploring the literary output and background of a nucleus of women writers in Lebanon during the war, titles her first chapter 'Danse Macabre'. So, incidentally, does Theodor Hanf (1993) in cataloguing the various stages and rounds of fighting.

son. In Lebanon, today, there are two Lebanons . . . (quoted by Awwad, 1976: 137)

Gamesmanship after all involves, literally, the internalization of the necessary social skills – those of tact, deftness, acumen, quick-wittedness – for handling and rearranging situations to one's own advantage. It conjures up images of Byzantine manoeuvring, manipulation, deals and quid-pro-quos. Everything, including the most cherished values and resources, becomes negotiable. Lebanese entrepreneurship, particularly in its reckless form of speculation and risk-taking, seems guided more by Adam Smith's 'invisible hand' than by rational long-term planning.

These factors too are not unmixed blessings. While they may account for much of the resourcefulness and enterprise associated with Lebanon's 'success story', they also make acceptable the use of ploys and other ethically and intellectually dubious means to achieve desired ends. Clientelistic politics, the survival of subversive patronage, graft, nepotism, corruption are all by-products of such practices. Those who stand to benefit from the spoils and excesses of this form of deranged 'social Darwinism' will naturally resist any system that undermines their jealously guarded privileges. Spokesmen of the radical left, heralding revolutionary change as the panacea that will cure society of its inherent foibles and moral weaknesses, admitted that even an organized revolt stood little chance of undoing the deep-seated structure of vested privileges. Writing again in the late 1960s Gibran Majdalani has this to say:

> The realisation of the aims of a real revolution conflicts with vested interests and with apparatuses which were set up to protect those interests. It is unreasonable to those who are profiting from the present state of affairs voluntarily to give up those things which give them their power and their material and political potentialities. Those who are 'eating the cheese' (as they say) in any system will oppose any attempt at radical change because change implies the liquidation of their privileges and positions of influence and the threatening of their interests. The form of opposition to which the leaders and protectors of any system will resort determines, in the last resort, the method of revolution. (quoted by Awwad, 1976: 138)

4. The most edifying and enabling feature of a playground is, without doubt, its convivial and gregarious character. In part because of the survival of many primordial and intimate social networks, the Lebanese have long displayed a proclivity for festive, light-hearted and fun-loving experiences. If one were to single out a national pastime, it would be feasting, with its associated carefree social gatherings and companionship. Time and budget analysis reveals that an inordinate amount of time and resources is devoted to ceremonial activities, social visiting and frequent contacts with close circles of family and friends. Such contacts are invaluable sources of social and psychological support, particularly in times of public distress. As the public world becomes more savage, menacing and insecure, people are more inclined to seek and find

refuge and identity in the reassuring comforts of family and community. So intense and encompassing are these attachments that the average Lebanese recognizes hardly any obligations and loyalties beyond them. Here lie many of the roots of deficient civility and the erosion of the broader loyalties to public welfare and national consciousness.

Once again, what enables at one level disables at another. At the local and communal level, conviviality is a source of group solidarity and an avenue for vital socio-psychological and economic supports. At the national and public level, it can lead to parochialism and oppression. Compassion for and almost obsessive preoccupation with micro-interests coexist with (are indeed a by-product of) disinterest or indifference for others. Nowhere is this more apparent than in the character or functioning of voluntary associations. The concern for public welfare continues to be inspired and mobilized on sectarian, communal or factional grounds. Hence national and broader societal problems such as child and family welfare, mental health, orphanages, the aged, delinquency, poverty, protection of the environment and habitat and concern for the threatened architectural, archaeological and cultural heritage, and other such public issues, are all articulated as parochial and segmented problems. Indeed, the character of voluntary associations, their membership, financial resources and organizational leadership continue to reflect sub-national loyalties. Even interest in competitive sports, normally the most benign and affectively neutral and transcending of human activities, has been lately pulverised into bitter and acrimonious sectarian rivalries.

5. Finally, Lebanon is recognized and treated as a 'playground' by the multitudes who perceive it and seek it as a popular resort. The country's captivating topography, scenic beauty, temperate climate, historic sites, colourful folklore, reinforced by an aggressive infrastructure of commercial, financial, medical and cultural facilities, have made it an all-year-round tourist attraction, a popular amusement centre and summer resort.

As a national industry, tourism and related services always served to invigorate the Lebanese economy. Early in the 1950s it already comprised the most important invisible export; earning more than half of the value of all exported merchandise (see Gates, 1998: 117–80). Revenue from tourism grew fourfold in the period 1968–74, to provide 10 per cent of the gross domestic product. (Owen, 1988: 37) By the outbreak of hostilities in 1975 it was contributing significantly (at least $40 million annually) to GNP and thus offsetting the unfavourable trade balance. It opened up society further and enhanced the receptivity of isolated communities to diverse cultural contacts.

There was, however, a darker side to tourism and Lebanon's image as a resort centre. It exacerbated further the lopsidedness of the Lebanese economy by rechannelling vital resources into largely unproductive sectors of the economy. The country was increasingly becoming a nation of services, middlemen, agents, idle rentiers and hotel keepers. Popular resorts invariably became tempting spots for venial and not-so-venial attractions. Lebanon was hardly a paragon of virtue in this regard. It had its full share of houses of ill-repute, casinos, gambling parlours, nightclubs, discos, bars, escort bureaus and other dens of wickedness.

The trouble was that this phenomenon placed a blemish on the country's national character. As a 'merchant republic' Lebanon became a country obsessed with and too eager to please and serve others, with all the cruel ironies that such ingratiation and servility often do to society's self-esteem. Artisans, villagers and farmers abandoned some of their venerated crafts, vocations and sources of traditional status to capitalize on the transient rewards of tourist-affiliated activities. Many became idle much of the year awaiting the seductive promises of a quick and sizeable windfall generated by the influx of 'resorters' during the brief summer months. Others wallowed in aimless indolence.

It is easy to see how tourism, underlain by the ethics of a mercantile culture, could deepen further the inauspicious consequences of rampant commercialism and the vulgarization of some of the cherished values and institutions. As a result, society at times displayed the most lurid features of a bazaar and an amusement park, where the impulses for fun and profit are there for all to see. Practically everything and anything can be put up for sale or converted into a sleazy tourist attraction. Every entity and human capacity is conceived as a resource for the acquisition of profit or as a commodity to be sold to the highest bidder. This is most visible in the ruthless plunder of Lebanon's scenic natural habitat and dehumanization of much of its living space. Hardly anything is spared: shore lines, green belts, public parks and private backyards, suburban villas, historic sites and monuments . . . they are all giving way to more intensive forms of exploitation to enhance the fashionable attributes of their resort.

Bibliography

Abi Nader, S. 1972. *Collection of Lebanese Laws*. Code No. 59/71 (September 13) (Beirut: Lebanese Company for Printing and Publications).

Abu Lughod, Janet. 1961. 'Migrant Adjustments for City Life: The Egyptian Case', *American Journal of Sociology*, 67 (July), pp. 22–32.

Adam, Hannah. 1817. *A Dictionary of Religions and Religious Denominations* (Boston: Cummings and Hilliard).

Adams, C. F. 1856. *The Works of John Adams: Second President of the United States* (Boston: Little, Brown and Co).

Adorno, T. 1973. *Philosophy of Modern Music* (New York: Seabury Press).

Ajami, Fuad. 1998. *Dream Palaces of the Arabs* (NewYork: Pantheon Books).

Albrow, M. 1997. 'Travelling Beyond Local Cultures', in J. Eade, ed., *Living in the Global City* (London and New York: Routledge).

Alcalay, Ammiel. 1993. *After Jews and Arabs: Remaking Levantine Culture* (Minneapolis: University of Minnesota Press).

Alger, C. 1988. 'Perceiving, Analyzing and Coping with the Local-Global Nexus', *International Social Science Journal*, 117 (August).

Almond, Gabriel and James Coleman, eds. 1960. *The Politics of Developing Areas* (Princeton, NJ: Princeton University Press).

—— and G. Bingham Powell, eds. 1966. *Comparative Politics: A Developmental Approach* (Boston: Little Brown and Co.).

American Board of Commissioners for Foreign Missions (ABCFM). 1861. *Memorial Volume of the First Fifty Years* (Boston: ABCFM).

—— 1817. *Annual Reports* (Boston).

—— 1819. *First Ten Annual Reports* (Boston: ABCFM).

—— 1827. *Annual Reports*.

Anderson, C. R. 1952. *Naval Wars in the Levant* (Princeton, NJ: Princeton University Press).

Anderson, Rufus. 1861. *Memorial Volume of the First Fifty Years of the American Board of Commissioners for Foreign Missions* (Boston: ABCFM).

—— 1869. *Foreign Missions: Their Relations and Claims* (New York: Charles Scribner and Co.).

—— 1872. *History of the Missions of the ABCFM to the Oriental Churches*, 2 vols (Boston: ABCFM).

Andover Theological Seminary. 1833. *Memoirs of American Missionaries* (Boston: Pierce and Parker).

Antonius, George. 1983. *The Arab Awakening* (London: Hamish Hamilton).

Apter, David. 1965. *The Politics of Modernization* (Chicago: University of Chicago Press).

—— 1968. 'The Role of Traditionalism in the Political Modernization of Ghana and Uganda', in David Apter, ed., *Some Conceptual Approaches to the Study of Modernization* (Englewood Cliffs, NJ: Prentice Hall), pp. 133–35.

Arendt, Hannah. 1958. *The Human Condition* (New York: Doubleday Anchor Books).

Aron, Raymond. 1957. *The Opium of the Intellectuals* (New York: W. W. Norton and Co).

Avi-Ran, Reven. 1991. *The Syrian Involvement in Lebanon Since 1975* (Boulder, CO: Westview).

Awwad, T. Y. 1976. *Death in Beirut* (London: Heinemann).

Azar, Edward. 1984. *The Emergence of New Lebanon: Fantasy or Reality.* (New York: Praeger).

Badr, Habib. 1992. 'Mission to Nominal Christians', unpublished Ph.D. dissertation (Princeton, NJ: Princeton Theological Seminary).

Baer, G. 1982. *Fellah and Townsmen in the Middle East* (London: Frank Cass).

Barber, Benjamin. 1996. *Jihad vs. McWorld* (New York: Ballantine Books).

Barber B. and A. Inkeles. 1971. *Continuity and Changes in Japanese Society* (Boston: Little, Brown and Co.).

Barlow, Joel. 1970. *The Work of Joel Barlow*, 2 vols (Gainesville, FL: Scholars' Facsimiles and Reprints).

Bartlett, S. C. 1972. *Historical Sketches of the Missions of The American Board* (New York: Arno Press).

Barton, James. 1918. *The Christian Approach to Islam* (Boston: Pilgrim Press).

—— 1925. 'The Impact and Influence of Western Civilization on the Islamic World', in John R. Mott, ed., *The Moslem World of Today* (New York: George H. Doran), pp. 3–29.

Beaver, R. Pierce, ed. 1966. *Church, State and the American Indian* (St Louis, MO: Concordia Publishing House).

—— 1967. *To Advance the Gospel* (Grand Rapids: Eardman).

Beidelman, T. O. 1982. *Colonial Evangelism* (Bloomington, IN: Indiana University Press).

Bellah, Robert N. 1971. 'Continuity and Change in Japanese Society', in B. Barber and A. Inkeles, eds, *Stability and Change* (Boston: Little, Brown and Co.), pp. 377–404.

Belling, Willard. 1960. *Pan-Arabism and Labor* (Cambridge, MA: Harvard University Press).

Bendix, Reinhard. 1967. 'Tradition and Modernity Reconsidered', *Comparative Studies in Society and History*, 9 (April), pp. 292–346.

Bennett, Clinton. 1996. *In Search of the Sacred: Anthropology and Study of Religions* (London, Cassell).

Berger, B.M. 1966. 'Suburbs, Subcultures, and the Urban Future', in Sam Bass Warner, ed., *Planning for a Nation of Cities* (Cambridge, MA: MIT Press), pp. 143–62.

Berger, Morroe. 1957. *Bureaucracy and Society in Modern Egypt* (Princeton, NJ: Princeton University Press).

Berger, P., B. Berger and H. Kellner. 1973. *The Homeless Mind* (New York: Random House).

Bettelheim, B. 1960. *The Informed Heart* (Glencoe, IL: The Free Press).

Beyhum, Nabil et al. 1992. *I'mar Beirut wal-Fursah al-Dhai'ah* (Rebuilding Beirut and Lost Opportunity) (Beirut: Rami al-Khal).

Bienen, H. 1984. 'Urbanization and Third World Stability', *World Development*, vol. 12, No. 7, pp. 661–91.

Bigelow, John, ed. 1887. *The Complete Works of Benjamin Franklin* (New York: Putnam's Sons).

Bill, James and Carl Leiden. 1984. *Politics in the Middle East*, 2nd edn (Boston: Little, Brown and Co.).

Black, Perry. 1966. *The Dynamics of Modernization: A Study in Comparative History* (New York: Harper and Row).

Bliss, Edwin Munsell. 1897. *A Concise History of Missions* (New York: Fleming Revell Co.).

Bond, Alvin. (1828). *Memoir of Rev. Pliny Fisk* (Boston: Crocker and Brewster).

Bonine, Michael. 1976. 'Urban Studies in the Middle East', *Middle East Studies Association Bulletin*, 10 (October), pp. 1–37.

Bosch, David. 1991. *Transforming Missions: Paradigm Shifts in Theology of Missions* (New York: Orbis Books).

Boulding, E. 1992. 'Introduction', in K. Rupesinghe, ed., *Internal Conflict and Governance* (New York: St Martin's Press).

Bourdieu, P. 1977. *Outline of a Theory of Practice* (Cambridge: Cambridge University Press).

Bouyer-Bell, J. 1987. *The Gun in Politics: An Analysis of Irish Political Conflict, 1916–1986* (New Brunswick, NJ: Transaction).

Bové, A. Paul, ed. 2000. *Edward Said and the Work of the Critic: Speaking Truth to Power* (Durham and London: Duke University Press).

Bradbury, Malcolm. 1964. 'Uncertainties of the British Intellectual', *New Society*, No. 117 (December 24), pp. 7–9.

Braudel, Fernand. 1979. *The Perspective of the World* (New York: Harper and Row), vol. 3.

Brockner, J. and J. Rubin. 1985. *Entrapment in Escalating Conflicts* (Springer Verlag).

Brookfield, H. C. 1972. *Colonialism, Development and Independence* (Cambridge: Cambridge University Press).

Brown, Gordon. 1944. 'Missions and Cultural Diffusion', *American Journal of Sociology*, vol. 50, pp. 214–19.

Brown, L. Carl, ed. 1973. *From Medina to Metropolis* (Princeton, NJ: Darwin Press).

Brzezinski, Z. 1993. *Out of Control: Global Turmoil on the Eve of the Twenty-First Century* (New York: Scribner).

Calinescu, M. 1987. *Five Faces of Modernity* (Durham, NC: Duke University Press).

Carlyle, Thomas. 1841. *On Heroes and Hero Worship* (New York: Charles Scribner's Sons).

Carroll, Bernice A. 1980. 'Victory and Defeat: The Mystique of Dominance', in S. Albert and E Luck, eds, *On the Endings of War* (Port Washington, NY: Kennikat Press).

Cernea, Michael. 1981. In M. Atir, B. Holzner and Z. Suda, eds, *Directions of Change: Modernization Theory, Research and Realities* (Boulder, CO: Westview Press).

Chevalier, D. 1971. *La Société du Mont Liban à l'époque de la Révolution Industrielle en Europe* (Paris: Librairie Orientaliste).

Collelta, N. J. 1975. 'The Use of Indigenous Culture as a Medium for Development: The Indonesian Case', *Prisma*, 1 (November).

Collins, R. 1974. 'The Three Faces of Cruelty: Towards a Comparative Study of Violence', *Theory and Society*, 1, pp. 415–40.

Conway, Mercure. 1906. *My Pilgrimage to the Wise Men of the East* (Boston: Houghton Mifflin).

Coser, Lewis. 1965. 'America's Intellectuals: The Twin Temptation', *New Society*, No. 120 (January 14), pp. 10–13.

Cooke, Miriam. 1988. *War's Other Voices: Women Writers on The Lebanese War* (Cambridge and New York: Cambridge University Press).

Coolidge, A. C. 1908. *The United States as a World Power* (New York: Macmillan).

Cranston, Maurice. 1965. 'Paradox of the French Intellectual', *New Society*, No. 119 (January 7), pp. 12–14.

Curtis, George Williams. 1856. *The Howdaji in Syria* (New York: Harper).

Dahrendorf, R. 1990. 'Has the East Joined the West?, *New Perspective Quarterly*, 7, No. 2 (Spring), pp. 41–43.

Dahl, Mary Karen. 1987. *Political Violence in Drama* (Ann Arbor, MI, U.M.I. Research Press).

Daniel, Robert L. 1964. 'American Influences in the Near East Before 1860', *American Quarterly*, vol. 16 (Spring), pp. 72–84.

Davies, R. H. 1973. 'Interpreting the Colonial Period in African History', *African Affairs* vol. 72, pp. 383–400.

Davis, Natalie. 1975. *Society and Culture in Early Modern France* (Stanford University Press).

Denis, James. 1872. *A Sketch of the Syrian Mission* (New York: Mission House).

—— 1872a. *Christian Missions and Social Progress* (New York: Fleming and Revell Co.).

Desai, A. R., ed. 1971. *Essays on Modernization of Underdeveloped Societies*, vol. 1 (Bombay: Thacher and Co.).

—— 1971. 'Need for Revolution of the Concept', in A. R. Desai, ed., *Essays on Modernization of Underdeveloped Societies*, vol. 1 (Bombay: Thacher and Co.), pp. 474–548.

Deutsh, Karl. 1961. 'Social Mobilization and Political Development', *American Political Science Review*, 55 (September), pp. 493–514.

Di Muccio, R. B. A. and J. Rosenau. 1996. 'Turbulence and Sovereignty in World Politics: Explaining the Relocation of Legitimacy in the 1990s and Beyond', in Z. Milnar, ed., *Globalization and Territorial Identities* (England: Avebury).

Douglas, M. 1966. *Purity and Danger* (Harmondsworth: Penguin Books).

Doxiadis, K. 1968. *Existics* (London: Hutchinson).

Durkheim, Emile. 1964. *The Division of Labor in Society* (Glencoe, IL: The Free Press).

Dwight, Theodore. 1864. 'Conditions and Character of Negros in Africa', *Methodist Quarterly Review* (January), pp. 77–90.

Earle, Edward. 1927. 'Early American Policy Concerning Ottoman Minorities', *Political Science* Quarterly, pp. 337–67.

Eickelman, D. 1981. *The Middle East: An Anthropological Approach* (Englewood Cliffs, NJ: Prentice Hall).

Eisenstadt, S. N. 1964. 'Breakdowns of Modernization', *Economic Development and Cultural Change*, 12 (July), pp. 345–67.

—— 1966. *Modernization: Protest and Change* (Englewood Cliffs, NJ: Prentice Hall).

—— 1973. *Traditional Patrimonialism and Modern Neopatrimonialism* (Beverly Hills, CA: Sage).

—— 1974. 'Studies of Modernization and Sociological Theory', *History and Theory*, vol. 13.

—— 1974. 'Reflections on a Theory of Modernization', in A. Rivken, ed., *Nations by Design* (NewYork: Anchor Books), pp. 35–61.

Elias, Norbert. 1988. 'Violence and Civilization: The State Monopoly of Physical Violence and its Infringement', in John Keane, ed., *Civil Society and the State* (London and New York: Verso).

Ellin, N. 1997. *Architecture of Fear* (New York: Princeton Architectural Press).

Elsbree, O. W. 1928. 'The Rise of the Missionary Spirit in New England, 1780–1815', *New England Quarterly*, vol. 1, pp. 295–322.

Emerson, Rupert. 1960. *From Empire to Nation: The Rise of Self-Assertion of Asian and African Peoples* (Boston: Beacon Press).

Erikson, K. 1976. *Everything in its Path: Destruction of the Community in the Buffalo Creek Flood* (New York: Simon and Schuster).

Esman, Milton J. 1990. *Ethnic Politics* (Ithaca, New York: Cornell University Press).

Esman, Milton and I. Rabinovitch, eds, *Ethnicity, Pluralism and the State in the Middle East* (Ithaca, NY: Cornell University Press).

Executive Board of Major Projects for the City of Beirut. 1968. *Comprehensive Plan Studies for the City of Beirut* (Beirut: J. S. Saikali).

Feierabend, I.K. and R. L. Feierabend. 1966. 'Aggressive Behaviors Within Polities, 1948–1962: A Cross-National Study', *Journal of Conflict Resolution*, 10, No. 3 (September), pp. 249–71.

Fernea, Elizabeth Warnock. 1985. *Women and the Family in the Middle East* (Austin, TX: University of Texas Press).

Festinger, L. 1957. *A Theory of Cognitive Dissonance* (Evanston: Row, Peterson).

Field, James A. 1969. *America and the Mediterranean World* (Princeton, NJ: Princeton University Press).

—— 1974. 'New East Notes and Far East Queries', in John K. Fairbank, ed., *The Missionary Enterprise in China and America* (Cambridge, MA: Harvard University Press).

—— 1991. *From Gibraltar to the Middle East* (Chicago: In Print Publications).

Finnie, David. 1967. *Pioneers East: The Early American Experience in the Middle East* (Cambridge, MA: Harvard University Press).

Fischer, C. 1982. *To Dwell Among Friends: Personal Networks in Town and City* (Chicago: University of Chicago Press).

Fisk, Pliny. 1819. 'The Holy Land: An Interesting Field of Missionary Enterprise', Sermon before the Departure of the Palestine Mission (Boston: Samuel T. Armstrong).

Foss, John. 1798. *A Journal of Captivity and Suffering of John Foss; Several Years a Prisoner in Algiers* (Newbury: A. Morch).

Foucault, M. 1975. *The Birth of the Clinic* (New York: Random House).

Frank, Andre. 1971. *Sociology of Development and Underdevelopment of Sociology* (London: Pluto Press).

Friedman, Thomas. 2000. *The Lexus and the Olive Tree: Understanding Globalization* (New York: Doubleday).

Fück, J.W. 1962. 'Islam as an Historical Problem in European Historiography since 1800', in B. Lewis and P.M. Holt, eds., *Historians of the Middle East* (London: Oxford University Press), pp. 303–14.

Fukuyama, F. 1989. 'The End of History', *The National Interest*, 16 (Summer).

Gabriel, R. H. 1950. 'Evangelical Religion and Popular Romanticism in Early 19th Century America', *Church History*, vol. XlV (March), pp. 34–37.

Gans, H. 1970. *People and Plans* (New York: Basic Books).

Garfinkel, H. 1967. *Studies in Ethnomethodology* (Englewood Cliffs, NJ: Prentice-Hall).

Gates, Carolyn L. 1998. *The Merchant Republic of Lebanon: Rise of an Open Economy* (London: I. B. Tauris).

Gay, Peter. 1993. *The Cultivation of Hatred* (New York: W. W. Norton and Co.).

Geertz, Clifford. 1968. *Agricultural Involution: The Process of Ecological Change in*

Indonesia (Berkeley, CA: University of California Press).

—— 1971. 'After the Revolution: The Fate of Nationalism in the New States', in *Stability and Change* (Boston: Little, Brown and Co.), pp. 357–76.

—— 1973. *The Interpretation of Culture* (New York: Basic Books).

Gellner, Ernest and John Waterbury, eds. 1977. *Patrons and Clients in Mediterranean Societies* (London: Duckworth).

Gellner, Ernest. 1973. 'Post-Traditional Forms in Islam', *Daedalus* (Winter), 102 (1), pp. 191–206.

—— 1984. 'Forward', in Said Arjomand, ed., *From Nationalism to Revolutionary Islam* (London: Macmillan).

—— 1987. *Culture, Identity and Politics* (Cambridge: Cambridge University Press).

Genberg, D. 1997. 'The Mutagenic Maquette of Beirut: A Real Estate Claim to a City' (unpublished paper).

Gendzier, Irene. 1985. *Managing Political Change: Social Scientists and The Third World* (Boulder, CO: Westview Press).

Ghoussoub, Mai. 1998. *Leaving Beirut: Women and The Wars Within* (London: Saqi Books).

Gibb, H. A. R. 1962. *Studies on the Civilization of Islam* (Boston: Beacon Press).

Gibbon, Edward. 1932. *The Decline and Fall of the Roman Empire* (New York: The Modern Library).

Girard, René. 1977. *Violence and the Sacred* (Baltimore: Johns Hopkins University Press).

Goffman, E. 1961. *Stigma: Notes on the Management of Spoiled Identity* (Englewood Cliffs, NJ: Prentice Hall).

Goodell, Fred Field. 1826. 'Attack of the Greeks from Beyroot and the Consequences of it', *Missionary Herald*, vol. XXII, pp. 345–58.

—— 1853. *The Old and the New: On the Changes of Thirty Years in the East, with some Allusions to Oriental Customs as Elucidating the Scriptures* (New York: Dodd).

—— 1861. *They Lived Their Faith* (Boston: ABCFM).

Grabill, Joseph L. 1971. *Protestant Diplomacy in the Middle East* (Minnesota Press).

Greene, J. K. 1916. *Leavening the Levant* (Boston).

Grossman, Dave. 1998. *On Killing* (Diane Publishing Co.).

Gulick, John. 1967. *Tripoli: A Modern Arab City* (Cambridge, MA: Harvard University Press).

Gurr, T. R. 1980. *Handbook of Political Conflict* (New York: Free Press).

Gusfield, Joseph. 1967. 'Tradition and Modernity: Misplaced Polarities in the Study of Social Change', *American Journal of Sociology*, 72 (January) pp. 351–62.

Habermas, J. 1989. *The Structural Transformation of the Public Sphere* (Cambridge, MA: MIT Press).

Hall, Gordon. 1818. *The Conversion of The World*, 2nd edn (Andover: ABCFM).

Halpern, Manfred. 1963. *The Politics of Social Change in the Middle East and North Africa* (Princeton, NJ: Princeton University Press).

Hanf, Theodor. 1993. *Coexistence in Wartime Lebanon: Decline of a State and Rise of a Nation* (London: I. B. Tauris).

—— 1995. 'Ethnergy: on the Analytical Use and Normative Abuse of the Concept of "Ethnic Idendity"', in Keebet Von Berda-Bechman and Utrecht Verknyten, eds., *Nationalism, Ethnicity and Cultural Identity* (Utrecht: Utrecht University).

Harb, el-Kak, M. 1998. 'Transforming the Site of Dereliction into the Urban Culture of Modernity: Beirut's Southern Suburb', in P. Rowe and H. Sarkis, eds., *Projecting Beirut* (Munich: Prestel Verlag).

Harik, I. 1968. *Politics and Change in a Traditional Society, Lebanon, 1711–1845* (Princeton, NJ: Princeton University Press).

Harris, William. 1997. *Faces of Lebanon: Sects, Wars and Global Extensions* (Princeton, NJ: Markus Wiener Publishers).

Harvey, D. 1973. *Social Justice and the City* (London: Edward Arnold).

Harvey, J. and G. Weary, G., eds. 1985. *Attribution: Basic Issues and Applications* (Academic Press).

Hassanain, Nagdi. 1975. *The Sahara, Revolution and Promise: The Story of Tahrir Province* (Cairo: General Book Organization).

Havel, V. 1985. *The Power of the Powerless: Citizens Against the State* (New York: M. E. Sharpe).

Hayword, John. 1843. *The Book of Religions* (Boston, MA: John Hayword).

Hewston, M. 1983. *Attribution Theory* (London: Blackwell).

Hiss, Anthony. 1990. *The Experience of Space* (New York: Vintage Books).

Hitti, Philip. 1957. *Lebanon in History* (London: Macmillan and Company).

Hobsbaum, E. 1972. *Bandits* (Harmondsworth: Penguin Books).

Hobson, J. A. 1965. *Imperialism* (Ann Arbor, MI: Ann Arbor Paperbacks).

Hooker, E. W. 1839. *Memoir of Mrs Sarah Lanman Smith* (Boston: Perkins and Marvin).

Hopkins, Charles H. 1940. *The Rise of the Social Gospel, 1865–1918* (New Haven, CT: Yale University Press).

Horowitz, Donald. 1985. *Ethnic Groups in Conflict* (Berkeley, CA: University of California Press).

Hourani, Albert. 1974. 'Western Attitudes Towards Islam', University of Southampton: The 10th Montefiore Memorial Lecture.

Hozelitz, B. I. 1961. 'Tradition and Economic Growth', in R. Bribanti and J. Z. Spengler, eds, *Traditions, Values and Economic Development* (Durham, NC: Duke University Press), pp. 83–113.

Hudson, Winthrop. 1961. *American Protestantism* (Chicago: University of Chicago Press).

Huizinga, Johan. 1949. *Homo Ludens* (London: Routledge and Kegan Paul).

Humphreys, David. 1804. 'Poems on Happiness', in *Miscellaneous Works* (New York).

Huntington, Samuel. 1966. 'The Political Modernization of Traditional Monarchies', *Daedalus*, 39 (Summer), pp. 760–66.

—— 1968. *Political Order in Changing Societies* (New Haven, CT: Yale University Press).

Hutchinson, William R. 1987. *Errand to the World* (Chicago: University of Chicago Press).

Ignatieff, Michael. 1994. *Blood and Belonging: Journeys into the New Nationalism* (New York: Farrar, Straus and Giroux).

Ikle, Fred Charles. 1971. *Every War Must End* (New York: Columbia University Press).

Illich, Ivan. 1980. *Tools for Conviviality* (New York: Harper and Row).

Inkeles, Alex. 1966. 'The Modernization of Man', in Myron Weiner, ed., *Modernization: Dynamics of Growth* (New York: Basic Books), pp. 151–66

Irving, Washington. 1849. *Mahomet and his Successors* (New York: The Cooperative Publishing Society).

Irwin, Ray. 1931. *The Diplomatic Relations of the US with the Barbary Powers* (Chapel Hill, NC: University of North Carolina).

Issawi, Charles. 1973. *Issawi's Laws of Social Motion* (New York: Hawthorn Books).

—— 1982. *An Economic History of the Middle East and North Africa* (New York: Columbia University Press).

Jacobs, J. 1961. *The Death and Life of Great American Cities.* (New York: Random House).

Jaspers, J., F. Fincham and M. Hewstone, eds. 1983. *Attribution Theory and Research* (Academic Press).

Jedlowski, P. 1990. 'Simmel on Memory', in M. Kaern, B. S. Philips and R.S. Cohen, eds, *George Simmel and Contemporary Sociology* (Dordrecht: Kluwer).

Jessup, Rev. H. H. 1910. *Fifty-Three Years in Syria* (New York: Fleming H. Revell Co.).

—— 1886. 'The Natûr at the Cedars of Lebanon', *El Arz* (Beirut: The American Press).

—— 1847. *Syrian Home Life* (New York: Dodd and Mead).

—— 1873. *The Women of the Arabs* (New York: Dodd and Mead).

—— 1879. *The Mohammedan Missionary Problem* (Philadelphia: Presbyterian Board of Publications).

—— 1884. 'Foreign Missions', sermon delivered at the opening of the General Assembly of the Presbyterian Church, Saratoga, May 15 (Friends of Foreign Missions).

Kakar, Sudhir. 1996. *The Colors of Violence* (Chicago and London: University of Chicago Press).

Kaplan, Jay. 1980. 'Victors and Vanquished: The Postwar Relations', in S. Albert and E. Luch, eds, *On the Endings of War* (Port Washington, NY: Kennikat Press), pp. 72–117.

Kaplan, Robert. 1993. *The Arabists* (New York: Free Press).

Keane, John. 1996. *Reflections on Violence* (New York: Verso).

Keen, Sam. 1986. *Faces of the Enemy: Reflections of the Hostile Imagination* (New York: Harper and Row).

Kelman, H. 1987. 'On the Sources of Attachment to the Nation', paper presented at the meeting of the International Society of Political Psychology, San Francisco, July 6.

Kerr, M. 1959. *Lebanon in the Last Years of Feudalism, 1840–1866* (Beirut: American University of Beirut).

Khalaf, Samir. 1971. 'Family Associations in Lebanon', *Journal of Comparative Family Studies* (Autumn), pp. 235–50.

—— 1977. 'Changing Forms of Political Patronage in Lebanon', in E. Gellner and J. Waterbury, eds., *Patrons and Clients* (London: Duckworth).

—— 1979. *Persistence and Change in Nineteenth Century Lebanon* (Beirut: American University of Beirut and Syracuse University Press).

—— 1987. *Lebanon's Predicament* (New York: Columbia University Press).

—— 1989. 'Besieged and Silenced: The Anguish of the Lebanese People', in *Prospects for Lebanon* (Oxford: Center for Lebanese Studies).

—— 1991. 'Ties That Bind', *The Beirut Review*, 1, No. 1 (Spring), pp. 32–61.

—— 1993a. *Beirut Reclaimed* (Beirut: Dar Al-Nahar).

—— 1993b. 'Culture, Collective Memory and the Restoration of Civility', in D. Collins, ed., *Peace for Lebanon: From War to Reconstruction* (Boulder, CO: L. Rienner).

—— 1995. 'Communal Strife in Global Politics', in M. Esman and S. Telhami, eds., *International Organization in Ethnic Conflict* (Ithaca, NY: Cornell University Press), pp. 101–25.

—— 1997. 'Protestant Images of Islam: Disparaging Stereotypes Reconfirmed', *Islam and Christian-Muslim Relations*, vol. 8, No. 2, pp. 211–29.

—— 2001. *Civil and Uncivil Violence* (New York: Columbia University Press).

Khalaf, S. and P. S. Khoury, eds. 1993. *Recovering Beirut* (Leiden: E. J. Brill).

Khalaf, Samir and Per Kongstad. 1973. *Hamra of Beirut: A Case of Rapid Urbanization* (Leiden: E. J. Brill).

Khalidi, Mustafa and Omar Faroukh. 1957. *al-Tabsheer wa al-Isti'mar fi al-Bilad al-Arabiyyah* (Beirut: published by the authors).

Khatchadorian, H. 1961. 'The Mask at the Face', *Middle East Forum* (February).

Khuri, F. 1975. *From Village to Suburb* (Chicago: University of Chicago Press).

Konrad, G. 1984. *Antipolitics* (New York: Harcourt Brace Jovanovitch).

Labaki, Boutros and Khalil Abu Rjeily. 1993. *Bilans des Guerres du Liban, 1975–1990* (Paris: Editions L'Harmattan).

Lasch, Christopher. 1977. *Haven in a Heartless World* (New York: Norton and Company).

—— 1988. 'The Communitarian Critique of Liberalism', in C. E. Reynolds and R. V.

Norman, eds, *Community in America: The Challenge of Habits of the Heart* (Berkeley: University of California Press).

Latourette, Kenneth Scott. 1949. *Missions and the American Mind* (Indianapolis: National Foundation Press).

Lauer, Robert. 1982. *Perspectives on Social Change* (Boston: Allyn and Bacon).

Laurie, Thomas Rev. 1866. *Historical Sketch of the Syrian Mission* (Boston: ABCFM).

Legum, Colin. 1964. 'Africa's Intellectuals: The Thin Black Line,' *New Society*, No. 118 (December 31), pp. 6–10.

Lerner, Daniel. 1962. *The Passing of Traditional Society* (Glencoe, IL: The Free Press).

Levi-Strauss, C. 1963. *Structural Anthropology* (New York: Basic Books).

Levy, Marion. J. 1953/4. 'Contrasting Factors in the Modernization of China and Japan', *Economic Development and Cultural Change*, vol. 2, pp. 161–97.

Lewis, Bernard. 1993. *Islam and the West* (New York: Oxford University Press).

Lewis, John. 1969. 'The Social Limits of Politically Induced Change,' in Chandler Morse et al., eds, *Modernization by Design* (Ithaca, NY, and London: Cornell University Press).

Lindsay, Rao H. 1965. *Nineteenth Century American Schools in the Levant: A Study of Progress* (Ann Arbor, MI: Malloy Lithoprinting).

Lipset, S. 1959. 'American Intellectuals: This Politics and Status', *Daedalus* (Summer), pp. 467–73

London Jews Society. 1825. *Annual Report.*

Lowenthal, D. and H. Prince. 1964. 'The English Landscape', *Geographical Review*, 54, pp. 304–46.

Lynch, K. 1960. *The Image of the City* (Cambridge, MA: MIT Press).

Lynch, William F. 1853. *Narrative of the United States Expedition to River Jordan and the Dead Sea* (Philadelphia : Blanchard and Lea).

MacCannell, D. 1989. *The Tourist: A New Theory of the Leisure Class* (New York: Schocken).

Mach, J. E. 1979. Foreword to V. E. Volkam, *Cyprus: War and Adaptation, A Psychoanalytic History of Two Ethnic Groups in Conflict* (University of Virginia).

—— 1988. 'The Enemy System', *The Lancet* (January).

Maclean, Norman. 1989. *A River Runs Through it* (Chicago: University of Chicago Press).

Makdisi, J. S. 1990. *Beirut Fragments* (New York: Persea Books).

Makdisi, Ussama. 2000. *The Culture of Sectarianism* (Berkeley: University of California Press).

Manganaro, E. S. 1994. *Bearing Witness: Recent Literature from Lebanon* (Madison, NJ: Fairleigh Dickinson University).

Mannheim, Karl. 1960. *Ideology and Utopia* (London: Routledge and Kegan Paul).

Marvin, Garry. 1986. 'Honor, Integrity and the Problem of Violence in the Spanish Bullfight', in David Riches, ed., *The Anthropology of Violence* (Oxford: Blackwell), pp. 118–35.

Mazrui, Ali. 1968. 'From Social Darwinism to Current Theories of Modernization', *World Politics*, 21 (October), pp. 68–83.

Melikian, L. and L. Diab. 1974. 'Stability and Change in Group Affiliations of University Students in the Middle East', *Journal of Social Psychology*, 93, pp.13–21.

Melko, M. 1990. *Peace in our Time* (New York: Paragon House).

Melville, Herman. 1966. *Melville in the South Seas* (New York: Dover).

Messarra, A. N. 1988. *The Challenge of Coexistence* (Oxford: Centre for Lebanese Studies).

Micaud, Ellen. 1978. 'Urbanization, Urbanism, and the Media in Tunis, *International Journal of Middle Eastern Studies*, 9 (November), pp. 431–47.

Midlarsky, M. 1992. *The Internationalization of Communal Conflict* (New York: Routledge and Kegan Paul).

Miles, George. 1850. *Mohammed, the Arabian Prophet: A Tragedy in Five Acts* (Boston: Phillips, Sampson and Co.).

Mills, C. Wright. 1959. *The Sociological Imagination* (New York: Oxford University Press).

Milnar, Z. 1996. *Globalization and Territorial Identities* (England: Avebury).

The Missionary Herald. 1824, 1825, 1826, 1827, 1830, 1834, 1837.

The Missionary Review of the World. 1889.

Le Monde. 1984.

Montgomery Watt, W. 1961. *Islam and the Integration of Society* (London: Routledge and Kegan Paul).

Morison, Samuel Eliot. 1965. *The Intellectual Life of Colonial New England* (Ithaca, NY: Cornell University Press).

Morse, Chandler. 1969. 'Becoming vs. Being Modern: An Essay on Institutional Change and Economic Development', in Ashford Morse et al, eds, *Modernization by Design* (Ithaca, NY: Cornell University Press), pp. 238–82.

Morton, Daniel D. 1832. *Memoir of Rev. Levi Parsons: First Missionary to Palestine From the United States* (Burlington, VT: Goodrich).

Moynihan, P. 1993. *Pandaemonium* (New York: Oxford University Press).

Mueller, J. 1989. *Retreat From Doomsday: The Obsolescence of Major War* (New York: Basic Books).

Munroe, James Phinney. 1915. *The New England Conscience* (Boston: Gorham Press).

An-Nahar. 1997. January, 14 and 24; February, 4 and 19.

Nash, J., J. Dandle and N. Hopkins, eds. 1976. *Popular Participation and Social Change* (The Hague: Mouton Publishers).

Nasr, Salim. 1978. 'The Crisis of Lebanese Capitalism', *MERIP*, No. 73 (December), pp. 3–13.

—— 1993. 'New Social Realities and Postwar Lebanon', in S. Khalaf and P. Khoury eds, *Recovering Beirut* (Leiden: E. J. Brill).

Nasr, Sami. 1976. *The Arabs and the English* (London: Longman).

Neill, Stephen. 1966. *Colonialism and Christian Missions* (New York: McGraw-Hill).

Nichols, Roy. 1956. *Advance Agents of American Destiny* (University of Pennsylvania Press).

Nietzsche, Friedrich. 1968. *Twilight of the Idols* (Harmondsworth: Penguin Books).

Nisbet, Robert. 1967. *The Sociological Tradition* (New York: Basic Books).

Omvedt, Gail. 1971. 'Modernization Theories: The Ideology of Empire', in A. R. Desai, ed., *Essays on Modernization of Underdeveloped Societies* (Bombay: Thacher and Co.), pp. 119–27.

Owen, Roger. 1988. 'The Economic History of Lebanon, 1943–1974: The Salient Features', in Halim Barakat, ed., *Toward a Viable Lebanon* (London: Croom Helm), pp. 27–41.

Oxtaby, W. G. 1980. 'Westen Perceptions of Islam and the Arabs', in M. Hudson and R.. Wolfe, eds, *The American Media and the Arabs* (Washington, DC: Georgetown University).

The Panoplist. 1819. vol. Xl (Boston).

Parsons, Levi. 1819. 'The Dereliction and Restoration of the Jews', sermon before the departure of the Palestine Mission (Boston: Samuel T. Armstrong).

Petran, Tabitha. 1987. *The Struggle for Lebanon* (New York: Monthly Review).

Phillips, Clifton Jackson. (1969). *Protestant America and the Pagan World* (Cambridge, MA: Harvard East Asian Monographs).

Picard, Elizabeth. 1996. *Lebanon, a Shattered Country: Myths and Realities* (New York: Holmes and Meier).

Pinderhughes, C. A. 1979. 'Differential Bonding: Toward a Psychophysiological Theory of Stereotyping', *American Journal of Psychiatry*, vol. 136, No. 1 (January), pp. 33–37.

Polk, W. 1963. *The Opening of South Lebanon, 1788–1840* (Cambridge, MA: Harvard University Press).

Porath, Y. 1966. 'The Peasant Revolt of 1851–61 in Kisrawan', *Asian and African Studies*, 2, pp. 77–157.

Pye, Lucian W. 1966. *Aspects of Political Development: An Analytical Study* (Boston: Little, Brown and Co.).

Qurtas, Wadad. 1983. *Dhikrayat* (Reminiscences) (Beirut).

Rabinow, P. 1989. *France Modern* (Cambridge, MA: MIT Press).

Ragheb [Southall], I. 1969. 'Patterns of Urban Growth in the Middle East', in Gerald Breese, ed., *The City in Newly Developing Countries* (Englewood Cliffs, NJ: Prentice Hall), pp. 104–26.

Randal, Jonathan. 1984. *Going All the Way* (New York: Vintage).

Ray, William. 1821. *Poems on Various Subjects* (Auburn: Doubleday).

Ricœur, Paul. 1967. *The Symbolism of Evil* (New York: Harper and Row).

Riggs, Fred. 1964. *Administration in Developing Countries: The Theory of Prismatic Society* (Boston: Houghton Mifflin).

Riggs, Rev. Henry H. 1931. 'Beginnings at Beirut', *Centennial of Constantinople Station* (Constantinople: Near East Mission of the American Board).

Riesman, David. 1959. 'The Academic Career: Notes on Recruitment and Colleagueship', *Daedalus* (Winter), pp. 152–57.

Rivkin, A. 1968. *Reflections on a Theory of Modernization* (New York: Anchor Books).

Rorty, Richard. 1989. *Contingency, Irony and Solidarity* (Cambridge: Cambridge University Press).

Rule, James. 1988. *Theories of Civil Violence* (Berkeley: University of California Press).

Rupesinghe, K. 1992. 'The Disappearing Boundaries Between Internal and External Conflict', in K. Rupesinghe, ed., *Internal Conflict and Governance* (New York: St Martin's Press).

Rustow, Daukward and Robert Ward. 1964. *Political Modernization in Japan and Turkey* (Princeton, NJ: Princeton University Press).

Rutgers University. 1990. *Proceedings of Conference* on 'How Civil Wars End' (March 2–4).

Safe, Joe. 2000. 'The State of Human Rights in Lebanon, 1999' (Beirut: Foundation for Human and Humanitarian Rights).

Said, Edward. 1978. *Orientalism* (New York: Pantheon Books).

—— 1983. *The Word, The Text and The Critic* (Cambridge: Harvard University Press).

—— 1991. 'Identity, Authority and Freedom: The Potentate and the Traveler', *Transition*, 54, pp. 2–18.

—— 1993. *Culture and Imperialism* (New York: Alfred A. Knopf).

—— 1996. 'Orientalism and After', in Peter Osbourne, ed., *A Critical Sense: Interviews with Intellectuals* (London: Routledge).

Salam, Assem. 1972. 'Town Planning Problems in Beirut and its Outskirts', in John Taylor, ed., *Planning for Urban Growth* (New York: Praeger), pp. 109–20.

Salibi, Kamal. 1965. *The Modern History of Lebanon* (London: Weidenfeld and Nicolson).

Sarkis, Hashim. 1993. 'Territorial Claims: Post-war Attitudes Towards the Built Environment', in S. Khalaf and P. Khoury, eds, *Recovering Beirut: Prospects of Urban Reconstruction* (Leiden: E. J. Brill).

Scarry, Elaine. 1985. *The Body in Pain: The Making and Unmaking of the World* (New York: Oxford University Press).

Schlesinger, Arthur, Jr. 1974. 'The Missionary Enterprise and Theories of Imperialism', in

John Fairbank, ed., *The Missionary Enterprise in China and America* (Cambridge, MA: Harvard University Press), pp. 336–76.

Schopenhauer, Arthur. 1951. *Essays* (London: George Allen and Unwin Ltd).

Schumpeter, J. A. 1947. *Capitalism, Socialism and Democracy* (New York: Harper and Brothers).

Scruton, R. 1987. *A Land Held Hostage* (London: The Claridge Press).

Segal, Charles and D. Stineback. 1977. *Puritans, Indians and Manifest Destiny* (New York: Putnam).

Sennett, R. 1990. *The Conscience of the Eye* (New York: Alfred Knopf).

Seton-Watson. 1964. *Nationalism and Communalism: Essays, 1946–1963* (London: Methuen).

Seurat, Michel. 1985. 'Le Quartier de Bab Tebbané à Tripoli (Liban): étude d'une 'asabiyya urbaine', in CERMOC, *Mouvements communautaires et espaces urbains au Machreq* (Beirut: CERMOC), pp. 45–86.

Sha'ban, Fuad. 1991. *Islam and Arabs in Early American Thought* (Durham, NC: The Acorn Press).

Al-Shaykh, Hanan. 1986. *The Story of Zahra* (London: Pan Books).

Al-Shidiaq, T. 1954. *Akhbar Al-Ayan Fi Jabal Lubnan* (Beirut: Lebanese University).

Shils, Edward. 1961.'Further Thoughts on Tradition and Modernity', in *The Problems of Afro-Asian States* (Congress for Cultural Freedom).

—— 1965. *Political Development in the New States* (The Hague: Mouton).

—— 1971. 'Tradition,' *Comparative Studies in Society and History*, vol. 13, pp. 22– 59.

Shklar, J. 1982. *Ordinary Vice* (Cambridge, MA: Harvard University Press).

Show, P. E. 1937. *American Contacts with the Eastern Churches, 1820 – 1870* (Chicago IL: The American Society of Church History).

Sinai, R. 1971. 'Modernization and the Poverty of the Social Sciences', in A. R. Desai, ed., *Essays on the Modernization of Underdeveloped Societies* (Bombay: Thacher and Co.), pp. 53–75.

Singer, Milton. 1972. *When a Great Tradtion Modernizes* (New York: Praeger).

Smilianskaya, I. M. 1972. *Al-Harakat Al-Fullahiyyah Fi Lubnan* (Peasant Uprising in Lebanon) (Beirut: Dar al-Farabi Press).

Smith, Chad Powers. 1954. *Yankees and God* (New York: Hermitage House).

Smith, Eli. 1832. *Trials of the Missionary*, address delivered in Park Street Church, October 24 (Boston: Crocker and Brewster).

—— 1840. *The Missionary Character*, address delivered before the Society of Inquiry, April 1.

Smith, K. and D. Berg. 1987. *Paradoxes of Group Life* (Jossey-Bass). Smith, Tony. 1985. 'Requiem or New Agenda for Third World Studies', *World Politics*, vol. 37, No. 4 (July), pp. 532–61.

Smith, Wilfred, C. 1955. 'The Intellectuals in the Modern Development of the Islamic World', in S. N. Fisher, ed., *Social Forces in the Middle East* (New York: Cornell University Press), pp.19–22.

Sovani, N. V. 1969. 'The Analysis of Over-Urbanization', in Gerald Breese, ed., *The City in Newly Developing Countries* (Englewood Cliffs, NJ: Prentice Hall), pp. 322–30.

Spear, Robert. 1901. *Presbyterian Foreign Missions* (Philadelphia: Presbyterian Board of Publications).

Spencer, H. 1874. *The Study of Sociology* (New York: D. Appleton and Co.).

Spring, Gardiner. 1829. *Memoir of Samuel John Mills* (Boston: F.C. Bridgman and Allen).

Srinivas, M. N. 1971. 'Modernization: A Few Queries', in A. R. Desai, ed., *Essays on Modernization of Underdeveloped Societies*, vol. 1 (Bombay: Thacher and Co.) pp. 138–48.

Stauth G. and B. S. Turner. 1988. 'Nostalgia, Postmodernism and The Critique of Mass Culture', *Theory, Culture and Society*, vol. 5.

Stivers, William. 1986. *America's Confrontation with Revolutionary Change in the Middle East 1948–1983* (London: Macmillan).

Storr, Anthony. 1968. *Human Aggression* (New York: Bantam).

Swalha, Aseel. 1997. 'Glocalization: Community Responses to Global Initiative in Ayn al-Mryseh', unpublished paper.

Swidler, Ann. 1986. 'Culture in Action', *American Sociological Review*, vol. 51, No.2 (April), pp. 273–86.

Tibawi, A. L. 1963. 'The American Missionaries in Beirut and Butrus Al-Bustani', St Antony's Papers, No. 16, *Middle Eastern Affairs* (London: Chatto and Windus), pp. 132– 82.

—— 1966. *American Interests in Syria: 1800–1901* (Oxford: Clarendon Press).

Tilly, Charles. 1978. *From Mobilization to Revolution* (New York: Random House).

Tipps, Dean. 1973. 'Modernization Theory and the Comparative Study of Societies: A Critical Perspective', *Comparative Studies in Society and History*, vol. 15, pp. 199–226.

Tisdall, Rev. W. C. 1907. 'Islam and Christian Missions', *Church Missionary Review*, 57 (April), pp. 206–10.

Touraine, A. 1981. *The Voice of the Eye* (Cambridge: Cambridge University Press).

Tuéni, Ghassan. 1992. 'Beirut, our City . . . A Legacy which Generates Capital', *An-Nahar* (February 2).

Turner, B. 1987. 'A Note on Nostalgia', *Theory, Culture and Society*, vol. 4 (1).

Turner, John, ed. 1987. *Rediscovering the Social Group* (Oxford: Blackwell Publishers).

Tyler, Royall. 1797. *The Algerine Captive*, edited by Jack Moore (Gainesville, FL: Facsimiles and Reprints), pp. 49–51.

Vander Werff, Lyle L. 1977. *Christian Missions to Muslims: The Record* (South Pasadena, CA: William Carey).

Volkan, V. D. 1979. *Cyprus: War and Adaptation: A Psychoanalytic History of Two Ethnic Groups in Conflict* (Charlottesville: University Press of Virginia).

—— 1979. 'The Need to Have Enemies and Allies: A Developmental Approach', *Political Psychology*, 6, pp. 2.

von Grunebaum, G. E. 1966. 'Islam: The Problem of Changing Perspective', in Lynn White, Jr, ed., *The Transformation of the Roman World* (Berkeley: University of California Press).

Wagner-Pacifici, R. and B. Schwartz. 1991. 'The Vietnam Veteran Memorial: Commemorating a Difficult Past', *American Journal of Sociology*, 97, No. 2 (September), pp. 376–420.

Walzer, Michael. 1991. 'The Idea of a Civil Society', *Dissent* (Spring), pp. 293–304.

Warwick, Donald. 1982. *Bitter Pills: Population Policies and their Implementation in Eight Developing Countries* (New York: Cambridge University Press).

Washburn, L. K. 1878. 'Who are Christians?', *The Index* (October), pp. 518–520.

Waterbury, John. 1983. *The Egypt of Nasser and Sadat: The Political Economy of Two Regimes* (Princeton, NJ: Princeton University Press).

Watt, William Montgomery. 1991. *Muslim-Christian Encounters* (London: Routledge).

Weaver, R. 1963. 'Major Factors in Urban Planning', in Leonard Duhl, ed., *The Urban Condition* (New York: Basic Books), pp. 97–112.

Webber, M. 1963. 'Order in Diversity: Community without Propinquity', in L. Wings, ed., *Cities and Space: The Future Use of Urban Land* (Baltimore: Johns Hopkins Press).

Welch, C. E. 1967. 'The Comparative Study of Political Modernization', in C. E. Welch, ed., *Political Modernization* (Belmond, CA: Wadsworth Publishing Co.).

Wertheim, W. F. 1971. 'The Way Towards Modernity', in A. R. Desai, ed., *Essays on the*

Modernization of Underdeveloped Societies (Bombay: Thacher and Co.).

Wherry, E. M., S. M. Zwemmer and M.A. Myleria, eds. 1911. 'Islam and Missions: Being Papers Read at the Second Missionary Conference on Behalf of the Mohammedan World at Lucknow', January 23–28.

Whyte, W. F. 1943. *Street Corner Society* (Chicago: University of Chicago Press).

Willhelm, S. M. 1962. *Urban Planning and Land-Use Theory* (Glenceo, IL: The Free Press).

Williams, Robin. 1981. 'Legitimate and Illegitimate Uses of Violence', in Gaylin, Macklin and Powledge, eds, *Violence and the Politics of Research* (Plenum), pp. 23–45.

Willner, Ann. 1964. 'The Undeveloped Study of Political Development', *World Politics*, 16 (April), pp. 468–82.

Wilson, K. B. 1992. 'Cults of Violence and Counter-Violence in Mozambique', *Journal of South African Studies*, vol. 18, No. 3 (September), pp. 527–82.

Wilson, Rodney. 1979. *The Economics of the Middle East* (London: Macmillan).

Winslow, Charles. 1996. *Lebanon: War and Politics in a Fragmented Society* (London/New York: Routledge).

Wirth, L. 1938. 'Urbanism as a Way of Life', reprinted in Richard Sennelt, *Classic Essays on the Culture of Cities* (New York: Prentice Hall, 1969).

Wood, Forrest. 1990. *The Arrogance of Faith* (New York: Alfred Knopf).

Worcester, Samuel. 1815. *Paul on Mars Hill: Or a Christian Survey of the Pagan World* (Andover, MA: Flagy and Gould).

Wriston, Walter. 1992. *The Twilight of Sovereignty: How the Information Revolution is Transforming our World* (New York: Scribner, Maxwell Macmillan).

Wuthnow, R. 1991. 'The Voluntary Sector: Legacy of the Past, Hope for the Future', in R. Wuthnow, ed., *Between States and Markets* (Princeton, NJ: Princeton University Press).

Yahya, Maha. 1993. 'Reconstituting Space: The Aberration of the Urban in Beirut', in S. Khalaf and P. S. Khoury, eds, *Recovering Beirut* (Leiden: E. J. Brill).

Young, Iris. 1990. *Justice and Politics of Difference* (Princeton, NJ: Princeton University Press).

Zur, O. 1987. 'The Psychohistory of Warfare: The Co-Evolution of Culture-Psyche and Enemy', *Journal of Peace Research*, vol. 24, No. 2, pp. 125–34.

Zwemer, S. M. 1906. *The Mohammedan World of Today* (New York: Fleming H. Revell).

—— 1907. *Islam, a Challenge to Faith: Studies on the Mohammedan Religion and the Needs and Opportunities of the Mohammedan World from the Standpoint of Christian Missions* (New York: Student Volunteer Movement for Foreign Missions).

Index